From Berlin to Baghdad

From Berlin to Baghdad

America's Search for Purpose in the Post–Cold War World

Hal Brands

THE UNIVERSITY PRESS OF KENTUCKY

Publication of this volume was made possible in part by a grant from the National Endowment for the Humanities.

Scholarly publisher for the Commonwealth,
serving Bellarmine University, Berea College, Centre
College of Kentucky, Eastern Kentucky University,
The Filson Historical Society, Georgetown College,
Kentucky Historical Society, Kentucky State University,
Morehead State University, Murray State University,
Northern Kentucky University, Transylvania University,
University of Kentucky, University of Louisville,
and Western Kentucky University.

Editorial and Sales Offices: The University Press of Kentucky
663 South Limestone Street, Lexington, Kentucky 40508-4008
www.kentuckypress.com

12 11 10 09 08   5 4 3 2 1

Library of Congress Cataloging-in-Publication Data
Brands, Hal, 1983–
From Berlin to Baghdad : America's search for purpose in the post–Cold War world / Hal Brands.
p. cm.
Includes bibliographical references and index.
ISBN 978-0-8131-2462-9 (hardcover : alk. paper)
1. United States—Foreign relations—1989– 2. World politics—1989– 3. War on Terrorism, 2001– I. Title.
JZ1480.B645 2007
327.73—dc22   2007030936

This book is printed on acid-free recycled paper meeting
the requirements of the American National Standard
for Permanence in Paper for Printed Library Materials.

Manufactured in the United States of America.

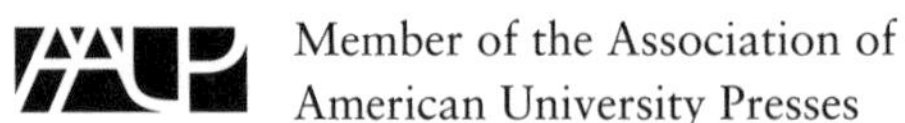

Contents

Abbreviations

ABM	Anti-Ballistic Missile (Treaty)
ASEAN	Association of Southeast Asian Nations
CFE	Conventional Forces in Europe
CIA	Central Intelligence Agency
CTBT	Comprehensive Test Ban Treaty
CWIHP	Cold War International History Project
FDCH	Federal Document Clearing House
FOIA	Freedom of Information Act
GATT	General Agreement on Tariffs and Trade
GDR	German Democratic Republic
ICBM	intercontinental ballistic missile
ICC	International Criminal Court
INF	Intermediate Nuclear Forces (Treaty)
JCS	Joint Chiefs of Staff
MFN	most favored nation
NAFTA	North American Free Trade Agreement
NATO	North Atlantic Treaty Organization
NMD	national missile defense
NPT	Non-Proliferation Treaty
NSA	National Security Archive
NSC	National Security Council
NSD	National Security Directive
NSPD	National Security Presidential Directive
NSS	*National Security Strategy*
OPEC	Organization of Petroleum Exporting Countries
PDD	Presidential Decision Directive
PDF	Panama Defense Forces

PFP	Partnership for Peace
PLO	Palestine Liberation Organization
PNTS	permanent normal trade status
RPF	Rwandan Patriotic Front
START	Strategic Arms Reduction Treaty
TMD	theater missile defense
UN	United Nations
UNISOM	UN Mission for Somalia
UNITAF	UN Task Force
WMD	weapons of mass destruction
WTO	World Trade Organization

Acknowledgments

I would like to thank the staffs of the Hoover Institution, the Library of Congress, the National Security Archive, and the George Bush Presidential Library (Debbie Wheeler in particular) for their help in locating many of the documents cited in this book. Thanks also to the Undergraduate Research Office at Stanford and the International Security Studies program at Yale, both of which subsidized my research, and to Anthony Lake for permission to view his papers.

John Gaddis and Barton Bernstein helped me formulate and rework some of the ideas that went into this book. Stephen Metz and an anonymous reader for the University Press of Kentucky offered valuable comments on the manuscript. Steve Wrinn and Anne Dean Watkins shepherded the book through the review process. A special thank-you goes to my dad, for his encouragement and willingness to serve as a sounding board.

Introduction

"We have found our mission and our moment," said George W. Bush on September 20, 2001.[1] Although Bush was referring to the launching of a global "war on terror," his words also signaled that the decade of incoherence known vaguely as the post–Cold War era was at a close. As the president identified a monolithic enemy and defined the next great calling of U.S. foreign policy, he declared an end to a twelve-year period that had been notable mainly for its lack of a diplomatic paradigm such as Bush now proposed. At the dawn of a new millennium, the president stated, the United States had once again located its purpose in international affairs.

The present volume treats the period between 1989 and 2006, exploring the ways in which the disappearance of the Cold War model of U.S. diplomacy affected the development of policy during those years. While much has been written on certain aspects of U.S. security strategy during the 1990s and beyond,[2] comprehensive studies of the period are scarce.[3] Accordingly, this book serves two purposes. First, it presents an account of U.S. foreign policy that, though not exhaustive, comes closer to being a full and critical examination of the relevant issues than is available elsewhere.[4] Second, it offers an interpretation of U.S. diplomacy that places the various events of the period in the broader context of the transition from Cold War to post–Cold War to war on terror.

As this study makes clear, much of this span (1989–2001) was more remarkable for what it was not (the Cold War) than for what it was (no one was really sure). During this period, the United States' interaction with the world lacked the defining peril and mission that had given structure to U.S. policy during the superpower confrontation and would do so again during the war on terror. Although U.S. strategists were at no loss to articulate particular policies or potential replacements for the doctrine that had been rendered superfluous by the end of the Cold War, there emerged no overall conception of foreign policy as structured or durable as anticommunism and containment. In many ways, the passing of bipolar rivalry had robbed the United States of its diplomatic raison d'etre, and the long decade following 1989 represented an attempt to come to grips with that loss.

This is not to say, of course, that certain goals and issues were not consistently present in U.S. diplomacy during the 1990s. The end of the Cold War and the fading of expected challenges from Germany and Japan left the United States with global preeminence, and each post–Cold War president sought, in one way or another, to protect that position.[5] As some recent studies have demonstrated, certain policies and tendencies of earlier eras—the promotion of free trade and global openness, for instance, or the notion that the United States had a moral and practical obligation to act as a world leader—carried over into this period as well.[6]

Yet, having objectives and power does not necessarily equate to having a coherent grand strategy (much less a domestic consensus in support of that strategy), and this was certainly the case during the 1990s. Aims and ideas were in no short supply during this decade; what was lacking was a strategy that incorporated these interests into a coherent and politically sustainable framework. It was this absence of a workable overall strategy, not a dearth of priorities or complete geopolitical bewilderment, that characterized the United States' post–Cold War experience.

On the whole, U.S. foreign policy in the period under consideration followed a cyclical pattern, from moral and logical certitude to confusion and back. The Cold War and the war on terror constitute the end points of this journey; the decade between, the road traveled. At the start and finish, the United States' international existence was (to most Americans, anyway) clear and unambiguous, while the connecting years were characterized by much greater uncertainty. The end of the Cold War led to the ambiguity that followed, while the often chaotic 1990s contained the sources of coherence's eventual resurrection. The onset of the war on terror was, in this sense, a return to the firmness and conviction that had vanished twelve years prior.

For the greater part of this study's chronology, though, the post–Cold War disorganization of the middle period was dominant. This characteristic exerted a significant—and at times profound—influence on the politics and practice of U.S. policy. In the diplomatic realm, simplicity's end produced both positive and negative results. In certain instances, freedom from the rigidity of the Cold War was all to the good, as flexibility could be the better part of wisdom in dealing with a world that seemed considerably more complex than its geopolitical antecedent. At other points, however, the intricacies of post–Cold War diplomacy seemed more bane than boon. Navigating the rough waters of international politics without a reliable rudder could be quite challenging. In the absence of a firm overall strategy, policy makers lost sight of the relationships among various policies, or they concentrated on regional affairs without reference to the larger global picture. Whatever the net effect, by the start of the twenty-first century, it was difficult to deny that the lack of an all-purpose strategic reference point had greatly impacted the conception and implementation of U.S. diplomacy.

The results of the Cold War's demise were no less notable in the political and rhetorical realm. When American politicians could no longer use anticommunism as a lever for obtaining public consent to foreign policy, they were forced to attempt new justifications for the U.S. role abroad. At times, presidents and their advisers enunciated new conceptions of strategy in an effort to restore the broad agreement on the basic premises of U.S. policy that had prevailed for much of the Cold War. More often, though, this narrative was lacking between 1989 and 2001, and domestic consensus waned as a result. More than simply a strategic problem, the relatively disjointed state of U.S. policy in the 1990s had domestic political ramifications as well.[7]

At each major turning point between the end of the Cold War and the beginning of the war on terror, in fact, the dilemmas of shaping a post-bipolar foreign policy were present. As the superpower confrontation hastened to a close in 1989 and 1990, Americans established the intellectual boundaries of foreign policy debate for the approaching decade. Public commentators eulogized the single-mindedness and purpose of U.S. policy during the Cold War and averred that these virtues would be crucial to the success of future security strategies. Other observers noted with some ambivalence the waning of an era in which the nation's international role had been obvious and (to Americans) morally fulfilling. Together, these themes would dominate American thought on foreign policy in the decade to come.

As the seemingly inchoate state of international relations in the early 1990s became apparent, politicians and policy makers paid heed to the legacies of the Cold War and containment by nominating new organizing principles of U.S. diplomacy. On one level, their motives were strategic and represented an effort to set a firm course for U.S. policy in what looked to be a chaotic world. During the early 1990s, Washington had a stake in events in every major region of the globe, confronting issues involving trade and arms control and problems ranging from humanitarian crises to ethnic conflict to full-scale war. Operating in these circumstances, decision makers reasonably concluded that they simply could not manage foreign policy without a structured conception of threats, interests, and priorities. A coherent scheme of U.S. statecraft, they believed, was imperative if the nation's leaders were to effectively target intelligence and diplomatic resources, shape military forces to meet new challenges, and decide which issues were most deserving of their limited attention. As George H. W. Bush said in 1991, the nation needed "new guideposts" for its international efforts.[8]

At the same time, these attempts at doctrine making were as much political as they were geopolitical. For both the elder Bush and Bill Clinton, the absence of consensus was just as troubling as the absence of coherence with respect to foreign policy. The end of the Cold War had fractured Americans' long-standing agreement on the end point of U.S. diplomacy, giving rise to dissent and debate on the essentials of the nation's international role. This state of affairs greatly complicated the presidential management of foreign policy and, in the words of Anthony Lake, Clinton's first national security adviser, threatened to unleash "neo-know-nothing" isolationism or other "irrational" ideas in the body politic. Accordingly, both Bush and Clinton aimed to impose order on a fragmenting public sphere by reestablishing a foreign policy consensus that, they believed, would result only from the articulation of an agreed-upon vision for U.S. involvement abroad.[9]

Yet the dual political and strategic challenges of foreign policy were difficult to overcome. American interests proved too diverse to be managed by a single-minded policy, and domestic consensus was hard to come by when no imminent threat to U.S. security loomed. Despite Bush's and Clinton's best efforts between 1990 and 1994, there emerged no successor to containment during this period.

This failure led Clinton to rethink the prevailing intellectual precepts of foreign policy. Shown the potential for a complex world to wreak havoc on a narrow strategy, Clinton repudiated his conceptual inheritance and stressed flexibility rather than strict prioritization in his second-term diplomacy. Here too, though, the rhetorical and practical exigencies of post–Cold War diplomacy confounded the president. If the intricacies of international affairs prevented the successful implementation of a simplistic policy, those intricacies also demanded at least a minimum of internal structure in foreign relations. As became apparent when Clinton failed to appreciate the connections between various policies and broader strategic goals, inconsistency could be no less pernicious than reductionism. The rhetorical effects of Clinton's new approach were similarly deleterious. Just as he had feared during his first term, the lack of a widely accepted notion of American purpose invited domestic discord on the particulars of foreign policy. Unable to provide a compelling narrative of the U.S. role in world affairs, Clinton soon found that basic components of his diplomacy were open to challenge.

So traumatic was Clinton's experience that it served as a cautionary example for his Oval Office successor. George W. Bush entered office promising to restore "a great and guiding goal" to foreign policy, and following September 11, 2001, the president got a chance to make good on his pledge.[10] In the year after 9/11, Bush crafted a broad and rhetorically appealing strategy—vaguely and somewhat simplistically referred to as the "war on terror"—calculated both to provide direction to U.S. policy and to ensure the long-term support of the domestic audience. Again confronted by dangerous and seemingly implacable enemies, and once more offered a morally and logically attractive worldview, the United States returned to the type of easily comprehensible foreign policy it had lost with the end of the Cold War. In terms of conceptual certainty and moral assuredness, U.S. policy had come full circle.

As the war on terror unfolded, though, it was hard to escape the reality that simplicity was not the cure-all that so many observers had believed it would be. In some instances, the contradictions that had plagued Clinton's diplomacy during the 1990s persisted, despite the apparent cohesiveness of Bush's policies. Bush's statecraft proved less seamless in practice than it had looked in conception, and the president's top priorities occasionally came into conflict with one another. At other points, the moral and rhetorical strictures of Bush's strategy were poorly suited to dealing with events outside of this newly dominant paradigm. On the domestic scene, too, the war on terror had ill effects, as politicians oversimplified the world situation and U.S. policy as the price of consensus and turned the political sanctity of the conflict to their own ends. By Bush's second term, developments both at home and abroad called into serious question the efficacy of the administration's strategy. If incoherence had been perilous, coherence seemed little less so.

As U.S. policy returned to logical minimalism, Americans could be forgiven for questioning whether the development was a positive one. Many of the problems of the 1990s remained, and those that had vanished had merely been replaced by equally bemusing quandaries. Managing foreign policy was still difficult, singular purpose or no, and the tension between domestic politics and diplomacy had simply assumed a new form. By 2006, the keen observer might have wondered whether the conundrums of the 1990s had their origins in the post–Cold War international environment or whether these issues had deeper roots in the practice and politics of U.S. foreign policy.

Indeed, as one looks more closely at the similarities (from the American perspective, that is) between the Cold War and the war on terror, it becomes difficult to shake the notion that the dilemmas encountered by American policy makers during the 1990s go to the heart of U.S. political and foreign policy style. In a country with such vast aims and influence, some connecting logic is required to make comprehensible the diverse tenets of U.S. globalism; in a democracy as pluralistic as the United States', intellectual simplicity and moral clarity are often the keys to domestic consensus. As they confronted these realities in the 1990s, Americans thus wrestled with the inescapable imperatives of the political and diplomatic system they had created. More than just a reaction to an unexpected turn of international events, the war on terror represented an attempt to resolve this larger dilemma.

Two disclaimers on the focus and method of this book may be helpful at the outset. With respect to method: For the sake of (relative) brevity, I have not attempted a comprehensive treatment of each of the issues described in the following pages. Rather, I sketch their general outlines and essential elements and relate them to the broader themes running through this volume—that is, the search for a governing foreign policy paradigm from 1989 to 2001, and the assertion of a new doctrine following 9/11. In other words, this book traces the relationship between specific policies and broader conceptions of security strategy, exploring how the latter played out in the former and the former influenced the latter.

In terms of focus, this is a story of *American* policy and strategy. This is not to say that I ignore or minimize the policies of or conditions in countries with which the United States interacted between 1989 and 2006; quite the opposite. Detailing the conception and implementation of foreign policy obviously requires an understanding of these subjects, and as far as possible, I have attempted to provide that understanding. From an analytical standpoint, however, my focus remains on Washington, on how U.S. officials (correctly or incorrectly) perceived the world and attempted to deal with it.

1

Beyond the Cold War?

By 1988, more than forty years had passed since Americans had known anything other than the Cold War as the defining aspect of their relationship with the world. Containment, the grand strategy that governed the United States' part in this conflict, was omnipresent in the practice and conception of foreign policy. Though there was no shortage of debate over the when, where, and how of containment, the what and why were largely above challenge. For four decades, the Cold War had dominated foreign policy, providing structure and coherence to the American worldview.[1]

Indeed, the Cold War was so familiar to Americans that many observers were ambivalent about its seemingly imminent demise in the late 1980s. Though a reprieve from Armageddon was obviously to be welcomed, there were intellectual, ideological, and practical reasons to greet the cessation of the superpower contest with trepidation. Broadly speaking, the Cold War offered a sense of certainty. For decades, Americans had known what they stood for and who the enemy was, and the prospect of an end to this certitude was less than alluring. On a practical plane, the termination of the Cold War threatened to unleash what would be a wrenching transformation in the conceptual and bureaucratic foundations of foreign policy. New assumptions would be required, new arrangements necessary. The U.S. worldview, rooted in a relatively straightforward conception of geopolitics, would have to adapt. The more one thought about it, the more the Cold War's end appeared to be less than an unmitigated good.

Whether Americans desired the change or not, the Cold War disappeared by mid-1990. A U.S.-Soviet relationship that had warmed in the mid-1980s improved with surprising speed, erasing many of the diplomatic strains and symbols of East-West hostility that had characterized the conflict. Although George Bush and his advisers often seemed to do their best to deny it, the Cold War was unquestionably dead.

Americans subsequently claimed victory in the four-decade struggle. The conclusion of the Cold War, most commentators assumed, was proof that U.S. policy, when guided by vision and pursued with conviction, could produce brilliant results. Dissenters decried the triumphalism, pointing to containment's social, economic, and moral costs, but theirs was a minority view. Americans accentuated the positive aspects of the Cold War experience, lauding the simplicity and purpose of U.S. policy and the clarity and structure of the era now gone. In doing so, they set a daunting precedent for whatever came next as the organizing principle of U.S. diplomacy and made it clear that the passing of the old order was to be regretted as much as welcomed.

Great Expectations?

When Bush entered the White House in early 1989, he inherited a situation unique in the post–World War II era: the possibility that the Cold War might soon be over. After shocking no one by embarking on a policy of confrontation toward Moscow during his first term, Ronald Reagan had surprised nearly everyone by becoming the great conciliator in his second. Reagan and Soviet chairman Mikhail Gorbachev put on a display of high-profile summitry between 1985 and 1988, substantiating the smiles and handshakes with progress in arms control and other issues. When Reagan left office in 1989, he and Gorbachev had made strides toward the Strategic Arms Reduction Treaty (START) and consummated the Intermediate Nuclear Forces (INF) Treaty, a proposal that had evolved during the second half of the 1980s from a propaganda ploy to a serious measure barring the deployment of medium-range missiles in Europe.[2]

This reduction in U.S.-Soviet tensions constituted a sea change from the relationship's nadir in the late 1970s and early 1980s, and it prompted heretofore radical ruminations about the future. Might the superpowers be moving beyond the diplomatic iciness and incessant competition of the Cold War? Strategist-turned-iconoclast George Kennan, who had played no small part in the origins of the conflict, thought so. "The Cold War is outdated," he wrote in 1988. Meaningful sources of tension had largely vanished with the gains of the 1980s, he argued, and the United States' interests now lay in locking in the recent positive changes in the Soviet system rather than opposing Moscow at every turn. "The notion of containment is today irrelevant," he contended. "The Soviets have dropped the Cold War mentality. Now, it's up to us to do the same thing."[3]

Others, less sanguine about glasnost, perestroika, and the prospects for U.S.-Soviet cooperation, were not so eager to call off the Cold War. After all, Moscow retained its grip on Eastern Europe, controlled a massive military machine, and funded leftist forces in Central America. Jeanne Kirkpatrick, a former Reagan official and prominent neoconservative, feared that Americans were too quick to accept Gorbachev's blandishments. Moscow's conciliatory behavior of late was to be welcomed, she acknowledged, but given the totalitarian nature of Soviet politics, the changes were likely to be temporary. "While there is evidence to suggest that totalitarian systems are capable of change, there is so far no example of such a regime evolving into something different," she wrote. "They have either continued or ended in war." If Americans declared the Cold War over and lowered their guard, Kirkpatrick implied, they did so at their peril.[4]

Kirkpatrick was hardly alone in her pessimism. Even among those who found Kirkpatrick excessively gloomy, there was disagreement about whether the end of the Cold War was to be celebrated or mourned. On one side, commentators such as Kennan were happy to see the conflict nearing an end. The Cold War had overtaxed the U.S. economy, led to a perilous nuclear standoff, and generally made life difficult over the past forty years. For other observers, however, the apparent winding down of superpower tensions was bittersweet.

Francis Fukuyama, for one, was more ambivalent than triumphal. To be sure, the end of the Cold War was an astounding victory in his view, representing something even more decisive than the United States vanquishing international communism: "the end of history." As Moscow's internal struggles and foreign policy retrenchments illustrated the bankruptcy of Marxism-Leninism, Fukuyama wrote in

1989, the world was witness to the "unabashed victory of economic and political liberalism." From the great ideological conflicts of the twentieth century, he argued, had emerged "the universalization of Western liberal democracy as the final form of human government." This was a positive outcome, of course, far preferable to the possibility of liberalism crumbling under the successive challenges of fascism and communism. For the foreseeable future, Fukuyama predicted, there would be a peace of sorts, as competing ideologies no longer drove nations to war. Yet to Fukuyama, this prospect seemed to rob international relations of their vitality. "The end of history will be a very sad time," he wrote. With no ideological competitors, Americans (and other peoples) would have nothing left to fight for. Nations would conduct their affairs rather listlessly, without any of the passion that had made the Cold War so much fun. "The struggle for recognition, the willingness to risk one's life for a purely abstract goal, the worldwide ideological struggle that called forth daring, courage, imagination, and idealism, will be replaced by economic calculation, the endless solving of technical problems, environmental concerns, and the satisfaction of sophisticated consumer demands," he predicted plaintively. With no competing ideology against which to define themselves, Fukuyama implied, Westerners would lose their international reason for being. "I can feel in myself, and see in others around me, a powerful nostalgia for the time when history existed," he wrote. Above all, post-history would be monotonous. Not until a new, great ideological conflict arose would international affairs regain their ability to inspire. "Perhaps this very prospect of centuries of boredom at the end of history will serve to get history started once again."[5]

Fukuyama's eulogy for history touched on certain misgivings about the potential passing of the Cold War. Though the conflict had been profoundly—at times murderously—dangerous, it had also given Americans a sense of purpose. Beyond resisting Soviet expansion, the West had carried the mantle of political and economic liberalism during the twilight struggle. The end of the Cold War would remove the Soviet danger, but it would also terminate this defining mission. In this sense, Americans had less reason to look forward to the post–Cold War era than Kennan might have argued.

What Fukuyama hinted at, neoconservative columnist Charles

Krauthammer stated explicitly. Krauthammer did not think that the Cold War was over in late 1988, but he could see its end on the horizon. "For the first time in the postwar period," he believed, "it is possible to foresee an end to the cold war—on Western terms." Although this was cause for enthusiasm, Krauthammer joined Fukuyama in looking to the future with foreboding. Beyond closing out the Cold War, he argued, Americans had to "figure out what to do next." This task gave Krauthammer pause. Krauthammer looked at the Cold War, and international relations more broadly, in much the same manner as Fukuyama. In this view, foreign policy was not just about interaction between states; it was also a means of forging national identity and meaning. "Nations need enemies," he wrote. "Take away one, and they find another. . . . Parties and countries need mobilizing symbols of 'otherness' to energize the nation and to give it purpose." The Soviet Union had filled this role for much of the Cold War, allowing Americans to conceive of their own ambitions in opposition to communist slavery. With that conflict over, the United States would have to look elsewhere for enemies, and the preliminary results were not reassuring. Failing to find a foe as menacing as the Soviet Union, American politicians had turned to assailing emergent economic powers such as Japan and West Germany, nations that were not antagonists but allies of the United States. According to Krauthammer, this worrisome trend was likely to continue when the Cold War came to a conclusive finish. "As the Soviet threat declines we can expect the bashing of trading partners to increase as politicians look for new ways to define nationalism and exploit its appeal." After the Cold War, Krauthammer feared, Americans would find it more difficult to direct their international efforts toward worthwhile ends.[6]

As Americans debated whether the Cold War was in fact over, they were thus somewhat uneasy about the prospect of an affirmative response. The superpower conflict had provided purpose to U.S. foreign policy, given meaning to the American role abroad, and helped define the nation's identity. Although an end to the Cold War seemed promising in terms of limiting the prospect of nuclear war, it also discomfited those who recognized the considerable benefits of the struggle. That Americans were already showing signs of confusion about post–Cold War foreign policy hardly reassured writers such as

Krauthammer. In some respects, then, leaving the Cold War behind was not especially appealing. Departing from the clarity of the past, Americans would confront an uncertain (and, in Fukuyama's mind, utterly boring) future.

Beyond Containment?

There was little consensus on whether the Cold War was over, but the mere fact that informed observers were seriously contemplating the notion signaled that U.S.-Soviet relations might be at an important crossroads. This prospect seemed all the more likely as Bush prepared to take office in late 1988 and early 1989. In the months after Bush's election, Gorbachev called for continued progress in U.S.-Soviet relations. Gorbachev desperately needed to lower defense costs and attract Western economic assistance to keep the Soviet system solvent, and he saw tighter links with Washington as a means of accomplishing both these tasks. In December, Gorbachev stunned U.S. observers by announcing the withdrawal of 500,000 Soviet troops from Eastern Europe. He subsequently continued the peace onslaught by removing Soviet forces from Afghanistan, pressing for additional steps toward arms control, and supporting economic and political reforms in the Soviet Union and Eastern Europe.[7]

During the transition period and the first weeks of his presidency, Bush and his advisers debated what these developments meant for the Cold War's future. Within the State Department, run by longtime Bush associate James Baker, the optimists held sway. Ambassador to the Soviet Union Jack Matlock thought the time had come to "lead [Moscow] into a partnership." By deepening U.S. economic ties with the Soviet Union, he believed, the United States could "accelerate Soviet reforms in a direction consistent with our interests." Influential voices in Washington counseled even more audacious strategies. Dennis Ross, a trusted Baker aide, urged his boss to exploit Gorbachev's cooperativeness to fundamentally reshape U.S.-Soviet affairs. "We're entering a period that is really unlike any we've seen throughout the whole postwar era," he told Baker in December 1988, "and this is not the time to put our thinking in a straitjacket." Bush should push Gorbachev to permit greater liberalization in Eastern Europe, Ross argued. "The division of Europe symbolizes the continuation of the cold war," he wrote. "If we are entering a new era and if there is a great new potential, we ought to be willing to deal with that key symbol." At a potential watershed, the United States must not be afraid to "dream big dreams."[8]

Ross's approach did not lack for vision, but others in the administration considered the proposal overly trusting of Gorbachev's public pronouncements. Unfortunately for Ross, the pessimists included National Security Adviser Brent Scowcroft, Bush's closest adviser. Scowcroft, whose cold warrior instincts had been honed during the decline of détente in the Ford administration, was more of a hardliner than most of Bush's aides; he once denounced the INF Treaty as "a defeat for us in that we got rid of a useful weapon system while the Soviets got rid of one they wouldn't need in any event." Just after Bush took office in January 1989, Scowcroft threw cold water on any hope for an early rapprochement. "The Cold War is not over," he said. Gorbachev's conciliatory gestures were little more than attempts to divide the North Atlantic Treaty Organization (NATO) and kill Euro-American solidarity with kindness, Scowcroft suspected. "He's interested in making trouble within the western alliance and I think he believes the best way to do it is a peace offensive."[9]

Scowcroft won the immediate argument. Bush slowed the previously torrid pace of U.S.-Soviet diplomacy in order to study Gorbachev's intentions and, just as important, his prospects for survival in the Kremlin hierarchy. In February, Bush ordered a comprehensive review of policy toward Moscow and announced in dramatic fashion at a joint session of Congress a "pause" in relations with the Soviet Union. Citing the dictates of "prudence and common sense," Bush stated that he would "proceed with caution" in engaging Gorbachev. "The fundamental facts remain," he explained, "that the Soviets retain a very powerful military machine in the service of objectives which are still too often in conflict with ours." Wary of embracing Gorbachev's calls for cooperation, Bush was in no hurry to move beyond the Cold War.[10]

Bush's pause lasted the better part of three months as the administration considered its options. Ross advocated engagement, urging Baker and Bush to press Gorbachev for further political reforms in the Soviet Union and Eastern Europe. This was no small request, Ross acknowledged, but Gorbachev's emphasis on reform would make it difficult for the Soviet leader to refuse fresh proposals. "Gorbachev's 'new thinking' gives us a point of leverage in this regard," Ross contended. The State Department adviser also noted what had become a growing headache for the administration during the pause: with Gorbachev scoring public relations coups throughout the West by broaching intriguing initiatives and declaring the Cold War over, Bush faced accusations of not keeping pace with the chairman. According to Ross, an engagement policy would "attack the fundamental assumption of [Gorbachev's] strategy—the notion that Gorbachev can appeal to Western publics better than we can."[11]

As in January, however, other advisers argued for a more conservative approach. A Central Intelligence Agency (CIA) estimate completed in April confirmed that Gorbachev was interested in a warmer relationship with Washington, but it predicted that the Soviet leader might not be able to maintain his hold on power. "There are too many unknowns to determine whether Gorbachev will be able to control the process he has started, or if it will increasingly come to control him," the study stated. Even if Gorbachev retained control, domestic crises might distract the Soviet leadership from foreign policy, leading to prolonged bouts of indecision that would presumably frustrate an engagement strategy. In a gloomier scenario, "a growing perception within the leadership that reforms are threatening the stability of the regime could lead to a conservative reaction." In sum, Bush would be wise not to deepen his involvement with a leader whose days in power might be numbered.[12]

When the administration's policy review was completed in early May, it reflected both sides of the internal debate. National Security Directive (NSD) 23 spoke grandly of a new era in U.S.-Soviet relations, stating, "We may be able to move beyond containment to a U.S. policy that actively promotes the integration of the Soviet Union into the existing international system." At the same time, the document made it clear that the onus for creating a warmer atmosphere would remain on Moscow. Far from outlining steps that Bush would take to facilitate rapprochement, NSD 23 described a series of "conditions" for Gorbachev to meet if he truly desired better relations. These tests were stern and extensive, ranging from renouncing Marxist theories of international relations to allowing self-determination in Eastern Europe. Furthermore, the directive rejected an immediate departure in U.S. policy. "We will not react to reforms and changes in the Soviet Union that have not yet taken place, nor will we respond to every Soviet initiative," Bush wrote.[13]

The public enunciation of NSD 23 was similarly restrained. In a commencement address at Texas A&M University on May 12, Bush stressed the phrase "beyond containment" and, in a nod to concerns that he not appear to falter in the public relations battle, announced his intention to revisit the "Open Skies" proposal of the 1950s, which would allow U.S. and Soviet reconnaissance planes to traverse the airspace of the other country. The conservative aspects of NSD 23 were also apparent, however, as Bush emphasized that the achievement of an improved relationship "requires the Soviet Union to take positive steps." Only after Gorbachev accepted the conditions imposed by NSD 23 would the Soviet Union receive the fruits of U.S. friendship. For Moscow to end the Cold War, it had to concede defeat.[14]

Indeed, the policy outlined in NSD 23 and the Texas A&M speech was essentially a continuation of the cautious position of early 1989. The basically conservative nature of Bush's policy became all the more evident when State Department adviser Curtis Kamman revealed that going "beyond containment" did not necessarily entail ending containment. "Containment is not an adequate explanation for the policy toward the Soviet Union," he explained. "It is not an adequate policy in itself." In other words, the administration's strategy was containment plus conditional cooperation, rather than cooperation in place of containment. Four months into his presidency, Bush remained circumspect in his handling of Gorbachev, showing little inclination to undertake a serious departure in U.S.-Soviet relations.[15]

For all of Bush's and Scowcroft's concerns about Gorbachev, there seems to have been a psychological component to their reluctance to accept that the Cold War might be in its terminal phase. In retrospect, one can detect a certain unease within the administration about the possibility of a revolution in foreign policy. Everything that Bush and Scowcroft had learned about international relations over the past forty-five years had been a product of the Cold War. When the conflict ended, Scowcroft wrote in his memoirs, "We were suddenly in a unique position, without experience, without precedent." Though Scowcroft was speaking of his state of mind in 1991, rather than 1989 or 1990, it is not difficult to imagine that he and other officials might have had similar apprehensions while at the precipice of the unknown. Looking back, Matlock believed that Bush had been "uncomfortable with change," a characteristic hardly conducive to rapid reconciliation with Moscow. Even in 1989, the administration had begun to think about how the end of the Cold War might radically reshape foreign policy. As the conflict wore down, National Security Review 12 stated, the United States would be confronted by new "challenges and uncertainties." Baker elaborated in his own memoirs. When Bush assumed office, he wrote, the world was undergoing profound geopolitical turmoil. "In the midst of such a revolution, most long-held assumptions and strategies had to be changed radically, if not junked altogether." Baker (predictably) considered himself better prepared to handle the transition than most, but he made it clear that the end of the Cold War presented a wrenching departure from the known and familiar.[16]

The potentially traumatic effects of the Cold War's demise went beyond the intellectual. Aside from dominating the worldview of U.S. policy makers, the superpower struggle defined the institutional context in which they worked. Military capabilities, diplomatic tools, intelligence resources, the rules of domestic debate on foreign policy, even the structure of the "national security state" were products of this conflict. The bipolar contest, according to Scowcroft, "shaped our assumptions about international and domestic politics, our institutions and processes, our armed forces and military strategy." Whatever the international environment looked like after the Cold War, the change would likely require a massive overhaul of American statecraft.[17]

In this sense, concluding the Cold War did not seem especially appealing. After a half century, the conflict brought familiarity and relative certainty to the practice of foreign relations. That the Cold War had become, in certain regards, comfortable for U.S. officials and public commentators was evident as they expressed unease about what might follow. The roadblocks to a new order of things were not only political and strategic but mental and institutional as well.

The Tiananmen Interlude

As Bush struggled to decipher U.S.-Soviet relations, developments in Asia further taxed his diplomatic acumen. In April and May, tens of thousands of Chinese students gathered in Beijing's Tiananmen Square to mourn the death of reformer Hu Yaobang. Solemnity turned to protest in mid-May, when Gorbachev's arrival for a summit evoked a glaring contrast between the new Soviet openness and China's continuing repressiveness. "In the Soviet Union they have Gorbachev," went one slogan. "In China, we have whom?" When the atmosphere in Tiananmen soured in late May, U.S. officials feared a confrontation between the government and the protesters.[18]

In certain respects, Bush was more enthusiastic about improving relations with China than with the Soviet Union at the outset of his presidency. A former China hand himself (he had served in Beijing in the mid-1970s), Bush raised eyebrows by making an extended stopover in Beijing shortly after announcing the pause in the Cold War's main event. Personal affinities aside, Bush had sound reasons for drawing closer to China. China's exploding economy seemed to beg for foreign investment, and Bush sought Chinese assistance in stemming missile proliferation.[19]

On a broader level, Bush hoped to preserve the long-standing balance among the United States, the Soviet Union, and China. In practice, this meant ensuring that the United States remained ahead of Moscow in forging positive ties with China. In this regard, early 1989 represented a crucial point for U.S.-Soviet-Chinese affairs, as Gorbachev's visit to Beijing raised the specter of normalized Sino-Soviet relations and closer cooperation between the two powers. "China does not want to fall too far behind as Washington's ties with Moscow improve," warned the State Department. Though few advisers predicted a renewed Sino-Soviet partnership along presplit lines, U.S. officials guarded against the possibility by attempting to remain in China's good favor. When Chinese foreign minister Wan Li traveled to the United States in May, ambassador to Beijing James Lilley advocated "keeping the strategic picture in play" during the visit. Conferring with Wan in May, Bush affirmed his pro-Beijing policy, telling the foreign minister, "I am personally committed to further development and expansion of U.S.-China relations during my Administration."[20]

While Wan was meeting with Bush in Washington, however, China's internal situation turned ugly. Embassy officials reported "deep and widespread public sentiment against corruption and for democracy throughout China," as protests in Tiananmen and elsewhere grew in scope and intensity. The CIA detected signs that Beijing was preparing a major response.[21] After attempts at compromise between the students and the government failed, the Chinese leadership grew desperate. Premier Li Peng feared a coup or the widespread breakdown of governmental authority unless Beijing was able to "stabilize" the situation. Chinese leaders recognized that harsh measures might endanger relations with the West, but this was a secondary concern when the future of the regime seemed in doubt. Li and his associates opted to crush the protests, and the People's Liberation Army rolled into Tiananmen Square on the night of June 3, killing and injuring thousands.[22]

The crackdown put Bush in an uncomfortable position. In May, he had (albeit weakly) registered his concern that Beijing might use force. Adding to his dilemma was the fact that by the time violence erupted in early June, the Tiananmen protesters had largely won the admiration of the U.S. public. Americans naturally sympathized with the pro-democracy demonstrators, and their fascination only increased after the students erected a replica of the Statue of Liberty in late May. This support for the demonstrations turned to apprehension and then disgust as the situation in Beijing deteriorated. Americans received firsthand accounts of the carnage from television news coverage and the reporting of Western correspondents in China. Particularly riveting was the saga of the solitary protester who halted an advancing column of tanks by planting himself in the path of the lead vehicle. News cameras stationed on the rooftops of nearby buildings relayed the drama to American living rooms, while newspapers ran vivid stories about the encounter. The *New York Times* provided a full account of the episode, a "blocking game that could not have been played out more precisely with a coach calling the plays." With the public captivated by the unfolding events in Beijing and horrified by the Chinese government's seemingly indiscriminate use of force, there was no shortage of U.S. commentators demanding a stern response. Appearing on NBC's *Face the Nation* on June 4, Congressman Stephen Solarz (D-N.Y.) advocated sharp punishment for "a government that engages in the wanton slaughter of its own people."[23]

Although Bush shared the revulsion of many domestic observers, he felt constrained in his response. With U.S.-Soviet relations still a strategic question mark, Bush had little desire to create another dilemma by jeopardizing Sino-American ties. "Don't disrupt the relationship," former president Richard Nixon cautioned. "What's happened has been handled badly and is deplorable, but take a look at the long haul." Bush's thoughts were much the same. "China is back on track a little with the Soviets," he confided to his diary, "and they could indeed come back in much stronger if we move unilaterally against them and cut them off from the west."[24]

Bush proceeded cautiously in the days following the massacre, condemning China's actions while stressing his desire to put the incident in the past. He struck a careful balance in public on June 5, deploring the "bloody and violent attack on the demonstrators" but, in the same breath, emphasizing "our long-term interests . . . in China." Eschewing stronger measures such as imposing economic sanctions or severing diplomatic ties, Bush confined his punitive steps to a suspension of military sales and a temporary (and almost immediately breached) prohibition of high-level contact between the two countries.[25]

Bush subsequently retreated from even this tepid stance, working behind the scenes to salvage the relationship with a Chinese regime notoriously sensitive to criticism of its internal affairs. On June 7, Lilley informed Chinese representatives that Bush "sees long-term value in the bilateral relationship." Bush made a personal plea for conciliation, appealing to Deng Xiaoping to receive an envoy "who could speak with total candor to you representing my heartfelt convictions." Deng assented, and Scowcroft and Deputy Secretary of State Lawrence Eagleburger made a secret trip to Beijing in late June and a public visit in December, both times stressing Bush's desire to move forward. In preparation for the second visit, the embassy in Beijing proposed that Scowcroft toast the Chinese leadership in words leaving little doubt that the administration was willing to put Tiananmen behind it: "We need to seek solutions—and preferably quick solutions—to the difficulties which now confront us. We need, in a word, to restore forward momentum."[26]

These efforts were only partially successful. Chinese leaders saw value in good relations with Washington, and the two nations had forged strong economic, cultural, and military ties during the 1980s. American technology and capital remained crucial to China's economy, military sales (which Bush had recently suspended) allowed Beijing to modernize its air force, and educational exchanges provided China with several hundred trained computer scientists and engineers each year. At the same time, Beijing placed a higher priority on internal stability than on warm ties with the United States, and with the Soviet threat to China fading, it felt less compelled to seek a strong Chinese-American partnership. Accordingly, Scowcroft and Eagleburger made little progress during their visits to China, and Beijing refused to budge on human rights.[27]

The political climate in Washington was also unfavorable to rapprochement. During the summer of 1989, Congress imposed additional sanctions on Beijing, and Bush came under fire for his leniency toward China. Although certain voices believed that Bush had been right to opt for moderation, a greater (and louder) number thought that his policy was an expression of either cowardice or callousness. The president's policy, charged one critic, was "pathetically weak." When Scowcroft visited Beijing in December 1989 in search of reconciliation, other critics contended that the president's foreign policy had lost all moral sensitivity.[28]

Aside from causing public relations problems for Bush, the Tiananmen incident had two important effects on U.S. perceptions of foreign policy in mid-1989. In the short term, the episode dimmed hopes that a peaceful and triumphant end to the Cold War was imminent. The killing of pro-democracy protesters in China served as a sobering reminder that Eastern European reform movements might meet a similar fate. Tiananmen "reminds us how readily communist leaders can still resort to brute force when their power is threatened," cautioned a *Washington Post* columnist. With Tiananmen in the background, U.S. views of the situation in Eastern Europe took on an air of greater uncertainty.[29]

The public response also illustrated the beginning of a change in U.S. views of China. With the Cold War apparently moving toward a conclusion in the summer of 1989 (in many American minds, at least, if not in Bush's view), Americans began to see Beijing less as a necessary counterweight to Moscow and more as a regime that needed confronting in its own right. Underlying their outrage at the events in Tiananmen Square was the sense that the coming demise of the Cold War should also entail the end of the alliance with the devil that the United States had engaged in since 1972. For those commentators who saw U.S.-Soviet affairs moving away from confrontation, the justification for befriending China and ignoring its repressive practices was bankrupt. Bush's failure to share this view made him unwilling to pursue a sharp response to Tiananmen, but it also increased his vulnerability to charges of being morally obtuse. Just as Tiananmen illustrated to Bush the continuing dictates of Cold War diplomacy, it also showed how the expected end of that conflict could complicate the domestic selling of foreign policy.

First Steps

Bush's restraint in dealing with China looked wise at the outset, because in May and June 1989, U.S.-Soviet relations remained rocky. As Bush attempted to refocus on Moscow amid Tiananmen's din, he found the going rougher than he had hoped. In particular, Bush was clearly losing the public relations battle with Gorbachev. The president's "beyond containment" speech had aimed to refute the idea that Gorbachev was doing the heavy lifting in ending the Cold War, but its skimpiness of substance elicited little praise from domestic observers. The *New York Times,* a vocal advocate of better U.S.-Soviet ties, called the speech "long on vision and short on content" and challenged Bush to match Gorbachev's efforts at reconciliation.[30]

The fact that Gorbachev had staked a claim to leadership of the Atlantic world was a sore spot for the administration, and U.S. officials occasionally failed to disguise their frustration. Asked in mid-

May about the latest of the Soviet leader's inventive proposals, press secretary Marlin Fitzwater responded by impugning Gorbachev's sincerity. He charged that Gorbachev was merely "throwing out, in a kind of drugstore cowboy fashion, one arms control proposal after another." Although few observers understood Fitzwater's obscure reference, many more recognized its pejorative intent. First criticized for inaction, the White House now came under fire for name-calling.[31]

Having failed to capture the public's imagination in both the United States and Europe, Bush shifted to a more aggressive strategy of engagement. On May 24, the president announced a new arms control initiative. The Conventional Forces in Europe (CFE) proposal entailed 20 percent reductions in NATO and Warsaw Pact forces on the Continent. The logic of CFE was rooted in both the realities of East-West diplomacy and the imperatives of alliance politics. From a military standpoint, the pact would lessen Moscow's ability to launch an attack on Western Europe and decrease the Kremlin's political leverage on the eastern side of the continent. This latter effect would encourage further reform in the Warsaw Pact countries, Baker argued, freeing "the political process in Eastern Europe from the heavy weight of an excessive Soviet military presence." At the same time, CFE was a public relations maneuver as much as anything else. With Gorbachev still besting Bush in the European popularity contest, the administration used CFE to dispel the notion that the president was unable to match the chairman in vision and ingenuity. Announcing CFE, Bush stressed (and perhaps exaggerated) the bold nature of the proposal, saying, "Our aim is nothing less than removing war as an option in Europe." Well received at home and at a NATO summit in late May, CFE gave the administration a needed public boost.[32]

The impetus for engagement gained strength in June and July. On June 15, West German chancellor Helmut Kohl telephoned Bush after meeting with Gorbachev in Bonn. Gorbachev was eager to cooperate on CFE, Kohl reported, and seemed "serious in his desire for establishing better relations." After a trip to Eastern Europe in July, Bush heeded Kohl's counsel. Returning to Washington aboard Air Force One, he drafted a secret message to Gorbachev proposing an initial meeting between the two statesmen "without thousands of assistants hovering over our shoulders." Reflecting both his own caution and a desire for a successful summit, Bush downplayed the need to achieve concrete results, focusing instead on the imperative to build trust. "I just want to reduce the chances there could be misunderstandings between us," he wrote. Gorbachev accepted, and the two leaders eventually agreed to meet in Malta in late 1989.[33]

While making overtures to Gorbachev, though, Bush remained circumspect in his dealings with Moscow. In particular, he refused to commit to concrete support for the reform process in Eastern Europe. Because the division of Europe was the most enduring symbol of the Cold War (and because there were plenty of Polish Americans in the United States), Bush was under pressure to hasten declension in the Soviet bloc by providing economic assistance to the region's liberalizers. Yet the administration was wary of undermining Soviet control of Eastern Europe, for a number of reasons. Tiananmen had raised the possibility that acting assertively in the area might invite a Soviet crackdown. "No one, probably not even the Soviet leaders themselves, could give you the exact limits of Soviet tolerance for the reform process in Eastern Europe," cautioned Kamman. The CIA also warned against an aggressive program, predicting that "Western actions that could be presented by [Gorbachev's conservative] opponents as attempts to 'take advantage' of Soviet internal instability could hurt Gorbachev" and increase the chances of a hard-line reaction. More broadly, many U.S. officials remained unconvinced of Soviet good intentions. "We need a track record," National Security Council staffer Condoleezza Rice stated. "We have been burned before."[34]

Only in the late summer and fall of 1989 did Bush warm to the idea of a fundamental change in U.S.-Soviet relations. Between August and December, a cascade of events in Eastern Europe made it difficult for U.S. officials to doubt Gorbachev's bona fides. During early 1989, the Eastern European communist regimes had seen their legitimacy erode substantially. Moscow's insistence that neighboring regimes emulate Soviet reforms had loosened constraints on dissent, and Gorbachev's refusal to suppress the antigovernment agitation that resulted allowed it to reach crisis proportions. In the following months, Eastern Europeans challenged the authority of their governments, and beginning in August, communism in the region simply collapsed.[35] Moscow acquiesced in the formation of a noncommunist government in Poland, a clear sign that the vaunted "Brezhnev Doctrine" was dead.[36] Czechs and Hungarians subsequently overturned their communist governments. Soviet officials again sat on the sidelines, with Anatoly Chernyaev, Gorbachev's confidant, looking forward to "the total dismantling of world socialism" as "inevitable and good." In October, Czechoslovakia opened its borders, and thousands of East Germans fled through the conduit to West Germany. Fears of a Soviet crackdown mounted, but the end result was precisely the opposite. Confronted by hordes of protesters on November 9, East German border guards declined a confrontation, and television news programs treated their viewers to the unexpected sight of German youths taking sledgehammers to the Berlin Wall. In December, Gorbachev yet again declined to intervene in an uprising, allowing Romania to exit the communist bloc. Through both its actions and its assurances to U.S. officials, the Soviet leadership clearly demonstrated its willingness to permit sweeping change in the Warsaw Pact countries.[37]

In the United States, this series of events evoked triumphal declarations that the Cold War had come to a close. "Freedom is on the march in Eastern Europe and the Soviet Union," wrote the *St. Louis Post-Dispatch.* "It has pushed the Humpty Dumpty of political oppression and economic failure off the wall, and there is no way to piece him back together." The fall of the Berlin Wall, which had been the starkest symbol of the Cold War, provoked particularly strong reactions. "The tragic cycle of catastrophes that first convulsed Europe 75 years ago, embracing two world wars, a Holocaust and a cold war, seems at long last to be nearing an end," stated the *New York Times.*[38]

Gorbachev did his best to make sure that the impression stuck. Meeting Bush at Malta in early December, he promised that under no circumstances would Moscow forcibly intervene in Eastern Europe. This assurance and the ongoing succession of events in the region went some distance in softening Bush's view of the Soviet leader. Reciprocating Gorbachev's gestures, Bush pledged "to avoid doing anything that would damage your position in the world." Afterward, Bush told Kohl that the summit had resulted in a warmer personal relationship between the two statesmen. "The most contentious issues were discussed without rancor," Bush remarked. "This could have been a shouting match, but it was very calm."[39]

Still, the president's suspicions had not disappeared entirely, and the Malta summit also reflected this cautious approach. Aiming to keep Gorbachev off guard, Bush refused to commit to a formal agenda for the meeting and fired off a dizzying set of initiatives at the outset. The strategy was Baker's, who believed that such tactics would forestall the type of Gorbachev peace onslaught that gave U.S. leaders migraines. The idea made sense in terms of keeping the Soviet leader on the defensive, but it also precluded a substantive breakthrough on the various arms control issues at hand. At times, the conversations were strained, such as when Gorbachev and Bush discussed continuing Soviet support for the Castro regime in Cuba and left-wing forces in Central America. At the end of the summit, too, it became clear that there remained some aloofness in the U.S. stance. Gorbachev proposed a joint communiqué stating that he and Bush had come "to a common conclusion that the period of cold war was over." Even after the fall of the Berlin Wall, Bush did not wish to commit to such a bold statement. He demurred, declaring that Gorbachev "can speak for himself" and leaving the chairman to make the declaration alone. In Bush's view, prudence remained a virtue.[40]

Berlin and Beyond

By late 1989, the momentum of events in Europe began to overwhelm whatever chariness Bush still felt. Beyond creating the impression that the Cold War had come crashing down, the fall of the Berlin Wall immediately raised the prospect of German reunification. Kohl had been considering the notion since midsummer, and the swelling influx of refugees from the East made the idea loom larger. Speaking to Bush on November 10, Kohl warned that the German Democratic Republic (GDR) faced an existential crisis. "For a few weeks people will wait to see if the reforms come and if there is no light at the end of the tunnel they will run away from the GDR in great numbers," he said. Kohl was right; tens of thousands of refugees fled East Germany in the last weeks of 1989. Because many of these emigrants were among the GDR's technical and intellectual elite, the East soon faced the possibility of economic collapse.[41]

For Bush, reunification carried both promise and peril. On the one hand, it would drive a final stake into the heart of the Cold War by gutting the Warsaw Pact and removing the separation of Germany as a marker of superpower hostility. On the other hand, reunification might be profoundly destabilizing. Gorbachev desired to preserve the Warsaw Pact on a voluntary basis and was deeply concerned about the economic, diplomatic, and military strength that a reunified Germany would enjoy. In November, he warned Bush that any attempt to rejoin East and West would have serious consequences for U.S.-Soviet relations. Western attempts to deny "the existence of two German states," he told the president, "would bring about not only the destabilization of the situation in Central Europe, but also in other parts of the world." American officials were also concerned. Matlock and others believed that pushing ahead on reunification could cause Gorbachev to lose credibility in the eyes of Soviet conservatives and possibly touch off a hard-liner revolt.[42]

Reunification was no less touchy a subject in Western European capitals. For Europeans with long memories, the idea that Germany would again become the most populous, prosperous, and powerful state between Moscow and the Atlantic was cause for concern. French president François Mitterand regularly warned that reunification could disrupt the continental equilibrium. British prime minister Margaret Thatcher sharply opposed the notion of a single Germany. Reunification could "destabilize everything," she believed. They must remember, she told Bush at one point, that "Germany was surrounded by countries most of which it had attacked or occupied on mainland Europe in the course of this century." In late 1989 and early 1990, Thatcher colluded with Mitterand and Gorbachev to slow the reunification initiative and stated publicly that union should wait at least a decade.[43]

Certain U.S. commentators were also apprehensive. Although polls revealed two-to-one support for reunification, prominent observers opposed the initiative. *New York Times* writer William Safire cautioned that Germans had a "cultural character flaw" in the form of "the tendency . . . to look the other way when moral values are threatened." The editors of Safire's paper issued a more understated warning, writing of the difficulties that might arise from the creation of a "new fatherland of 80 million Germans."[44]

Bush thus proceeded slowly. The president had actually taken an initial step toward supporting reunification even before the Berlin Wall came down. After being assured by Kohl in late October 1989 that rumors of post-reunification revisionism were "absolute nonsense," Bush told a reporter that Germany's "unshakeable" commitment to NATO would mitigate any dangers posed by reunification.[45] Now that a single Germany was a real possibility, though, Bush was more deliberate, aiming to restrain movement on the subject until the situation in Europe stabilized. "The euphoric excitement in the U.S. runs the risk of forcing unforeseen action in the USSR or GDR that would be very bad," he told Kohl. "We will not be making exhortations about unification or setting any timetables. We will not exacerbate the problem by having the President of the United States posturing on the Berlin Wall."[46]

Kohl agreed to be patient, but the growing German clamor for reunification soon forced his hand. On November 28, without informing Bush, Thatcher, or Gorbachev, Kohl explicitly declared his support for reunification and outlined a "Ten-Point Plan" for deepening ties between East and West Germany. As Bush had feared, Kohl's unilateral move annoyed Gorbachev, who complained that the chancellor was "in too much of a hurry." Bush too was irritated, and he admonished Kohl that such actions threatened to upset the delicate balance among Germany, the Europeans, and the superpowers. "Gorbachev's chief problem is uncertainty," he told Kohl. "We need a formulation which doesn't scare him, but moves forward." The key was to "avoid things which would make the situation impossible for Gorbachev." Kohl reassured Bush on this point, telling him, "I will not do anything reckless. I have not set up a timetable for reunification."[47] Satisfied, Bush publicly supported reunification at a NATO meeting in early December. A "gradual" process that occurred "in the context of Germany's continued commitment to NATO" would receive U.S. backing, he pledged.[48]

This statement set the pattern for U.S. policy during early 1990. Bush supported Kohl publicly and in his dealings with Moscow, but he took a more cautious stance in private, working to minimize the contentiousness of the German question and the concerns it inevitably raised in Moscow and other European capitals. When Kohl traveled to Moscow in February 1990 to negotiate with Gorbachev, Bush gave the chancellor a letter restating U.S. approval of the process, but he also sought to reassure the Soviet leader that a reunified Germany would not necessarily be a Germany with complete freedom of action. "Assuming unification takes place," Baker told Gorbachev shortly before Kohl's visit, "what would you prefer: a united Germany outside NATO and completely autonomous, without American forces stationed on its territory, or a united Germany that maintains its ties with NATO, but with the guarantee that NATO jurisdiction or troops would not extend east of the current line?" In other words, if Moscow acquiesced to reunification, Bush would ensure that Germany did not slip the restraining hand of NATO. In a similar vein, Bush encouraged Kohl to make concessions that would ease Soviet, Eastern European, and NATO fears. The chancellor should guarantee the Oder-Neisse boundary with Poland, Bush told Kohl, to lessen fears of a revisionist Germany and deprive reunification opponents of a propaganda tool. "The Soviets seem to be trying to stir up trouble on this border issue," he advised.[49]

Through early 1990, Bush's steady approach seemed well calibrated to the delicate situation surrounding reunification. Gorbachev pledged in February to support reunification in principle, a concession that stemmed from both Bush's support of the initiative and Kohl's promise of extensive economic aid to Moscow. The British, French, Soviet, and U.S. foreign ministers subsequently agreed on a "two plus four" mechanism for negotiating reunification, whereby the two German states would discuss internal issues while the four former allies would settle the international aspects of the question. (Paris, London, Moscow, and Washington had treaty rights in Germany stemming from the settlement following World War II.)

In February and March, however, the pace of events in Germany threatened to overtake the president's diplomacy. On February 13, Kohl informed Bush of his plan to create an economic union between Bonn and Berlin. The GDR was near collapse, Kohl said, "and I do not see a light at the end of the tunnel." Bush supported the idea but cautioned the West German leader not to provoke Kremlin conservatives. "We need to talk and see where we need to be more flexible and where we need to be more firm," he said. Developments on the ground continued to push the process forward in the following weeks. On March 15, Kohl told Bush that the economic union would have to proceed quickly, because only the stabilization of East German currency could stem the "exodus" of refugees. Sensing Bush's concern, Kohl reassured the president that "under no circumstances will we make [reunification] a *fait accompli*." Later, however, the chancellor hedged this guarantee. "The population here and in the GDR want movement," he said. "If they don't get it, they will run around the situation." East German elections on March 18 brought pro-Kohl forces to power, adding to the intensity of pro-reunification sentiment. By late March, reunification appeared inevitable.[50]

Bush again found himself in an awkward situation. Even with the United States backing reunification, a four-power agreement on Germany's international, military, and alliance status did not appear to be close at hand. The major sticking point was the NATO question. Although Gorbachev was willing to go along with reunification, the Kremlin was vehement in its preference for a weakened Germany that would not have the support of the world's most powerful alliance. In April, the Communist Party leadership directed Foreign Minister Eduard Shevardnadze to "firmly state our negative attitude to the participation of the new Germany in NATO" at upcoming conferences with U.S. diplomats. Instead, Germany should become a "non-aligned state." For Bush, this proposal was unacceptable. Keeping Germany within NATO was "vitally important for European security and stability and for the U.S.," he told Kohl. A nonaligned Germany would be free to pursue an independent foreign policy, whereas a Germany within NATO would still be subject to the constraints of an alliance dominated by the United States. If Germany were not a full member of NATO, reunification lost much of its allure.[51]

Bush and Gorbachev therefore appeared to be on a collision course as the two leaders prepared for a summit in Washington in June. The main U.S. goal at the conference was to conclude the long-delayed START, and neither Bush nor his advisers saw much hope of overcoming Soviet objections to German membership in NATO. "I don't think there will be any major surprises" on the German question, Rice predicted. In this regard, she believed, Washington would be much like Malta, with Bush and Gorbachev feeling each other out on the issue to facilitate later, substantive negotiations between Baker and Shevardnadze.[52]

Gorbachev, however, thrived on confounding expectations, and in Washington he pulled a real stunner. When Bush suggested that the Helsinki Final Act of 1975 left the issue of alliance status to the German people, Gorbachev unexpectedly agreed. (East and West Germans overwhelmingly favored joining NATO.) Bush and Scowcroft were shocked. If Gorbachev's position held, it would remove the largest obstacle to reunification on Western terms. But, having visibly angered the other members of the Soviet delegation, Gorbachev backtracked, maneuvering away from his statement. By the end of the conference, Bush and his advisers were unsure whether the agreement remained valid. In a meeting with congressional leaders, Bush reported Gorbachev's consent but added, "We'll see how this works out in practice."[53]

However tenuous Gorbachev's promise seemed in early June, the pledge ultimately held. With the East-West economic union approaching on July 1, Bonn promising substantial economic aid if Moscow went along with reunification, and Baker vowing that a united Germany would remain accountable to NATO, Gorbachev decided to strike a deal before reunification went ahead without him.[54] During June and July, the two-plus-four group met to resolve the remaining issues, namely, Soviet-proposed restrictions on German military capabilities. At the first meeting on June 22, Shevardnadze took a firm position, demanding curbs on German armaments and NATO operations within the new country. "So much for German sovereignty," Baker quipped after seeing Shevardnadze's proposals. The British representative urged Baker to "walk Moscow back from extreme approach Shev articulated today." In a concession that seemed minor at the time but later took on greater significance, the group agreed to forswear eastward expansion of NATO as the price of keeping a united Germany within the alliance. It also suggested that Germany voluntarily restrict its military capacity to preserve both the military balance in Central Europe and the appearance of German sovereignty.[55]

Appeased on these issues, Shevardnadze retreated from his more controversial demands, and by mid-July, a final settlement was in sight. Reunification occurred on October 3, less than a year after the fall of the Berlin Wall and sooner than all but the most optimistic observers might have predicted.[56]

Demise of the Old Order

The series of events that occurred between November 1989 and October 1990 constituted fatal blows to the Cold War order. This climactic phase of the conflict commenced with the fall of the Berlin Wall and the sudden collapse of the Eastern European regimes in late 1989, a striking transformation of European politics that brought home to Americans both the possibility and the reality of change. In a common analysis, one esteemed observer characterized these developments as "momentous, irreversible, and truly epoch-making."[57]

German reunification confirmed this feeling. Reunification erased the artificial division of Germany and the Continent that had been so symbolic of the Cold War, and it clarified that a new geopolitical structure was taking shape. The fact that the union had taken place essentially on NATO's terms, as opposed to the type of neutralization arrangement favored by Moscow and practiced with Austria in 1955, also hinted that the power dynamics of the U.S.-Soviet relationship and European diplomacy had changed fundamentally.

For those who believed that the end of the Cold War would herald a period of unpredictable change, the intricacies of German reunification must have seemed a confirmation of their convictions. Involving the reorganization of arrangements that had long been thought immutable, and occurring more rapidly than nearly anyone had anticipated, reunification was fraught with unforeseen issues and the emergence of conflicts that had long simmered beneath the surface of the Cold War. The debates in the United States and Europe over Germany's future illustrated the anxiety caused by these changes. Likewise, the fact that Bush sometimes positioned himself as a mediator between Bonn and Moscow did not fit neatly within existing customs. Indeed, the awareness of this novelty often guided Bush's policy toward reunification. As State Department adviser Robert Zoellick put it, "We did not want a treaty that either singularized or discriminated against Germany, but frankly we also did not want one that did the same against the Soviet Union for fear that that would plant the seeds for future problems."[58]

As a politician who made *prudence* his watchword, Bush was noticeably averse to public declarations that the Cold War had ended. With reunification impending, however, Bush reflected briefly on the larger meaning of a united Germany. "Forty-five years of conflict and confrontation between East and West are now behind us," Bush said in a televised address to a German audience. "In this past year, we've witnessed a world of change for the United States, for the united Germany, for the Atlantic alliance of which we are a part."[59] Opinion surveys showed that Bush was not alone in this conclusion. A poll taken even before reunification was complete showed that most Americans had accepted Kennan's advice and abandoned the Cold War mind-set. A majority pronounced the conflict "mostly over," and only a quarter of those surveyed viewed the Soviet Union as an enemy. By 1991, 65 percent of Americans considered the Soviet Union an *ally* of the United States.[60]

As a good sport and a statesman who still needed Moscow's friendship, Bush resisted for a time the temptation to claim victory. But as a candidate for reelection in 1992, he could not hold out forever. When his campaign lagged in midyear, Bush and Baker lost their modesty, looking to take credit for "winning" the Cold War. Democrats scoffed at these claims. Bill Clinton, Bush's opponent in 1992, joked that "the notion that the Republicans won the cold war alone reminds me of the rooster who took credit for the dawn."[61]

Neither Clinton nor Bush was entirely correct (or objective) in his assessment, but each was partially correct. As Clinton pointed out, Bush had played little or no role in initiating U.S.-Soviet rapprochement. Bush had entered office with Gorbachev already conducting a full-scale peace offensive and, if anything, may have slowed the reconciliation with his deliberate—at times standoffish—approach. At crucial points, too, it was Kohl or Gorbachev who pushed for change, not Bush. In this view, it seems more appropriate to say that events drove the president rather than the other way around.

Yet whatever his hesitance to initiate change, Bush proved masterful in managing it. German reunification was a complex problem fraught with potential dangers for the United States, the Soviet Union, the Western European nations, and not least Germany itself. Resistance to the idea was strong (if latent, in some areas) in Europe and the United States, and many of Bush's own advisers feared that reunification would prejudice Gorbachev's hold on power. Nonetheless, the president ultimately found a formula that was acceptable to the major players and helped consummate the process with greater alacrity than most commentators thought possible. Vision Bush may have lacked, but tactical adroitness he showed in no short supply. Luck, timing, and skill were all involved in the end of the Cold War.

Claiming Victory

Had there been a winner of the Cold War? The question provoked a good deal of discussion in 1990 and 1991. Perhaps predictably, Gorbachev chose not to delve into the issue. "The Cold War is behind us," he said. "And let us not wrangle over who won it."[62] For the Soviet leader, the end of the Cold War represented U.S.-Soviet cooperation, not the triumph of one side over the other. Not surprisingly, given the circumstances of the conflict's end, most Americans disagreed. "The good guys won," of course, wrote *Boston Globe* columnist David Wilson. In certain respects, that conclusion was eminently reasonable. After all, it was hard to conceive of a more satisfying way to terminate a war than to have virtually all outstanding issues resolved on one's own terms.

Having claimed victory, Wilson and other observers searched for the source of the triumph. In most cases, the answer involved praise for the durability and consistency of U.S. policy. The single-mindedness of containment, rather than the decrepitude of the Soviet system or Gorbachev's efforts, had been crucial. "No Thermopylae, no Actium, no Lepanto, no Waterloo, nor any Gettysburg, Anzio or Tarawa caused this wonderful change," wrote Wilson. "Rather it was the firm, unwavering dedication of millions of Americans who backed the Truman Doctrine and the Marshall Plan, endured the bitter cold of the Chosin Reservoir in Korea and brutal combat in Pleiku and Hue and the Delta, in taxes paid and missions flown and blood shed and steady pressure over generations that brought the communist structure finally crashing down." Chief Justice William Rehnquist agreed. The determining factor, he declared, was the fact that America "has had the courage of its convictions and stood firm in its policy for half a century." When conducted with foresight and perseverance, Rehnquist and others argued, U.S. diplomacy could move mountains.[63]

This view was a common one. Many observers believed that the clarity and strength of U.S. policy had been the keys to the successful conclusion of the Cold War. Charles Horner, a former State Department official, bemoaned the liberal tendency to say otherwise. What had to be appreciated, he wrote, was "the role played by the application of American and allied power during the past four decades in bringing about its proclaimed objective of forcing changes upon the Soviet Union that would make it less dangerous to the world." In this view, the source of the Cold War's end was not Gorbachev in the late 1980s but Kennan four decades earlier. Kennan's prescription of an unyielding application of containment "has turned out to be eerily prophetic, both in its analysis of the Soviet system and in its forecast of how a policy of Western resistance to Soviet expansion would work," Horner wrote.

> Kennan saw Soviet expansion as the product of essentially irreconcilable internal contradictions, irreconcilable because their resolution would change the regime fundamentally. He advocated a Western response—containment—which he defined as "the adroit and vigilant application of counterforce at a series of constantly shifting geographical and political points." And now suppose, he continued, "that the Western world finds the strength and resourcefulness to contain Soviet power over a period of ten to fifteen years. What does that spell for Russia itself?" His answer was that our counterpressures would "promote tendencies which must eventually find their outlet either in the breakup or the gradual mellowing of Soviet power." . . . Kennan imagined this might take fifteen years; it took forty instead.

Victory, Horner argued, had simply been a matter of time.[64]

In some cases, the celebration began even before the reunification of Germany. *New York Times* columnist A. M. Rosenthal, writing in the wake of the Washington summit, considered those who seemed willing to concede a draw wrongheaded. "Some American specialists on the Soviet Union now say that the Western buildup against the Soviets was never necessary—just look at how the empire collapsed," he wrote. Clearly, this was nonsense. "Gentlemen, go tell that to the Poles, the Hungarians, the Czechs. They know that without the growth of Western armed power and the necessity to match it, the Kremlin could have gone on controlling the evil empire for more decades, staving off collapse by sucking out the resources of the colonies." The Cold War, Rosenthal argued, had been part of the twilight struggle between "freedom and slavery." Freedom had won, in part because of its inherent superiority, but also because it had been supported by the full force of American strategy.[65]

Other commentators looked at the history of the Cold War and conceded that the United States had not always pursued anticommunism with full vigor. At times, they acknowledged, Washington had been enticed by the allure of a less confrontational policy. These instances, however, merely confirmed that the advocates of persistent containment had been right all along. "The West may not always have acted with the necessary consistency or resoluteness in its dealings with the Soviet Union," explained Radio Free Europe director Arch Puddington. "But neither, in the end, did the free world permit the anti–cold war brigade's prescriptions to take root. If those prescriptions had prevailed, the Cold War would almost certainly still be on, and the collapse of Communist totalitarianism would have been delayed instead of being hastened." In this view, the instances of weakness were merely the exceptions that proved the rule.[66]

Dissenting voices attempted to mellow the triumphalism but were roundly shouted down. Kennan, a hero to many who claimed triumph in the Cold War, ridiculed the notion that U.S. policy had been the determining factor in the outcome of the struggle. "The suggestion that any Administration had the power to influence decisively the course of a tremendous domestic political upheaval in another great country on another side of the globe is simply childish," he wrote. Equally appalling to Kennan was the idea that the United States had won anything of note by its participation in a conflict as all-consuming as the Cold War.

> Nobody—no country, no party, no person—"won" the cold war. It was a long and costly political rivalry, fueled on both sides by unreal and exaggerated estimates of the intentions and strength of the other

> party. It greatly overstrained the economic resources of both countries, leaving both, by the end of the 1980s, confronted with heavy financial, social, and, in the case of the Russians, political problems that neither had anticipated and for which neither was fully prepared.[67]

Kennan made a good point, but his analysis was too uninspiring for most mainstream observers. Besides, Kennan's argument had profoundly troubling implications for the last forty years of U.S. history. If communism had been rotten from the start, why had the United States paid such a high price to defend against it? Not wishing to delve into such questions, the American majority adhered more closely to the triumphalist formulation. (For those commentators who cited Kennan as a prophet, the aging diplomat's conversion was slightly more disconcerting but could perhaps be explained by the fact that Kennan had spent too much time on campus after leaving government.) In a development that would have ramifications for domestic debate on foreign policy throughout the next decade, the general conclusion was that a simple and forceful policy had been integral to overcoming the challenges of international affairs. The Cold War was over, American observers maintained, because the United States had shown enough vision and resolve to win.

At the Cold War's close, two major themes dominated U.S. perceptions of world politics. One was somewhat pessimistic. The idea that the United States would abandon a state of affairs in which Americans had forty years of experience and enter a decidedly less familiar era was cause for some apprehension. As commentators such as Baker, Scowcroft, and Krauthammer gave it more thought, they likely realized that the moral and strategic certainty of the Cold War might be scarce in the new order. If the present was any indication, the years following would offer far fewer absolutes. The Tiananmen incident had made it clear that the justifications for U.S. policy were already outdated, and domestic observers displayed little patience with the continuation of cold power politics as the Cold War's exceptional circumstances seemed to fade. German reunification was equally novel and demonstrated the possibility of overturning the arrangements and assumptions that had taken root over the prior half century. The stability, moral conviction, and conceptual comfort that had emerged from the Cold War, it appeared, were wasting assets as the superpower confrontation mellowed.

The second theme was not nearly so discouraging. Americans' generally laudatory assessment of containment amounted to a collective affirmation of the potential of U.S. diplomacy. According to this school of thought, foreign policy could be staggeringly successful if backed by the requisite vision and determination. Washington's strategy had been clear and (for the most part) rigorously implemented, or so went much of the thinking, and the result had been victory over what one observer termed "the most puissant enemy we or anyone had ever known." Strength and purpose, in the form of an agreed-upon goal and relentless pursuit of that objective, were assumed to be the elements that ensured the effectiveness of U.S. foreign policy. By 1991, containment's legacy was established. As Americans moved away from the Cold War, they set an elevated standard for evaluating the successor to that doctrine.[68]

Combined, these ideas formed what would become the U.S. foreign policy mind-set of the early 1990s. Simplicity and forcefulness were virtues; complexity and irresoluteness were to be avoided. Drawing both consciously and unconsciously on the Cold War experience, Americans would seek to re-create the certainty and clarity that had seemingly prevailed for the preceding forty-five years. They would attempt to identify themes of international relations as clear-cut as the clash between liberalism and communism, to articulate strategies as logically firm and rhetorically persuasive as containment. Their efforts represented the psychological residue of the Cold War and the apparent lessons of that conflict for U.S. foreign policy. As the post–Cold War era unfolded, the past served as prologue.

2

Peace Elusive

For a brief time, it looked as if the end of the Cold War might bring the United States something in the way of a peace dividend. Having acquiesced only reluctantly in the military buildup necessitated by the Cold War, Americans asked for their money back when the conflict came to a close. After the Berlin Wall fell in late 1989, the Defense Department came under increasing pressure to cut spending. Partly in response to this criticism, and partly in the hope of staving off additional slashing, Pentagon planners completed a plan for post–Cold War military reform in early August 1990. Bowing to demands for fiscal austerity, the document called for significant changes in the size and composition of the military. From the current level of 2.1 million troops, the number of soldiers, sailors, and airmen in uniform would fall by 25 percent over the next half decade. Overseas deployments, the heart of the United States' conventional defense posture during the Cold War, would drop dramatically. At least 80,000, and possibly up to 200,000, U.S. troops would depart Europe, with the potential for greater reductions elsewhere. The cutting was not limited to manpower, either; the navy would have to part with several aircraft carriers and keep its remaining fleets closer to home. As domestic observers had hoped, these cutbacks entailed a decrease in the defense budget. The initial amount was small, only 10 percent, but it would increase substantially as the cuts proceeded.[1]

Underlying these reductions was a sense that the end of the Cold War had reduced both the number and the intensity of security threats to the United States. After the CFE cutbacks and the collapse of the Warsaw Pact, the Pentagon calculated, it would take Moscow up to two years to mount an invasion of Europe. In a broader sense, the end of the superpower rivalry appeared to mean that the United States no longer had to be prepared to oppose aggression any place, any time. The Defense Department might not have agreed with this formulation, but the politicians who had to defend the Pentagon's budget did. On August 2, Bush publicly endorsed the department's downsizing plans. The United States, he said, was now free from "the levels of confrontation that marked the depths of the cold war," and the long-oversized defense establishment could shrink accordingly. With the superpower conflict over, Bush implied, the United States had found some measure of respite from foreign danger.

Bush was not entirely optimistic, though. Hours before he spoke, Iraqi tanks had rolled into Kuwait, conquering the entire nation. Although the dimensions of the crisis were not yet apparent, it was clear that Iraqi domination of one-fifth of the world's oil supply (Iraq's share plus that of Kuwait) threatened U.S. strategic interests and economic well-being. Bush therefore balanced his enthusiasm for defense cuts with a warning that U.S. security in the post–Cold War world was far from assured. "The world remains a dangerous place," he cautioned.[2]

At the dawn of the post–Cold War era, the administration thus oscillated between hope and foreboding with regard to the future of world affairs. Bush was optimistic about prospects for peace but nervous about the rise of new threats. Within six months, the former theme had receded entirely, and the latter had become the notion of the day. As the post–Cold War world took shape, it was reasonable to inquire what the United States had gained through its victory in the superpower conflict—certainly not peace or calm. With half a million U.S. troops massed in the Persian Gulf in a conflict that rivaled Vietnam in size if not in duration, it was difficult to shake the idea that the end of the Cold War had simply replaced one type of insecurity with another. The Bush administration soon warned that the world was still full of villains who had the Cold War Kremlin's bad intentions if not its awesome capabilities, and the Pentagon gained ground in its fight to preserve the size and strength of the armed forces. As the Cold War gave way to an uncertain new era, the United States seemed little more secure than before.

Spurred by war in the Persian Gulf, U.S. policy makers and public observers weighed the proper response to these new dangers. The post–Cold War world was still plenty perilous, they concluded, and the United States needed a security strategy that would guide the nation through this turbulent era, just as containment had shepherded it through the trials of the superpower conflict. As the events of 1990 and 1991 gave rise to discussions of the imperatives of post–Cold War diplomacy, Americans increasingly looked to containment as an exemplar of what that policy should be. Drawing on the lofty appraisals of containment that were commonplace at the time, they concluded that a similarly comprehensible and single-minded strategy was needed to navigate this new age of upheaval. As the outlines of the debate on post–Cold War foreign policy came into focus, containment's legacy was as influential as ever.

Invading Panama

Although the Gulf War ultimately proved to be the United States' formative post–Cold War experience, the nation's first military conflict in the new era actually came several months prior to August 1990. In December 1989, 26,000 U.S. troops invaded Panama, overturned the government of local strongman Manuel Noriega, installed a civilian leadership, and brought Noriega to the United States to face drug-trafficking charges.

The confrontation with Noriega had long been brewing. The military leader-turned-dictator had once been cozy with the Reagan administration. Oliver North and National Security Adviser John Poindexter cultivated Noriega, then head of the Panama Defense Forces (PDF), as an anti-Sandinista influence in Central America, and the general was on the CIA payroll during the mid-1980s. The relationship soured in the second half of the decade, when Noriega became deeply involved in the international cocaine trade, occasionally aided left-wing forces in Central America, denounced the United States as an imperial power, and assumed the role of dictator in Panama. Certain U.S. officials favored forcing Noriega from power, but amid the Iran-contra scandal, Reagan declined a full confrontation with the general. He took a conciliatory tack instead, offering to drop federal drug charges or perhaps bribe Noriega in return for the general's exit from Panama.[3]

These efforts came to naught, and when Bush took office, he initiated a more aggressive strategy. There were several reasons for the change in policy. The leadership of the Panama Canal Control Commission was scheduled to be transferred to Panamanian hands on January 1, 1990, and Bush was unwilling to cede Noriega any measure of influence over the strategically vital waterway. U.S. intelligence also indicated that Noriega had ties to Fidel Castro and El Salvador's leftist Farabundo Marti Liberation Front, additional black marks against the general.[4]

The rising prominence of counternarcotics operations in U.S. policy provided another reason to seek Noriega's ouster. The prevalence of drug use and drug-related crime in the United States had become a major political issue during the late 1980s. The vast majority of cocaine entering the United States came from Latin America, and as the winding down of the Cold War freed American officials to tend to new problems, the administration began to attack the supply side of the equation. In 1989, Bush approved an ambitious counternarcotics strategy that entailed giving economic and military aid to Latin American governments willing to tamp down on cocaine smuggling (Honduras, Colombia, and Peru received roughly $5 billion) and strengthening interdiction efforts in the Caribbean and along the U.S. border. American forces also participated directly in the antidrug efforts of Colombia, Peru, and other regional governments, and Washington assumed a sterner posture toward regimes that were considered uncooperative. The United States, Bush wrote in NSD 18, would pursue international drug cartels "wherever and however they choose to operate."[5]

U.S.-Panama relations deteriorated further in early 1989. With Panamanian elections scheduled for May, Bush's advisers feared that Noriega would set aside the voters' verdict and continue his reign. "Noriega will not have an election only to lose it," an aide warned. Michael Kozak, head of the State Department's Latin America desk, urged Bush to take action if Noriega indeed "stole" the election. The economic sanctions currently in place against Panama would not suffice, Kozak believed. "If we want Noriega out, we must act ourselves," preferably by encouraging disgruntled PDF officers to mount a coup.

"If the PDF has not acted by September 1," Kozak wrote, "the President should order Noriega's removal."[6]

When, as expected, Noriega disallowed the results of the May election and prepared to install his own candidates in power, Bush responded with a campaign of psychological warfare. In July, he invoked an article of the Panama Canal Treaty that allowed U.S. forces to move throughout the country to conduct training missions, and they undertook a number of exercises aimed at rattling Noriega. The Pentagon also replaced a cautious head of the U.S. Southern Command with General Maxwell Thurman, who favored a more vigorous anti-Noriega campaign. Vice President Dan Quayle visited Guatemala in June, urging the Guatemalan government to pressure Noriega to resign. "Time is short," he warned. "Noriega must go." When Noriega installed a puppet government in September, Bush ratcheted up the pressure by breaking off relations with Panama.[7]

Noriega was not easily toppled, however, and by early fall, James Baker favored removing him by force. Special forces could execute a "surgical strike" against Noriega, or U.S. troops in the Canal Zone could mount an invasion of the country. The Pentagon demurred, citing the lack of a "morally and legally acceptable justification" for violating Panamanian sovereignty. Because Noriega had scrupulously avoided threatening the canal, there was no pretext for invasion under the Panama Canal Treaty, and international law offered little justification for invading another country to enforce U.S. statutes. Moreover, Bush still hoped that the PDF would act. Such an occasion did in fact arise in October, when Major Moises Giroldi asked for U.S. assistance in executing a coup. He would detain Noriega, he promised, if U.S. forces would block pro-Noriega troops from coming to the rescue. This was the opportunity Bush had been seeking, but at the last minute, he wavered. Joint Chiefs of Staff chairman Colin Powell thought that the operation sounded "like amateur night." Thurman agreed, deeming the scheme "ill-conceived, ill-motivated, and ill-led." Bush thus withheld U.S. support from the major, and the coup collapsed. Although Giroldi captured Noriega, he inexplicably allowed him to call in reinforcements, and the general soon regained his hold on power.[8]

Giroldi's failure pushed Bush closer to a collision with Noriega.

The Panamanian dictator tightened his control of the PDF in the wake of the coup, and U.S. officials realized that another putsch was unlikely. Bush's decision not to support Giroldi occasioned much criticism, and even congressional allies castigated the president for his timidity and blundering. Senator Jesse Helms (R-N.C.) labeled the administration "a bunch of Keystone Kops, bumping into each other," while Congressman Henry Hyde (R-Ill.) lamented that "we look indecisive, vacillating, and weak."[9]

Having been made to appear feeble and foolish, Bush moved toward a tougher policy. The administration's credibility in the "war on drugs" was at stake, and Bush wanted to set a strong precedent in counternarcotics policy. Powell, too, had come to favor a more assertive stance. Though generally anti-interventionist in orientation, Powell thought that it might be in Washington's best interests to strike against Noriega. The United States should demonstrate that it had the will to use force in the post–Cold War era, he thought, with a brief but decisive operation in Panama. By the fall of 1989, Powell favored letting international observers know that, as he put it, the "superpower lives here." Within the administration, Baker and his aides began to cultivate support for an invasion.[10]

The climax came in mid-December. Noriega proclaimed himself "maximum leader" of Panama and declared war on the United States. His "Dignity Battalions" stepped up their harassment of U.S. soldiers in Panama. On December 17, pro-Noriega forces killed an American officer, injured another, and assaulted the wife of the second officer. These developments outraged Bush. Shortly thereafter, the president pronounced himself "extraordinarily frustrated" that he had been unable to remove Noriega from power. On December 17, Bush opted for military action. The only remaining question was what form the strike would take. A surgical strike aimed only at Noriega was a possibility, but Bush resolved instead for a much larger initiative. "We can never be certain where Noriega is at any particular time," said Brent Scowcroft, so the only way to be certain that he fell from power was to invade and occupy Panama. Powell also favored an invasion, arguing that the PDF was rampant with corruption and that any action taken in Panama should be overwhelming and decisive. "If you're going to get tarred with a brush," he argued, "you might as well take down the whole PDF . . . pull it up by the roots." Bush approved a full-scale invasion, hoping to move quickly enough to capture Noriega and prevent PDF loyalists from dispersing into the countryside to take up guerrilla warfare.[11]

Operation Just Cause commenced on December 20. Word of the operation had leaked beforehand, and CNN broadcast footage of U.S. soldiers deploying from Fort Bragg, North Carolina. In Panama, the actual fighting was brief. The invasion began with air strikes against the PDF, followed by an airborne assault and the movement of U.S. forces out of the Canal Zone. A short firefight at the PDF barracks was sufficient to persuade the majority of Noriega's soldiers to surrender, and the only major combat took place at Panama's international airport, where loyalists waged a fierce struggle against U.S. troops. After the fighting ended, the invasion took on a somewhat comedic quality. Noriega fled, barely escaping capture at a Dairy Queen in Panama City before taking refuge in the papal nunciature. U.S. troops surrounded the building, blaring rock music (which Noriega reputedly detested) and staging anti-Noriega demonstrations in the hope of persuading the now-fallen leader to surrender. After several days he capitulated and was spirited to the United States to face drug charges. Bush quickly installed a new government (the leaders who had been deprived of victory in the May elections) and promised aid for the reconstruction of Panama's economy (which had largely been wrecked by the sanctions). All told, U.S. losses were 23 dead and 322 wounded; the PDF lost 314 soldiers, and more than 200 civilians died in the fighting.[12]

For Bush, the invasion was a clear victory. Although many Latin American leaders objected to this violation of Panamanian sovereignty, Bush's domestic approval rating soared to 79 percent. The consequences were more mixed for the Panamanians. The vast majority were happy to be rid of Noriega, but Panama remained beset by economic stagnation and drug trafficking in the years that followed.[13]

From a U.S. perspective, the Noriega episode reflected concerns both traditional and new. The invasion contained elements familiar to any number of U.S. interventions in Latin America: concern over the Panama Canal, Castro's shadow, and an aversion to anti-American leaders. At the same time, the invasion showed the emergence of new issues that had come to the fore as American priorities shifted with the end of the Cold War. The war on drugs had gained prominence in the late 1980s and played a major role in Bush's antipathy to Noriega. Powell's concern with the United States' credibility and post–Cold War reputation was also a product of the changing realities of international affairs. The invasion additionally illustrated that, assertions that the Cold War had given way to a new era notwithstanding, military conflict and the use of force would remain central to U.S. policy. The intervention was no less demonstrative of Bush's own qualities. A tendency to personalize confrontations and a desire not to appear weak were on display in U.S.-Panamanian relations during 1989. Whatever his caution in moving to end the Cold War, the president would take decisive action when he perceived a challenge.

A Bad Lesson

These characteristics soon resurfaced in a larger confrontation in the Persian Gulf. On August 2, Iraqi president Saddam Hussein launched a lightning strike against Kuwait, his oil-rich neighbor to the southeast. In a single stroke, Hussein now controlled roughly one-fifth of the world's proven petroleum reserves, and Iraq was poised to put a hammerlock on both Gulf politics and a world economy that was heavily dependent on Middle Eastern crude.

The invasion of Kuwait caught the administration flat-footed. With Baker and his advisers immersed in the details of German reunification, the United States had neither expected Hussein to act nor seriously attempted to deter him from following through on the menacing noises he had made toward Kuwait in July. For much of the previous year, in fact, U.S. officials had wrestled with the question of what the Cold War's end meant for policy toward Iraq and the Gulf. Following the Iranian revolution and the Soviet invasion of Afghanistan in 1979, Bush and his Oval Office predecessors had adhered closely to the Cold War scheme of regional competition in the Persian Gulf. Maintaining a steady supply of Gulf oil, U.S. officials believed, meant keeping a stable balance among the various regional powers and minimizing openings for Soviet influence. In practice, this meant aligning with Iraq. Though Hussein's rule was odious and his tendency to play the superpowers off one another annoyed Washington, his antagonism toward Iran qualified the Iraqi leader as a (dubious) member of the free world. During the Iran-Iraq War, the Reagan administration had supported Baghdad just enough to prevent an Iraqi defeat.[14]

Bush initially showed no inclination to reevaluate the relationship. Despite concerns about Iraq's chemical arsenal and nuclear ambitions, Bush affirmed his desire for close ties with Baghdad in September 1989. Citing the familiar dictum that "the Soviet Union or any other regional power with interests inimical to our own" must not be allowed to dominate the Gulf, NSD 26 approved the continuing accommodation of Hussein. The practical implications of NSD 26 were apparent shortly thereafter, when the Department of Agriculture released $500 million in export credits to Baghdad despite signs of Iraqi financial malfeasance in the program.[15]

As Hussein denounced the U.S. presence in the Middle East and developed advanced weapons programs in late 1989 and early 1990, however, American officials had second thoughts about Gulf policy. The Iraqi leader's bad behavior coincided with improved U.S.-Soviet relations and Moscow's new low profile in the Middle East. Besides withdrawing from Afghanistan, the Kremlin had retrenched substantially in the Middle East, cutting aid to its former allies and reducing its participation in the East-West competition for influence in the region. Combined with Hussein's intransigence, the lessening of the bipolar imperative for good relations with Iraq pushed U.S. strategists toward a new conception of Gulf policy. As one adviser noted in January 1990, "Our changing relationship with the Soviet Union is altering the East/West setting" in the region, and Washington was no longer forced to tolerate Iraq's outrages as the price of zero-sum competition. What was needed was a "containment policy" toward Iraq—a strategy that would decrease Baghdad's role in regional affairs and provide for sharper responses to future violations of the U.S. code of Middle Eastern conduct.[16]

Other advisers warned against such a harsh policy, fearing that a break with Iraq would impair U.S. commerce and strain the complex strategic situation in the Gulf. By June 1990, these conflicting views on Iraq had muddled U.S. policy. A statement by Assistant Secretary of State John Kelly on June 15 demonstrated this uncertainty. "Now and in the future Iraq will play a major role in the Gulf," Kelly said. "That role may be for good or for ill."[17]

Ill seemed closer to the mark in July, as Saddam Hussein exploited a pricing dispute within the Organization of Petroleum Exporting Countries (OPEC) to make threats toward Kuwait. The wealthy emirate had drilled for oil on the Iraqi side of the border, Hussein alleged, and kept petroleum prices low as a means of impoverishing Iraq. In the last ten days of July, Hussein massed troops near the Kuwaiti border. Although Bush desired to keep Hussein from overrunning Kuwait, the ambivalence of his Iraq policy compromised the clarity of U.S. warnings to Baghdad. On July 24, Baker instructed Ambassador April Glaspie to inform Hussein of U.S. concerns about Iraqi hostility toward Kuwait but also noted, with emphasis, that "we take no position on the border delineation issue." Perceiving an opening, Hussein played on the weak U.S. stance with contradictory statements. The Iraqi dictator was conciliatory one moment, threatening the next. "We don't want war because we know what war means," he told Glaspie on July 25. "But do not push us to consider war as the only solution to live proudly and to provide our people with a good living." Hussein's statements were sufficiently hedged to allow U.S. officials to interpret them as they pleased. Glaspie, who favored a soft policy toward Iraq, chose to believe that Hussein would not take military action. "Saddam has blinked," she concluded.[18]

Saddam had done nothing of the sort. The Iraqi leader had grown desperate since the end of the Iran-Iraq War. Iraq's oil exports had fallen dramatically. Baghdad had amassed debts of $80 billion, and inflation soared 40 percent annually. Hussein's modernization program ground to a halt, and various segments of Iraqi society grew restive. Opposition leaders demanded elections, and there were rumors of a possible military coup. After Kuwait, Egypt, and other Arab countries refused to cancel Iraq's war debts, and negotiations on oil prices and the border issue failed, Hussein moved toward war. "Iraq is in a state of economic warfare," he said. Invading Kuwait would bring new oil revenues, he calculated, persuade the Arab states to forgive Baghdad's arrears, and ameliorate discontent within Iraq. In late July, the Iraqi embassy in Washington reported "few risks" of a strong U.S. response to an invasion, and on August 2, 140,000 troops and 1,800 tanks rolled into Kuwait. The Kuwaiti army, which contained just four ill-trained and ill-equipped brigades, put up only meager resistance, and Iraqi forces overran the country within the day.[19]

The invasion stunned Bush and his advisers, who had expected, at most, a limited incursion into the disputed border zone. The strike simultaneously threw into sharp relief the flabbiness of U.S. policy toward the Gulf and showed that threats to U.S. security had not abated with the end of the Cold War. In one day, Hussein had been able to menace the U.S. position in the Gulf and threaten the vitality of the international economy. Even more troubling, Washington feared that Hussein might not stop at the Kuwaiti border. "Saudi Arabia looks like the next target," commented Lawrence Eagleburger.[20]

Faced with this sobering situation and future prospects that were bleaker still, Bush was inclined toward a vigorous response. At a National Security Council (NSC) meeting on August 3 (and after some early public hesitation by Bush, who on August 2 had denied to reporters that he planned to send troops to the Gulf), there emerged a consensus that the United States could not allow Hussein to dominate the Gulf and its precious resources. "There is too much at stake," Scowcroft said. Secretary of Defense Dick Cheney agreed, putting the issue in stark terms. Hussein "has clearly done what he has to do to dominate OPEC, the Gulf and the Arab world," Cheney said. "He is only 40 kilometers from Saudi Arabia, and its oil production is only a couple of hundred kilometers away. If he doesn't take it physically, with his new wealth he will still have an impact and will be able to acquire new weapons, including nuclear weapons." Cheney concluded gravely, "The problem will get worse, not better." The invasion promised to have serious economic consequences as well. "The financial markets are down badly," reported Treasury Secretary Nicholas Brady shortly thereafter. "The price of oil is rising."[21]

Beyond the immediate dangers it posed, the Gulf crisis seemed a foreboding presage of the post-bipolar era. Filling in for Baker (who was abroad) during the early days of the crisis, Eagleburger believed that Hussein's actions predicted a chaotic future. The end of the superpower conflict had depolarized regional politics around the world, he thought, giving local actors the freedom to challenge the existing order. "This is the first test of the post [cold] war system," he told the

NSC on August 3. "As the bipolar contest is relaxed, it permits this, giving people more flexibility because they are not worried about the involvement of the superpowers. . . . If [Hussein] succeeds, others may try the same thing. It would be a bad lesson."[22]

The post–Cold War era was not off to an auspicious start. With German reunification still two months away, Bush already faced a challenge to Middle Eastern and international stability. Having defined the stakes as nothing less than control of the Gulf, domination of the world's most valuable resource, the health of the U.S. economy, and the geopolitical shape of things to come, the administration brought its diplomatic and military resources to bear. In Mongolia at the time of the invasion, Baker hit on the idea of a joint U.S.-Soviet statement condemning Hussein's assault and calling for an immediate withdrawal. To prevent the post–Cold War world from turning anarchical, he told Shevardnadze, Moscow and Washington must "send a signal that together we have entered a new era and . . . demonstrate that when a crisis develops, we're prepared to act swiftly and affirmatively in a meaningful way."[23]

Given Moscow's traditional ties to Baghdad, Soviet cooperation was far from assured, but the Kremlin quickly agreed to Baker's proposal. The Soviet leadership, in desperate need of Western technology, trade concessions, and economic aid, could hardly refuse. As Baker hurried to Moscow, Soviet and U.S. diplomats agreed on a tough statement, which the secretary of state and the foreign minister issued shortly thereafter. "Governments that engage in blatant aggression must know that the international community will not acquiesce in nor facilitate that aggression," the document read.[24]

Moscow's cooperation made a strong multilateral response to the invasion possible. With Soviet consent, U.S. diplomats won United Nations Security Council approval of a series of resolutions calling for an Iraqi withdrawal and imposing harsh economic and military sanctions on Baghdad. On a military level, too, the administration took almost immediate action. Powell recommended deploying U.S. troops and planes to Saudi Arabia as a deterrent to any further Iraqi advance. At an NSC meeting on August 5, Scowcroft agreed. "Now is the time to get the Saudis everything we have," he said.[25]

The next week, Cheney traveled to Riyadh in an effort to win approval for a massive deployment of U.S. troops. The Saudis initially balked, fearing that Bush's resolve might wane if it became clear that ejecting Saddam Hussein from Kuwait or defending the Saudi kingdom would come at a high cost in American blood. In this case, the United States might withdraw, leaving the Saudis to face Hussein's wrath alone. Bush's advisers were well aware of this hurdle. The Saudis "don't know what we are willing to do," Chief of Staff John Sununu said. "We have to define at a minimum a package of steps we could commit to Saudi Arabia." Cheney arrived in Riyadh with assurances that the United States did not intend to leave the Gulf before the situation was resolved to Saudi and U.S. satisfaction. Persuaded of American intentions, the Saudis agreed to allow U.S. forces into the country. On the home front, Bush also hinted publicly that Iraqi forces would be leaving Kuwait, one way or another. "This will not stand," he told reporters. "This will not stand, this aggression against Kuwait."[26]

Bush's strong response to the invasion marked a departure from long-standing patterns in U.S. policy and international relations more broadly. The level of collaboration in the UN Security Council between the United States and the Soviet Union was especially striking. Throughout the Cold War, Moscow's UN ambassadors had been known as "Mr. Nyet" for their tendency to veto U.S.-sponsored resolutions. The Kremlin's willingness to break with Iraq, a former client state, was equally significant, as it facilitated Bush's attempts to line up other former Soviet allies for the anti-Hussein coalition. With the sole exception of Jordan, the Arab countries rallied around the introduction of UN sanctions and U.S. power into the Iraq-Kuwait conflict. (Their decision was made easier by American largesse. Egypt, for instance, received a large debt-forgiveness package.) For those observers who still sought confirmation of the Cold War's end even after the July agreement on German reunification, the sight of the United States and its former global antagonist aligning on the same side of a conflict over oil and regional hegemony should have sufficed.

The American stance was also revolutionary in that it reversed more than a decade of U.S. strategy in the Gulf. Bush's condemnation of the invasion and his determination to undo the Iraqi conquest repudiated the former American reliance on Iraq as a stabilizing presence in the Gulf and entailed a departure in U.S. policy toward the region. Whatever the outcome of the crisis, there could be no return to the status quo ante between the United States and Iraq. With Baghdad and Washington now foes, Bush would have to find some other means of securing U.S. interests in the Gulf.

This aspect of the crisis indicated the wrenching nature of post–Cold War geopolitics and also demonstrated how the end of that conflict had loosed the bonds on American power. During the Cold War, a similarly forceful response would have been considerably more difficult, because Washington surely would have feared that a threatened Iraqi regime might turn to Moscow for support. In the short run, this probably would have resulted in raised U.S.-Soviet tensions (or a weaker U.S. response); in the long run, it almost certainly would have produced a tighter Iraqi-Soviet relationship. The thawing of the superpower chill and Bush's confidence that the Kremlin would not be the beneficiary of a strong U.S. stance opened new possibilities for American policy makers, providing options that would not have been feasible just half a decade earlier.

Yet if some aspects of the crisis seemed promising, the immediate picture looked dark. Saddam was unapologetic, dashing hopes that he might withdraw from Kuwait voluntarily. The economic outlook was grim; the Treasury Department predicted that the protracted loss of Kuwaiti and Iraqi oil would seriously hamper domestic prosperity. Confirmed in the inclination to remove Hussein's troops from Kuwait (the fear that they would move into Saudi Arabia faded as U.S. troops deployed), Bush settled in for an armed standoff. On August 20, he approved NSD 45, which stated that the United States intended to secure "the immediate, complete, and unconditional withdrawal of all Iraqi forces from Kuwait" and outlined a series of diplomatic, economic, and military steps toward that end. Coupled with Bush's earlier reaction to the crisis, NSD 45 essentially committed the administration to remove Hussein's forces from Kuwait by whatever means necessary.[27]

As the administration set its stance, Bush and Baker sought additional foreign support. Having won international plaudits by initially working through the United Nations, Bush took full advantage of that goodwill in an attempt to defray the costs of Operation Desert Shield. In late August, he announced that he expected other nations that benefited from secure access to Gulf oil to "bear their fair share" of the burden.[28] In the following weeks, Baker and other U.S. officials visited dozens of countries, soliciting military, financial, and diplomatic assistance (wags dubbed the exercise the "tin cup tour"). For the most part, their efforts met with success. Most Arab states interpreted the Iraqi invasion as a threat to the political and military balance in the region and, with the exception of Jordan, rallied to the cause. Thatcher saw the crisis in much the same light as Bush, and she often appeared eager for a confrontation. Mitterand and Kohl hoped that a strong international showing would convince Hussein to withdraw from Kuwait. Japan, Korea, and other U.S. allies in the Far East cooperated because of their own reliance on Gulf crude.[29]

All told, Baker's efforts produced a formidable coalition. Washington supplied the bulk of the ground troops (roughly 200,000 through late October), but coalition states provided nearly half the total allied force. London sent 45,000 troops, including an armored division and five tactical fighter wings. Paris committed 10,000 troops, an aircraft carrier, and three fighter groups. Saudi Arabia committed 40,000 soldiers; Egypt, another 35,000; Syria, 20,000; Pakistan, 10,000; and Kuwait, 7,000. Thirty-six nations provided military assistance, with capitals from Buenos Aires to Wellington contributing air and naval forces. On the financial side, Saudi Arabia and Kuwait each allotted roughly $13 billion to the cause. Japan gave $10 billion, and Germany about two-thirds of that. In all, Baker eventually collected $48 billion from the coalition members, or nearly half the overall cost of operations Desert Shield and later Desert Storm. Other nations participated in other ways. Turkey did not contribute troops to Desert Shield but did tighten the economic noose by closing oil pipelines running from Iraq. By mid-September, the U.S.-Iraq conflict had gone international.[30]

The administration also mustered domestic backing. Appearing before the Senate Foreign Relations Committee, Baker spoke in tones of peril. At issue in the Gulf, he argued, was U.S. economic security in the post–Cold War era. "It is about a dictator who, acting alone and unchallenged, could strangle the global economic order," sending the United States into "the darkness of depression," Baker warned. Addressing a joint session of Congress on September 11, Bush pointed to both the immediate and long-term consequences of the crisis. Beyond its immense economic and strategic impact, he declared, the Gulf crisis would determine the shape of post–Cold War geopolitics. Whereas inaction would lead to a future of danger and uncertainty, a strong collective response could set a useful precedent for international stability. "Out of these troubled times," he intoned, "a new world order can emerge: a new era—freer from the threat of terror, stronger in the pursuit of justice, and more secure in the quest for peace." Together, Baker's scare tactics and Bush's lofty vision proved effective. Despite some grumbling, there was strong public support for the initial deployment to the Gulf. A month after the invasion, the United States and Iraq seemed headed for a collision.[31]

Into the Storm

As Bush raised the stakes in public, U.S. officials privately considered what the crisis meant for Washington's post–Cold War posture in the Gulf. Beginning in late August, the president's advisers recognized what had been implicit in the U.S. stance all along: that taking a hostile stance toward Saddam Hussein necessitated a departure in Middle East policy. The invasion of Kuwait—and Bush's response—had destroyed the balance of power in the Gulf, and new postcrisis arrangements would be needed to ensure the stability of the area. By late August, the administration accepted that this meant removing Iraq as a regional power. In a memo to Baker, UN Ambassador Thomas Pickering stated that Bush could not now "accept any solution in which Saddam Hussein remains in power; Iraq is heavily armed and developing sophisticated weapons, and able, as a result, to bully and threaten its neighbors." Unless Iraq were substantially weakened, Pickering argued, Gulf security would remain tenuous. The problem was not necessarily the Iraqi president himself but rather his current capabilities. "While Saddam is a dangerous catalyst in an Iraq which is malevolent," Pickering wrote, "it is his military strength, power, and his economic potential that are concerning, not his personality." Pickering eventually lost the argument about the desirability of removing Hussein, but his cable nonetheless refocused the debate on the long-term consequences of intervention in the Gulf.[32]

Regardless of how expansively the president defined his objectives, it soon appeared that achieving them would require the use of force. With Hussein defiant, the chances for a peaceful resolution seemed to diminish each day. In late October, Bush moved toward creating the offensive capability necessary to eject Iraqi forces from Kuwait. Although this proposal had been in circulation for some time, the proximate catalyst for Bush's decision was a cable from Riyadh on October 29. The message warned of looming time constraints on offensive action. Due to the political fragility of the coalition, the likelihood of inclement winter weather, and the need to avoid fighting during the Muslim holy month of Ramadan (March 1991), officials urged Bush to make the necessary political, diplomatic, and military arrangements as soon as possible.[33]

For Bush and his top advisers, the decision to take this offensive option did not require extensive soul-searching. Deploying the extra troops needed to remove the Iraqis from Kuwait followed logically from Bush's stark definition of what was at stake in the Gulf and his earlier commitment to reverse Iraqi aggression. At a meeting with Powell, Cheney, Scowcroft, and others on October 30, the president agreed to send 200,000 additional troops to Saudi Arabia. On November 8 (after the midterm congressional elections), Bush made the decision public.[34]

Using force may have been acceptable to Bush, but selling the idea abroad took greater effort. Many of the nations that had initially supported confronting the Iraqi president were not enthusiastic about the prospect of the United States flexing its military muscle in the Gulf. Moreover, from a multilateral perspective, additional diplomatic steps were necessary to legitimize military action against Iraq. Placing a premium on the international consensus and the burden sharing afforded by UN backing, Bush sought that organization's sanction in resolving the crisis. A Security Council resolution authorizing the use of force against Saddam Hussein was therefore a prerequisite for offensive action.

During the first two weeks of November, Baker visited London, Paris, Moscow, and various Middle Eastern destinations to line up support for the UN initiative. Arab backing was solid, with Riyadh particularly eager to use force. Saudi officials were worried about how

Hussein's power and military capabilities would affect their own security (Baker recalled that the royal family "wanted [Saddam] destroyed") and strongly supported the resolution. Egypt did likewise. China's foreign minister was uneasy about providing a showcase for U.S. power in the Gulf but conceded that a force resolution might be useful as a diplomatic lever; he also implicitly acknowledged that Beijing was in Bush's debt for his nonresponse to the Tiananmen Square incident. Shevardnadze and Gorbachev, who had always favored negotiating with Hussein, were initially cool to Baker's entreaties. They warmed to the proposal, however, as the secretary explained the need to send a strong signal to Hussein and reassured them that the United States still preferred a peaceful solution. The secretary's friendship with Gorbachev and Shevardnadze was crucial, allowing him to overcome their initial reservations. "My own sense is that in the end they will go along with us," Baker reported. Britain and France posed less of a problem, with neither government offering serious resistance. (Thatcher was ready for war even without UN sanction.) The Security Council soon authorized the coalition to use force if Hussein did not withdraw by January 15, 1991.[35]

As Bush prepared for war, the broader implications of the crisis came into focus. In particular, Bush's advisers now embraced the idea that Gulf policy would require a thorough overhaul. "We cannot restore the status quo ante," concluded the State Department. In place of its traditional reliance on Iraq, the United States must take an increased role in Gulf politics. "A post-crisis security architecture must be rooted primarily in the region but will still have to be reinforced from the outside," the report stated. U.S. military support for the Gulf states "will be the cornerstone on which the other parts of the structure rest." Washington would now have a heightened commitment to Gulf security.[36]

In some ways, this realization made a military resolution to the crisis more attractive. After all, a voluntary Iraqi withdrawal would reduce the coalition's will to confront Hussein and maintain the sanctions currently aimed at Baghdad. Perhaps more important, a diplomatic resolution would allow elite Iraqi military units to escape unscathed. A military conflict, in contrast, would allow the United States to lance the Iraqi boil once and for all. The Defense Intelligence

Agency predicted that the coalition would inflict devastating damage on the Iraqi military in the event of a major conflict. In this scenario, "Iraqi forces would be rendered essentially combat ineffective against coalition forces for a period of weeks or months." No less notable, military action would likely "lead to the fall of Saddam Hussein." Hussein's demise and the destruction of the Iraqi armed forces would remove a serious threat to regional stability and clear the way for a Pax Americana in the Gulf. Additionally, such a development would permit a reduction in the American postwar presence in the region. If large-scale combat occurred, another analysis noted, Iraq's capabilities would be diminished to such an extent that "U.S. peacetime presence of ground troops would not be necessary." In certain respects, war had become preferable to peace.[37]

This diminishing interest in a negotiated settlement was evident as war loomed in late December and early January. At the end of 1990, U.S. officials worried that Hussein might fracture the coalition by agreeing to a partial pullout or by making his withdrawal contingent on reciprocal concessions. The purpose of U.S. diplomacy in the pre–January 15 period, the NSC Deputies Committee concluded, should be to "ensure that any Iraqi attempts to weaken the international coalition would fail." In early January, Bush maintained his hard-line stance, discouraging a Soviet peace initiative. Rather than looking to avoid war, Bush was determined to settle the crisis on U.S. terms.[38]

As the UN deadline approached, Bush focused on heading off any crises that might undermine this policy. Because Arab solidarity had been crucial to the U.S. response thus far, one of Bush's greatest fears was that Hussein might somehow drag Israel into the conflict. If he provoked Israel and the Israelis retaliated, for instance, the Arab nations might leave the coalition rather than side with their enemy. "A preemptive strike by Israel would be very bad," Bush bluntly told Israeli prime minister Yitzhak Shamir on December 11. Israel should leave the fighting to the coalition. "If he attacks you, or if an attack becomes apparent, we have the capability to obliterate his military structure," Bush promised. "We have a beautifully planned operation, calculated to demoralize him forever." Shamir made no commitments but pledged to work closely with Bush should hostilities ensue.[39]

The domestic scene posed similar difficulties. Although opposition to the initial defensive deployment had been limited, the prospect of a ground war was considerably more alarming to many Americans. After Bush announced the creation of an offensive capability in November, congressional criticism intensified. Many senators and congressmen were skeptical of Bush's claim that force was the only remaining option, and they favored giving the sanctions more time to work. In some measure, their reluctance stemmed from the fact that Bush had earlier touted the sanctions package as the most devastating international embargo ever placed on a nation and had expressed considerable optimism that economic coercion would force Hussein to withdraw. When the administration reversed course in December, claiming that the Iraqi leader was unlikely to bend unless confronted with overwhelming military force, certain congressmen were dubious. "Sanctions are running Iraq's economy into the ground," argued Senate Foreign Relations Committee chairman Claiborne Pell (D-R.I.). "I believe the passage of time is in our favor, not Saddam Hussein's."[40]

The legacy of Vietnam also weighed heavily on the minds of many congressmen. Fearing another quagmire, congressional observers invoked the history of the Indochina conflict. "We must recall the lessons of the Vietnam war," warned one senator who hoped to "Arabize" the conflict rather than "lose a single GI" in a foreign quarrel. As Bush moved toward war, another representative referenced the infamous Gulf of Tonkin resolution in decrying Bush's "Gulf of Persia" formula "to plunge America into a war." Such sentiments were not confined to Capitol Hill. Polls showed that two-fifths of Americans considered it either "very likely" or "somewhat likely" that war with Iraq would become "another prolonged situation like the Vietnam conflict."[41]

Bush realized that these fears constituted a serious psychological roadblock to using force against Saddam Hussein. Even at the highest levels of the administration, there was much worry about the Vietnam analogy. Bush himself confessed to a preoccupation with the "Vietnam syndrome" and desperately hoped to avoid "the agony and the ugliness" associated with an inconclusive and bloody war. Accordingly, when Bush sought congressional authorization in early January to use force against Iraq, he made a concerted effort to ease congressional fears on this count. In meetings with the congressional leadership, Bush rejected historical analogies to the present situation. "If we must use force it will be decisive," he promised. "The parallels to Vietnam do not and will not bear scrutiny." To a group of senators, he pledged to "act in a manner designed to keep U.S. and allied casualties to a minimum."[42]

Beyond attempting to alleviate these anxieties, Bush reminded legislators of the immense stakes in the Gulf. "Saddam is using every day that passes to continue his brutal destruction of Kuwait," he told congressional officials in early January. "We also pay a high economic price for every day that passes. And Saddam is using time to upgrade his military forces and to develop unconventional weapons. Should war come, waiting could result in higher U.S. and allied casualties." If the United States failed to confront Hussein now, he argued, the consequences would be dire.[43]

Making the case for war also required Bush to demonstrate that he had exhausted all options that might preserve the peace. On January 9, Baker met with Iraqi foreign minister Tariq Aziz for a final round of negotiations. Baker was pessimistic about the chances for success, and with good reason. The secretary arrived without any new incentives for the Iraqis to retreat and simply restated Bush's demand for an immediate withdrawal. Intending to convince Aziz of the hopelessness of Iraq's predicament, Baker treated the foreign minister to a briefing on the coalition's war plan. After an aide displayed photos of Iraqi military installations and government buildings that would be targeted, Baker warned, "If Iraq chooses to continue its brutal occupation of Kuwait, it will choose a military confrontation which it cannot win." Baker's approach was long on sticks but short on carrots, and the meeting ended in a deadlock.[44]

Although Baker's mission failed, his efforts were useful to Bush in persuading the domestic audience of Hussein's intractability. The congressional debate raged almost until the UN deadline, with pessimists claiming that a war would result in 10,000 American deaths. The vote on January 12 was the closest in U.S. history on a decision to go to war. The bill passed easily in the House (250 to 183), but Bush won in the Senate with only a slim majority (52 to 47). Margin of victory aside, however, Bush had his authorization, and the administration avoided a constitutional crisis on the eve of war.

January 15 came and went without an Iraqi withdrawal, and the coalition began air strikes the next day. Shortly before the air war began, Bush signed NSD 54, which outlined U.S. objectives in the conflict. The directive illustrated both the expansiveness of Bush's aims and the drastic shift in policy toward Baghdad over the last year. NSD 54 called for nothing less than Iraq's destruction as a regional power. The directive demanded the elimination of the elite Republican Guard and made it a coalition objective to "weaken Iraqi public support for the current government." Having come into office committed to maintaining good relations with Iraq, Bush now endorsed a policy meant to destroy that regime.[45]

Give War a Chance

The war started on January 16 as coalition forces launched a devastating aerial assault against targets in Iraq and Kuwait. U.S., British, French, and Saudi planes averaged 1,800 sorties per day in an air campaign that lasted one and a half months. Although U.S. commanders initially feared that Iraq's air defense systems would take a heavy toll, the alliance seized air superiority almost immediately. Cruise missiles and F-117A stealth fighter-bombers wrecked Iraq's air defense capability during the first two nights of combat, and what remained of the Iraqi air force fled to Iran. With aerial supremacy won, the coalition turned to striking Republican Guard units in Kuwait and southern Iraq, as well as (unsuccessfully) attacking Iraq's Scud missiles. U.S. and allied planes also targeted Iraqi infrastructure, destroying roads, railways, communication grids, water and electrical plants, and government installations. Thanks to the widespread use of precision-guided munitions, Western observers were treated to bomb's-eye views of these attacks, following the weapon to its target. The air war inflicted severe hardship on Iraqi troops and civilians at relatively minimal cost to the coalition, which lost only about sixty planes.[46]

Once the air war commenced, Bush's basic diplomatic problem was to hold the coalition together long enough to allow (mostly) U.S. forces to achieve the goals outlined in NSD 54. The foremost obstacle was the involvement of Israel. As Bush and his advisers had feared, Hussein attempted to split the coalition along Arab-Israeli lines. Beginning in January, Iraq rained Scud missiles on Israeli cities in the hope of inciting a response. Bush, Baker, and Scowcroft pressured Shamir to forgo retaliation and dispatched batteries of Patriot air defense missiles to Israel to afford some protection to Israeli citizens. (The protection turned out to be mostly illusory, as the Patriots were spectacularly ineffective.)[47]

As the attacks continued, Shamir's restraint wore thin. Several times, the prime minister seemed to be on the brink of military action. On February 11, Israeli defense minister Moshe Arens visited Bush in the Oval Office and painted a bleak picture. "Israelis are on edge living with fear," he said, and "the result is a sense we're at war." Israel would have to strike back, Arens told the president. For Bush, this was a nonstarter; the perception that Israel had joined the coalition would be disastrous for allied unity, he argued. "We understand the risks for the coalition," Arens conceded. But for Israel, the time was quickly approaching "when there will be no alternative." Though Bush was sympathetic to Arens's concerns, he took a hard line against Israeli action. He doubted that Israel could bring a new dimension to the coalition's efforts and told Arens that he found it hard to believe that "you can do something we can't." Besides, he argued, any contribution from Israel would be overshadowed if the coalition splintered before the United States could destroy Hussein's army or, better yet, his government. "I am trying to get rid of one of your greatest enemies," Bush reminded Arens. Perhaps the thought of getting rid of Hussein did the trick, because Shamir's government refrained from entering the fray.[48]

A challenge of a different sort arose as Bush prepared to augment the air campaign with a ground invasion of Iraq and Kuwait. Hoping to avoid full-scale hostilities (in which a Soviet-supplied army would be humbled by U.S. weapons) and bolster Moscow's international prestige in the face of decreasing Soviet power, Gorbachev proposed a compromise: Hussein would guarantee that his troops would be out of Kuwait by a certain date in return for a cessation of hostilities and a promise that Iraqi forces would not be attacked while retreating. Scowcroft found the idea unacceptable. "If Saddam withdrew with most of his armed forces intact, we hadn't really won," he believed.[49] Bush sided with Scowcroft, telling the Soviets that there could be no cease-fire "before a massive withdrawal from Kuwait was underway."[50]

Gorbachev persisted, and on February 21, he announced an agreement whereby Iraq would withdraw following a cease-fire; then, once two-thirds of Hussein's troops had left Kuwait, the Security Council would lift the sanctions. Bush again refused to negotiate, so Gorbachev presented yet another idea. This time, the withdrawal would begin immediately and conclude within three weeks, at which point the sanctions would be removed. Although the deal effectively fulfilled the Security Council's requirements, Bush deflected the proposal. He thanked Gorbachev for his counsel but made his position clear: "I don't feel inclined to wait."[51] Having committed to undermining Hussein's regime and destroying Iraq's military power, Bush was uninterested in a negotiated settlement. "If they crack under force, it is better than withdrawal," he told Powell when the chairman of the Joint Chiefs of Staff reported that a delay in the start of the ground war might make an invasion unnecessary. With diplomatic obstacles to a military solution out of the way, Bush ordered the invasion to begin on February 24.[52]

From the start of the ground war, it was obvious that the coalition's military plan aimed to do far more than expel Iraqi forces from Kuwait. The frontal assault on Kuwait was a mere feint, designed to lure nearby Republican Guard units into battle. Once the Guard engaged, a sweeping American "left hook" would drive across southeastern Iraq and encircle the forces in the forward theater. Once they were trapped, these units would be decimated by U.S. airpower and armor. In effect, the invasion would liberate Kuwait in the process of destroying Iraq's military and Hussein's hold on power.

The breadth of the military plan, Bush's aversion to diplomatic solutions, U.S. plans for the postwar Gulf, and the expansive scope of NSD 54 all point to a fundamental fact of U.S. policy: the Gulf War was not merely about liberating Kuwait and restoring U.S. economic security; it was also about removing the regional conditions that had allowed the current situation to arise. In some sense, the administration now saw the Iraqi occupation of Kuwait not only as a problem in itself but also as a symptom of a larger issue: the breakdown of the regional balance of power. The administration had realized as early as August 1990 that creating a situation that was friendlier to U.S. interests required more than the liberation of Kuwait; it entailed reducing Iraq's role in the Gulf. With this broader goal in mind, a narrow diplomatic solution to the standoff would not do, nor would a military operation limited to restoring Kuwait's freedom. To fully accomplish his goals, Bush needed to decimate Iraq's military and, hopefully, Hussein's government while restoring Kuwaiti sovereignty.

Begun on February 24, the ground attack proceeded largely as envisioned. The assault started with deception, as 18,000 American troops feigned an amphibious landing on the Kuwaiti coast to distract Iraqi forces and pull them deeper to the southeast. At roughly the same time, U.S. forces advanced somewhat cautiously across Kuwait's southern border, engaging Iraqi units while moving slowly enough to limit American casualties. As these attacks went forward, the main components of the U.S. plan unfolded far from the front lines. U.S. Central Command conducted five separate airdrops in Kuwait and Iraq, inserting troops whose goals were to both block reinforcements from reaching the forward theater and prevent Iraqi soldiers in Kuwait from escaping to the north. The left hook, consisting of some 200,000 soldiers who had covertly crossed more than 200 miles of desert in the run-up to the fighting, sliced into southwestern Iraq, rapidly encircling the Iraqi units.[53]

The attack was more successful than virtually any observer had predicted, and within four days, Powell and Central Command chief Norman Schwarzkopf favored ending the fighting. U.S. forces had freed Kuwait, they argued, and Bush should minimize further casualties by closing out the war. Moreover, news images of burned-out hulks of Iraqi vehicles caught attempting to flee north along the so-called Highway of Death created the troubling (but accurate) impression that U.S. forces were attacking a retreating enemy. From a broader perspective, Schwarzkopf believed that one more day of fighting would be sufficient to impair Iraq's military capabilities as specified in NSD 54. Bush and Scowcroft, mistakenly believing that the essential Republican Guard units had been lured into the trap and incapacitated, decided to halt the conflict immediately. (It later became clear that the left hook had worked too well, preventing the Republican Guard reserves from reaching the forward theater. This outcome haunted Bush when Hussein used his well-trained troops to sustain his regime.) Whatever desire Bush might have had to inflict additional punishment on Iraqi forces or to push on to Baghdad was tempered by the likely diplomatic fallout of such actions. By February 27, many of the allies wanted to conclude the conflict, and continuing the fighting meant risking the coalition. The coalition also lacked plans for an occupation of Iraq, and Scowcroft was wary of repeating the Vietnam experience of not knowing "what you're going to do before you go in." Within hours, a cease-fire was in effect. For the coalition, the human toll of Desert Storm amounted to 358 killed (about half of these in friendly-fire accidents) and slightly more than that number wounded. The cost for Iraq was exponentially higher. Estimates vary, but total Iraqi deaths were probably in the neighborhood of 100,000 soldiers and 35,000 civilians.[54]

Aftermath

From a tactical, political, and diplomatic standpoint, the Gulf War was an unquestionable triumph for Bush. Saddam Hussein was humiliated, Kuwait was liberated, and Americans celebrated their relatively painless victory. Now the steadfast commander in chief rather than the "wimp" his opponents had labeled him previously, Bush enjoyed a spike in his approval rating. As a final benefit, the shaky but ultimately unbroken U.S.-Soviet partnership against Hussein had pounded yet another nail in the coffin of the Cold War.[55]

In the aftermath of the conflict, though, Americans could be forgiven for having mixed feelings about the war and its ramifications. Hussein, whom Bush had earlier likened to Hitler, remained in power, his Republican Guard mostly intact. This outcome alone scotched much of U.S. planning for the postwar period and ensured the continuing tenuousness of Gulf security. Speaking to reporters, Bush did not conceal his disappointment. "We have Saddam Hussein still there," he explained, "the man that wreaked this havoc upon his neighbors." With Hussein retaining his iron grip on Iraq, the Gulf remained unstable.[56]

In another sense, the mere fact that the conflict had occurred meant that the post–Cold War world was likely to be an unfriendly place for some time to come. Instead of enjoying a golden peace after vanquishing the Soviet threat, the United States found itself deploying half a million soldiers halfway around the globe. Indeed, the Gulf War experience had been a chastening one for the United States. Hussein's incursion into Kuwait demonstrated that regional despots could hold the United States hostage economically in the post–Cold War era and showed that bipolarity's demise brought with it the potential for instability. Although the international community had responded effectively to this crisis, it was nonetheless a worrying precedent.

Actually, if the present situation was any indication, the new era might be even more dangerous and volatile than its predecessor. The Cold War, for all its pernicious effects, had been utterly predictable. Americans went to bed every night knowing that when they woke up (or if they woke up, during some of the conflict's tenser moments), their foreign policy compass would still point to Moscow. This was no longer true. The Gulf War showed not only that threats to the United States still existed but also that it was increasingly difficult to predict where those threats might emerge. Bush was cognizant that the Gulf crisis did not augur well for a kinder, gentler geopolitics. "In the emerging post–Cold War world," the 1991 *National Security Strategy* warned, "international relations promise to be more complicated, more volatile, and less predictable." From this perspective, the new strategic situation looked even more difficult to manage than the old.[57]

The bittersweet nature of the U.S. victory became all the more apparent as administration officials surveyed the security landscape of the early 1990s. Looking at various trends in international affairs, Bush and his advisers concluded that the end of the Cold War had caused as many problems as it had solved. Bipolar rivalry had restricted the potential for international violence over the past forty-five years, Bush believed, subsuming regional and local conflicts within the strictly bifurcated U.S.-Soviet order. The Cold War "held history captive for years, and it suspended ancient disputes, and it suppressed ethnic rivalries and old prejudice," he stated in the fall of 1991. As that confrontation ended, so did the stability it imposed. "While the collapse of communism has eliminated the major global clash of values, it has opened the way for nationalist, tribal, religious, economic and ethnic conflicts perhaps more than as before," concluded Pickering in one analysis. These dangers, as well as other hazards such as nuclear proliferation, would become more likely in the 1990s.[58]

In 1991, many of these issues coalesced in the chaotic last months of the Soviet Union. By the beginning of the year, the Soviet Union's political and social structure had begun to give way. Perestroika and glasnost, intended by Gorbachev to save the Soviet system, instead hastened its breakdown. Reforms designed to rejuvenate the Soviet economy and society, which had been in decline since the 1970s, instead rapidly knocked out the pillars that had sustained Russian communism. Gorbachev's retreat from Marxist-Leninist economic principles undermined the socialist ideal among Soviet elites, while the growth of civil associations and political dissent weakened the legitimacy of the state. The "loss" of Eastern Europe in 1989 had provoked recriminations that splintered the Soviet leadership (as had the withdrawal from Afghanistan) and sapped the will of the Red Army to use force as a tool of political and social control. Open discussion of the uglier aspects of the Soviet past, encouraged by Gorbachev, undermined morale and further weakened the state. As the power of the central authorities eroded, centrifugal forces pulled the union apart. Nationalism flared in Russia and the other republics, as citizens and political leaders sought to create new sources of authority. Long-building tensions in the Baltic exploded in early 1991, when Soviet troops violently suppressed unrest in Lithuania and Latvia.[59]

Western observers doubted that perestroika could survive. "The current center-dominated political system is doomed," warned the CIA. If left unchecked, current trends would cause the devolution of power to the republics and a transition to democracy. Alternatively, the hardliners might revolt and reassert control. Either way, "The Soviet Union is now in a revolutionary situation in the sense that it is in a transition from the old order to an as yet undefined new order."[60]

In Washington, the atmosphere was one of concern and confusion. In late 1990 and 1991, intelligence analysts produced a stream of gloomy and hedged assessments. "The Soviet Union is in the midst of an historic transformation that threatens to tear the country apart," one CIA report stated. In 1991, the predictions grew more pessimistic. While Gorbachev desperately sought to hold the Soviet system together with a new, voluntary union treaty, the CIA deemed his gambit unlikely to succeed. A right-wing coup could not be ruled out, but neither could the "fragmentation" of the country into a number of political entities. These reports offered little in the way of certitude; the CIA often projected its intelligence statements over a five-year period and admitted that "no one can know what the duration or ultimate outcome" of the current instability would be. It was unknown whether a potential breakup of the Soviet Union would be peaceful, or what types of governments might replace Moscow's authority in the republics.[61]

The possible fragmentation of a state armed to the teeth with nuclear and conventional weaponry was discomfiting to U.S. officials. No less reassuring were thoughts about what or who might replace Gorbachev if the Soviet government collapsed. Shevardnadze, a leading moderate, had resigned months earlier, taking many of the liberalizers with him. Russian president Boris Yeltsin looked promising to some U.S. media observers, but Gorbachev refused to deal seriously with him. Yeltsin also lacked stature in the eyes of Bush's top advisers. Scowcroft and his aides thought that Yeltsin had no "coherent program" for governing and dismissed the Russian as "a bombastic political lightweight."[62]

This dangerous and seemingly unpredictable situation presented Bush with a dilemma. Many U.S. commentators thought that the president should hasten the breakdown of Moscow's authority and encourage self-determination in the republics. A number of factors argued against this approach, though. Many of the republics seethed with ethnic tensions and lacked stable governments, and some stood to inherit Soviet nuclear weapons stationed on their territory. Moreover, support for declension could hurt Gorbachev, encouraging his reactionary foes to take action. It was a difficult situation, and Bush's response was hesitant. The president disapproved of Soviet actions in Latvia and Lithuania but ignored demands that he condemn Gorbachev's meddling or recognize the independence of the Baltic states. As the breakup of the Soviet Union loomed larger in July and August 1991, Bush again withheld support for the republics. The president backed Gorbachev's union treaty and, during a visit to Kiev in August, discouraged Ukrainian lawmakers from declaring independence.

Fearful of adding to the current instability, Bush declared that "Americans will not support those who seek independence in order to replace a far-off tyranny with a local despotism."[63] (For those who thought that the Soviet republics stood on the brink of a democratic revolution akin to the one that had swept Eastern Europe, Bush's speech was a betrayal. Columnist William Safire famously labeled it "Chicken Kiev.")[64]

Additional perils soon arose. Gorbachev's inability to restore order or stabilize relations with the republics led hard-liners to turn against the Soviet chairman. Gorbachev lost the loyalty of many high-ranking officials in June and July, and in the second half of August, the plotters staged a putsch. The Soviet military detained Gorbachev at his Black Sea resort while a "Gang of Eight" took power in Moscow. Bush struggled to formulate a response amid a stream of fragmentary and occasionally contradictory reports from abroad: the Estonians had moved for independence; Soviet troops had stormed Riga; Gorbachev was dead or injured; tanks had attacked Soviet parliament. Scowcroft thought that the coup would succeed and argued that Bush should not "burn our bridges" with the new leadership. Accordingly, the president referred to the coup only as "extraconstitutional" and refrained from placing himself firmly on Gorbachev's side. Bush gradually took a firmer stance, but only after this initial hesitation. As it turned out, though, the Soviet system was beyond redeeming. Loyalists under Yeltsin refused to acknowledge the authority of the hard-liners. (It hardly helped the Gang of Eight's cause that one of its spokesmen showed up at a press conference visibly drunk.) The army rallied to Yeltsin, and the coup unraveled. From there, events moved rapidly. At Cheney's urging, Bush extended diplomatic recognition to the Baltic nations in the hope of encouraging a peaceful breakup of the Soviet Union. Gorbachev's political base eroded, as did the legitimacy of the Soviet state. The coup actually hastened this process, as it discredited the Red Army and the KGB, the only institutions capable of restoring order. Nationalist agitation increased, and with Gorbachev unable to establish a new union compact and unwilling to use force against the republics, the system collapsed. The republics split from the union over the last months of 1991, and on December 25, the Soviet state simply ceased to exist.[65]

Although Americans certainly welcomed the death of Moscow's communist regime, they also recognized the more disturbing implications of the Soviet demise. The breakup of the Soviet Union underscored the peril and disorder that seemed omnipresent in the early 1990s. The episode itself had taken Americans by surprise and lent credence to the notion that the next era would be one of uncertainty. Additionally, the Soviet collapse contributed to many of the new security problems that U.S. officials had recently identified. Moscow did in fact bequeath nuclear weapons to Ukraine and other republics, many of the new regimes were far from stable, and nationalism and ethnic disputes appeared to be on the upswing in the region. "We see the potential for conflict as rising," stated CIA director Robert Gates. In a common assessment, another observer opined that "the still-fragmenting, nuclear-armed shards of the world's last great empire represent an unknown as daunting and potentially dangerous as Columbus' 'Indies' must have seemed."[66]

Assessments like these painted a less than rosy picture of the future. During 1991 and 1992, U.S. officials concluded that the post–Cold War security environment was just as dangerous as its antecedent. Although the existential threat to the nation had disappeared, it had been replaced by a number of less predictable challenges. Moscow "is no longer the enemy," Bush said in late 1991. "The enemy is uncertainty. The enemy is unpredictability." If anything, overt violence was more likely than it had been during the Cold War. With the constraints of bipolarity gone, U.S. officials feared, crises would spring forth with greater frequency. "Regional crises and conflicts are likely to arise or to escalate unpredictably and on very short notice," Cheney warned in 1991. "This will require that we be able to respond, if necessary, very rapidly and often very far from home, and against hostile forces that are increasingly well-armed with conventional and unconventional capabilities." There would be no rest for the Cold War weary.[67]

Cheney's gloomy assessment looked prescient in 1991 and 1992 as regional, ethnic, and civil conflicts erupted in various locales. Yugoslavia dissolved into chaos, Somalia and other African nations lapsed into civil strife and humanitarian catastrophe, the central Asian republics teetered on the brink of anarchy, and, despite Bush's efforts in Panama and elsewhere, international drug trafficking continued virtually unimpeded. The sense that the United States had simply passed from one period of insecurity to the next took root in the administration, and it soon became clear that those who had hoped for a post–Cold War peace dividend would be disappointed. For the Defense Department, the Gulf War came along just in time to reverse the administration's plans for deep cutbacks. Showcasing a vast array of U.S. weaponry (including the most expensive and high-tech weapons in the Pentagon's arsenal), the conflict provided a near-incontestable argument against slashing the defense budget. Not surprisingly, the administration quickly discarded its earlier projections of substantially diminished outlays and called for much more modest reductions. Cheney said of the turnaround, "We based these sweeping reductions not on the somewhat sobering prospects of the early winter of 1991, when war loomed in the Gulf and Soviet reformers were under siege, but on the promise of change symbolized by the fall of the Berlin Wall 15 months earlier."[68]

Trimmers objected to the change of plans. They argued that whatever the current threats might be, they were certainly not on the level of the Soviet menace that had justified Cold War–era profligacy. Hussein-type characters were scary, they conceded, but not in the Armageddon-looming sense of the postwar years. The Pentagon batted these objections away. The world indeed lacked a hostile giant at the moment, Cheney and the defense brass conceded, but who knew what the future might hold? Hadn't the Gulf War proved that the international environment was utterly unpredictable? Following this logic, Powell contended that "uncertainty" deserved its own itemization in the defense budget. "There is the enduring reality of the unknown," he said, "the crisis that no one expects, the contingency that suddenly comes along."[69]

Cheney backed this assessment, arguing that the rapidity of change in the post–Cold War world meant that the United States had to be prepared for nearly any contingency. "People like to talk about a threat-based force, a threat-based strategy," he told the keepers of the purse strings in the House of Representatives. "But, of course, it is important for us to remember that it is very risky to place total confidence in our ability to predict future events. . . . In early 1990, I do not know anyone who predicted that by Labor Day the United States would be headed for war in the Persian Gulf." This being the case, global vigilance remained imperative. Future security, Cheney said, "will continue to depend in large measure upon our willingness to deploy forces overseas in Europe, Southwest Asia and the Pacific, and to maintain high-quality forces here at home." Far from providing a long-awaited peace, it seemed, the end of the Cold War had simply introduced the United States to a new type of international danger.[70]

The Debate Takes Shape

As this reality dawned on the nation, Americans began the search for a strategy that would guide them through a perilous world. In many cases, these efforts centered less on adapting to the emergent realities of international affairs than on seeking refuge in the experience of the past. Drawing on the positive appraisals of containment that were so common in 1990 and 1991, U.S. commentators proposed to re-create that policy's virtues in the nation's new diplomatic posture. Anticommunism had been a single-minded and easily understandable strategy, many foreign policy thinkers believed, and its replacement should follow suit. Despite the fact that the emerging security environment looked quite complicated and unpredictable, U.S. observers persisted in demanding a foreign policy that would make sense of an inchoate global arena. "The world is going to be messy in the decades ahead," predicted House Foreign Affairs Committee chairman Lee Hamilton in 1991. "We've got to begin to lay an intellectual base for U.S. involvement in the world, a rationale that people understand and support and around which you can build a consensus, as was done with containment." In Hamilton's view, the disorderliness of international politics made articulating an orderly vision of foreign policy all the more urgent.[71]

Other observers took much the same perspective, hoping for a singular vision akin to containment to define U.S. policy in the coming decades. In 1991 and early 1992, comparisons to the early Cold War were ubiquitous as policy makers and foreign-policy intellectuals looked backward in an attempt to move forward. Diplomatic thinkers anxiously awaited the arrival of a new doctrine as comprehensible and popular as its predecessor. "Now that the Cold War is over, we are looking for another X," said *Foreign Affairs* editor Peter Grose, in a reference to George Kennan's nom de plume, "someone who can come along and write the single article laying down the architecture that will shape our foreign policy for the next 40 years."[72]

If the idea that U.S. officials should be able to set down the nation's diplomatic course for the next two generations seems unreasonable in light of the U.S. foreign policy experience of the 1990s, relatively few observers saw much wrong with this formulation at the outset of the decade. As Americans accepted that the post-bipolar era would be dangerous and unstable, they demanded that officials in Washington replicate the experience of the Cold War in terms of providing constancy and understandability to the U.S. worldview. The degree to which containment's exalted status influenced thinking on the future of foreign policy was obvious from the analogies used by public commentators. To craft a new grand strategy, *New York Times* writer R. W. Apple believed, the United States needed great conceptual thinkers, giants in the mold of the early cold warriors. These statesmen had seen through the chaos of the postwar period and placed a firm hand on the United States' diplomatic rudder; similar vision and courage were imperative in the early 1990s. "Is there another Dean Acheson in the wings, ready to help in the recreation of world order?" asked Apple. Although containment was obviously no longer relevant as a policy, its legacy seemed as salient as ever.[73]

In the wake of the Gulf War and the fall of the Soviet Union, the basic intellectual themes that had taken root near the end of the Cold War found fertile ground. Those who thought that the end of bipolarity would complicate the practice of foreign policy seemed to be vindicated as new threats arose in place of the old. As Saddam Hussein had so emphatically illustrated, U.S. security (at least as Americans defined it) still hinged on developments in faraway places, and if the Gulf War was any indication, those developments might be more difficult to manage than ones of the foregone era. The notion that containment provided a model for a successful security strategy also prospered, and a successor to that doctrine was in high demand as the post–Cold War era unfolded. At the dawn of the 1990s, U.S. strategic thinking thus blended a recognition of new realities with an attachment to past verities.

There was tension between these foremost intellectual precepts of post–Cold War foreign policy. On the one hand, there was the belief that the new age was so dangerous because the menaces that inhabited it were diverse and unpredictable. On the other hand, there was the belief that the rigidity and structure of containment could serve as paragons for the security strategy of the future. In logical terms, these beliefs were incongruous: was not a simplistic policy inappropriate for a time of complexity and instability? From the start, the components of cognitive dissonance existed within the public debate.

If friction was a possibility, though, relatively few observers seemed to realize it. Amid the calls for a new doctrine in the mold of containment were comparatively few comments about the potential shortcomings of such a strategy in the world currently taking shape. If this absence seems glaring from the space of fifteen years, it was not nearly so obvious at the time. The logic of the day was more straightforward. Facing uncertainty regarding the international environment and the United States' role in it, public commentators and officials looked for a strategy similar to the one that had supposedly led them through their previous hour of peril. Given the common belief that the simplicity and forcefulness of containment had been integral to winning the Cold War, it was intuitive to seek a like-structured conception of U.S. purpose as a new era of danger unfolded.

3

The Search for Order

If containment was the standard for foreign policy, however, meeting that standard would be difficult indeed. During the Cold War, anticommunism had provided an intellectual structure to foreign policy, allowing U.S. officials to prioritize commitments and objectives according to a fairly (and often deceptively) uncomplicated calculus. Although this litmus test misinformed as often as it guided, it still served as a relatively straightforward means of evaluating individual initiatives. By 1991, there was no longer such an obvious measure of foreign policy. Instead of facing a single dominant threat, the United States now confronted multiple perils. Moreover, although each of these challenges was no doubt dangerous, none was sufficiently menacing to rivet American attention as the Soviet bogey had. This was a basic problem of public thought on foreign policy in the early 1990s: it stated that U.S. diplomacy should be clear and coherent but failed to identify a single overriding threat or objective that would make it so. When Americans demanded a replacement for containment, they therefore sought a strategy that would reduce an undeniably complex situation to a one-size-fits-all formula.

Anticommunism also left an imposing political legacy. For more than forty years, the Cold War had served as an almost unbeatable rhetorical device. The specter of Sovietism had provided an enduring domestic consensus in support of containment. The political strength of the doctrine was obvious throughout the Cold War, as ethically questionable policies and hundreds of thousands of U.S. casualties altered only the tactics, but not the basic premise, of the nation's security strategy.[1]

One source of containment's strength had been geopolitical, that is, the perception that Soviet foreign policy posed an imminent threat to U.S. interests and, indeed, lives. Roused by this danger, Americans accepted the globalist foreign policy, massive defense establishment, and intrusive internal practices that had previously been taboo except in times of war. Additionally, the perception of threat limited the boundaries of dissent from U.S. policy, confining this debate to the particulars (massive retaliation, flexible response, détente, and containment's other various incarnations) rather than the generalities (the need to confront and restrain Soviet power).

An equally potent wellspring of anticommunism's vitality had been its moral clarity. Containment was not simply a means of protecting America's interests but also an opportunity to further its ideals; it was a crusade against slavery and on behalf of freedom. The fact that Washington's chief antagonist held utterly foreign conceptions of government, personal liberty, and religion allowed Americans to see the international situation as a struggle between good and evil. This identification of U.S. diplomacy with an ultimate moral end captured the nation's tendency toward idealism and contributed substantially to the political durability of anticommunism. With the end of the Cold War, though, both the geopolitical and moral taproots of domestic support for foreign policy had vanished. The threat was gone; the mission accomplished.[2]

When U.S. officials attempted to fashion a new security strategy, they thus confronted a daunting precedent. In addition to identifying some organizing principle that would help them make sense of a world that looked more chaotic by the day, they had to relocate the sources of public consensus that had vanished with the close of the Cold War. Bush had entered office schooled in the verities of the U.S.-Soviet conflict, but it was this vastly different task that he faced in the second half of his term. As might have been expected, he struggled. Bush attempted to juggle the competing requirements of crafting a new strategy, but he ultimately failed to find a suitable balance between the diplomatic and political dictates of foreign policy. The president's idealistic rhetoric of human rights and democracy appealed to public observers but left his own strategists unmoved. A more pragmatic policy found support in the Pentagon but lacked public backing. As Bush left office, containment's replacement had yet to be found.

Starting Anew

By the midpoint of Bush's presidency, the administration had become anxious to adapt its diplomatic thinking to the new order of things. In one sense, this urgency reflected growing perceptions of disorder and danger in the international environment. Uncertainty was the dominant theme; Dick Cheney remarked that "we have good reason to wonder about what might come next" in world affairs. Brent Scowcroft was more pessimistic, worrying about the destabilizing impact of the Cold War's end. "The outlines of a very messy world" were in view, he believed.[3]

This impression grew stronger as the post–Cold War era unfolded. Regional conflicts in the Middle East, ethnic and civil strife in the Balkans and Africa, nuclear proliferation, and the prospect of post-Soviet chaos all loomed large in 1991 and 1992. "The final shape of the future is far from established," commented Robert Gates in early 1992. "We should expect continuing change and upheaval around the world." To ensure the nation's security, he believed, U.S. policies must "conform to the reality of an unstable, unpredictable, dangerously overarmed, and still transforming world."[4]

Watching this transformation unfold, the White House looked to reset its priorities. "The old [defense] strategy that has dominated our thinking for so many years" had become irrelevant with bipolarity's end, Cheney argued. Without a new plan for managing foreign policy, Bush's advisers feared, the complexity of the dawning era would overwhelm U.S. officials. To manage the array of original dangers and reemerging threats that characterized the early 1990s, the administration needed a clear idea of American interests and capabilities, a framework that would structure the allocation of scarce resources and allow U.S. officials to focus on the most important matters. "Our new era brings with it a new need for new guideposts, for solutions and approaches that keep pace with the times," said Bush.[5]

The need for new ideas also stemmed from the recent breakdown of the fifty-year consensus on foreign policy. With Sovietism defeated, domestic agreement on the basic underpinnings of U.S. strategy began to disintegrate. Between 1990 and 1992, public debate on foreign policy showed the emergence of a new discord not only about specific initiatives but also about the nation's fundamental diplomatic philosophy. Some observers looked to the Gulf War as precedent, arguing that the end of U.S.-Soviet hostility made possible the long-delayed realization of collective security. Political scientist Bruce Russett argued in 1991 that international cooperation against aggression could "change the parameters of the global order to something more favorable than existed under the prior status quo." Calling for the establishment of a permanent UN army, Russett pointed to coalition action against Iraq as proof of the Security Council's ability to work for "the maintenance of peace in a new world order." For Russett, the United Nations was the key to post–Cold War peace.[6]

Hardly, replied neoconservatives such as Charles Krauthammer. Dismissing the prevalent idea that multipolarity would replace bipolarity, Krauthammer argued that the United States stood at the pinnacle of global affairs. Germany and Japan, rising powers in the late 1980s, "have generally hidden under the table since the first shots rang out in Kuwait," he derided. The end of the Cold War had led not to the diffusion of power but rather to its centralization. "The immediate post–Cold War world is not multipolar," he wrote. "It is unipolar. The center of world power is the United States, attended by its Western allies." Disdainful of those who contended the opposite, Krauthammer had even less patience for commentators who placed their faith in the United Nations. "The United Nations is guarantor of nothing," he wrote. It was the United States that had assembled the coalition and led the fight against Saddam Hussein, not some nebulous organization that "can hardly be said to exist." The solution to post–Cold War instability was not UN-imposed collective security but a Pax Americana. Only the United States had the power to create order from chaos. "If America wants stability, it will have to create it," Krauthammer concluded. "The alternative to unipolarity is chaos."[7]

The neoconservatives were not united in their support for an assertive foreign policy, though. Jeanne Kirkpatrick, never shy about the need for diplomatic activism during the Cold War, sounded a distinctly different note in 1990. Following in the intellectual footsteps of Paul Kennedy, whose widely read book *The Rise and Fall of the Great Powers* had predicted in 1987 that the United States would soon succumb to "imperial overstretch," Kirkpatrick advocated a circumscribed approach to world affairs. With the Soviet Union defeated, she argued, the United States' real problems were domestic. Shouldering the burdens of foreign affairs, however necessary that task might have been when the Soviets wanted to conquer the world, had distracted the United States from critical social and economic issues at home. The end of the Cold War offered the opportunity to tend to these concerns. "It is time to give up the dubious benefits of superpower status," she wrote. The United States would be best served by abandoning its globalist pretensions and becoming "a normal country in a normal time."[8]

The paleoconservatives agreed. Pat Buchanan, formerly a speechwriter for Richard Nixon, advocated the closest thing to outright isolationism. "With the Cold War ending, we should look . . . with a cold eye on the internationalist set," he wrote, "never at a loss for new ideas to divert U.S. wealth and power into crusades and causes having little or nothing to do with the true national interest of the United States." Buchanan scorned the idea that the nation needed an activist foreign policy to ensure its defense. "Blessed by Providence with pacific neighbors, north and south, and vast oceans, east and west, to protect us, why seek permanent entanglement in other people's quarrels?"[9]

Though many believed that such sentiments had been forever discredited by Pearl Harbor, Buchanan's argument appealed to a surprising number of Americans. During the 1992 presidential campaign, Texas billionaire Ross Perot picked up the banner of retrenchment with his emphasis on decreasing U.S. commitments abroad. "Our highest foreign-policy priority is to get our house in order and make America work again," Perot declared. Perot's appeals resonated in some quarters; the candidate received 19 percent of the national vote and likely would have done better had he not dropped out of the race temporarily.[10]

The fragmentation of public debate on foreign policy, and especially the relative prevalence of isolationist sentiment, was profoundly troubling to Bush and his top aides. In the 1991 *National Security Strategy,* the administration warned against retrenchment. "In the

1920s, judging that the great threat to our interests had collapsed and that no comparable threat was evident, the Nation turned inward," the document reminded. "That course had near disastrous consequences then and it would be even more dangerous now." During the next two years, Bush's public statements frequently betrayed a fear of a creeping isolationism that would render the nation vulnerable to lurking threats. "Anyone who says we should retreat into an isolationist cocoon is living in the last century," he said.[11]

For Bush, domestic concerns therefore merged with the fear of international instability, spurring the administration to enunciate a new doctrine. Order was needed in U.S. policy abroad and public debate at home. As the Cold War gave way to something new, Bush and his advisers looked for a solution to the confusion and disagreement that surrounded them.

Catchphrase Diplomacy

Bush's first opportunity to chart this new course came in August 1990. While the president was pondering the dictates of national security and public consensus, he found himself in need of a justification for taking the nation to the brink of war with Saddam Hussein. For Bush, the rationale was clear: the future shape of the Middle East, access to oil, and the United States' economic vitality were at stake. Yet the president's advisers feared that the public audience would not be receptive to appeals based solely on cold pragmatism. Bush needed a higher purpose, something to motivate the idealists. Early in the crisis, Colin Powell hinted at this problem. The need to confront Hussein was a given, he argued. "The question is how do you lay it out to the public."[12]

This question seemed especially important in the aftermath of the initial deployment to Saudi Arabia. With both houses of Congress in Democratic hands, Bush was hardly assured of legislative support for Desert Shield. Within weeks, in fact, Democrats attacked the president's policy. Senator Bob Kerrey of Nebraska, a leading Democratic voice on foreign affairs, pronounced himself "profoundly uneasy about the instant deployment of over 100,000 American troops, sold to the American people on false assertions that Saddam Hussein is

Adolf Hitler, that our way of life is at clear and present danger, that we have as much at stake as we did in World War II." Although public approval of Bush's policies held, nagging questions remained. Strong majorities of Americans believed that Bush's desire for a showdown stemmed from selfish economic concerns, with only 24 percent agreeing that "a moral principle" was the president's primary motivation. The potentially dangerous effect of this notion was confirmed when James Baker said that the crisis was about "jobs," and critics decried the administration's lack of altruism. In these circumstances, a unifying rationale for Desert Shield seemed all the more necessary.[13]

In late August, Bush and Scowcroft hit on an answer to both the immediate problem and the larger need to reestablish a consensus on foreign policy. After retreating to the president's summer home in Maine to discuss the Gulf crisis, Bush and Scowcroft coined a phrase to justify U.S. involvement in the Iraq-Kuwait dispute as well as continued participation in post–Cold War international relations: the "New World Order." In their memoirs, Bush and Scowcroft claimed that the term signified a belief that the thawing of the Cold War had raised the prospect of greater international cooperation against the various forms of disorder that threatened in the early 1990s. The point, said Scowcroft, was to take advantage of the "collapse of the U.S.-Soviet antagonisms" to "build an order beyond [the Gulf] crisis." With the Cold War over, the United States could mobilize UN support in combating aggression and resolving humanitarian crises and ethnic conflicts. In this respect, the New World Order was, as Bush put it, "a challenge to keep the dangers of disorder at bay."[14]

There may have been a geopolitical component to the New World Order, but at its heart, the notion was a domestic political creation. Although Bush and Scowcroft certainly believed that the concept could be useful in dealing with the challenges of international affairs, the national security adviser conceded in 1991 that the main rationale for the term was less noble. It was, he told a reporter, merely a "catchphrase." As would soon become clear, the expression was useful in offering an attractive purpose for U.S. involvement in the Gulf, but less so for actually encapsulating the president's overall conception of policy.[15]

During the Gulf crisis, the catchphrase's domestic political value was most salient. Fearing a rise in opposition to Desert Shield and Desert Storm, Bush's political advisers focused on providing an appealing rationale for U.S. policy. After reading a draft of a presidential address to be delivered at a joint session of Congress on September 11, White House aide Andrew Card wrote, "My thought—needs a bit more punch." Another adviser composed an outline of themes for the speech. The paper built on Bush's original conception of the New World Order, emphasizing the moral as well as the geopolitical connotations of the phrase. "Out of these troubled time, a new world order will emerge," it stated. "With the course we have charted, we can not only reverse the Iraqi aggression. We can also establish a cooperative precedent—making the post–Cold War era freer from the threat of terror; and making the community of nations stronger in the pursuit of justice, and more secure in the quest for peace."[16]

Bush's joint session address borrowed liberally from these suggestions, placing a moral and ethical slant on the New World Order. Indeed, the more Bush referred to the New World Order, the more he stressed its idealistic—rather than its practical—meanings. Addressing Congress, Bush made only passing reference to the demise of U.S.-Soviet competition and the consequent prospects for multilateral action, focusing on the grander moral import of the New World Order. "Today that new world is struggling to be born, a world quite different from the one we've known," he declared. "A world where the rule of law supplants the rule of the jungle. A world in which nations recognize the shared responsibility for freedom and justice. A world where the strong respect the rights of the weak." Given this exalted language, observers could be pardoned for interpreting the New World Order largely as a moral statement.[17]

The idea was popular at first, and as the crisis dragged on through late 1990 and early 1991, the administration returned to the theme. After Bush announced that the U.S. mission in the Gulf had gone from defense to offense, he again had to consider the prospect of public or congressional repudiation. Although ramping up the pressure on Hussein was not an unpopular move, there remained considerable public anxiety over the prospect of war. Forty percent of those surveyed thought it "very likely" or "somewhat likely" that military action would turn into "another prolonged situation like the Vietnam conflict." Many congressional observers reacted negatively to the offensive deployment, especially after Bush asked for authority to use force in early January. Influential Minnesota senator Paul Wellstone accused Bush of a "rush to war," and Representative James McDermott (D-Wash.) predicted that military conflict would result in "perhaps tens of thousands of deaths and casualties."[18]

In light of these concerns, Bush and his spokesmen placed a heavy reliance on the moral appeal of the New World Order. Often, they could not resist endowing the term with grandiose meanings. Making a conscious effort to stay "on message," the White House Cabinet Affairs Office created "communications packages" outlining themes for U.S. officials to stress when dealing with the media. These packages generally minimized the geopolitical connotations of the New World Order in favor of its moral themes. "Morally, we must act so that international law, not international outlaws, governs the post–Cold War world," stated one version of the package. "We must act so that justice, not brutal force, governs this new era." Law, justice, and freedom: these notions quickly became the public face of the New World Order.[19]

As crisis turned to war, the moral undertones of the New World Order were ubiquitous. In press conferences and speeches, Bush rarely missed an opportunity to remind his audience that the Gulf War was about more than the Gulf; it was about the principles that would govern international relations after the Cold War. In a victory speech on March 6, 1991, he portrayed the war in the Gulf as a first step toward a just international order. Urged on by NSC staffer Richard Haass and aides who scoured the addresses of Winston Churchill and Woodrow Wilson for lofty ideas and choice phrases, White House speechwriters gave Bush's remarks an exalted air. He stated grandly:

> Now, we can see a new world coming into view. A world in which there is the very real prospect of a new world order. In the words of Winston Churchill, a world in which "the principles of justice and fair play protect the weak against the strong." A world where the United Nations—freed from cold war stalemate—is poised to fulfill the historic vision of its founders. A world in which freedom and respect for human rights find a home among all nations.[20]

With the Gulf War over, though, what would become of the New

World Order? The president had not given it much thought, hardly considering what the term actually meant in practice. This paucity of substance was obvious as Bush avoided delving into the specifics of the New World Order during and after the Gulf crisis. Bush rarely touched on the concrete aspects of the notion, with the exception of an instance in February when he asserted that the New World Order would feature a "revitalized peacekeeping function" of the UN Security Council. The shallowness of the idea annoyed those advisers who had to deal with the details of everyday policy. One State Department official complained that the term was "a buzzword for nothing."[21]

What the New World Order lacked in meaning, however, it more than made up for in style. The term's emphasis on morality and justice appealed to those looking for a new U.S. role in the world. The New World Order, argued conservative commentator Joshua Muravchik, offered the prospect of a more humane system. "This Pax Americana will rest not on domination but on persuasion and example as well as power," he wrote enthusiastically. "It will consist not of empire but of having won over a large and growing part of the world not only to the joys of jeans and rock and Big Macs but also to our concept of how nations ought to be governed and to behave." Having earned such glowing reviews, Bush refused to part with the phrase, and when pressed to elaborate on the still-vague New World Order, he duly responded. In April, Bush reinforced the Wilsonian underpinnings of the doctrine in a speech at the Air War College. "The new world order really is a tool for addressing a new world of possibilities," Bush declared. "This order gains its mission and shape not just from shared interests but shared ideals." These ideals encompassed "a set of principles that undergird our relations: peaceful settlement of disputes, solidarity against aggression, reduced and controlled arsenals, and just treatment of all peoples."[22]

Generalities aside, this speech gave away little in terms of how Bush planned to pursue his vision. Solidarity against aggression was fine in the abstract, but it was another thing altogether once the shooting started. In September, Bush gave slightly more body to the New World Order, advocating an enhanced UN role in resolving disputes and supporting human rights. "For the first time," he announced, "we have a real chance to fulfill the UN Charter's ambition of working 'to save succeeding generations from the scourge of war, to reaffirm faith in fundamental human rights.'" The speech was again light on specifics, but Bush seemed to envision the United Nations playing a key role in encouraging nations to honor the ideals of the New World Order. "Where institutions of freedom have lain dormant, the United Nations can offer them new life," he said.[23]

Still, the New World Order was long on rhetoric and short on substance. The practicalities of the idea were unmentioned, the moral connotations undiminished. Whatever its shortcomings, however, the "catchphrase," as Scowcroft referred to it, accomplished its purpose. Although support for U.S. policy in the Gulf waxed and waned during the run-up to war, public commentators eventually embraced the notion that the conflict was about something grander than money, oil, and power. Bush's emphasis on human rights was particularly popular. One poll showed that 58 percent of respondents viewed "protecting and defending human rights in other countries" as "very important," with another 33 percent labeling it "somewhat important." Editorial comment on the New World Order was favorable as well, as the idea garnered praise from the *New York Times* and other media outlets.[24]

Perhaps more important, the New World Order was successful in sparking optimism about the future of U.S. involvement overseas. Bush's rhetoric put the now-fleeting sense of hope engendered by the end of the Cold War to good use, giving Americans something to look forward to in post–Cold War foreign policy. Although self-described "realists" shook their heads and derided American naïveté, other observers were more receptive to the idea that U.S. policy could embody ideals as well as interests. A writer for the *Boston Globe* surveyed the public mood at war's end and concluded that the president's rhetoric "seemed to capture a widespread sense that the world had indeed reached some kind of turning point." There were signs that the domestic audience embraced Bush's high-toned principles as cornerstones of U.S. diplomacy. A poll taken in June 1991 revealed that 80 percent of those surveyed advocated the multilateral use of force against a regime that used unconventional weapons or violated the sovereignty of another country. More striking still, 91 percent believed that a dictator who violated the human rights of his own citizens represented a grave danger to international order. As a justification for the Gulf War and U.S. foreign policy, the New World Order was a hit.[25]

The Pragmatists Object

Ironically, public enthusiasm for the New World Order exceeded the administration's willingness to pursue the ideas Bush espoused. During 1991 and 1992, it became apparent that many of Bush's advisers (as well as Bush himself) were not persuaded by the centrality of international justice or the rationale for a morals-oriented, multilateralist foreign policy. In the end, the pragmatists triumphed, leaving the New World Order bankrupt both practically and politically.

Even at the outset, Bush's top advisers had not believed that the New World Order was as all-encompassing as the president publicly portrayed it to be. In 1991, Scowcroft complained that he had lost control of his own creation. Public commentators, he believed, were attributing "too much specificity" to the New World Order, giving it meanings he had never intended. For Scowcroft, the idea had been mainly a rhetorical abstraction, not a definitive conception of policy. The principles that the doctrine supposedly embodied, he conceded, were "not all that clear." The New World Order was "not a specific road map with intersections and left turns and right turns and ups and downs." The notion had some relevance in terms of the ability of the United States and the Soviet Union to work together in extraordinary circumstances, he said, but little more. In short, the New World Order was no firm guide for U.S. policy, and certainly not to the morally grandiose extent of Bush's public statements.[26]

Baker was no more enamored of the concept. Despite its expansive connotations, the New World Order was actually a rather narrow conception of U.S. interests. In early 1992, Baker explained to the Senate that the nation had a wide variety of objectives in the post–Cold War world. Washington should limit the proliferation of nuclear, chemical, and biological weapons (weapons of mass destruction); seek stability in the former Soviet Union and other strategically important areas; attend to regional conflicts; expand opportunities for free trade; redefine NATO's mission for the 1990s; and promote democracy. These aims were numerous and potentially contradictory, and they defied easy expression in a phrase such as the *New World Order.* The United States had a number of goals, Baker implied, and would need a number of strategies to meet them.[27]

Internal antipathy to the New World Order became clearer as U.S. officials delved into the specifics of the idea. Bush's public statements to the contrary, many of the president's advisers had grave reservations about the peacekeeping and humanitarian missions thought to be central to the New World Order. For certain officials in the State and Defense departments, peacekeeping was a black hole rather than a new mechanism for securing peace and justice. If the United States became embroiled in civil or ethnic conflicts, they feared, it would find itself trapped in bloody and inchoate situations without end. Accordingly, the State Department imposed strict tests for determining when and how Washington would support UN peacekeeping operations. "We do not view UN peacekeeping as the savior of lost causes, to be thrown into a crisis willy nilly when all else fails," State Department official John Bolton reassured the Congress. Peacekeeping missions should "have as clearly defined a mandate as possible," a fixed duration, and be "tied to a process which will clearly lead to a resolution of the underlying problem." Bolton envisioned U.S. intervention only in cases in which the issues were clear-cut and not particularly intractable. This stance implied a commitment to peacekeeping that was far smaller than Bush had hinted in his public statements.[28]

The Pentagon was equally hostile to the type of missions that might fall within the purview of the New World Order. As Powell and Cheney grappled with the already difficult task of adapting U.S. military power to the post–Cold War era, they had little desire to dilute that might by excessive adventurism. In 1991 and 1992, Powell repeatedly emphasized that the role of the military was to defend vital U.S. interests, not to act as the guarantor of human rights or other ideals that were, at best, peripheral to national security. The "U.S. National Military Strategy," Powell stated, "is straightforward and simple: avoid fighting wars, deter aggression. Should deterrence fail, defend the vital interests of the United States and our friends in a world that is going to be very uncertain and will have major elements of instability for years to come." Powell did not say so explicitly, but it was clear that this definition left little room for peacekeeping or interventions in defense of high principles.[29]

Powell, who had a near-visceral aversion to this type of action, soon emerged as a chief opponent of the New World Order. Powell's formative military experience had been the Vietnam War, and he resolved never to repeat the mistakes of his predecessors. "As a mid-level career officer," he recalled, "I had been appalled at the docility of the Joint Chiefs of Staff, fighting the war in Vietnam without ever pressing the political leaders to lay out clear objectives." In Powell's view, the United States should avoid the limited, open-ended interventions that had led to catastrophe in Vietnam and that seemed likely to result from attempts to deal with the ethnic and human rights crises of the early 1990s. Involvement in limited war, with political objectives that were hazy at best, seemed a surefire recipe for long-term commitments to conflicts whose very nature prevented the military from taking the steps necessary to win. "The Armed Forces of the United States exists to win if sent in harm's way," Powell argued, not to act as a global constabulary in situations with little direct import for national security. Furthermore, he warned, civil wars and ethnic conflict were like quicksand: one might enter with the intention of only dipping a foot but end up totally immersed. When certain officials suggested U.S. intervention in the Bosnian civil war in 1992, Powell was quick to point to the lessons of Vietnam. "I get nervous when so-called experts suggest that all we need is a little surgical bombing or a limited attack," he warned. "When the desired result isn't obtained, a new set of experts then comes forward with talk of a little escalation. History has not been kind to that approach."[30]

Powell eventually refined his anti-interventionism to a science, or, to be more accurate, a doctrine. By 1992, Powell had adopted and slightly refashioned the ideas of former secretary of defense Caspar Weinberger. Late that year, the Joint Chiefs of Staff chairman published an article in *Foreign Affairs* outlining rigid criteria for whether the United States should intervene in a given conflict. "Is the political objective we seek to achieve important, clearly defined and understood?" he asked. "Have all other non-violent policy means failed? Will military force achieve the objective? At what cost? Have the gains and risks been analyzed? How might the situation that we seek to alter, once it is altered by force, develop further and what might be the consequences?" Under these conditions, U.S. involvement in anything short of a major war in a region of crucial strategic or economic importance looked unlikely. To make sure that everyone got the point, Powell subsequently elaborated his dislike for excessive interventionism:

> When the political objective is important, clearly defined and understood, when the risks are acceptable, and when the use of force can be effectively combined with diplomatic and economic policies, then clear and unambiguous objectives must be given to the armed forces. These objectives must be firmly linked with the political objectives. We must not, for example, send military forces into a crisis with an unclear mission they cannot accomplish—such as we did when we sent the U.S. Marines into Lebanon in 1983. We inserted those proud warriors into the middle of a five-faction civil war complete with terrorists, hostage-takers, and a dozen spies in every camp, and said, "Gentlemen, be a buffer." The results were 241 dead Marines and Navy personnel and a U.S. withdrawal from the troubled area.[31]

As Powell's, Bolton's, Baker's, and Scowcroft's views on U.S. political and military strategy indicated, there was little internal support for the type of policies implied by the New World Order. The idea worked in a rhetorical and political sense, but not in terms of its applicability to the day-to-day imperatives of U.S. policy. This tension simply pointed back to the reality that although the New World Order contained a certain geopolitical logic, Bush and Scowcroft had conceived the idea mainly as a justification for foreign policy, rather than as a coherent policy itself. Only because Bush sold the notion so well did it achieve widespread recognition as doctrine. In practical terms, though, the New World Order was empty from the start.

What New World Order?

What Scowcroft's skepticism and Powell's twist on the Weinberger Doctrine implied, the U.S. reaction to a series of humanitarian crises in 1991 and 1992 illustrated more pungently. In several instances, Bush showed a marked lack of enthusiasm for intervention in conflicts that appeared to be ideal test cases for the New World Order, instead choosing to stay on the sidelines when vital interests were not at stake. By the end of his term, it was difficult to deny that cautious pragmatism had carried the day over the idealism of the New World Order.

The first of these crises erupted in Yugoslavia in June 1991. Since the death of dictator Tito in 1980, Yugoslavia had been a country in decline. Without a dominant personality to hold the multinational state together, long-latent social and political tensions among Yugoslavia's constituent republics reappeared, and the process accelerated in the late 1980s. As in the Soviet Union, the collapse of the communist regime in Belgrade led to a rise in nationalist agitation. Opportunistic politicians, most notably (but not only) Serbia's Slobodan Milosevic, exploited this rising nationalism for their own ends, and Yugoslavia began to disintegrate. During 1990 and 1991, Milosevic's calls for the creation of a "Greater Serbia" that would include those parts of neighboring republics inhabited by Serbs created widespread insecurity. The spark came in May 1991, when Serbia refused to relinquish its hold on Yugoslavia's federal presidency. Fearing a power grab, Croatia and Slovenia declared independence. The Yugoslav army, which was 70 percent Serb, retaliated, attacking border posts before moving into Croatia and Slovenia proper. Although a ceasefire stopped the fighting in Slovenia by late summer, the violence continued in Croatia. The civil war raged on, claiming thousands of lives by late 1991.[32]

The CIA, State Department, and National Security Council had all known for months that bloodshed was likely in the Balkans. "Signs are increasing of a military move against Croatia and Slovenia," one NSC adviser warned in January 1991. When the feared scenario played out in July and August, it soon became clear that Milosevic was the chief culprit in the escalating violence. Although Bush had been reluctant to say exactly what the New World Order was, there was an uneasy feeling that it did not include allowing leaders like Milosevic to brutalize their neighbors on the basis of ethnicity. "The issue in Yugoslavia is the illegitimate use of force for armed ends," wrote the editors of the *New York Times*. "The last time that happened, the president said such aggression could not stand."[33]

For Bush, however, the civil war in Croatia lacked the economic or strategic import that would justify U.S. involvement. The killing might be troubling from a moral perspective, but it did not threaten national security or prosperity. "I've told our top people, 'We don't want to put a dog in this fight,'" Bush confided to his diary as the conflict began. "It's not one that we have to mastermind. . . . This concept that we have to work out every problem, everywhere in the world, is crazy." In other words, Bush had written off Croatia and the major premise of the New World Order. In his memoirs, Baker was equally blunt in explaining why there was no impetus for intervention: "Milosevic had Saddam's appetite, but Serbia didn't have Iraq's capabilities or ability to affect America's vital interests, such as access to energy supplies." Washington remained aloof from the war in Croatia, allowing the European Community to take the lead with threats and peace missions that provided little respite for those being slaughtered. When U.S. action came, it was limited to support for an arms embargo on the entire region, a step that essentially codified Serb military superiority.[34]

The Balkan crisis worsened in early 1992. Since the start of the war a year earlier, Bosnian leader Alija Izetbegovic had attempted to stay clear of the fighting, neither allying with Serbia nor moving toward independence. When Milosevic emerged as the dominant figure in what was left of Yugoslavia, this position became untenable. Milosevic's calls for Bosnian Serbs to join Greater Serbia had created grave tensions among Bosnia's Serb, Muslim, and Croat populations, and Izetbegovic feared that inaction would mean the end of Bosnian autonomy. By early 1992, Serbia and Croatia had claimed more than three-quarters of Bosnia's territory as their own, and Milosevic and Croatia's Franjo Tudjman had in fact secretly agreed to divide the republic between them. In March, Bosnia's Muslim faction opted for independence, and the Serbs again responded by invading.[35]

Even when the fighting spread to Bosnia and the bloodshed worsened, Bush and his advisers remained opposed to intervention. State Department official Margaret Tutweiler implicitly challenged the tenets of the New World Order, dismissing the notion that the United States had a moral imperative to intercede. "Where is it written that the United States government is the military policeman of the world?"

she asked. Also discouraging intervention was a belief that the Balkan conflict was ultimately intractable. Ethnic wars, Bush thought, sprang from deep-seated hatred and were therefore not amenable to outside solutions. "You have ancient ethnic rivalries that have cropped up as Yugoslavia is dissolved or getting dissolved," he argued. "It isn't going to be solved by sending in the 82nd Airborne."[36]

Moreover, by 1992, Bush adhered to Powell's minimalist view of military intervention. From this perspective, the situation in Bosnia did not satisfy the criteria for U.S. involvement. Asked about intervention in October 1992, Bush replied, "I won't do that until the military, Colin Powell, Cheney, come to me and say, 'Here's what we need to do. Here's what our mission is. And here's how those kids are going to get out.' Vietnam, we didn't do it that way. We made a big mistake. Saudi Arabia, we did do it the way I say, and something good happened." By late 1992, the lessons of Vietnam had become omnipresent in Bush's statements on Bosnia and other areas rife with ethnic strife. "I learned something from Vietnam," he said. "I am not going to commit U.S. forces until I know what the mission is, until the military tell me that it can be completed, until I know how they can come out." Powell's views had become Bush's, removing whatever impulse for intervention there might have been.[37]

The New World Order absorbed another setback in late 1991. A year earlier, in December 1990, Haiti had ended decades of dictatorship and corrupt rule with the election of President Jean-Bertrand Aristide. But as Aristide attempted to implement an ambitious social reform program in 1991, his power eroded. The Haitian upper class objected to his redistributive economic policies, and poorer elements believed that the reforms had not come quickly enough. After Aristide attempted to purge the military of old-regime loyalists, he lost the support of that institution, and the situation in Haiti unraveled. Aristide sanctioned the use of violence against his opponents, and in September 1991, a group of military officials staged a successful putsch.[38]

For Bush, the coup posed a number of political and diplomatic problems. The president had praised Aristide's election as a signal of Haiti's turn away from tyranny, and the small Caribbean country was an example of the rising tide of democracy that Bush so liked to reference when ostracizing Castro or talking about the New World Order.

Aristide's own actions also ensured that the coup was prominent in American thinking, as his flight from Port-au-Prince to Washington (and subsequent authorship of op-ed pieces urging intervention) served as a visible reminder of Haiti's setback.

Bush initially took a strong stance against the coup. He affirmed his support for Aristide and scorned Haiti's military henchmen. Baker stated that the United States was committed to opposing the new regime of General Raoul Cedras, saying pointedly, "This coup must not and will not succeed." As with Croatia and Bosnia, Haiti seemed to many domestic observers to be a test of Bush's sincerity. As one writer for the *New York Times* phrased it, "The coup in Haiti has put the Bush administration and its talk of a new world order on the spot: can it do any less to restore a democratically elected Government next door in the Caribbean than it did to put a feudal monarch back on the throne in Kuwait?"[39]

The answer was yes. Although the administration took a firm public position on the coup by breaking diplomatic relations and suspending economic aid to Haiti, it proved unwilling to take more assertive steps. When rumors spread that military intervention would be necessary to return Aristide to office, Bush immediately nixed the idea. "There's a lesson out there for all Presidents, and the lesson I've learned is that you've got to be very, very careful of using United States forces in this hemisphere."[40] Administration spokesmen pointed to Panama in 1964 and the Dominican Republic in 1965 as cautionary examples, warning of the deleterious effects of interventionism. Bush's newfound respect for the sovereignty of the nations of Latin America and the Caribbean seemed suspect, given that he had ordered the invasion of Panama two years earlier under similar circumstances. More likely, Bush had little enthusiasm for sending troops into battle when no tangible interests were at stake. There was no Panama Canal in Haiti, and U.S. economic involvement in Haiti was minimal. New World Order or no, democracy's reversal in Haiti was not reason enough for a strong response.

Bush's reaction to the coup culminated in the implementation of economic sanctions at the end of October. The president expressed confidence that the combination of moral opprobrium and financial pain would cause Cedras to yield. Within the administration, though, most advisers thought otherwise. Assistant Secretary of State Bernard Aronson warned that the sanctions would probably prove ineffective. "This is not a scalpel. It is much more like a sledgehammer," he said. "It is clear that Haiti will feel the effect of the sanctions. But whether or not those who hold de facto power and those who hold the guns will respond by agreeing to negotiate President Aristide's return is not clear." In essence, sanctions were more useful as proof that the United States was doing something about Haiti than as an actual remedy to the situation.[41]

The gap between rhetoric and reality in Haiti specifically and in the New World Order in general was too great for domestic observers to ignore. As the sanctions failed to have the desired effect, newspaper commentators criticized Bush's timorous response to the coup. A *Washington Post* columnist complained that Haiti "never mattered much to the policy makers of the Cold War, and it seems to count even less in the New World Order." Bush's credibility sustained another blow when he ordered the Coast Guard to deny Haitian refugees asylum. The White House claimed that federal law demanded this response because the refugees did not face political persecution in Haiti. That story seemed dubious, however, after seventy-three refugees were arrested immediately upon their return to Haiti in December 1991.[42]

Even in the face of growing pressure, the administration remained opposed to intervention in Haiti. There was some talk in early 1992 of an expedition under the aegis of the Organization of American States, but this venture quickly crumbled (the only state with any interest in the undertaking, Costa Rica, lacked a military). Bush's tepid policy received a fitting summation in March 1992, when the chief State Department official for human rights matters resigned over policy differences. The Cedras regime remained in power through the end of Bush's presidency.

The New World Order received a third major test in late 1992. A civil war in Somalia had led to political and social chaos in that country and quickly devolved into a humanitarian catastrophe. The fighting disrupted food supplies and any semblance of normal economic activity, and rival clans seized international aid as a means of controlling the civilian population. The conflict wrecked Somalia's infrastructure, reducing much of Mogadishu to ruins. In 1992, starvation killed roughly 300,000 Somalis, and upward of 1 million more fled the country.

In late November, Bush responded to the crisis by ordering U.S. troops into Somalia under UN auspices to oversee the distribution of food and medical supplies. Here, it seemed, the president had finally embraced the principles of the New World Order. Still, it was hard to escape the impression that Bush's motives in Somalia were as much political as humanitarian. Bush responded to the crisis only after the *New York Times* and other major news outlets shamed the administration for its previously inadequate response.[43] Further belying claims of disinterested humanitarianism was the fact that policy makers had resisted internal pressure for intervention for nearly a year. The State Department Bureau of African Affairs and the U.S. Agency for International Development had been urging a relief mission for months but had received little response from Baker or from Lawrence Eagleburger. Even after the Office of U.S. Disaster Assistance warned in May that two-thirds of Somalia's population of 6.5 million faced "the threat of starvation due to the effects of civil strife," the country remained off Bush's agenda.[44]

When the decision to intervene finally came in November 1992, it stemmed from motives that were hardly altruistic. Under mounting criticism for its concurrent failures to resolve the situations in Bosnia and Somalia, the State Department decided that intervention in one of the two areas was politically imperative. Assistant Secretary of State Robert Gallucci presented Eagleburger (now acting secretary, since Baker had agreed to manage Bush's struggling reelection campaign) with a choice between Somalia and Bosnia. Seeing the former mission as the easier of the two to manage, Gallucci recommended Somalia, and Eagleburger concurred.[45]

The administration's framing of Bosnia and Somalia as an either-or proposition illuminated Bush's dilemma with the New World Order. The president had no strategic motive for intervention in either locale and most likely would have preferred that neither of these situations intrude on his foreign policy. Yet Bush's idealistic rhetoric had created public expectations about the shape of his diplomacy, expectations built on the same moralistic streak of the American polity that

Bush had exploited to sell the New World Order. In the end, then, the action that finally afforded a limited measure of credibility to the New World Order demonstrated not Bush's humanitarianism but the runaway rhetoric of the doctrine.

This lack of genuine enthusiasm was obvious at the time of Bush's decision. The president made little pretense that intervention would restore Somalia to a working civil society. Illustrating the political considerations underlying Operation Restore Hope, Bush attempted to impose a January 19, 1993, withdrawal date for the mission. This restriction made sense in terms of not bequeathing an ongoing commitment to the incoming Clinton administration, but it had little relevance to the situation on the ground. Certain officials recognized that a mission of such short duration would be little more than a palliative for Somalia's suffering. Smith Hempstone, the ambassador to Kenya who had done as much as anyone to bring Somalia to Bush's attention, decried the limits on the project. "It will take five years to get Somalia not on its feet but just on its knees," he said. The intervention would keep "tens of thousands of Somali kids from starving to death in 1993 who, in all probability, will starve to death in 1994."[46]

As if to reinforce the idea that Somalia did not herald a departure in humanitarian intervention, Bush took steps to emphasize the extraordinary nature of the mission. On November 24, just one day after deciding to intervene, the president approved NSD 74, which guided U.S. policy on "peacekeeping and emergency humanitarian relief." The document implied that the United States would avoid using its own troops in such missions, instead contributing only "unique" capabilities such as airlift, logistics, and communications assistance. In a literal sense, the United States would do the heavy lifting, but in human and political terms, the task would fall to others. In short, Somalia represented a one-time exception to the Powell Doctrine and NSD 74, not the belated triumph of the New World Order.[47]

By late 1992, critics caught on to the fact that the New World Order was more catchphrase than reality. As Bosnia lapsed into chaos and Bush refused to sanction intervention, popular commentators pointed out the superficiality of the notion. Anthony Lewis, a longtime liberal columnist for the *New York Times,* repeatedly charged during the 1992 campaign that Bush's timidity had destroyed the

New World Order: "Whoever has a chance to question George Bush in the first debate should surely ask: Why had you not met the first post–Cold War challenge to decency and humanity in Europe? Is this your idea of the new world order?" By and large, the distance between Bush's ideals and pragmatic inclinations had wrecked the credibility of the New World Order.[48]

At the end of his presidency, Bush too seemed resigned to the collapse of the notion. In his speeches, Bush dismissed the idea that the United States could fashion a coherent policy based on moral tenets. "There can be no single or simple set of guidelines for foreign policy," he conceded in addressing the inconsistency between intervening in Somalia and leaving Bosnia to its fate. For Scowcroft, this news was all to the good. Since 1991, the national security adviser had resisted the idea of the New World Order as it developed in public thought, arguing that the United States should deal with international and ethnic conflict "flash point by flash point," rather than in a preset, systematic manner. Even as U.S. troops landed in Somalia in December 1992, the New World Order was dead.[49]

Hegemony and Its Discontents

If humanitarianism, democracy, and justice were not to be the ends of post–Cold War foreign policy, what was? For a group of Defense Department advisers, the end of the Cold War had afforded the United States an opportunity of a different sort. With its rival superpower destroyed, Washington now had a preponderance of power in international affairs. China was a rising power, as were India, Japan, and Germany (though reunification slowed the German economic dynamo, and Japan had entered a decade-long recession), but superpower status for these countries was still in the distance. For the present, the United States reigned supreme.

In early 1992, Pentagon strategists took this reality to heart in drafting a defense strategy for the rest of the twentieth century. In March, the Defense Department completed a version of its "Defense Planning Guidance" statement for 1994–1999.[50] Whereas the New World Order had emphasized ideals over interests, the Defense Planning Guidance was pure power politics. According to the document, the first-order priority for the United States was to use its position of strength to ensure that no enemy rose to the level of the former Soviet threat. "This is a dominant consideration . . . [and] requires that we endeavor to prevent any hostile power from dominating a region whose resources would, under consolidated control, be sufficient to generate global power," the report stated. Along these lines, the United States would strengthen its European and Asian alliances and retain the capability to fight two major regional wars at once. Promoting human rights and the peaceful settlement of disputes was, if anything, an ancillary concern. The document made limited provision for humanitarian intervention, but only as a means of "addressing selectively those wrongs which threaten not only our interests, but those of our allies or friends, or which could seriously unsettle international relations." The draft, which appeared to border on advocating preventive war against potential regional hegemons, was a muscular assertion of American might, essentially a blueprint for U.S. domination of the international order. Power, not principle, was to be at the base of national security strategy.[51]

While the Pentagon advocated strategic preeminence, Bush and his economic advisers considered the financial foundations of U.S. power. The second key to American strength, they argued, was maintaining and expanding the system of free trade that ensured domestic prosperity. "Our national power . . . ultimately rests on the strength and resilience of our economy," stated one planning document. At the Republican National Convention in August 1992, Bush put the matter directly. "The defining challenge of the '90s is to win the economic competition," he declared. "We must be a military superpower, an economic superpower, and an export superpower." An ardent free-trader, Bush believed that the strength of the U.S. economy hinged on its ability to market American products abroad. For Bush, the issue was simple: trade "means more jobs." Just as in security matters, isolationism on trade matters would therefore make the United States more, not less, vulnerable.[52]

Trade issues took on added significance in 1991 and 1992. A recession that began in 1991 persisted longer than most economists had expected, and the nation's economic woes dominated public debate in the run-up to the 1992 election. Unemployment jumped, reaching 7.5

percent in midyear, and economists predicted that it might take several years for employment to return to prerecession levels. Addressing the economic downturn, Bush stressed that restoring prosperity required selling an ever greater amount of goods abroad. The theme of U.S. economic diplomacy, he declared, was "jobs, jobs, jobs."[53]

The centerpiece of Bush's trade agenda was the North American Free Trade Agreement (NAFTA). The pact established a free trade zone between the United States and Mexico and Canada and required a sharp reduction of commercial barriers by the participants. Bush went ahead with the negotiations in 1990, after Mexican diplomats assured U.S. officials that, despite some "worrisome" indications of financial instability in Mexico, the economy of America's southern neighbor was basically sound. Bush made completion of the agreement a principal aim of his last two years in office, and he portrayed NAFTA as a key component of his economic program. The pact would have "a monumental effect on the quality of life here in the United States over the next decade," he assured skeptics. "Every billion dollars in trade means 20,000 more jobs."[54]

Yet, whereas the New World Order had been greeted more enthusiastically in public than within the administration, free trade and the Pentagon's proposed strategy were more convincing to Bush and his advisers than to the domestic audience. Most often, observers objected to the notion that liberalized trade would increase national prosperity. Despite Bush's repeated perorations, many commentators concluded that opening the U.S. economy would hurt American workers rather than help them. As unemployment remained high through mid-1992, anti-NAFTA spokespersons claimed that the agreement would only exacerbate current economic problems. Trade unions and blue-collar workers were particularly vehement in savaging NAFTA. When Pat Buchanan pledged during the 1992 primaries to "stop foreign imports putting guys up here out of jobs," his denunciations of NAFTA in particular and of free trade more broadly won support from the Republican Right. On the left, Missouri representative Richard Gephardt, who had strong ties to organized labor, predicted that NAFTA would "hasten the exodus of U.S. jobs to Mexico and drag down the wages of manufacturing workers." With unemployment in the nation's ten largest states above 8 percent in mid-1992, these attacks had a powerful effect. In the general campaign, Ross Perot authored the most memorable condemnation of Bush's commercial program, claiming that NAFTA would result in "a giant sucking sound of jobs being pulled out of this country." By mid-1992, free trade had become a political albatross for Bush and, his opponents charged, another example of the president's preoccupation with international affairs at the expense of domestic problems.[55]

Just as troubling for many public observers was the Pentagon's conception of national defense strategy. After a draft of the Defense Planning Guidance statement became public in March 1992, it came under fire for its unvarnished emphasis on raw power. The *Washington Post* declaimed the draft's "muscle-flexing unilateralism," and others commented that the document appeared to be a plan for U.S. domination of the global scene. In response to this criticism, Bush distanced himself from the draft, claiming not to have read it. The Defense Department soon backtracked, releasing a revised draft that discarded the bold language of the original. The final document focused on strengthening U.S. alliances rather than subduing regional powers and generally took a more subdued tone. For the moment, the Pentagon's blueprint for U.S. hegemony went unheeded.[56]

From a political perspective, the basic problem with the Pentagon's plan was that it contained little that appealed to the impulses and perceptions that drive American support for an assertive foreign policy. Grounded in cold geostrategic logic, the Defense Planning Guidance found little resonance with a public that had just recently shown such enthusiasm for the New World Order. Even in its characterization of the international environment, the Defense Department's plan was politically lacking. The global arena seemed plenty dangerous in 1992, but there was no single overriding threat to U.S. interests. (In fact, many of the most powerful nations were U.S. allies.) The Defense Planning Guidance thus created the impression that the United States would be imposing its will on lesser powers that presented only peripheral threats to national security. The defense strategy therefore made domestic observers uncomfortable. Until officials could identify an imminent peril to the nation and provide a sense of moral purpose for U.S. involvement in the world, they would have trouble compelling support for their policies.

The Bush administration's attempts to define a post–Cold War policy ended in frustration. The New World Order had seemed promising as a new American mission, but it suffered from the marked disadvantage of lacking the confidence of its creators. Bush's pragmatic inclinations eventually caught up to his idealistic rhetoric, sinking the New World Order amid recriminations from disillusioned domestic commentators. The Pentagon's strategy was more to the liking of administration hawks, but its language and content were too bold for the public consciousness. Free trade was somewhat more agreeable, but the fact that 61 percent of the 1992 presidential vote went to candidates who were either opposed or lukewarm to NAFTA showed strong resistance to Bush's economic principles. Strategic vision and political acceptability never met, and no durable expression of national purpose had emerged by the end of Bush's term. The rhetorical and practical void created by the Cold War's collapse persisted at the beginning of 1993. After a half century, American globalism had hit a midlife crisis.

Although Bush's presidency did not provide a new American grand strategy, it at least gave hints as to the requirements of producing one. The challenge of constructing post–Cold War foreign policy went beyond prioritizing objectives abroad and identifying clarity in an inchoate world. These were necessary, to be sure, but so was persuading the domestic audience that whatever strategy an administration arrived at was worth pursuing. As Bush's experience indicated, this would be a formidable challenge. With no obvious menace to U.S. safety, successive administrations would have to seek new justifications for foreign policy. The incoming administration thus had a dual assignment: provide an organizing principle for its diplomatic efforts, and market that principle successfully at home. The new president had to bridge the gap between diplomacy and domestic politics, crafting a strategy that would bring both coherence and consensus to foreign policy.

4

The Successor to Containment

Bush's lack of commitment to the New World Order had been one problem with his attempt to define a new U.S. mission; the imperatives of the U.S. political system posed another. Just weeks after U.S. forces finally arrived in Somalia, lending some (but not much) credibility to Bush's doctrine, the presidency changed hands. Bill Clinton thus assumed the task of shaping foreign policy in what, for lack of a better term, was still awkwardly referred to as the post–Cold War world.

In some respects, Clinton seemed less likely than his predecessor to meet this challenge. Whereas Bush was a seasoned diplomat in his own right, Clinton's knowledge of foreign affairs was limited to course work at Georgetown and Oxford. Bush's aides were well-respected pros; Clinton's advisers sometimes seemed better suited to college seminar halls or congressional caucusing. Clinton had one important advantage over Bush, however: his lack of prior experience made the transition from Cold War to post–Cold War less traumatic. Bush's training and background had made it difficult for him to adjust to the new order of things, as evidenced by his inability to determine what came next for U.S. policy. Clinton, less rooted in the truisms of superpower competition, was more of a blank slate.

Moreover, the problems that had been so vexing for Bush had come into clearer focus by the time of Clinton's inauguration. From the start, Clinton and his aides knew that in addition to organizing foreign policy, they had to frame it in a manner that was rhetorically persuasive enough to win the support of skeptical observers at home. The new administration was quick to realize that both the practice and the politics of foreign policy were at issue, and it tailored its diplomacy accordingly.

During his first year in office, Clinton sought to overcome the political half of this challenge by casting U.S. policy in ideals that appealed to Americans on an intuitive and emotional level. The administration wrapped its diplomacy in the rhetoric of human rights, prosperity, and democracy, hoping to capture the attention of the domestic audience and sell Americans on the notion that U.S. leadership was integral to maintaining the external and economic security of the country. Based on Wilsonian and Carteresque aims that, in principle at least, were practically indisputable, Clinton's strategy appeared promising in terms of sustaining public support for foreign policy.

In practical terms, too, Clinton's approach seemed calculated to meet the exigencies of post–Cold War affairs. "Enlargement," as Clinton called it, promised to provide a consistent worldview and lend cohesiveness to U.S. aims. The end of the Cold War had removed old constraints on multilateral diplomacy and intervention and highlighted the rising importance of economic issues. At the same time, currents in scholarly thought emphasized the strategic benefits of good governance. As an organizing principle, enlargement therefore appeared to be well matched to the international conditions of the 1990s. At the outset of Clinton's presidency, it seemed that U.S. policy might have found its post-bipolar footing.

The Politics of Human Rights

The origins of enlargement were as much domestic as foreign. During the 1992 campaign, Clinton articulated what would eventually become the dominant themes of his foreign policy. Although Bush's record on international affairs was fairly impressive and Clinton largely avoided the topic, Richard Holbrooke, Anthony Lake, and Sandy Berger, the candidate's foreign policy advisers, believed that the incumbent was vulnerable on human rights issues. Holbrooke focused on Bush's refusal to intervene in Bosnia, calling the administration's response "weak and inadequate." Clinton seized on the allegation that Bush had been passive in confronting challenges to democracy and the rule of law and readily played the foil to the president's detached pragmatism. "We need to be a force for freedom and democracy," Clinton argued in one presidential debate. "We need to use our unique position to support freedom, whether it is in Haiti or China or any other place." At another point, Clinton alluded caustically to Scowcroft's trips to Beijing after the Tiananmen Square incident. "It is a mistake for us to do what this administration did when all those kids went out there carrying the Statue of Liberty in Tiananmen Square, and Mr. Bush sent two people in secret to toast the Chinese leaders and basically tell them not to worry about it."[1]

Clinton's fundamental complaint against Bush was that the president was preoccupied with power politics and therefore neglected the moral foundations of U.S. power. "I think there is an inconsistency in a lot of his actions," Clinton said in 1992, "because of the pull between the impulse, the deep American impulse, to support freedom and democracy and his own preference for stability in his relationships with foreign leaders in a given area." Such practices might have been unavoidable during the Cold War; with the United States involved in a global struggle against a supposedly implacable enemy, amorality was a necessary evil. For Clinton, though, the end of the Cold War lessened this imperative. Here was an opportunity, he contended, to emphasize principle over simple pragmatism. In the post–Cold War world, interests could give way to ideals.[2]

At times, the candidate's attacks approached the level of a new conception of foreign policy. According to Clinton, the end of the Cold War had produced an urgent need "to assert a new vision for our role in this dynamic world." Citing Bush's failure "to offer a compelling rationale for America's continued engagement in the world," Clinton charged that the administration had "invited a new birth of isolationism on the left and the right." Faulting Bush for his tendency to privilege "prudence without purpose," Clinton called for a foreign policy representative of American ideals. It was the nation's calling, he insisted, to lead "a global alliance for democracy as united and steadfast as the global alliance that defeated communism."[3]

Rhetoric aside, during the campaign, it often appeared that Clinton was more concerned with winning votes at home than protecting freedom and liberty abroad. Although Clinton berated Bush for his diplomatic failures, he did not go so far as to advocate robust military intervention on behalf of these virtues. Stung by Bush's counterattacks, which portrayed Clinton as "naïve" about the realities of international diplomacy and "reckless" in his willingness to use force, the Arkansas governor stopped short of enunciating a comprehensively interventionist strategy for foreign affairs. Clinton must take care, warned one campaign adviser, not to look the "woolly-haired idealist intent on butting into the affairs of other countries all over the world, no matter how remote their connection to American national interests." Heeding this advice as the campaign neared its conclusion in October 1992, Clinton took a tone nearly identical to that of his opponent in arguing against U.S. involvement in "the tribal wars of Somalia." At this point, support for human rights and democracy was more electoral bludgeon than anything else.[4]

Even as a campaign tool, Clinton's stance on foreign affairs was understated. To Bush's chagrin, the candidate turned the election away from a discussion of foreign policy (where Bush was strong) and toward a referendum on the state of the domestic economy (where he was not). At the outset of 1992, few observers gave Clinton better than an outside chance of winning the presidency, but the campaign mantra of adviser James Carville ("It's the economy, stupid") and the surprisingly strong showing of Ross Perot proved to be Bush's undoing. With the economy struggling and Perot splitting the conservative vote, Clinton slipped into the White House.

Carter Redux?

Once elected, Clinton warmed to the principles he had espoused during the campaign. In part, this change owed to the fact that president-elect Clinton was no longer so vulnerable to the charges of recklessness and naïveté that had dogged candidate Clinton. With the election over, Clinton was also free of the fear that talking about foreign policy would simply play to his opponent's strength.

The composition of the new president's National Security Council, arrived at largely by default, also privileged a human rights–based strategy. Clinton and transition chief Warren Christopher initially tended toward a more restrained foreign policy, looking to Joint Chiefs of Staff (JCS) chairman Colin Powell as a potential secretary of state. Powell, known for his reluctance to use force except in exceptional circumstances, might have been the wet blanket for Clinton that he had been for Bush's New World Order. Unfortunately for Clinton, Powell refused to assume new responsibilities under a president who, in Powell's view, had given "no clear idea" of his stance "on foreign policy or defense issues." Senator Sam Nunn, the top Democratic foreign affairs hand in Congress, also rebuffed Christopher's overtures.[5]

These initial missteps presented a problem for Clinton and Christopher. Both were wary of filling the National Security Council with Carter administration retreads (which was somewhat ironic, given that Christopher had been Carter's undersecretary of state), but after twelve years of Republican tenancy of the White House, there was a dearth of Democratic foreign policy talent. Reluctantly and with great hesitation (it took the president-elect nearly two months to settle on a foreign policy team), Clinton turned to his campaign staff, most of whom were, in fact, former Carterites, and other Carter-era officials. Christopher, a Democratic stalwart whom Clinton knew and trusted, came on as secretary of state. In foreign policy circles, Christopher was known for his negotiating skills rather than his strategic vision; he was, most observers believed, more of a Baker than a Kissinger.[6]

Like Christopher, UN Ambassador Madeleine Albright was a product of the Carter administration, where she had acquired the interest in human rights that was so common among her former colleagues. Unlike the typical Carterite, though, Albright was not shy about using military force. A protégé of Zbigniew Brzezinski, who himself had often seemed out of place in the Carter White House, Albright was an enthusiastic interventionist, willing to commit U.S. troops to fight for the principles propounded by the new president. Furthermore, as a Czech émigré who knew well her homeland's tragic past, Albright was a vigorous advocate of preventive, multilateral diplomacy. "As students of history, we all studied the League of Nations period," Albright said, as she urged an expanded U.S. role in UN peacekeeping and conflict prevention. "I remember every time I studied it I would think, how is it possible that these people watched what was going on and did not do anything about it?"[7]

Albright, who employed a take-no-prisoners approach to internal debate, occupied a position with newly enhanced authority under Clinton. The UN ambassador had not traditionally wielded great influence; Lyndon Johnson had used the post as a means of keeping prominent Democrats Adlai Stevenson and Arthur Goldberg around without actually having to listen to them. However, reflecting his stress on democracy, human rights, and international cooperation, Clinton endowed the position with greater power, making Albright a member of both the cabinet and the NSC. The promotion was doubly important. As a matter of appearances, being on the NSC gave Albright greater power within the administration and lent weight to her views. On a practical level, the promotion meant that Albright got invited to the important meetings, including those of the NSC Principals Committee (normally consisting of the UN ambassador, secretaries of state and defense, JCS chairman, and national security adviser).

The post of national security adviser went to Anthony Lake, another Carterite and a campaign adviser to Clinton. Lake too had a reputation as a moralist, having quit the Nixon administration in protest over the bombing of Cambodia in 1970. An outspoken critic of Nixon and Kissinger, Lake had been repelled by their relentless amorality and "realism." "I retain the belief that I found so attractive in the Kennedy years," he explained at the time, "that problems created by man can at least be ameliorated by man, and that we must try." After Lake's selection as national security adviser, Beltway observers predicted that he would join Christopher as a cautious influence on internal debate, but the NSC chief's words hardly comported with these forecasts. "I want to work to end every conflict," he declared early on. "I want to work to save every child."[8]

Yet Lake mixed his idealism with a healthy dose of practicality. His and Albright's support for democracy and human rights was predicated on strong trends in contemporary social science and public thought. As professors of the history or practice of international relations, both Lake and Albright subscribed to the idea of the "democratic peace," which held that democracies rarely, if ever, warred with one another. Democracies had greater institutional and political capabilities for dispute resolution and placed a higher value on human life, or so the theory went. "To the extent democracy and market economics hold sway in other nations," Lake claimed in 1993, "our own nation will be more secure, prosperous, and influential." Asked at one point to describe U.S. policy, Lake answered, "pragmatic neo-Wilsonianism," a response that indicated both the strategic and the moral appeal of building democracy and protecting human rights. "Principles without pragmatism is posturing," he continued, "and pragmatism without principles becomes rudderless opportunism."[9]

Rounding out the inner coterie was Defense Secretary Les Aspin, former chairman of the House Armed Services Committee. Aspin posed a sharp contrast to the Bush administration's tendency for the Pentagon head to jealously guard against military overcommitment. Under Bush, for instance, Cheney had clashed with the interventionists, often siding with Powell in asking hard questions about plans to use force. Aspin, something of a visionary in the mold of Albright and Lake, was less inclined to kill his colleagues' fun. In early 1993, Aspin confirmed that he would sanction the use of force "even when vital interests are not at stake." In the post–Cold War world, he said, one could not easily separate security matters from humanitarian issues or problems of conscience; these concerns all resided along the same "continuum." In the case of Bosnia, for instance, security and humanitarian issues were indivisible. "It's not a clear case of either or," he said in advocating a more assertive stance. Predictably, Aspin's interventionism irritated Powell, who by early 1993 rarely agreed with his boss on policy issues.[10]

If the intellectual predilections of Clinton's advisers encouraged a policy based on human rights and democracy, the internal dynamics of the staff reinforced these themes. Christopher, the most cautious of Clinton's counselors, rarely took an active role in internal debate, living up to his reputation as a negotiator rather than a strategist. Albright and Lake, both humanitarian hawks, were the beneficiaries. They dominated internal deliberations during Clinton's early years in office and quickly became visible public proponents of administration policies. Clinton's own initial tendency to take a hands-off approach to foreign affairs added to Lake's and Albright's sway. Administration political guru Dick Morris referred to Lake's influence as a "regency," implying that Clinton maintained only nominal control of the process.[11]

The Logic of Enlargement

Despite his tendency to shrink from policy debates, Christopher did contribute two crucial bits of wisdom to Clinton's diplomatic thinking. The first was a reaffirmation of the consensus that had emerged during the latter half of the Bush years: that the United States needed a new, overarching grand strategy. Citing many of the same issues that had begun to command attention between 1990 and 1992 (nuclear proliferation, humanitarian crises, ethnic conflict, drug trafficking, terrorism), Christopher asserted that the nation faced a challenge similar to that encountered in the late 1940s—that is, the challenge of "shaping an entirely new foreign policy for a world that's fundamentally changed." To effectively target its resources, the United States needed a clear picture of its interests and priorities. Coherence was imperative in managing the complexity of post–Cold War affairs, Christopher believed. "We cannot afford to careen from crisis to crisis," he said; otherwise, the diversity of the international environment might discombobulate presidential diplomacy.[12]

Christopher's second contribution pertained to the domestic side of foreign policy. With a background in domestic politics, Christopher was well aware of the connections between consensus at home and policy effectiveness abroad. The new secretary was convinced that, whatever the focus of Clinton's diplomacy, it had to encompass themes that the domestic audience understood and believed in. The end of the Cold War had unleashed the isolationism latent in the American body politic, prompting questions about why the United States needed to maintain an active international role in the absence of a threat to the nation's survival. "It is not enough," Christopher contended, "to articulate a new strategy. We must justify it to the American people. . . . The unitary goal of containing the Soviet Union's power will have to be replaced by more complex justifications to fit the new era." For Christopher, coherence and persuasiveness would be key to the success of U.S. policy.[13]

Christopher's dicta gained support from the president's top advisers. Lake, for one, had a similar conception of the challenges facing the administration. Not since the 1940s had U.S. policy "not had a single defining issue against which it could define itself," he believed. The task for Clinton, therefore, was "to define the questions and provide the answers" regarding U.S. involvement abroad. The administration would have to reset American priorities in some cohesive fashion, lest the complexity of the international environment render U.S. diplomacy confused and ineffective.[14]

This need was as pressing in the domestic aspect of foreign policy as it was in the international, Lake believed. Americans had to understand and accept their president's conception of foreign affairs for the policy to have any level of endurance, because international relations inevitably entailed a diplomatic, financial, and human price. "It can be costly when you get involved" in foreign disputes, Lake conceded. Moreover, the end of the Cold War had given rise to a "cacophony of voices" on the domestic scene, each urging different and often divergent views of the nation's foreign commitments. What Clinton needed, therefore, was a strategy persuasive and attractive enough to give structure to domestic debate and defeat the "neo-know-nothing isolationists."[15]

Clinton was initially reluctant to subscribe to Lake's and Christopher's counsel. As a diplomat, the president was troubled by the idea that, no matter how complex the situation, U.S. policy had to be straightforward and simple in order to gain the support of the domestic audience. As a politician, though, he conceded that his advisers had a point. Early in his presidency, Clinton philosophized on the rhetorical and practical exigencies of foreign policy. "The Cold War was helpful as an organizing principle," he told adviser Strobe Talbott, "but it had its dangers because every welt on your skin became cancer." Talbott agreed, as did Talbott's mentor George Kennan. Reminding Talbott of the "great and misleading oversimplification of analysis and policy" resulting from the canonization of containment, Kennan urged the administration to eschew catchphrase diplomacy. Clinton should express U.S. policy in a "thoughtful paragraph or more, rather than trying to come up with a bumper sticker." Told of Kennan's advice, Clinton replied, "That's why Kennan's a great diplomat and scholar and not a politician." Deciphering the intricacies of international affairs was only half the battle in devising foreign policy, Clinton realized. Equally important was being able to explain foreign policy to one's constituents. "You've still got to be able to crystallize complexity in a way people get right away," he said. "The operative problem of the moment is that a bunch of smart people haven't been able to come up with a new slogan, and saying that there aren't any good slogans isn't a slogan either."[16]

When the administration unveiled Clinton's approach to foreign affairs in early 1993, its concern with internal and rhetorical cohesiveness was evident. In January, Christopher outlined the administration's vision, emphasizing the themes that had proved attractive in the early 1990s. The end of the Cold War, he began, gave the United States "the opportunity to create a new strategy to direct America's resources at something other than superpower confrontation." The United States could now turn away from the hard pragmatism of power politics and promote ideals as well as interests. Active support for democracy and human rights, Christopher stated, would be the main pillar of U.S. diplomacy. By spreading these virtues abroad, the administration would make the international environment more hospitable to the United States. "Support for human rights and democracy abroad can and should be a central tenet of our efforts to improve our own security." American efforts on behalf of good governance and human rights would not be limited to moral suasion, however. The "discreet and careful use of force" would play a key role in U.S. policy, Christopher promised. Aspin seconded this stance, telling the Senate Armed Services Committee that the Powell-Weinberger Doctrine "might set the threshold for using force too high for many of the problems that the United States will face in the post–cold war era."[17]

Predictably, this position raised eyebrows among those still schooled in the lessons of Vietnam. If the United States liberalized its guidelines for military action, they feared, it would soon confront quagmires anew. In Aspin's opinion, though, military policy in the 1990s would not be captive to the rigidity that had characterized U.S. strategy during the postwar period and led to disaster in Vietnam. "One of the arguments that kept us going in Vietnam . . . was the concern about how would the Soviets look on this thing if we backed out," he explained. "So, what that meant was that you could never start with the use of force without being willing to see it all the way through because there was always the concern that . . . the Soviets [would] misread your resolve or your allies [would] misread it." With the dictates of credibility and superpower competition no longer in operation, Aspin believed, the danger of being unable to escape a Vietnam-type situation had markedly decreased. "There is no more Cold War and there is no more Soviet Union," he argued. "There is less concern now about . . . are we going to be perceived to have lost our will." If the United States found itself in a losing intervention in the 1990s, Aspin believed, it could simply withdraw. In this more permissive context, it was not necessary to govern the use of force so strictly. Humanitarian intervention could therefore rise to the forefront of foreign policy.[18]

The second component of Clinton's program was to be economically oriented and focused on advancing national prosperity by opening markets abroad. "For too long we have made economics the poor cousin of our foreign policy," Christopher said. The new administration would make expanding U.S. commercial opportunities a key part of national security policy, he vowed, and would "harness our diplomacy to the needs and opportunities of American industries and workers." Clinton, Christopher promised, would make up the economic ground lost under Bush with "diplomacy that seeks to assure access for U.S. business to expanding global markets."[19]

In a certain sense, Clinton's emphasis on trade as a coequal component of foreign policy was rooted in a post–Cold War fad in geopolitical thinking. The strategic and physical threat to the United States, observers assumed, had been vanquished with the Soviet Union's demise. In its place, though, had arisen the danger that the United States would be overtaken in economic power. Americans could not help but notice that two former enemies and then protégés, Germany and Japan, had risen to near economic superpower status by the early 1990s. U.S. officials and politicians increasingly feared that these nations could translate their financial might into international political dominance. The durability of American power, it seemed, would depend not on the strength of U.S. arms but on the strength of the U.S. economy. Jeffrey Garten, undersecretary of commerce for much of Clinton's first term, argued in 1993: "A more effective international economic policy, based heavily on increased trade competitiveness, will enhance U.S. influence around the world at a time when our military assets will be deployed with decreasing frequency." For Clinton, the task was to ensure continued American power by attending to the nation's economic imperatives as well as its strategic needs.[20]

Yet Clinton's emphasis on trade was as much political as strategic. Language aside, there was nothing original about the president's international economic policy. After all, Bush had negotiated NAFTA, and his thinking on the relationship between free trade and national prosperity had been practically identical to Clinton's. (Bush had actually been a more vigorous exponent of free trade than Clinton, as evidenced by their respective stances on NAFTA. Whereas Bush had supported the pact outright, Clinton had hesitated until voters demanded that he take a stance.[21] Even then, he had insisted that side agreements would be necessary to protect U.S. workers and the environment.) Going back further still, U.S. diplomacy had long been informed by efforts to find new outlets for surplus production. According to some critics, this tendency accounted for much of U.S. foreign policy over past decades.[22] During the Cold War, this search for markets had been a subtext to anticommunism, but by 1993, the main text no longer existed. Free trade remained a focus of foreign policy, but it assumed greater rhetorical prominence as alternative themes faded away. Clinton's emphasis on the search for markets was thus less a change of policy than a means of filling the post–Cold War rhetorical gap in American diplomacy.

Having defined the ends of U.S. policy, the administration turned to outlining the means. On the economic side, Clinton promised to bring NAFTA to a conclusion, protect domestic employment by adding a labor standards protocol to the pact, and negotiate new opportunities in the booming Japanese market. Regarding humanitarian intervention and support for democracy, Albright presented the administration's approach in late January. The great danger of the post–Cold War era, Albright stated, was "fragmentation," or the prospect that the easing of bipolar constraints would encourage ethnic and civil strife. To promote democracy and human rights, she argued, the United States must intercede when fragmentation threatened. National security policy, Albright explained, would include peacekeeping in places that were recovering from internal conflict, such as Cambodia, and "peacemaking" in areas where ethnic or civil war threatened the rule of law or human rights, such as the Balkans.

The obvious problem with this approach was that it would be dangerous and costly. Washington needed a means of defraying the human and financial expense of an interventionist strategy. In Albright's view, the United Nations was an ideal fit for this role. The United States could exert its moral leadership through that international body, a strategy that would lend legitimacy to U.S. intervention and conduce to burden sharing, as it had during the Gulf War. The institution would act, Albright was fond of saying, as a "force multiplier." Furthermore, she argued, the current global environment was propitious to multilateral diplomacy. With the end of the Cold War and the diminishing likelihood of Russian vetoes, the United Nations could take an enlarged—and presumably impartial—role in punishing aggressors and restoring peace. "We have an opportunity for the United Nations to reflect our greatest hopes and work for our needs," Albright stated boldly.[23]

Reflecting the administration's early penchant for catchphrases, Albright coined a term to represent this vigorous U.S.-UN partnership: *assertive multilateralism.* Months later, Lake merged the two tenets of Clinton's foreign policy into a single term, *enlargement,* signifying the administration's desire to enlarge the community of free-market democracies. As they took office, Clinton's advisers offered a new vision of (and, no less important, a new term for) U.S. foreign policy to replace the principles that had given way at the end of the Cold War.

Opening Moves

The first months of Clinton's presidency were well matched to the principal themes of his diplomacy. The continuing catastrophe in Bosnia seemed to beg for U.S. intervention, and the emerging debate over NAFTA compelled Clinton to prove that freer commerce was the key to renewed prosperity at home.

Free trade's first test came just as Clinton assumed office, with the opening of intensified public discussion of NAFTA. Campaigning as a pro-trade "New Democrat" in 1992, Clinton had—after considerable hesitation—offered tentative support for the pact, insisting on side agreements with Mexico that were meant to safeguard U.S. jobs and environmental standards. With Perot predicting that NAFTA would be an economic disaster for the United States, Clinton had been circumspect in his support for the agreement to avoid offending organized labor and environmentalists, two key Democratic blocs. After the election, the president dispatched negotiators to secure the side agreements, which were finalized in mid-1993. Satisfied on this count and safely in the White House, Clinton removed the qualifiers from his backing of NAFTA. On January 30, he announced to his cabinet that he would make a strong push for congressional approval of the pact.[24]

Clinton's support of NAFTA was controversial among Democrats, but there was a double logic to the president's stance. First, NAFTA appealed to the long-standing belief that prosperity at home required finding new markets abroad. "We know that economic growth depends as never before on opening up new markets overseas and expanding the volume of world trade," Clinton said. By making inroads into Mexico and Canada, markets that were crucial to U.S. industry and agriculture, NAFTA would be a major advance in this quest. "The potential that it represents for opening markets in this hemisphere is absolutely incredible," remarked Deputy Secretary of State Clifton Wharton.[25]

There was a strategic rationale for NAFTA as well. According to this argument, political influence would follow greater economic involvement in foreign countries. If the United States rejected free trade, these nations would look elsewhere for diplomatic partners. Christopher contended that NAFTA's failure "would send a chilling signal about our willingness to engage in Latin America at a time when so many of our neighbors are genuinely receptive to cooperation with the United States." As this statement indicated, the administration believed that NAFTA was a precursor to trade agreements with other Latin American countries. The success of NAFTA would presumably lead to similar pacts across the Americas, increasing U.S. influence throughout the hemisphere. In April 1993, Clinton played on a familiar American worry, referencing Japan's success in this regard. "If you look at what Japan and other countries in the Pacific are doing to reach out in their own region, it's a pretty good lesson to us that we had better worry about how to build these bridges in our own area," he said.[26]

Whatever the arguments for NAFTA, securing congressional approval of the agreement promised to be difficult. NAFTA faced strong opposition from manufacturing and service employees who feared that their jobs would migrate south if the agreement passed. Secretary of Labor Robert Reich, charged with selling the pact to organized labor, discovered the intensity of this resistance. "NAFTA is crap," declared Bill Ford, a House leader with deep ties to the AFL-CIO. Across the country, labor came out against NAFTA. "We worked our asses off to elect Bill Clinton," one labor representative told Reich. "I'll be goddamned if my members are going to lose their fucking jobs on some vague promise by Mexico to improve their labor standards." Environmental groups also withheld their support, claiming that NAFTA would allow firms to exploit Mexico's lenient environmental regulations.[27]

Debate over NAFTA peaked in the late summer and fall of 1993, as progress on the side agreements raised the prospect of a congressional vote in the near future. Passage was seen as a near certainty in the Senate, so the contest centered in the House. Anti-NAFTA groups rolled out the standard arguments against the pact, often buttressing their claims with xenophobic or nativist appeals. Representative Bernard Sanders (I-Vt.) alleged an unholy alliance between U.S. and Mexican elites. "Why is it that the Mexican Government, dominated by 30 super-rich families who own 50 percent of Mexico's wealth and control 60 percent of their Gross National Product, are putting an unprecedented $40 million into a pro-NAFTA lobbying effort?" he asked. "The answer is obvious. If NAFTA passes, it will be even easier than now for American companies to flee to Mexico and hire workers for starvation wages."[28]

Pro-trade advocates stressed the benefits of the pact, marveling that critics seemed willing to ignore Mexico's new interest in free trade. One commentator pointed out that, under NAFTA, "Mexico agrees to do almost everything of an economic nature that the United States ever wanted it to do," such as lifting trade barriers and obstacles to foreign investment. Paul Krugman, a prominent economist, acknowledged that the economic gains were minimal but contended that rejecting the pact would irreparably damage U.S.-Mexico relations: "For the United States, NAFTA is essentially a foreign policy issue."[29]

Perhaps, but at its core, the debate over NAFTA was purely political. Within Congress, many arguments for or against the pact were rooted less in economic or strategic calculus than in electoral self-interest. Representatives with large constituencies of manufacturers or farmers supported the accord; those who owed their election to blue-collar workers did not. By early fall, the latter group appeared to have the upper hand. With the anti-NAFTA forces strong, the fate of the agreement hinged on Clinton's prestige and willingness to bargain for votes. Well suited for politicking of this sort, Clinton embraced the challenge. He met congressional leaders more than ten times between September and November, trading horses and rolling logs. A Florida congressman offered to trade his vote for the extradition of a criminal from Mexico. Louisiana representatives demanded guarantees that their state's economy would not be swamped by sugar imports. Esteban Torres (D-Calif.), head of the House Hispanic Caucus, received federal loans for working-class Californians who might be hurt by NAFTA.[30]

Still, with more than thirty representatives undecided as of mid-November, the outcome was in doubt until days before the vote. The White House made a final push, with Vice President Al Gore taking on NAFTA archenemy Perot in a televised debate. Gore performed well, with most observers concluding that he had bested Perot. In the end, Clinton eked out a victory. The final tally was 234 to 200 in favor of NAFTA, and the party breakdown confirmed that Clinton had put his trade program ahead of Democratic unity. Clinton drew more than half his support from Republicans, while Democrats opposed the pact by more than two to one.[31]

Free trade in the Clinton administration was off to an auspicious start and received an added boost in mid-1994 with the completion of the long-stalled Uruguay Round of the General Agreement on Tariffs and Trade (GATT). Combined, NAFTA and GATT validated Clinton's identity as a free-trade Democrat and demonstrated the president's commitment to the economic half of his nascent foreign policy doctrine. In his first major economic test, Clinton had seemingly won acceptance of the free-trade principles he considered integral to U.S. diplomacy. NAFTA's passage carried political benefits for the president as well. Pundits credited Clinton with securing ratification of the trade pact, giving the president a sorely needed victory. Early on, Clinton looked vindicated in his quest to elevate economic openness as a practical and rhetorical marker of foreign policy.[32]

Unassertive Multilateralism

On the diplomatic and military side of enlargement, however, the going was rockier. Within the first four months of Clinton's presidency, the administration discovered the difficulties of pursuing an interventionist policy. Struggling to manage a humanitarian crisis in Europe, Clinton learned that spreading human rights and democracy did not come cheaply in political, bureaucratic, or diplomatic terms.

The continuing civil war in Bosnia offered an early challenge for Clinton's policy. In 1992, Serb offensives continued despite repeated European attempts to broker a cease-fire. In the second half of that year, Serb troops blockaded and shelled Sarajevo, eliciting both international and domestic calls for action to relieve the besieged Bosnian Muslim communities. During the 1992 campaign, Clinton had encouraged these demands for intervention. In stump speeches, the candidate had condemned Bush's failure to halt "a deliberate and systematic extermination of human beings based on their ethnic origin." Clinton proposed to stabilize the situation by lifting the UN-imposed arms embargo to allow foreign countries to replenish the Croats' and Bosnian Muslims' dwindling materiel and by using NATO airpower to punish Serb outrages.[33]

After the election, certain of Clinton's advisers supported this "lift-and-strike" option. During the transition, Holbrooke urged Lake to intervene. "Bosnia will be the key test of American policy in Europe," he wrote. A hawk himself, Lake was sympathetic to Holbrooke's proposal, and opinion polls showed majority support for providing aid to the Bosnian Muslims.[34]

Unfortunately for Holbrooke and Lake, lift-and-strike had a number of flaws that discouraged Clinton from enacting the plan.

Christopher and Aspin both initially opposed air strikes or taking sides in Bosnia, believing that doing so would only intensify the conflict. Powell was especially skeptical of the efficacy of lift-and-strike. Asked by Clinton whether air strikes would halt the Serbs, Powell curtly responded, "Not likely." As the situation in Bosnia deteriorated in early 1993, the fractiousness within the NSC worsened. At a series of meetings in late January and early February, Powell clashed with Lake and Albright. Powell predicted that a major infusion of ground troops would be necessary to enforce a settlement on the warring parties, but he refused to sanction intervention until Clinton defined a clear political objective and exit strategy. Albright favored immediate action and soon grew frustrated with Powell's opposition. "What's the point of having this superb military that you're always talking about if we can't use it?" she demanded.[35]

Domestic political considerations also dampened Clinton's enthusiasm for plunging into the Bosnian mire. Although large numbers of Americans supported intervention, the vast majority believed that the first months of Clinton's presidency should be devoted to domestic affairs. Polls showed that only 2 percent of respondents thought that foreign relations should be Clinton's top priority, with much larger percentages preferring that the president focus on the economy or other domestic issues. Even traditionally internationalist observers agreed that it was time to look inward. In a piece outlining the challenges facing the president, the *New York Times* opined that Clinton's "mandate runs toward correcting a domestic legacy of drift and neglect."[36]

Clinton felt the same way. After winning the 1992 election, he famously pledged "to focus like a laser beam on this economy," and during the transition, his staff prepared an ambitious agenda that included an economic stimulus package, measures to balance the federal budget, and health care reform. In these circumstances, Clinton had good reason to shy away from foreign adventures. An entanglement that turned messy (as Powell repeatedly asserted would happen in Bosnia) would expose the president to early criticism from a constituency that wanted primary attention to focus on internal concerns, depleting his political capital just as he advanced a number of domestic initiatives.[37]

Together, the lack of consensus within the administration and the political risks of intervention discouraged Clinton from going ahead with lift-and-strike. Clinton would neither impose unity on a divided NSC nor wager his domestic agenda on a throw of the dice abroad, and plans for humanitarian action in the Balkans stalled as a result.

As Clinton retreated from intervention in early February, the situation in Bosnia took another turn. Under the auspices of the European Union, former secretary of state Cyrus Vance and former British foreign secretary David Owen devised a peace plan calling for the creation of a ten-canton Bosnian state based on a prewar distribution of ethnic populations. Although a number of European governments supported the plan, Clinton and Christopher were cold to the proposal. In many respects, the Vance-Owen plan looked like a sellout, as it did nothing to punish the Serbs for their brutal policies. The administration disliked the idea "in principle," according to Lake. Domestic opinion was equally hostile. The *Washington Post* opined that Vance-Owen "raises a vision of a larger and more violent Lebanon." After meeting with the envoys in early February, Christopher refused to endorse the scheme.[38]

The administration now found itself in a bind, however. Having decided that military intervention was impracticable, Clinton could hardly reject diplomatic initiatives as well. Clinton disliked Vance-Owen, but he disliked the idea of doing nothing even more. By mid-February, the president had warmed to Vance-Owen as the best of bad options. On February 10, Christopher announced that the United States would participate in upcoming negotiations on Vance-Owen and hinted that American troops might enforce a settlement. Two weeks later, Christopher explicitly stated that U.S. backing for a settlement "includes possible U.S. military participation."[39]

Even as the administration took a stronger position on Bosnia, however, its ambivalence was obvious. In announcing their backing of Vance-Owen, Clinton and Christopher had made U.S. participation in a peacekeeping mission contingent on there being a peace to keep. Should Vance-Owen fail, the United States would basically be released from its pledge of military support. This conditionality gave Clinton's policy a fatal flaw, as the Serbs could preclude U.S. intervention by simply refusing to sign on to Vance-Owen. This scenario eventually played out, as Belgrade rejected the plan in May.

Clinton's public statements further exposed his halfhearted approach to intervention. In an attempt to compel Serb acquiescence in Vance-Owen, Clinton spoke boldly in February and March on the U.S. commitment to peace in Bosnia. If the Serbs proved intransigent on Vance-Owen, Clinton implied, he might rescind the arms embargo and reconsider lift-and-strike. "We're going to have to look at some actions to try to give the Bosnians a means to at least defend themselves," he said. Other presidential statements, however, which probably reflected the divisions within the NSC, contradicted Clinton's tough talk. Weeks earlier, Clinton had made it clear that the United States would not intervene without European backing. "The United States cannot proceed here unilaterally," Clinton stated, essentially making American action subject to the veto of European capitals that were hesitant to send their troops into a potential bloodbath. Further weakening his position, Clinton maintained that "the whole issue of ground troops . . . is not on the table at all." In late March, Clinton again hedged on whether U.S. troops would enforce a cease-fire. By this point, the U.S. position had lost nearly all credibility.[40]

Given this weakness, it was hardly surprising that the Serbs rejected Vance-Owen. By late April, it was clear that the peace plan would founder on Belgrade's opposition. With Clinton's diplomatic efforts headed for failure, certain advisers encouraged a reappraisal of U.S. policy. Observers returning from Bosnia apprised Clinton of the worsening predicament of the Bosnian Muslims and recommended a greater U.S. role in ending the conflict. At roughly the same time, Christopher's anti-interventionism incited a mutiny at Foggy Bottom. A dozen European area experts drafted a letter to the secretary in which they deplored "Western capitulation against Serbian aggression" and urged intervention. Albright soon joined in, calling for air strikes against the Serbs. At an NSC meeting on April 20, however, Powell again played the spoiler, disputing the notion that bombing could enforce a cease-fire. "You punish from the air, you do not enforce from the air," he stated.[41]

Unlike in January, though, Powell's opposition was no longer decisive. Clinton's failure to implement anything resembling an effective strategy had become a public relations nightmare for the president, who was portrayed by reporters as indecisive and unable to enact his agenda. In Clinton's actions, wrote a *New York Times* columnist, "There is no sign of any policy that might actually stop Serbian 'ethnic cleansing.'" Frustrated by this criticism and his own ineffectiveness, Clinton took bolder measures. At a principals meeting on May 1, Clinton approved lift-and-strike, opting to end the embargo and begin NATO attacks on Serb artillery positions. Powell still believed that air strikes would be ineffective, but, perhaps sensing that caution was not the watchword of the Clinton administration, he dropped his explicit opposition to the plan. With this fragile consensus established, Clinton dispatched Christopher to Europe to rally support for the UN resolution needed to lift the embargo and begin air strikes.[42]

Yet by the time Clinton approved lift-and-strike, the plan was less a fully supported initiative than an attempt to save the administration's public credibility. Powell's repeated criticism had laid bare the shortcomings of the scheme, which, according to the JCS chairman, might do more harm than good. Consequently, when Clinton finally took action, there was little enthusiasm for lift-and-strike among top administration advisers, and even the president was ambivalent. Announcing Christopher's European mission, Clinton took the rare step of stating that the United States would implement the plan only if the NATO allies and the UN Security Council agreed. "Europe must be willing to act with us," Clinton said. "We must go forward together."[43]

Clinton had again compromised his own policy, and few were surprised when Christopher's trip failed utterly. The British and French governments opposed lift-and-strike on the grounds that the plan might expose European peacekeepers in Croatia to Serb reprisals. Furthermore, critics asked, what if the plan worked too well and gave the Croats or Bosnian Muslims a decisive military advantage? Might they go beyond recovering lost territory and emulate Serb practices? Moscow also opposed lift-and-strike; the Kremlin favored the Serbs and had no desire to deepen NATO involvement in an area of traditionally Russian influence. With three-fifths of the Security Council against the plan and Clinton willing to allow the Europeans to dictate the outcome, lift-and-strike stalled. The French rejected the proposal outright and instead suggested the creation of UN-protected "safe havens" to shelter refugees. Returning to Washington in mid-May, Christopher reported "stiff resistance" to lift-and-strike and informed Clinton that the plan would die unless he insisted that London, Paris, and Moscow cooperate. Not wishing to jeopardize European relations, Clinton demurred, and by late May, the plan was dead. In its place, Christopher announced a "Joint Action Plan" for Bosnia (the watered-down French proposal of two weeks previous).[44]

The demise of lift-and-strike concluded Clinton's first brush with Bosnia. As plans for intervention faded, so did hope for a quick resolution to the conflict. Vance-Owen was moribund, having been rejected by the Serbs and abandoned by Washington, and the Joint Action Plan soon proved to be every bit as ineffective as it looked. Serb offensives and atrocities continued, but the president remained reluctant to intercede. In a letter to Senate leaders, Clinton implied that he would make U.S. intervention contingent on the prior support of Congress, a prospect that was unlikely at best.[45]

In embarrassing fashion, Bosnia had exposed the shortcomings of Clinton's humanitarianism. The administration had looked hesitant and confused in its response to the crisis, unsure of how to implement its preferred policy or whether decisive action was even possible in the current political climate. On controversial issues such as Bosnia, it now appeared, Clinton would have to devote greater effort to creating consensus and enacting the premises of enlargement. Internal disagreement and a lack of political and diplomatic will had crippled the Bosnia policy, and it seemed that the administration needed a firmer conception of its own position on humanitarianism. In essence, Clinton needed to find a solid bureaucratic and political base on which to build a policy centered on human rights and democracy.

Refining Enlargement

If Bosnia highlighted the problems of Clinton's policy, it also suggested a solution. This frustrating experience, which alerted the president and his inner circle to the perils of uncertainty and ambivalence, spurred an effort to define more exactly the U.S. stance on humanitarian intervention. What emerged was a rhetorical and practical strengthening of the doctrine that produced a firmer foundation for Clinton's policy and anointed enlargement as containment's legatee.

The administration began a review of its policy on humanitarian intervention even before Christopher's trip to Europe provided a humiliating—though not entirely inappropriate—conclusion to Clinton's initial involvement with Bosnia. This review, meant to "ensure that issues of development and democracy building are effectively integrated into our foreign policy," culminated in the completion of Presidential Decision Directive (PDD) 13 in the summer of 1993.

In mid-July, Frank Wiesner, the assistant secretary of defense for peacekeeping and democracy (by no coincidence, a new position created under Clinton), informed the Senate Armed Services Committee of the basic outlines of the directive. An ongoing and deepening intervention in Somalia, which, under Clinton's watch, had evolved from a simple relief mission to an effort to rebuild Somali society, was an example of the type of mission that would define U.S. policy in the 1990s. Wiesner stated, "We have got to consider a broad range of interventions from diplomatic, military, right through to the nation-building subjects that we are facing today in so many instances." No longer would peace missions be "ancillary" to the dominant themes of foreign policy, he said. In the post–Cold War era, these activities "will lie right at the core of our activities."[46]

When signed by Clinton on July 14, PDD 13 approved an ambitious expansion of U.S. humanitarian efforts worldwide. The directive authorized U.S. support of UN intervention in case of "sudden and unexpected interruption of established democracy or gross violations of human rights" and made it clear that Washington would back such missions "politically, militarily, and financially." PDD 13 went far beyond anything Bush had approved during his dalliance with the New World Order. Most important, it removed previous strictures on U.S. involvement, stating that American participation in humanitarian missions would no longer be limited to noncombat functions. Instead, U.S. force would be at the center of these efforts.[47] Bosnia, which had exposed the internal and external constraints on multilateral peace operations, had not chastened the administration; rather, it had led Clinton to recommit himself to supporting human rights and the rule of law.

Although PDD 13 represented a clear victory for Lake and Albright, it also contained a significant concession to Powell and the minimalists. At the Pentagon's insistence, PDD 13 ruled out U.S. participation in a UN "Rapid Reaction Force." The idea for a UN army dated to 1992, when Secretary-General Boutros Boutros-Ghali had proposed to give the world organization its own peacekeeping force. The *New York Times* and other partisans of the New World Order had approved of the idea, and Clinton had championed the scheme as part of his campaign platform.[48] After the election, though, Powell quashed the notion. "As long as I am Chairman of the Joint Chiefs of Staff," he said, "I will not agree to commit American men and women to an unknown war, in an unknown land, for an unknown cause, under an unknown commander, for an unknown duration."[49]

Powell's objections aside, PDD 13 signaled a heightened commitment to humanitarianism. During the summer of 1993, State Department and White House officials further elaborated the policy. Albright reaffirmed her support for assertive multilateralism. "We are going to have to open our minds to broader strategies in international forums," she said. "We need to project our leadership where it counts long before a smoldering dispute has a chance to flare into the crisis of the week." Undersecretary of State Roy Tarnoff outlined differences between the familiar idea of peacekeeping and the new notion of peacemaking, a term that found frequent expression in PDD 13 and other official statements. *Peacekeeping* implied managing a settled situation, while *peacemaking* (also called *peace enforcement*) entailed imposing the settlement. "Peace enforcement requires a combination of diplomacy and force," Tarnoff explained. Clinton publicly touted his reinforced humanitarian doctrine, calling the Somalia intervention "an important new chapter in the international annals of peacekeeping and international assistance." In mid-1993, humanitarianism was at high tide.[50]

The tide ebbed somewhat in July and August, as the administration encountered problems of implementation in Somalia. After several months of good luck in avoiding casualties, U.S. troops sustained their first notable losses in August, when a remote-detonated bomb killed four soldiers. Domestic uneasiness with the mission rose during midsummer, and Senator Robert Byrd (D-W.V.) called for a pullout of U.S. forces now that the original task of feeding Somalis had been accomplished.[51]

Growing public discomfort with the mission in Somalia was an ominous portent for an administration that had just approved a large-scale expansion of its humanitarian exertions. As Byrd and others called for Clinton to terminate the operation, the administration took steps to defend its policy. Clinton publicly backed UN action in Somalia, arguing that a successful strategy of human rights and good governance would inevitably encounter obstacles. "I think we are on the right path in Somalia," he averred, "but we have to have patience in nation-building." To allay fears of runaway multilateralism, Clinton also reassured the domestic audience that he did not intend to issue a blank check to the United Nations. In late September, Clinton imposed certain criteria for determining U.S. participation in peace enforcement missions, including that the United Nations identify a clear political objective at the outset. "If the American people are to say yes to UN peacekeeping," Clinton said, "the United Nations must know how to say no." Lake echoed this theme, stating that humanitarianism was not without limits. "There will be relatively few intra-national ethnic conflicts that justify our military intervention," he promised.[52]

Still, the administration would not discard the essence of its policy. Although the tactics of promoting human rights and democracy had changed somewhat, the basic purpose—and willingness to use force—remained. Even as Lake placed limits on interventionism in a major policy address at Johns Hopkins University in late September, he made clear its continuing relevance. "Where we can make a difference, as in Somalia and Northern Iraq," he said, "we should not oppose using our military forces for humanitarian purposes simply because these missions do not resemble major wars for control of territory." Albright hit the same notes, arguing that cooperation with the United Nations would act as a "force multiplier" and stating the administration's refusal to spell out "a checklist" to govern the use of force. As a pillar of U.S. foreign policy, armed humanitarianism was here to stay.[53]

Indeed, the administration went beyond reviving interventionism. In his Johns Hopkins speech, Lake merged the two dominant aspects of U.S. policy (free trade and humanitarianism) into a single, easily expressible doctrine. Using language sure to draw attention, Lake proclaimed Clinton's policy the long-awaited replacement for the United States' Cold War grand strategy. "The successor to a doctrine of containment must be a strategy of enlargement," Lake declared, "enlargement of the world's free community of market democracies." Lake packaged the two tenets of U.S. policy into this one phrase, arguing that the promotion of human rights and democracy complemented the expansion of opportunities for economic growth. As countries allowed greater economic liberalization, he believed, they would embrace political reform as well (and vice versa), thereby adding to the community of peaceful and cooperative states. Supporting democracy and the rule of law, Lake argued, would safeguard the spectrum of U.S. interests in the long term.

In making his point, the national security adviser drew on both moral and practical themes. The direction of U.S. foreign policy, he contended, would determine "whether Americans' real incomes double every 26 years, as they did in the 1960s, or every 36 years, as they did during the late 1970s and 1980s. . . . Whether the nations of the world will be more able or less able to address regional disputes, humanitarian needs, and the threat of environmental degradation." As he endorsed Albright's emphasis on working through the United Nations, Lake stated his hope that "the habits of multilateralism may one day enable the rule of law to play a far more civilizing role in the conduct of nations." In sum, enlargement was to be the next great organizing principle of foreign policy, framing U.S. interests in a fashion no less comprehensible than that provided by containment during the Cold War.[54] Proclaiming this doctrine to be the nation's post–Cold War grand strategy, the administration thus gave its answer to the question that had dominated public discourse on U.S. policy for the past three years.

Given containment's formidable legacy, Clinton's attempt to find a replacement did not lack for boldness. Yet how would enlargement fare in U.S. politics and international diplomacy? In principle, at least, the policy appeared likely to pass Christopher's litmus tests. The ideals were seemingly beyond challenge (who did not support democracy, human rights, or domestic prosperity?); the rhetoric was clear and comprehensible. In global terms, too, the end of the Cold War raised the possibility that the world was on the cusp of a revolution in economic openness and democratic government. In practice, however, there were already troubling signs. European reluctance to intervene in Bosnia did not augur well for enlargement; neither did unease with the mission in Somalia. The fracturing of the Democratic Party during the NAFTA debate and the contentiousness of free trade were also worrying presages. In mid-1993, it remained to be seen whether enlargement would go the way of containment or the New World Order.

5

Unmaking Enlargement

Unsettling portents aside, enlargement was at its high point in September 1993. Though criticism of humanitarian intervention in Somalia had surfaced during the summer, Clinton's affirmation of policy on UN missions allayed fears that the president would hand over U.S. sovereignty to the unelected bureaucrats of that international body. American troops were distributing food, hunting warlords, and building order in Somalia, making that country the first recipient of enlargement's benefits. On the economic side, the overall outlook remained fairly bright as well. NAFTA was en route to congressional approval, Clinton having cleared the way with his considerable political facility. Enlargement's rhetorical prominence was at its height, largely as a result of Anthony Lake's widely publicized speech, which anointed the doctrine as the postcontainment lodestar of U.S. policy.

Despite these auspicious omens, enlargement lay in tatters only a year later. Armed humanitarianism had been written off after a haunting misadventure in Somalia, which turned public observers away from the largely abstract attractions of interventionism and refocused their gaze on the painfully tangible costs thereof. Although it ultimately proved more durable than the politicomilitary aspect of enlargement, the economic half of Clinton's foreign policy also came under attack during this period. For groups to which free trade seemed more peril than promise, enlargement appeared poised not to safeguard domestic prosperity but to kill it. By late 1994, Clinton had retreated from his enthusiasm for humanitarian intervention and had lost momentum in the fight for international economic integration. Perhaps more telling, enlargement had lost its political currency, as Clinton no longer insisted that the doctrine was the new magnetic north for U.S.

policy. The term quickly fell out of use, reopening the void in foreign policy.

In some cases, enlargement's failure owed to the practical shortcomings of the strategy, such as the president's unwillingness to pursue his goals in the face of serious domestic resistance. At other points, the administration's ambitious objectives outran its resolve to commit the necessary level of military resources or political capital. Yet the flaws of enlargement went deeper than means and ends. Fundamentally, the decline of the doctrine stemmed from Clinton's inability to convince Americans that free trade, human rights, and democracy were sufficiently integral to U.S. security to justify any meaningful sacrifice in their pursuit. As the inevitable costs of intervention and economic openness became evident, so did the superficiality of public support for enlargement. *National interest* became the catchphrase of the day as domestic commentators shied away from bearing the burdens associated with the president's strategy. In the absence of a clear threat to American well-being, Clinton could not overcome the basic self-interestedness of U.S. politics in the post–Cold War era, and by late 1994, enlargement was stalled at home and abroad.

Nation Building

Enlargement's military proving ground was Mogadishu, where roughly 20,000 American troops had deployed in December 1992 as part of Operation Restore Hope. In contrast to the abortive effort in Bosnia, the U.S.-led United Nations Task Force (UNITAF) mission in Somalia proceeded smoothly at first. In late 1992 and early 1993, UNITAF noticeably improved conditions in and around the capital, reestablishing supply lines, delivering food, and ensuring that famine reached the proportions of only a minor catastrophe. By February, most observers concluded that UNITAF had accomplished its strictly defined mission of averting starvation and creating a logistical base for the delivery of aid. With UNITAF's task complete, the White House relinquished command of the international forces in Somalia to the United Nations.[1]

The transfer of power occurred in early May, as the UN Mission for Somalia (UNISOM) superseded UNITAF. Clinton reduced the number of U.S. troops under the new UN command by more than half and, at a homecoming ceremony on May 5, declared, "Mission accomplished." At this point, Somalia looked to be a clear victory for the new administration. Aside from saving lives, the intervention had proved popular at home, with optimistic observers concluding that the United States had charted a new course for international relations in the 1990s. The *New Yorker* rejected criticism of the mission on grounds that it did not serve vital interests, calling it a "moral advance" for American foreign policy.[2]

Even as Clinton reveled in UNITAF's success, however, there were indications that the mission was far from complete. Several thousand U.S. soldiers remained in Somalia as part of UNISOM, which took a broader view of its mandate than had its predecessor. UNISOM was charged with building civil society and creating the conditions for long-term stability in Somalia, a task vastly more difficult than the one that Bush had initially accepted. Affirming his humanitarian inclinations, Clinton did not challenge this expanded mission, announcing that U.S. protection would enable the Somalis "to complete the work of rebuilding and creating a peaceful, self-sustaining, and democratic civil society." Emergency relief had begun to sound like nation building.[3]

In early June, U.S. involvement in Somalia evolved again. The civil war that had originally necessitated UNITAF flared, and certain factions, upset that outsiders had curtailed their ability to seize food supplies, began to target the UN force. On June 5, Somali fighters under the command of warlord Mohammed Aideed ambushed and killed twenty-four Pakistani soldiers. The UN Security Council responded by passing a new resolution calling for UNISOM to punish those responsible for the attacks. Days later, another resolution singled out Aideed for arrest. The rapid deepening of the U.S. mission reached its logical conclusion on June 11, when U.S. forces raided Aideed-controlled territory. Colin Powell identified Aideed as the "strategic center" of the operation in Somalia, and the administration resolved to "keep pressure on" the warlord. Having entered Somalia as impartial bearers of relief, U.S. troops now found themselves in a thoroughly partisan role.[4]

As it became apparent that Somalia's happy ending had turned into a fratricidal struggle with U.S. soldiers at its center, domestic support for the mission frayed. U.S. participation in the attack on Aideed elicited questions from those who wondered what had happened to the limited commitment to Somalia. Writers for the *Washington Post* were harshly critical of the expanding mission. "Instead of bringing the wretched Aideed to his knees, the U.S. bombings have brought him to the microphone," asserted one columnist. The *New York Times,* which had earlier shamed Bush into action, now called for Clinton to set a withdrawal date.[5]

Despite these signs of unease, the overall state of opinion on the mission was not unfavorable, and Clinton refused to distance himself from UN aims in Somalia. In a June letter to congressional leaders, Clinton averred that U.S. forces would aid UNISOM in keeping order and punishing Aideed. At another point, he was bolder still, referring to Somalia as a precedent for humanitarian intervention. Announcing U.S. participation in the June 11 raid, Clinton hinted that peace enforcement would not be limited to Somalia. "The United States must continue to play its unique role in the world," Clinton declared, "but now we can increasingly express that leadership through multilateral means such as the United Nations."[6]

The administration's persistence was closely related to its concurrent expansion of plans for humanitarian intervention (discussed in chapter 4). The drafting of PDD 13 reinforced Clinton's and his advisers' inclination to undertake Somalia-type missions and, to some extent, probably steeled them to the limited dissent produced by the feeling that UNISOM was in no hurry to exit Somalia. Within the context of PDD 13 and the administration's summer statements on peacemaking, it is now clear that the growing U.S. role in Somalia was more than an example of "mission creep," as observers alleged at the time. Rather, U.S. policy in June and July 1993 was part of a broadened strategy of humanitarianism. Bosnia might have alerted the administration to the limits of multilateralism, but it ultimately failed to dissuade Clinton from promoting democracy and human rights.

The administration had overestimated public support for peace enforcement, however. In late summer, senators challenged the continuing U.S. presence in Somalia, to say nothing of potential future commitments. Senator Robert Byrd declared that with UNITAF's mission complete, it was time to get out of Somalia. South Dakota senator Larry Pressler complained that the United States had abandoned impartiality by attempting to disarm Aideed. "We are taking part in internal politics, so to speak, with our troops," he said, "and I predict it is going to lead us to lots of problems." The criticism mounted in August, when several U.S. soldiers were killed in Mogadishu.[7]

It was partly in response to these concerns that Clinton's inner circle mounted the public relations blitz that culminated in the promulgation of enlargement as the United States' post–Cold War foreign policy. Even at its rhetorical high point, though, this new strategy seemed unlikely to inspire the level of domestic support that had made anticommunism such an enduring doctrine. In the days after Lake's address, there were signs that enlargement had failed Warren Christopher's test of political viability. Although observers lauded the ideals of enlargement, the doctrine garnered a generally tepid response. For the most part, commentators doubted that the admittedly noble goals of enlargement were worth meaningful sacrifice. "The notion of 'enlargement' is pleasing," conceded the *Washington Post,* "but it does not fit easily within the country's evident current distaste for heavy risks and high costs in foreign engagement." *USA Today* approved of enlargement's principles but pointed out that the policy "doesn't satisfy the public desire for an easily understood basis for U.S. involvement abroad." Americans would demand a strategy more "hard-headed" than enlargement, opined another newspaper.[8]

Given Clinton's hope of re-creating a foreign policy consensus, the reserved public reaction to enlargement must have been troubling to the administration. As responses to Lake's speech indicated, domestic observers demanded concrete justifications for an active—and potentially costly—diplomatic role in the postcontainment world. What was missing from enlargement was a credible appeal to American self-interest, a widely accepted rationale for why intervention in Somalia and elsewhere was essential to U.S. security. As Lake himself admitted, human suffering did not pose a mortal threat to the United States or its interests. "There is now no credible near-term threat to America's existence," he conceded. Regional conflict, authoritarian regimes, and human rights violations were certainly morally troubling, but they lacked immediacy for U.S. observers. These threats seemed abstract, far away, and not especially menacing to national security. They were, in short, not particularly scary, and as such, they hardly seemed worthy of sacrifice.[9]

Enlargement had other flaws that became apparent in the fall of 1993. For one, Clinton's commitment to nation building in Somalia was not matched by his resolve to see the mission through. An obvious inconsistency of Somalia policy was the fact that Clinton endorsed an expanded mandate only after the majority of U.S. troops had been withdrawn. Additional problems arose when the Pentagon initially refused to deploy the armored vehicles and elite Ranger units thought necessary for the offensive against Aideed. Finally, miscommunication between UNISOM and Washington left U.S. troops pursuing Aideed after Clinton had sought to minimize the visibility of the military mission by focusing on diplomatic efforts to mollify the warring clans.[10]

The inadequacies of the Somalia policy converged on October 3, when an attempt to capture Aideed misfired and produced nineteen American deaths. The debacle was a searing experience for Americans, made all the more so by the fact that television news reports showed gruesome scenes of the bodies of U.S. soldiers being dragged through the streets of Mogadishu by mobs denouncing the foreign presence in their country. This defeat, magnified by the seeming omnipresence of those piercing images, produced a domestic revolt against the mission in Somalia. In the days after the battle, surveys revealed that only 31 percent of respondents favored keeping U.S. troops in Somalia until UNISOM's mission was complete. Congress turned against the intervention as well, revealing the shallowness of public support for humanitarian action. Representative Mitch McConnell (R-Ky.) issued a stinging condemnation of Clinton's strategy, saying, "Creeping multilateralism died in the streets of Mogadishu."[11]

More damaging still, other critics began to compare Somalia with Vietnam. Opposition to the open-ended nature of the mission, which had stayed at a simmer during the summer of 1993, boiled over after the battle of Mogadishu revealed that keeping troops in Somalia came at a significant human cost. One congressman now called on Clinton to "get his foreign policy act together before Somalia becomes another Vietnam." Senator Frank Lautenberg (D-N.J.) agreed, saying that the mission "evokes all sorts of recollections about what Vietnam looked like." In both houses of Congress, enlargement was now tainted by historical analogy.[12]

This growing apprehension that the conflict in Somalia might be simply a more arid version of the war in Vietnam was the kiss of death for Clinton's policy. Only behind-the-scenes maneuvering by the White House prevented Congress from demanding an immediate withdrawal, instead producing an agreement to bring U.S. forces home within six months. Chastened, the administration backtracked from its ambitious humanitarian plans. Appearing before the Senate on October 20, Madeleine Albright promised that the U.S. commitment to UN missions in general was "not open-ended." Her presentation was uncharacteristically pessimistic and presaged the deterioration of enlargement. "Clearly," Albright admitted, "the bipartisan consensus that so recently guided our approach to UN peacekeeping has broken down."[13]

Enlargement had turned into a political nightmare for Clinton. Having been criticized for indecision and inaction in Bosnia, he was now condemned for creating another Vietnam in Somalia. Enlargement had originated as a strategy designed to ensure domestic support for foreign policy; it now threatened Clinton's political standing at home. "Right now the average American doesn't see our interests threatened to the point where we should sacrifice one American life," he told aides. Coming in late 1993, at a time when Clinton had major domestic and economic initiatives in the offing, this realization was especially lethal to the strategy. Already involved in a struggle for health care reform and a bruising battle over NAFTA, Clinton could hardly shoulder another political burden by clinging to a policy that had become so unpopular. To do so might have risked the economic and domestic programs at the heart of his first-term agenda.[14]

Albright hoped to prevent Clinton from conciliating domestic sentiment by ditching his entire humanitarian agenda, but he proceeded to do just that. The first casualty was the scope of U.S. involvement in Somalia. "It is not our job to rebuild Somalia's society, or even to create a political process that can allow Somalia's clans to live and work in peace," Clinton declared in the wake of Mogadishu. U.S. troops spent the next six months biding their time until withdrawal. Clinton directed U.S. commanders in the region not to "create a provocation" that might spur renewed fighting and incur more casualties, and the administration may have even sent feelers to Aideed, encouraging the warlord to lay low until American forces were withdrawn.[15]

The retrenching did not stop there. Deeply troubled by the lack of a public stomach for peacemaking, Clinton ordered a new policy review on humanitarian intervention and UN relations. The study led to the expected results: minimizing U.S. involvement in peacekeeping and peacemaking. Eager to distance the administration from Somalia and humanitarian intervention in general, Lake made the findings public in early 1994. "Peacekeeping is not at the center of our foreign or defense policy," he reassured Americans. Departing sharply from the comments of U.S. officials during enlargement's heyday in mid-1993, Lake reaffirmed the traditional objective of the military: "Our armed forces' primary mission is not to conduct peace operations but to win wars." Finalized in May 1994, PDD 25 discarded the idealism and essence of enlargement, stating that Clinton would keep the "national interest uppermost" in defining foreign policy objectives. The July 1994 *National Security Strategy* also displayed this new realism, avowing, "Our national interests will dictate the pace and extent" of military operations. Clinton's experiment in peacemaking was over.[16]

Blinksmanship

The tragic irony of enlargement's demise was that it came just as events elsewhere in Africa illustrated the horrific potential of humanitarian crises left unchecked. In early 1994, just as PDD 25 took final shape, Rwanda relapsed into a civil war that rivaled Somalia's in terms of intensity and destruction. Reeling from the debacle in Mogadishu, however, the Clinton administration refused to take even minimal steps to halt the slaughter. Coupled with his weak response to a crisis in Haiti months later, Clinton's inaction in Rwanda left little doubt that he had abandoned the military side of enlargement.

The Rwandan genocide had its roots in the late 1980s and early 1990s. Rwanda's majority Hutu and minority Tutsi ethnic groups fought a civil war beginning in 1990, with the Tutsi-manned Rwandan Patriotic Front (RPF) using neighboring Burundi and Uganda as safe havens. As the RPF scored battlefield victories, Hutu leaders, including President Juvenal Habyarimana, exploited Rwanda's ethnic divisions in an attempt to roll back Tutsi influence. Backed by the radical Hutu Power movement, they drew on long-standing Hutu resentment of the Tutsi's favored status under the Belgian colonial regime and painted Tutsi civilians as RPF agents. Amid periodic anti-Tutsi violence perpetrated by Habyarimana's allies between 1990 and 1993, Hutu leaders created the civilian *interhamwe* militias as a means of solidifying their own power base. Tensions mounted in 1993. The RPF won a number of military triumphs and gained a favorable peace settlement, further threatening Habyarimana's position. In October, the murder of the Hutu president of Burundi by Tutsi extremists heightened fears that the RPF would not acquiesce in an equitable power-sharing arrangement. Hutu businesses began to import weapons, especially machetes, and in March 1994, Hutu Power leaders plotted mass attacks against Tutsi civilians. When Habyarimana died under mysterious circumstances on April 6, Hutu radicals enacted their plan. They first killed moderate Hutu officials, so as to fill the Rwandan government with Hutu Power supporters, and then initiated the widespread killings of Tutsi. By mid-April, genocide had become official policy.[17]

It was no secret in Washington that events in Rwanda had taken a deadly turn. Several months earlier, the CIA had predicted that a major conflict might erupt. On April 7, a day after the violence began, the CIA warned that "as Hutus in Rwanda seek revenge on Tutsis, the civil war may resume." A day later, the embassy in Kigali reported that "the Rwandan army is killing officials and Tutsis, and the UN is unable to control the situation." Pentagon analysts were blunter. An assistant secretary of defense thought it likely that, if the violence continued, "a massive bloodbath (hundreds of thousands of deaths) will ensue." The killing of ten Belgian peacekeepers, hacked to death while guarding the Hutu prime minister, focused the gaze of the UN community on the tragedy, which grew in scope with each passing day. By mid-April, the general dimensions of the violence were largely apparent.[18]

In Washington, Clinton never considered military intervention or even strong diplomatic steps that might have alleviated the spiraling violence. The genocide came at a particularly inopportune time for humanitarians, as PDD 25 was finalized at roughly the same moment. That document killed any internal impetus for intervention. The report took a pessimistic stance (no doubt informed by the experience in Somalia) on the utility of peacemaking, stating that civil conflicts "are particularly hard to come to grips with and to have an effect on from the outside, because basically, of course, their origins are in political turmoil within these nations. And that turmoil may not be susceptible to the efforts of the international community. So, neither we nor the international community have neither the mandate nor the resources nor the possibility of resolving every conflict of this kind."[19]

This assessment of the intractability of internal strife was new (Clinton had not been burdened by such concerns in Somalia) but powerful nonetheless. Lake, formerly an ardent interventionist, displayed no enthusiasm for a proactive stance. The National Security Council never convened a principals meeting to contemplate a U.S. role in Rwanda, and the State Department disbanded its Working Group for Rwanda after the successful evacuation of U.S. nationals in mid-April. After Somalia, strong measures in Rwanda were simply out of the question. The only direct action Clinton authorized in the crucial period between early April and mid-May was a UN arms embargo on Rwanda. This measure would have been laughable had the situation not been so tragic; arms shipments were of relatively little import when most of the killing was being done with machetes.[20]

Clinton's advisers and diplomats actually went beyond passivity and actively discouraged UN intervention. Fearing that international observers might demand more forceful measures, the administration sought to draw attention away from the conflict. During the Security Council debate on Rwanda in mid-April, U.S. representatives pressed for the withdrawal of UN peacekeepers as a favor to the Belgian government, which wanted to avoid further loss of life among its soldiers. Hoping to minimize public awareness of the crisis, the State Department forbade its officials to use the word *genocide* in reference to Rwanda. An Interagency Working Group cautioned against investigating the circumstances of the violence too closely. "Be careful," the officials wrote, a "genocide finding could commit the [U.S. government] to actually 'do something.'" The Pentagon was equally eager to avoid involvement. When midlevel State Department advisers attempted to persuade their Defense Department counterparts to consider a peace enforcement mission, the Pentagon officials refused. Moreover, Defense took the extraordinary step of refusing to jam Hutu radio broadcasts directing the *interhamwe* militias to their next victims, terming the idea "ineffective and expensive."[21]

Nor was there any public enthusiasm for intervention. For those who remembered the footage of mobs dragging dead U.S. soldiers through Mogadishu, it was not difficult to imagine a similar situation in Rwanda. More generally, Americans had lost their appetite for humanitarianism. A poll from late 1994 revealed that only 26 percent of the public saw protecting human rights as "very important" (a drop of more than 30 points from 1990). Once they had been shown the costs of intervention, Americans had decided that it was not such a good idea after all. In April and May, somewhere between 500,000 and 800,000 Tutsi lost their lives, most of them suffering a gruesome death by machete, and the killing ended only when the RPF eventually overran the country.[22]

Clinton's refusal to commit troops to Rwanda was understandable, if perhaps unfortunate; with a crisis brewing in North Korea and little public support for intervention, presidential enthusiasm for such a project would have been surprising. What was striking about Clinton's response, however, was his unwillingness to even consider the prospect and the lengths to which the administration went to discourage intervention of any sort. In fact, Clinton took advantage of the genocide to enunciate a new philosophy of humanitarian intervention. This doctrine barred U.S. forces from undertaking peace missions to countries embroiled in internal political or military disputes—that is, almost any country that would need peacekeepers. The lesson of Somalia, Clinton stated, was that "even a humanitarian mission will inevitably be caught up in the politics of a country, unless people are starving and dying because of a natural disaster." Clinton applied this idea to Rwanda, announcing that intervention was out of the question because "from what we read of the conflict between the Hutus and the

Tutsis . . . there is a political and military element to this." These statements confirmed the restrictive guidelines of PDD 25 and signaled that the military side of enlargement was truly bankrupt.[23]

Events in the summer of 1994 raised the prospect that Clinton might revive the now-discarded doctrine, but in the end, they merely provided additional evidence of the administration's newfound caution. Haiti, which had played a key role in Clinton's campaign attacks on Bush, was the site. Since the coup in 1991, the situation in Haiti had steadily worsened. Cedras's government clamped down on political activity, banning civil associations and suppressing dissent. Gangs allied with the regime conducted violent campaigns against suspected Aristide loyalists. Beatings were common, as were slayings with machetes. Haiti's civil society ground to a halt, and the already poor country became even more poverty-stricken. During 1992 and 1993, Haiti moved from being a diplomatic embarrassment for Washington to a full-fledged humanitarian crisis. Cedras's forces killed roughly 4,000 Haitians, 60,000 attempted to escape to the United States, and 300,000 became internal refugees.[24]

Like his predecessor, Clinton was slow to respond to the situation, initially repudiating his campaign promises by upholding Bush's refugee policy. It appeared that a peaceful resolution might be at hand in 1993, when UN mediation produced the Governor's Island accords, which laid out a plan for returning Haiti to civilian rule. Cedras soon reneged on the agreement, however, and he had members of Aristide's government murdered. The issue burst onto the U.S. scene in October 1993, when Haitian mobs prevented a group of U.S. and Canadian engineers under the UN flag from landing in Port-au-Prince.

Cedras's blatant rejection of the UN-brokered deal and affront to the United States evoked a few isolated calls for intervention to restore Aristide to power. If undertaken, such a project promised to be far less complicated than meddling in Somalia, Rwanda, or Bosnia. In Haiti's case, there were no ethnic issues to speak of, and U.S. intervention would entail simply removing Cedras and allowing Aristide to return, at which point Clinton could declare democracy restored. Furthermore, Cedras was unpopular, and there was little prospect of the civilian population supporting the despot. Despite the attractiveness of this proposition, Clinton showed little inclination to use force in late 1993. Although, as Lake noted, the president desired "strong action to scare [the] bad guys" in Haiti, after the embarrassment in Somalia, few administration officials were eager for a new conflict or confident that Congress would condone another military excursion to a troubled country. Even the normally hawkish Albright hewed to a cautious line, stating that Clinton would not initiate "an armed intervention that nobody wants." Instead, the administration continued the economic sanctions that had been in effect since the Bush years.[25]

Despite Clinton's best efforts to ignore the situation, the Haitian problem refused to go away. Evidence surfaced that, in addition to cutting off the faces of its citizens, the Cedras regime was involved in drug trafficking. The sanctions did not have the desired effect, wrecking the Haitian economy without loosening Cedras's hold on power. Confronted with the ineffectiveness of their policy, Clinton and Lake conducted a review of U.S. strategy in early 1994. Though rumors of an invasion swirled around Washington, the administration hesitated to move toward stronger measures. Distrust of Aristide was one component of this reluctance. The State Department alleged that Aristide and his supporters "consistently manipulate or even fabricate human rights abuses as a propaganda tool." Added to existing concerns, these new doubts ensured that the policy review ultimately reflected the same hesitance to use force that was apparent in Clinton's reaction to the Rwandan genocide. As State Department representative Lawrence Pezzullo put it at the conclusion of the study, the United States remained committed to a "peaceful, negotiated settlement" in Haiti. Clinton again took the course of least resistance, tightening the existing sanctions on Haiti in the hope of averting a military confrontation.[26]

This hope was more wishful than realistic; over the past two and a half years, various sanctions had failed to have any significant effect on Cedras, and there was little reason to expect that the next package of restrictions would be any more persuasive. To the surprise of few, Clinton's new policy enjoyed no greater success than his old one had, and certain advisers began to bang the drums for war. By mid-June, Undersecretary of State Strobe Talbott favored an invasion, but he failed to convince Clinton that the United States had exhausted diplomatic measures. In public, U.S. officials continued to deny that the use of force was being contemplated. The anti-interventionist position gained additional strength shortly thereafter, when the Senate passed a nonbinding resolution calling on the White House to secure congressional approval before committing troops to Haiti.[27]

As it became obvious in June and July that Cedras had no intention of bowing to U.S. and UN demands, international patience with the sanctions waned. The Security Council passed a resolution authorizing the use of force to remove Cedras from power, which the U.S. delegation supported. Nonetheless, strong voices in Washington continued to oppose an invasion. At a meeting in early August, Talbott again proposed military action and resurrected the rhetoric of enlargement by declaring that it would be immoral to allow Haiti to suffer any longer under Cedras's rule. Reactions to Talbott's argument showed the declining influence of such sentiments. According to a paraphrased account of the meeting, new Secretary of Defense William Perry (Aspin had resigned over the Somalia imbroglio) blasted Talbott's "strange morality." In Perry's view, "It would be immoral for the United States not to do whatever it could to avoid the deaths of American soldiers." Clinton sided with Perry, deciding that intervention would be "premature." The administration considered other means of resolving the crisis, including sending a UN envoy to negotiate, promising not to punish Cedras, or perhaps even bribing the regime to leave Haiti. Clinton still sought a way to avoid war.[28]

By early September, however, the crisis had become a major headache for the president. Having spoken grandly of a "hemisphere of democracies," Clinton could no longer ignore the fact that an authoritarian regime was thumbing its nose at the United States from the nearby Caribbean. Clinton's credibility was on the line; Lake argued that the "essential reliability" of U.S. policy was at stake. "We must make it clear that we mean what we say," he stated.[29] In mid-September, Clinton finally took a hard line, threatening to invade Haiti if Cedras did not step down. "Your time is up," Clinton declared on national television. "Leave now, or we will force you from power."[30]

Bold language to the contrary, Clinton had not yet committed to war. He had issued no deadline for Cedras's departure, leaving the timing of an invasion ambiguous. Clinton's subsequent actions further belied his bellicose rhetoric. On September 17, the president dispatched Powell (now retired), former president Jimmy Carter, and

Sam Nunn to negotiate Cedras out of power. Despite fears that Carter might fall into a protracted bargaining session, Clinton again refused to set a deadline for agreement. Carter's open-ended mission left little doubt that Clinton remained wary of intervention and confirmed the new conservatism of his foreign policy.[31]

Luckily for Clinton, the negotiations succeeded. Cedras caved when Powell informed him that U.S. forces would soon strike. The returning Aristide government "invited" U.S. troops to oversee the transition as Aristide reclaimed the presidency and, with U.S. assistance, set about the difficult (and still incomplete) process of rebuilding Haiti's economy and political system. Armed conflict avoided, Clinton could (and did) claim that he had delivered victory without incurring the costs of war.

Even so, critics were unimpressed. Leaked reports revealed internal disagreements and presidential indecision, adding to the impression that Clinton was a weak leader. *Time* cuttingly referred to Clinton's strategy as "blinksmanship," and *Newsweek* agreed that the president had "stumbled into a crisis." Inside and outside the White House, it was clear that the successful outcome in Haiti did not herald a return to interventionism. Somalia had killed enlargement; Rwanda and Haiti showed that resurrection was not in prospect.[32]

The Wages of Free Trade

Just as 1993 and 1994 proved decisive in determining the fate of humanitarian intervention, these years also witnessed a contest over the essence of Clinton's commercial program. The debate began favorably for the president, who garnered personal, political, and policy vindication by winning the NAFTA battle. The seeds of frustration took root in this victory, however, as the debate opened a veritable Pandora's box regarding free trade and domestic politics. By late 1994, with the Democratic ranks rent and Clinton's initiatives giving voice to opponents of free trade, his commercial agenda was in serious trouble. The visibility and decreasing effectiveness of Clinton's economic policies threw into sharp relief arguments for and against trade liberalization, providing a stern test of his integrationist rhetoric and the remaining tenets of enlargement.

Even at the acme of Clinton's trade success in late 1993, there had been ominous portents for the president's economic agenda. The debate over NAFTA had alienated key Democratic groups, including environmentalists and organized labor. The ramifications of this showdown became apparent in 1994, when Clinton attempted to win fast-track trade legislation. Fast track, which allowed the president to send foreign trade agreements to the Hill for expedited advice and consent, was considered integral to international economic policy by Clinton and his predecessors. Without it, the White House feared, trade pacts would become embroiled in domestic politics, resulting in watered-down agreements or amendments that would prove unacceptable to the United States or its trade counterpart.

NAFTA had been passed under the fast-track legislation accorded Bush in 1991, but the enabling law would expire at the end of 1994. Clinton sought a seven-year extension and tied the enacting legislation to the treaty concluding the Uruguay Round of GATT. The president viewed the two measures as linked indicators of progress toward freer trade and probably believed that appending fast track to GATT would improve the former's chances of approval. The administration predicted that Congress would be reluctant to reject what Clinton called "the biggest trade agreement in history," especially if the president made a strong push for the legislation.[33]

Yet Clinton misjudged the political climate. Opposition to GATT was surprisingly strong; opposition to fast track was even more so. The battle lines were roughly those drawn in the NAFTA debate, and in many ways, the contest over fast track turned into a referendum on the earlier agreement. Labor Democrats feared that fast track would allow Clinton to replicate NAFTA's pernicious consequences for domestic employment, and environmentalists reiterated their concerns about border jumping. "This administration cannot continue to dance to the tune of the corporate interests that seek to be able to move in a very mobile world from one country to another to seek the subsidy they receive in either human misery or environmental pollution," declared Congressman George Miller (D-Calif.). In the upper chamber, one senator charged that "U.S. living standards are being sacrificed to a bunch of failed policies and a slogan called 'free trade.'"[34]

By mid-1994, criticism of fast track had become so intense that it threatened to derail GATT as well. Attempting to save both initiatives, the White House downgraded its request, asking for a thirty-month extension of fast track. Even this concession was not sufficient to rescue the legislation. Faced with the prospect that insisting on fast track would prevent the passage of GATT, which Senator Patrick Moynihan (D-N.Y.) referred to as "the culmination of 60 years of American international trade policy," Clinton removed fast track from the GATT bill and thereby conceded defeat.[35]

Free trade's domestic popularity sustained another setback in late 1994 and early 1995. In Mexico, the Zapatista uprising and a series of political assassinations in 1994 triggered a crisis of investor confidence and sent the peso plummeting. A lax monetary policy compounded the structural shakiness of Mexico's economy, and the government was unable to right the situation. As foreign capital fled the country, it became apparent that Mexico would be unable to make debt payments scheduled for the beginning of 1995. American exports to Mexico, which had grown substantially since the passage of NAFTA, dwindled.[36]

To protect U.S. exports and financial interests, and to prevent the crisis from spreading to other Latin American countries, Clinton proposed a multibillion-dollar bailout for Mexico. Christopher defended the package, arguing that Americans had an "immense political and economic stake in Mexico's stability." An economic collapse would drive down exports, hurting U.S. companies, and it might trigger a flood of illegal immigrants to the United States. Many congressmen opposed the bailout and used the debate it occasioned as an opportunity to assail free trade and NAFTA for putting the United States in a position where a massive aid package was necessary to protect American investors and exporters. "Many of us who opposed NAFTA had deep fears that the state of the Mexican economy was not what Mexican leaders told us it was," chided Bernard Sanders. "I think that history has largely proved us to be right." When subpoenaed documents revealed that Treasury Department officials had shared these fears as early as 1993, the administration suffered additional embarrassment. Clinton eventually used his executive authority to authorize a $20 billion bailout, but on the U.S. domestic political scene, the damage was done.[37]

Clinton's problems did not stem solely from the domestic controversy provoked by free trade; he was also hurt by his occasional ineffectiveness as an opener of markets abroad. Having promised to achieve greater foreign market access for U.S. exporters, Clinton came under criticism when he failed to deliver. This issue was most salient in the administration's troubled dealings with Japan in 1993 and 1994. When Clinton took office, U.S.-Japan relations were widely viewed to be at a crucial point. Although Tokyo had been Washington's client during the Cold War, Japan's economic success in the 1970s and 1980s had skewed that relationship. By the late 1980s, Japan appeared to be on the verge of surpassing the United States in several important economic areas. If Japan established economic supremacy over the United States, could political dominance be far behind? What if, during a crisis, Tokyo gained leverage on Washington by threatening to withdraw Japanese investments from the United States? And if Japan was such an economic powerhouse, why did the United States heavily subsidize that nation's defense? Clinton had promised to get to the bottom of these matters, calling U.S.-Japan ties "our most important bilateral relationship" during the campaign.[38]

The belief that Japan pursued illiberal trade policies fueled the commercial animosity between the two countries, creating both an economic and a political incentive for U.S. politicians to take action. During the 1980s and early 1990s, the White House approached this problem cautiously, calling for greater access to Japanese markets but being careful not to start a trade war or alienate a close ally. Congressmen were less careful and, in some cases, seemed determined to do both. In the early 1990s, "Japanophobia" reached new heights. "The Cold War is over," Democratic presidential hopeful Paul Tsongas liked to say, and "Japan won." In this atmosphere, corrective action seemed a political necessity.[39]

By the time Clinton took office in 1993, the recent downturn in the Japanese economy made a solution seem all the more urgent. Since the Japanese asset bubble had burst in 1990, Tokyo's economic fortunes had taken a steady southward slide. The Nikkei (Japan's stock exchange) fell more than 50 percent between 1990 and 1992, and by 1993, it was clear to observers on both sides of the Pacific that the Japanese dynamo had slowed considerably. In a psychological sense,

Japan's bad fortune actually alleviated certain U.S. anxieties. In late 1991, nearly 50 percent of Americans had thought that Japan would be "the number one economic power in the world" during the next century, and only 30 percent had believed that the United States would remain on top in the rankings; by the end of the next year, these predictions had roughly reversed. With "Japan Inc." struggling, Americans felt somewhat more secure about their own economic future.[40]

In the main, however, Tokyo's difficulties exacerbated tensions with Washington. As earnings stagnated in Japan, the U.S. trade deficit ballooned. Japanese consumers purchased fewer U.S. goods, while Japanese companies compensated for the slack in domestic sales by sending more merchandise abroad. The trade imbalance between the two nations reached $44 billion in 1992, and during the first months of Clinton's term, it looked as though it might go even higher in 1993. Far from abating, calls for a U.S. response grew stronger at the outset of Clinton's presidency.[41]

Clinton agreed wholeheartedly with this advice. A more equitable trade relationship, he and his advisers reasoned, was desirable for multiple reasons. Closing the trade deficit was surely an end in itself, and reforming economic affairs between Washington and Tokyo would be a first step toward reshaping the broader U.S.-Japan relationship to reflect the changing dynamics between the two countries and in the world at large. Japan had reached adulthood after half a century of U.S. tutelage, the administration argued, and no longer merited special treatment. Assistant Secretary of State Winston Lord called for "a fresh global partnership with Japan that reflects a more mature balance of responsibilities." A victory in trade negotiations with Japan would also be a boon to enlargement and the president's economic program.[42]

After taking office, Clinton told the U.S. ambassador to Japan that securing increased market access would be a priority of his presidency. Within weeks of the inauguration, U.S. diplomats quietly pressured their Japanese counterparts to take measures such as lowering the Bank of Japan's discount rate (the interest charged on loans to commercial banks) as a means of stimulating imports. In public, Clinton's rhetoric was conciliatory but tough; while affirming the cooperative nature of affairs between the two countries, he stated bluntly that the trade gap "cannot continue." American negotiators, led by Mickey Kantor, sought a set of "objective criteria," or numerical indicators of the Japanese market share of U.S. goods, as a benchmark for measuring Tokyo's progress in allowing freer trade.[43]

Kantor's opposite numbers proved difficult to corner, however. Although the fact that the United States consumed one-third of Japanese exports made Tokyo keen to avert a trade war, there was also strong pressure in Japan not to accede to Clinton's wishes. The Gulf crisis of 1990–1991, during which Washington had solicited $10 billion from Tokyo to finance a conflict that many Japanese opposed, had created substantial tension. This had come on the heels of a number of occasions during the 1980s when American officials had pressured Japan to alter its trade policies and U.S. congressmen had (literally) taken axes to Japanese products on the Capitol lawn. The cumulative result was a backlash against cooperation with the United States. Japanese public opinion opposed compromise on trade issues, and Tokyo officials made clear their intention to take a firm stance. Foreign Ministry representative Masamichi Hanabusa declared that Japan should be "an equal partner" with the United States and promised that Tokyo would henceforth be "asserting itself a little more strongly."[44]

When trade negotiations opened in 1993, common ground was hard to find. Rejecting Washington's claims of unfairness, Japanese officials countered that low sales of U.S. exports were merely indicative that American goods were not competitive. Throughout 1993 and 1994, Kantor made little progress in five areas of chief importance to Clinton: autos, auto parts, insurance, telecommunications equipment, and medical supplies. The Japanese negotiators were elusive, pledging their commitment to free trade without making meaningful concessions. As the talks stalled, Clinton acknowledged that "Japan's offers made in these negotiations simply did not meet the standards" to which the administration was bound by its economic program and earlier promises.[45]

The already chilly climate of U.S.-Japan relations worsened in the summer of 1994. A weak dollar and a strong yen made the exchange rate less favorable for Americans, and the triumph of a socialist government in the Japanese elections hardly seemed a promising omen. A showdown loomed, as U.S. law mandated sanctions on Japanese products if there was no agreement by the end of July (the deadline was later extended to September). With a crisis imminent, Clinton discovered that he had talked himself into a corner. By pledging to open the Japanese market, he had raised domestic expectations of success. Support for this general goal, however, did not necessarily translate into support for the measures needed to achieve it. By midsummer, it appeared that a virtual declaration of economic hostilities might be necessary to wring significant concessions out of Tokyo. A trade war would hurt the United States as much as Japan, and enthusiasm for a tough stance dissipated accordingly. The *New York Times,* which generally supported Clinton's efforts, declared that market access was "not worth risking a trade war." Furthermore, Clinton needed Japanese support in a brewing confrontation with North Korea and could not jeopardize the overall relationship with Tokyo.[46]

The president was in an awkward position, and a meaningful agreement looked unlikely. Yet with U.S. sanctions in prospect, a deal was necessary. Failure to achieve a breakthrough by the end of the month would automatically result in what would likely be the first shot in a trade war: a crippling 100 percent duty on Japanese luxury cars. In the end, Clinton had to settle for what was at best a partial victory. The negotiators struck a deal at the last minute, but the language of the pact was so loose as to be almost meaningless. The most critical issue separating the two countries, auto imports, remained unresolved. Kantor tried to portray the agreement in the best possible light, calling it "results-oriented." The remarks of Kantor's Japanese counterpart showed the hollowness of that statement. "Our interpretation," he explained, "is if the U.S. products are really competitive in the world market, then their value and share in the Japanese market will certainly increase. That is not a result we can guarantee." In other words, Americans should stop making shoddy products. Widely seen as a setback in the United States, the agreement was hailed as a victory in Japan, and Tokyo's chief negotiator later parlayed this triumph into a successful run for prime minister.[47]

The failure to make any real progress in the trade talks was a setback for Clinton in several respects. The immediate result was that U.S. businesses and investors remained at a disadvantage in the lucrative Japanese market. In the political realm, Clinton faced criticism for failing to deliver on his promise to reshape the United States' relationship with Japan. "Clinton talked tough on trade," commented *Newsweek*. "But when the car talks came to a head, Washington blinked." More generally, the lack of progress in Japan and the defeat of fast track combined to undermine Clinton's accomplishments with NAFTA and GATT. The momentum created by these agreements slowed as other aspects of economic policy stalled, giving his trade program the distinct appearance of failure at the end of 1994.[48]

After NAFTA

Clinton's early setbacks had mixed effects on his subsequent commitment to free trade as a hallmark of foreign policy. Throughout his presidency, Clinton never wavered from the notion that prosperity was best achieved through international commerce. Between 1993 and 2000, the administration initialed nearly 300 trade agreements. In 1999, the deputy U.S. trade representative brushed off concerns about the failure of fast track, saying that the defeat had "not fundamentally impeded" Clinton's commercial program.[49]

In terms of free trade's status in the post–Cold War evolution of U.S. diplomacy, though, Clinton's economic policy failed to meet the standards imposed by its creator. The president's aim had been to establish trade as a rhetorical and practical pillar of foreign policy, but his initiatives provoked intense disagreement over the desirability of economic openness. If anything, U.S. opinion turned away from economic liberalism during the remainder of Clinton's presidency. An example of this trend came in 1997, when he again sought to obtain fast track. This time, it seemed, the administration had a stronger case. In contrast to 1994, when Clinton had had no specific agreement in mind when seeking the legislation, in 1997, his sights were set on concrete goals. Chile, its economy booming after the Chicago School's neoliberal reforms of the 1970s and 1980s, was going to receive NAFTA status. More ambitiously, Clinton sought to create a Free Trade Area of the Americas by 2005 and hoped to arrive at an inter-American summit in Santiago in 1998 armed with the necessary legislation.

The rationale for seeking fast track was much the same as it had been for NAFTA four years earlier. Free trade increased domestic prosperity, claimed Secretary of State Madeleine Albright, allowing U.S. firms to "break down barriers to American exports, create better jobs, and raise our standard of living." Strategic concerns also figured in the administration's calculations. If the United States did not open its economy to Latin American countries, Washington feared, Asian powers such as China would do so, increasing their commercial power and regional clout in the process. "We cannot afford to sit on the sidelines while other countries move ahead to take advantage of the growing market of Latin America," warned State Department adviser Jeffrey Davidow.[50]

By 1997, the administration also had a new argument for fast track. To many observers in the mid-1990s, the gradual integration of national societies and economies—referred to as *globalization*—appeared to be the inevitable outcome of international relations in the post–Cold War era (discussed in greater detail later). For the United States to maintain its position as a global leader, American officials argued, it must embrace this process. Fast track, as a symbol of the U.S. commitment to free trade, would be a good start. Fast track "is about more than economics," Clinton said in 1997. "It's about whether other countries will continue to look to the United States to lead to a future of peace and freedom and prosperity . . . or whether we will be viewed as somehow withdrawn from the world, not interested in leading it, and therefore not nearly as influential as we might otherwise be."[51]

In the fall of 1997, Clinton sent fast track to the House, where a vote was expected by the end of the year. Clinton called the bill a "no-brainer" and predicted that it would pass easily, but there were worrying signs as the debate began. A poll taken in September showed that only 36 percent of those surveyed favored fast track. Among opponents, there were two main objections to the legislation. For liberals, the vote on fast track turned into a second referendum on NAFTA. On the surface, this need not have been especially bad news for Clinton; most evaluations showed that the economic effects of the 1993 agreement had been minimal. But NAFTA's image suffered from the inherent political liability of all free-trade acts: the losses caused by a particular accord are almost always far more visible than the gains. In other words, lost jobs and picketing workers provide better news material than lower prices do. Esteban Torres, the California congressman whose support had been crucial in 1993, refused to back fast track, citing negative effects on wages and employment, and many union leaders took the same position.[52]

Liberal objections to free trade were nothing new. But the latest—and, for free-trade advocates, deeply troubling—development was conservative ambivalence about fast track. In 1993 and 1994, Republican cooperation had been crucial to passing NAFTA and GATT. Since then, however, the debate over free trade had changed. Conservatives had become increasingly apprehensive about linking the U.S. economy to other national and regional systems. The Mexican peso crisis and a financial meltdown in East Asia in 1997 had created the impression that interdependence threatened U.S. economic stability. Pat Buchanan, a self-styled "economic nationalist" who ran for president in 1992 and 1996, led the charge against a further expansion of free trade. "We are running into bailouts without end because of this global economy," he complained to Congress in November. NAFTA had forced Washington to rescue the Mexican economy; could additional free-trade agreements fail to have similar consequences?[53]

These objections proved powerful within the right wing of the Republican Party. Republican Speaker of the House Newt Gingrich warned that less than two-thirds of Republicans would support fast track, leaving Clinton short of the majority he needed. (In 1993, Republicans had backed NAFTA by more than three to one.) On the whole, conservatives had growing misgivings about free trade. A poll taken in November 1997 showed that one in three Republicans believed that free trade did more harm than good, an increase from earlier in the decade. With Republicans deserting the cause, fast track was doomed, and Clinton withdrew the legislation rather than suffer another defeat. The failure of fast track, the *Economist* remarked glumly, was "a worrying confirmation of America's current disenchantment with liberal trade." Indeed, polls showed that only a bare majority of Americans (52 percent) believed that free trade was beneficial, with nearly 40 percent seeing it as detrimental to domestic employment. Free trade was hardly the political winner Clinton had expected.[54]

Concerns about free trade spilled over into a larger—and equally contested—public discussion of globalization during Clinton's second term. In recent decades, and especially since the 1980s, the pace of global integration had quickened significantly. The end of the Cold War had ended the separation of Europe, and the resulting depolarization of international politics had eased divisions in other regions as well. The removal of these barriers and a concurrent revolution in information and communications technology combined to promote greater economic, political, and cultural ties among societies around the world. International commerce became easier, efforts to shield communities from outside influence became more difficult, and the general interconnectedness of nations increased markedly. By the mid-1990s, it was common to assume that the immutable outcome in the coming decades would be the erasure of national boundaries. As communications technology allowed near-instantaneous global intercourse, political, economic, social, and cultural frontiers would simply disappear. Globalization "can't be stopped," wrote *New York Times* columnist Thomas Friedman, one of the most widely read commentators on the subject. "It's inevitable."[55]

Globalization promised a number of benefits, especially in the economic realm. Interconnectedness would allow firms to do business in other countries, tapping new resources, capital, and labor supplies. Globalization would bring about standardized rules of international commerce, making it easier for businesses—U.S. and otherwise—to negotiate the intricacies of foreign trade. There would be political advantages as well. The breaking down of national barriers would reduce nationalism and facilitate multilateral endeavors, while increased global affluence would make war less likely. In general, proponents of this "Washington consensus" argued, globalization would enhance prospects for world prosperity and cooperation.[56]

Clinton came down firmly in favor of globalization. The administration contended that greater international openness was neither avoidable nor threatening. "Efforts to resist the powerful technological and economic forces behind globalization . . . are misguided and, in the long run, futile," argued Undersecretary of State Joan Spero. To fully realize the fruits of globalization, the United States must participate in the process in order to structure it and tailor it to U.S. interests.[57]

For the most part, high officials in other developed countries took the same position, and during the mid-1990s, international leaders worked to institutionalize globalization. European states moved toward financial and political integration, as the European Community became the European Union. On January 1, 1995, GATT became the World Trade Organization (WTO), a group devoted to regulating and facilitating trade between countries with market economies. During the second half of the decade, the WTO vetted applicants for admission, mediated trade disputes, and increasingly acted as a sort of governing body for world commerce.

Yet the movement toward global integration had a substantial backlash. The same interconnectedness that made it possible for firms to do business in faraway places also meant that a financial breakdown in one area could lead to instability around the globe, as happened when an economic crisis in East Asia spread to Russia and Latin America in 1997–1998. In other instances, increased international economic competition hurt the fortunes of established groups. The ability of companies to tap labor resources in other countries often meant that workers in developed nations found themselves out of work as their employers moved production facilities overseas. In poorer countries, workers without the skills and resources to take advantage of the "new global economy" were shut out of the process, locked into low-wage jobs and lacking upward mobility. All told, the 1990s saw a widening of the gap in wealth between developed countries and the third world and within most nations as well.[58]

Globalization was also destructive to existing social and cultural orders. The Internet and satellite dishes brought new ideas and values into societies, eroding traditional norms. The economic dislocations produced by unemployment altered social dynamics, leading to widespread feelings of anxiety. One analyst credited globalization with fostering a "palpable sense of insecurity" in countries around the world, as people worried that an invisible international system would determine their fates.[59]

These concerns produced a growing antiglobalization movement during the second half of the 1990s. Community leaders in India led boycotts of foreign goods and resisted the intrusion of outside ideas. Labor unions in Latin America and Europe railed against the loss of job security that came with economic openness. Environmentalists protested deforestation and pollution in developing countries, and activists criticized labor conditions in these nations. In France and Germany, anti-immigrant riots broke out as citizens attempted to shield their societies and economies from foreign influence. By mid-decade, there was growing pressure to slow or arrest the decline of national sovereignty. Beginning at roughly this time, protests and riots racked every major meeting of the Group of Eight, the WTO, and the International Monetary Fund.[60]

The debate over globalization was no less contentious in the United States. While the Clinton administration and the business and financial communities championed the process, there remained widespread fears about globalization. No less than Europeans or Asians, Americans worried that increased openness would corrode U.S. economic well-being and social cohesion. Opposition to globalization, wrote one columnist, "is summed up in a question you can hear all over America: If the economy is doing so well, why have I just been downsized out of a job and why do I feel like my community is eroding?" By the mid-1990s, prominent commentators had become openly skeptical of the phenomenon. Dani Rodrik, a Harvard economist, defended globalization but conceded that it had revealed a "deep fault line" between beneficiaries and victims of the phenomenon. Other analysts took globalization-bashing much further. One collective assessment began with an outright condemnation of the process:

> The euphoria [proponents of globalization] express is based on their freedom to deploy, at a global level—through the new global free trade rules, and through deregulation and economic restructuring regimes—large-scale versions of the economic theories, strategies, and policies that have proven spectacularly unsuccessful over the past several decades wherever they've been applied. In fact, these are the very ideas that have brought us to the grim situation of the moment: the spreading disintegration of the social order and the increase of poverty, landlessness, homelessness, violence, alienation, and, deep within the hearts of many people, extreme anxiety about the future.[61]

This statement may have taken the argument against globalization to the extreme, but it was an extreme that growing numbers of Americans were comfortable with during Clinton's second term. The most visible manifestation of antiglobalization sentiment came at a WTO summit in Seattle in late 1999. Although the occasion was most memorable for the anti-WTO riots by anarchists and other such groups, this violence obscured the fact that the summit served as a nexus for various forms of antiopenness advocacy. Peaceful demonstrators numbered in the tens of thousands, drawing their ranks from organized labor and environmental groups including the AFL-CIO, the Teamsters, and the Sierra Club. They castigated WTO officials for the secretive practices of the organization and raised concerns about the social, cultural, and economic effects of global openness. In a common assessment, a *Boston Globe* writer considered the events "a jarring reminder that many Americans are deeply insecure about what lies ahead as nations become more intertwined with the economies of their trading partners."[62]

Aiming to conciliate the antiglobalization forces, Clinton demanded that the WTO impose sanctions on nations with insufficient labor protections, and at times, he seemed to side with the peaceful demonstrators. "If we're going to have an open trading system," he allowed, "we have got to make it work for ordinary folks." The labor standards proposal marked a concession to those who feared that the availability of cheap foreign labor would lead to an exodus of manufacturing jobs from the United States, and it created another controversy at an already fractious summit. Egypt's trade minister promised "to block consensus on every issue if the United States proposal goes ahead." Developing countries strongly opposed the proposal, which would greatly raise the costs of production in the third world. The WTO meeting broke up after several unproductive days, a result that many media commentators and foreign diplomats attributed to Clinton's stance and the outpouring of antiglobalization opinion. In the aftermath, pro-trade observers admitted that events in Seattle had demonstrated the strength of protectionist feeling in the United States. The *Financial Times* saw the episode as part of a "powerful backlash against globalization," while the *New York Times* considered the summit's failure "a sharp setback, and perhaps a fatal blow" to Clinton's trade liberalization efforts.[63]

This mounting opposition showed that Clinton had not established the domestic backing necessary to enshrine free trade and global openness as defining principles of foreign policy. Discussing the status of U.S. trade efforts in 1999, Undersecretary of Commerce David Aaron was frank about the continuing controversy over integration and its effects. "The proven contribution of trade to our current prosperity has . . . not convinced most Americans of the value of trade," he admitted. Aaron was right; by 2000, a plurality of Americans believed that free trade did more harm than good.[64]

After 1994, Clinton largely bowed to this reality. To be sure, he extolled the benefits of free trade and pushed (with some success) for new economic agreements. At the rhetorical level, however, Clinton dropped the pretense that a strategy premised on economic openness could assume the political mantle once held by containment. *Enlargement,* formerly the public encapsulation of Clinton's foreign policy, quickly fell out of usage as the administration distanced itself from the term. Both connotations of the word were either discredited or controversial, as humanitarian intervention was decidedly out of vogue, and economic integration proved to be as much of a domestic liability as a means of inducing support for administration diplomacy.

In a basic sense, the oratorical emptiness of U.S. policy was probably more significant than the fact that Clinton would pursue trade agreements and, in rare cases, humanitarian intervention throughout his presidency. After all, the administration's insistence on formulating a new vision of foreign policy owed as much to domestic concerns as to international imperatives. Dropping enlargement, as Clinton did after 1994, was an implicit admission of failure in crafting a redefined U.S. mission abroad.

Polls taken at the midpoint of Clinton's first term confirmed that enlargement had failed to catch on. One survey revealed that no more than one-third of foreign policy elites or randomly polled citizens believed that defending human rights and democracy should be "a very important foreign policy goal." Likewise, free trade enjoyed little popularity. Although a majority of people approved of NAFTA, 83 percent opined that "protecting the jobs of American workers" (a virtue rarely attributed to the pact, or to economic openness in general) should be the foremost consideration. The lack of public interest in objectives that Clinton defined as vital, and the great concern with goals that his policies seemed to prejudice, meant that the president's approach to diplomacy was politically unsustainable. Enlargement, intended to carry the United States into the twenty-first century, was dead before Clinton completed his second year in office.[65]

At a certain level, enlargement's demise can be attributed to its own ineffectiveness. Although Clinton scored some successes in 1993 and 1994, they were overshadowed by his failures. On the plus side, NAFTA and GATT furthered Clinton's trade program. The threat to intervene in Haiti, however irresolute it might have been, was sufficient to remove Cedras from power. Less to the president's credit, Bosnia was an embarrassing failure, Somalia discredited interventionism, Rwanda gave the lie to Clinton's humanitarian pretensions, the U.S.-Japan trade talks were of dubious value, and fast track's defeat was a blow to plans for economic liberalization. Clinton's own lack of steadfastness hardly helped matters, and his decision not to mount a defense of enlargement in the wake of Mogadishu consigned the policy to its fate.

If these were the proximate causes of the strategy's downfall, there were also deeper sources of its repudiation. Clinton's optimism notwithstanding, there was simply no public enthusiasm for bearing the costs associated with enlargement. Domestic apathy on this count underscored a paradox of post–Cold War politics: although the international environment was sufficiently scary to prevent Americans from retreating from world affairs, it was not frightening enough to compel meaningful sacrifice from the domestic audience. In other words, although there were plenty of small or moderate threats to U.S. interests, there was no single menace great enough to overcome the nation's cost-averse nature. Clinton's policies sounded fine in principle, but in practice, they fared considerably worse. In the absence of a mortal threat to national security, Americans simply rejected the notion that they should part with blood and treasure (or, in the case of free trade, jobs) to further the ideals that Clinton championed.

Just as there was a dual nature to the crafting of a new diplomatic strategy, there were two aspects of the rhetorical-political half of this challenge. To elicit support for an activist strategy, the perception of threat was just as important as a feeling of moral rectitude. Until Americans believed that national security hinged on their willingness to pay the price of foreign policy, the public audience would remain fickle. Clinton's efforts at persuasion were long on morality but short on geopolitical necessity, and they stumbled on this reality. Five years after the end of the Cold War, the United States still sought containment's successor.

6

Whither Foreign Policy?

Forging a replacement for containment would be more difficult than it had initially appeared. But what if containment was not destined to have a successor of equal simplicity and political strength? Although this proposition had been heretical at the outset of the decade, by 1996, it looked quite likely. Even as enlargement crumbled, other developments in Clinton's on-the-job education in foreign policy cast doubt on the administration's earlier insistence on crafting a fully cohesive strategy. The debate over enlargement had dominated Clinton's early involvement in foreign affairs, masking broader geopolitical and policy trends. In particular, the very fact that Clinton had been unable to identify a dominant threat to U.S. interests raised questions about the basic precepts of 1990s foreign policy. If there was no single issue or confrontation at the heart of U.S. involvement abroad, perhaps a Cold War–style approach to diplomacy was less expedient than previously supposed. At a time when the global environment seemed considerably more diverse than at any point since World War II, maybe U.S. policy should lose its monolithic quality as well.

This issue grew more pressing during the mid-1990s. With the international arena proving every bit as complex as American observers had expected, U.S. policy necessarily transcended the boundaries of enlargement. Human rights and free trade were important to Clinton, but they did not encompass the totality of U.S. interests during his first term. Between 1994 and 1996, Clinton tackled wide-ranging issues in Asia, the Middle East, and Europe. In certain instances, the intricacies of regional relations undermined Clinton's initial policies and provided further proof of enlargement's impracticability. In others, the breadth of American aims confounded the application of any overarching strategy. At still other points, pursuing U.S. objectives in a given region complicated the broader practice of foreign policy.

These events had a turbulent effect on Clinton's diplomacy, the course of which provoked new discussion of the imperatives of post–Cold War grand strategy. Both specific policies and the overall conception of U.S. strategy were at issue as officials and informed observers took different lessons from Clinton's experience. At its heart, the controversy boiled down to a single, deceptively simple question: Was the post–Cold War world too complex to be governed by a single overall strategy akin to containment, or was such a strategy imperative to impose discipline on U.S. involvement in a complex world? In short, had coherence become irrelevant?

First Moves in East Asia

At the outset of his presidency, Clinton intended U.S.-Asia relations to showcase the possibilities of the post–Cold War era. He spoke glowingly of an "Asia-Pacific century" and revised the traditional Eurocentric approach of U.S. policy. Europe's decreasing strategic significance and the growing economic importance of the Pacific Rim created the perception that U.S.-Asian relations would be at the heart of foreign policy in the coming decades. "The engine of world economic growth is now in the Pacific," wrote two advisers during the 1992 campaign. The presence of established markets and emerging economies presented tantalizing opportunities for U.S. investors, and the White House made penetrating these markets its top priority in Asia.[1]

As economic concerns came to the forefront of U.S. policy, security issues receded. Aside from altering views of Asia's relative importance, the end of the Cold War promoted a reconceptualization of the U.S. role in the Far East. With Moscow and its proxies no longer seen as security threats in the area, perhaps the United States need not shoulder the heaviest burdens of regional security. Future Clinton adviser Richard Holbrooke argued in 1992 that "the removal of permanent American military facilities and troops from East Asia is probably inevitable."[2]

Along these lines, Washington refocused its gaze on economic concerns. American officials restated their commitment to Asian security but firmly declared their intent to embark on a new course in U.S.-Pacific relations. During his first visit to Japan, Clinton focused on trade, rather than security, when touting prospects for a "new Pacific community." At the State Department, Winston Lord downplayed regional security threats in the post–Cold War era. "There are problems of security," he conceded, "but, essentially, again compared to other regions, it is a fairly stable area." And in late 1993, Joan Spero explicitly acknowledged "the centrality of economics" in relations with the Pacific Rim.[3]

Clinton went only so far in de-emphasizing security. He slightly reduced U.S. forces in East Asia and reassured Japanese and South Korean audiences that the United States would not withdraw from the area. At the same time, it was clear that Washington meant to redistribute the costs of Asian security. Primarily, Clinton encouraged East Asian nations to look to regional forums such as the Association of Southeast Asian Nations (ASEAN) for security assistance. In the 1990s, Clinton contended, traditional forms of security cooperation had become less important. As the end of the superpower standoff released latent tensions, Asian nations would face new security issues: drug trafficking, ethnic tensions, and refugee flows, to name a few. The United States would deter outright aggression, Clinton promised, but ASEAN and other regional forums must deal with these emerging threats. "Asia is not Europe. The 1990s are not the Cold War," Secretary of State Warren Christopher told ASEAN representatives. "We need new regional security dialogues to meet common challenges" of the dawning age. By encouraging ASEAN to assume greater responsibility, Clinton's team reasoned, Washington could shed the more cumbersome obligations of its Asian relationships and devote new energy to trade.[4]

Human rights also played a major role in early U.S.-Asian affairs under Clinton. Applying the premises of enlargement (as well as Clinton's campaign rhetoric) to U.S. involvement in the area, the administration stated at the outset that it would shun regimes whose human rights practices were deemed inadequate. Although there were several East Asian governments that fit this description, the message was unmistakably directed at China. During the 1992 election, Clinton had promised to take a harder line toward Beijing. "I believe that our nation has a higher purpose than to coddle dictators and stand aside from the global movement toward democracy," he said.[5]

Early on, the president adhered to this notion in conducting China policy. Clinton pledged to reevaluate Beijing's most favored nation (MFN) trade status in light of its human rights violations. "Americans cannot forget Tiananmen Square," Lord told Congress, and he promised that Clinton would be circumspect in dealing with Beijing "until a more humane system emerges." Together, Clinton's human rights advocacy and his stress on economics signaled that enlargement would be prominent in U.S.–East Asian affairs.[6]

Clinton's first moves reflected the latter of these concerns. Washington normalized relations with Vietnam in 1994 and 1995 to take advantage of that nation's booming tourism market and offshore petroleum reserves. Even while consummating this new relationship, however, Clinton encountered obstacles to his plans for the region. First was the failure to pry open the Japanese market, which raised the possibility that economic cooperation might not be the future of U.S. relations with the Pacific Rim.

Concurrent to this setback, a crisis in the region further challenged Clinton's strategy. On the Korean peninsula, the end of the Cold War had introduced a new dynamic into the standoff between North and South. With the North no longer able to count on Russian aid, Kim Il Sung's philosophy of *juche,* or self-reliance, took on new meaning. In particular, it soon became clear that post–Cold War *juche* included possessing a nuclear deterrent. The North Korean nuclear program had originated in the 1960s, but in the late 1980s and early 1990s, the initiative became the focal point of Pyongyang's security posture. After the demise of the Soviet Union left Kim to face South Korea and the United States without the backing of his own superpower patron, he came to see nuclear weapons as a means of ensuring the survival of a destitute and isolated regime. During 1991 and 1992, North Korea intensified its nuclear efforts accordingly.[7]

By early 1992, U.S. intelligence officials perceived Kim's intentions. Discounting North Korea's accession to the Non-Proliferation Treaty (NPT) and its 1991 pledge to keep the Korean peninsula nuclear free, the Bush administration warned that the United States could not tolerate a North Korean bomb. Nuclear weapons in North Korea would create irresistible pressures for South Korea and Japan to follow suit, antagonizing China and, as State Department adviser Lynn Davis put it, causing "grave instability throughout Northeast Asia." Given the erratic and cash-strapped nature of Kim's regime, North Korea might also export its nuclear technology to Iran or terrorist groups. The administration refused to negotiate directly with Pyongyang but averred that its pressure was having the desired effect. "The North Koreans are finally getting the message," Davis assured Congress.[8]

That was not the case, and in 1993, Kim announced North Korea's withdrawal from the NPT. In response, Tokyo visibly hesitated before signing an extension of the NPT. Worried by these developments, Clinton endorsed Bush's formulation of the North Korean problem, stating that he would not allow Kim to go nuclear. Concern over Northeast Asian stability aside, the new administration saw its response as critical in deterring other regimes from pursuing the bomb. "Tehran is watching this," Davis said.[9]

Clinton initially eschewed bellicose rhetoric, focusing on economic and political inducements to modify North Korean behavior. South Korean and Japanese officials believed that "carrots will work better than sticks" in persuading Kim to retreat, U.S. diplomats reported. With Washington's two foremost East Asian allies favoring diplomacy, Clinton took a conciliatory tone. U.S. negotiators quietly raised the possibility of ending the embargo against North Korea and dangled the prospect of diplomatic recognition. In late 1993, Clinton promised to "reassess" the entire U.S.–North Korea relationship if Kim gave up his nuclear program.[10]

There were definite liabilities to this approach, not the least of which was the possibility that Kim was not negotiating in good faith. A CIA estimate from early 1994 put the odds at "somewhat better than even" that North Korea already had the bomb, raising fears that the negotiations might simply be a tactic to buy time for Kim's weapons program. Nonetheless, the administration maintained its nonprovocative stance. In February, Defense Secretary William Perry supported Clinton's approach to the building crisis, warning that a harsher response might alarm the sensitive North Korean regime and provoke a war of immense carnage. "I'm not anxious to precipitate the use of sticks," he said. A March 1994 white paper reaffirmed existing policy, as it spoke of "persuading" North Korea to change course and promised that after resolution of the crisis, "doors will open to better relations." As an added incentive, Clinton canceled U.S.–South Korean military exercises scheduled for the spring.[11]

Clinton's reluctance to move toward a firmer policy reflected both internal and external factors. Within the administration, there was no consensus on whether Kim was actually aiming toward a nuclear capability or merely wanted to better his bargaining position. The CIA and Defense Department took the former view, while the State Department and the White House inclined toward the latter. The North Koreans "want to see what they can squeeze out of people before they have to give in," predicted one official in late March. Even if Clinton had wanted to take stronger action, such as imposing UN sanctions on North Korea, he would have had trouble doing so. Because China controlled both a Security Council veto and a border with North Korea, Beijing's cooperation was crucial to ratcheting up the pressure on Pyongyang. While Chinese leaders had little desire to see North Korea go nuclear, they also feared that imposing sanctions might provoke Kim to lash out or, conversely, might prove so successful as to cause the fall of his regime. Neither of these scenarios was particularly reassuring to the Chinese leadership, and Beijing refused to move toward a more confrontational posture. Clinton bowed to this limitation, and in early 1994, he downgraded a UN warning to Kim from a resolution to a "statement" in order to keep Beijing on board.[12]

In May, however, pressure built for a stronger policy. Senators from both parties criticized Clinton's attempts to bargain with Kim. "We've been in this cat-and-mouse game with North Korea now for about the last fifteen months," remarked Republican presidential hopeful Robert Dole. George Mitchell, a leading Senate Democrat, supported economic sanctions, saying, "We cannot tolerate the actions that are occurring without any response at all." Attitudes were shifting within the administration as well. Perry believed that Pyongyang might already have nuclear weapons, and his public statements increasingly focused on using a combination of diplomatic inducement and military pressure to compel North Korea to reopen its nuclear plants to international inspectors. Clinton threatened UN sanctions if North Korea refused to yield. Reminded of Pyongyang's warning that it would consider sanctions an act of war, Clinton casually replied, "I don't really believe that." In early June, Clinton announced his intention to go to the Security Council with a sanctions resolution, but his plans were again complicated by Chinese reluctance. A spokesman for the Chinese Foreign Ministry implied that China would veto sanctions against North Korea, stating, "We do not favor the resort to means that might sharpen the confrontation."[13]

The crisis climaxed in early June, when North Korea ignored Clinton's warnings and diverted spent fuel rods from its nuclear reactors, a clear sign that it was moving toward a weapons capability. This development converted those officials who had earlier maintained that Kim's actions were mere diplomatic posturing. "Anyone who still believes the North Koreans are using their nuclear program as a bargaining chip has their head in the sand," said a CIA official. Clinton now feared that a negotiated deal might be impossible, and he convened a cabinet meeting to consider the sanctions option and the possibility of dispatching additional troops to South Korea. As rumors of war circulated, the situation turned bizarre. Acting on his own initiative, Jimmy Carter went to Pyongyang to negotiate. Carter subsequently announced (without White House authorization) that he had brokered a deal whereby the North Koreans would readmit inspectors if Clinton would no longer insist on sanctions. Furious that Carter had undercut his position, Clinton initially disavowed the ex-president's statements.[14]

Within days, though, Clinton reconsidered and publicly implied that he might accept Carter's deal if North Korea froze its nuclear program while new negotiations commenced.[15] The president likely realized that Carter's solution might be the only means of extricating the administration from a crisis that was spiraling out of control. Charles Larson, the commander in chief of U.S. Pacific forces, warned, "We have to be careful that we don't propel ourselves into a war that we're trying to prevent." The prospect of declining Chinese cooperation was a second argument in favor of Carter's solution. Quiet Chinese pressure on North Korea was widely considered crucial to persuading Kim to back down, and any escalation of the crisis risked alienating Beijing. After Carter returned to Washington for debriefing, Clinton agreed to negotiate with North Korea on the basis of the ex-president's deal, and in late 1994 (after Kim died and his son, Kim Jong Il, succeeded him), the two sides reached an agreement whereby North Korea suspended its nuclear program in exchange for U.S. technological and economic assistance. Shaky though it was, the pact held for the next several years.[16]

Reversing Course

The North Korean crisis had two major implications for Clinton's Asia policy. First, the shock of this episode combined with the failure of trade negotiations with Japan to halt Clinton's move away from a security-oriented approach to East Asia. The nuclear crisis signaled that East Asia would not necessarily be any more stable in the post–Cold War era than it had been in the past, while the U.S.-Japan trade talks showed that the economic going would be rougher than Clinton had expected. The 1995 *National Security Strategy* explicitly reversed the trend of his first two years in office, making security relations "the first pillar of our new Pacific community." In early 1996, negotiators revised the Japanese-American Security Agreement, with the United States pledging to maintain its current level of forces in East Asia and to deepen its relationship with Japan's Self-Defense Forces. U.S. security ties with Seoul received similar attention. By 1996, security issues had regained the prominence they had earlier lost.[17]

Second, the North Korean crisis underscored an emerging theme in administration debate over Asia: the idea that the United States would be wise to seek a partnership, rather than a rivalry, with China. Beijing had played a central role in moving the nuclear crisis toward a peaceful resolution, using its economic leverage and diplomatic clout to restrain both the United States and North Korea. The point was not lost on U.S. officials, who in late 1994 sought Chinese assistance in negotiating a permanent end to Pyongyang's nuclear program.[18]

China policy was a prime example of Clinton's troubled search for a workable approach to post–Cold War geopolitics. Early on, the president was rather indifferent to China's strategic significance, making little effort to engage the Asian giant. This initial distaste for cooperation stemmed partly from Clinton's desire to de-emphasize power politics in favor of human rights. Additionally, the end of the Cold War altered the long-standing rationale for a close partnership with Beijing. Clinton's first moves toward China reflected a new hostility, as he made it clear in 1993 that renewal of MFN status the following year would depend on Beijing's making significant advances in human rights.[19]

The elevation of moral over strategic and economic concerns worried Asia experts at the State Department and the National Security Council, who began to rethink the U.S. approach to China even before the Korean crisis demonstrated the benefits of Sino-American cooperation. It quickly became obvious that Clinton's policy toward China, though perhaps consistent with one aspect of enlargement, was incompatible with broader American concerns in Asia and the international economic realm. If Clinton planned to decrease the U.S. security presence in the Far East, for instance, would it be wise to simultaneously embark on a policy of confrontation toward the region's largest power? Similarly, if Clinton staked U.S. prosperity on the availability of foreign markets, how could he justify restricting commerce with a billion potential customers? The logical inconsistencies in Clinton's policy could not be ignored, and in mid-1993, the administration reviewed its stance toward China and Taiwan. Clinton cautiously moved toward warmer relations with the mainland, aiming to gradually reduce arms sales to Taipei and approving expanded high-level contacts with Beijing.[20]

These steps were minimal, in large part because Clinton had not given up on a showdown over human rights. In November, Christopher urged the president to warn Chinese premier Jiang Zemin of "the urgent necessity of early visible progress on human rights." In early 1994, Christopher visited Beijing, telling his hosts that their lack of responsiveness "certainly bodes ill" for MFN renewal.[21]

Yet the mid-1990s were not a propitious time to seek political liberalization within China. Whereas Tiananmen had provoked U.S. leaders to seek greater respect for human rights from Beijing, the incident had made the Chinese leadership more likely to refuse these entreaties. The mass protests of 1989, followed by the fall of Eastern European communism and the demise of the Soviet Union, led to a tightening of social controls in China. The specter of governmental collapse removed the impetus for reform, as Beijing focused on reconstructing and consolidating its authority. This "new authoritarianism" or "neoconservatism," as Chinese intellectuals termed it, emphasized order and development rather than liberalization. The human rights doctrine as a whole also seemed suspicious to Chinese policy makers. They feared that Western exhortations on the subject were really attempts to weaken unfriendly foreign regimes, as Li Peng put it, to "undermine the unity and racial harmony of other countries under the pretext of 'freedom,' 'democracy,' and 'human rights.'" In this climate, Beijing refused to allow Chinese dissidents freer rein, as Christopher discovered upon his arrival. "China will never accept the U.S. human rights concept," declared Li, who also warned that a cutoff of MFN status would hurt the United States more than it would China.[22]

Christopher's lack of progress combined with Beijing's growing strategic importance to promote a reevaluation of U.S. policy. Perry in particular was worried that a policy of hostility toward China would discourage Beijing from continuing its integration into the international economy and, in time, would create a new and powerful foe in the Far East. Washington could face a new cold war in Asia if it made an enemy of Beijing, he wrote, but "our security posture dramatically improves if China cooperates with us." On the economic side, revoking MFN status would be a disaster for American producers and consumers, as prices of Chinese imports would nearly double and U.S. firms would lose their toehold in China's market. Acknowledging these factors, Clinton delinked China's human rights practices from MFN renewal and granted the privilege in May 1994. Building on the earlier policy review, U.S. officials spoke of "comprehensive engagement" with China, with Lord promising dialogue "at all levels."[23]

This reversal of policy had limits, however, and there were indications that Clinton would be constrained in his new approach as well. Primarily, the about-face on human rights produced a backlash from critics who saw MFN renewal as a surrender to Beijing. A *USA Today* columnist, for one, bemoaned Clinton's tendency "to show weakness and accommodation" in China policy.[24]

Resistance to engagement grew stronger after the 1994 congressional elections, in which the GOP gained fifty-four seats in the Senate and eight in the House and took control of both chambers. This result, widely interpreted as a repudiation of Clinton, had pronounced implications for foreign policy. With Republicans now confident of their ability to challenge the president and hoping to retake the White House in 1996, Clinton faced a congressional majority that was eager to oppose him on diplomatic issues. Beginning in 1995, Republicans (as well as some Democrats) continually assailed engagement. Representative Douglas Bereuter (R-Neb.) pushed the "China Policy Act," which called for Clinton to condemn several aspects of Chinese behavior in a manner not at all hospitable to warm relations. There was strong House support for a more confrontational posture. "I don't think America should be in the business of licensing torture," said David Bonior (D-Mich.). "There is no moral or practical difference between trading with the PRC dictatorship and trading with the Nazis," agreed Chris Smith (R-N.J.). In this atmosphere, the measure passed easily.[25]

Anti-China sentiment converged with the ever-present issue of Taiwan to frustrate Clinton's policy. In mid-1995, the White House received a request from Taiwanese president Lee Teng-hui to visit the United States. Clinton and Christopher felt forced to agree, fearing that pro-Taiwan senators would (in Christopher's words) "work some mischief with the Taiwan Relations Act" if they refused. Beijing protested the decision, and the situation worsened after Lee gave an incendiary speech at Cornell University. Chinese leaders worried that Lee's trip signaled U.S. approval of a Taiwanese policy of "creeping independence," fears compounded by the fact that State Department spokesmen (in an accidental breach of protocol) referred to the Taiwanese leader as "President Lee." Outraged over the incident, the Chinese Foreign Ministry withdrew its ambassador from Washington.[26]

Clinton struggled to keep the relationship with China intact. The president sent a letter to Jiang promising that the United States did not support Taiwanese independence, and Perry gave a public articulation of the engagement doctrine in early 1996. Emphasizing the "inescapable conclusion that China is a power of global significance," Perry contended that the U.S. stance toward China would go far in determining the security environment of the coming decades. Perry rejected calls to contain China, arguing, "A China that feels encircled by U.S. containment policy is quite unlikely to cooperate on U.S. vital security objectives." Engagement, in contrast, would allow Washington and Beijing to work together on regional security matters such as North Korea. Clinton publicly affirmed Perry's position, predicting that relations with China would define the global landscape of the twenty-first century. "The direction China takes in the years to come, the way it defines its greatness in the future," he stated, "will help to decide whether the next century is one of conflict or cooperation."[27]

Unfortunately for Clinton, engagement remained liable to the vicissitudes of domestic politics and U.S.-Taiwan relations. The limitations of the strategy became clear in March 1996 when, in Taiwan's first democratic presidential election, Lee campaigned on a platform that came close to advocating independence. Beijing signaled its displeasure with military exercises and missile tests in the Taiwan Strait, and to show his support for Taiwanese sovereignty, Clinton sent two aircraft carrier battle groups to the area. The Chinese leadership was incensed, with certain officials believing that Clinton had "gone too far," but the crisis passed without serious incident. Nonetheless, tensions persisted. Arms sales to Taiwan remained a sticking point in U.S.-China relations, and the administration made no further progress with Beijing during the president's first term.[28]

Perhaps more than anything else, Clinton's experience in East Asia between 1994 and 1996 demonstrated the complexity of regional affairs and the corresponding irreducibility of foreign policy. The administration entered East Asian affairs determined to prioritize its interests according to the framework provided by enlargement, but it soon discovered that the economic and security climate of the Pacific Rim defied such an approach. This reality was obvious as early as 1994, and it underlay Clinton's decisions to reverse policy toward China and reelevate security concerns to the top of the agenda. East Asia simply refused to mold itself to Clinton's strategy.

In an objective sense, the administration was probably well-advised to discard its contradictory, oversimplified original strategy. To Clinton's chagrin, though, this course correction still invited criticism from domestic observers who were inclined to see the president as indecisive. To be sure, Clinton's public relations problems were partly of his own making. He had talked tough on human rights during the campaign, and when he backtracked, there was the inevitable backlash. The *New York Times* criticized Clinton's "embarrassing retreat," and other commentators attributed shifts in China policy to the president's alleged lack of "strong beliefs" regarding foreign policy. The same criticism was prevalent regarding Clinton's Asia policy as a whole. A writer for *Commentary* attributed Clinton's reversals to a "relentless subordination of foreign policy to domestic politics," and questioned whether there were any firm principles guiding U.S. diplomacy. Whereas flexibility was a virtue in East Asian affairs, it seemed to be a vice in domestic politics. Even as Clinton began to appreciate the necessity of a nuanced approach to foreign policy, he discovered that it carried a price.[29]

European Diplomacy

At the outset, European affairs presented a different challenge than did relations with East Asia. Whereas Clinton had outlined an ambitious policy for the Pacific Rim, his early vision for Europe was less expansive. The president initially distanced himself from Europe, making Asia his first international destination and remaining comparatively silent on continental affairs. Christopher's failure to convince the allies to follow Washington's lead on Bosnia in 1993 posed a stark contrast to the self-assuredness of U.S. policy during the Cold War, reinforcing the perception that, as one writer phrased it, U.S.-Europe relations had reached "the end of an era."[30]

Clinton's limited priorities for Europe centered not on NATO but on Moscow—in particular, on consolidating Russia's recent political and economic reforms. The transition had been troubled so far, with widespread corruption and economic stagnation impeding the process. Since the dissolution of the Soviet Union in late 1991, the atmosphere in Russia had been one of uncertainty. The economic and political order had collapsed along with the parent state, and through 1992, there emerged no consensus among Russian elites on the future of the country. That year saw bitter disputes over the pace of economic reform and sharp disagreement over what form the nation's political system should take. Boris Yeltsin and his allies called for a democratic presidential-parliamentary system, while others urged an authoritarian alternative. The situation neared chaos in 1992, with starvation threatening in some areas of the country and Russian authorities and former Communist Party members fighting in the streets of Moscow.[31]

Clinton and his advisers viewed this situation with alarm, fearing that, in the absence of a workable reform program, Russia might experience an authoritarian resurgence or perhaps emulate the Soviet implosion. In early 1993, Christopher asserted that U.S. interests lay with Russian liberals struggling to push their country toward democracy and a market economy. "We must say to the democratic reformers in Russia that the democratic nations stand with them," he argued. Democratization in Russia, the administration hoped, would ensure that the Cold War stayed won, provide security for Eastern Europe, allow Clinton to slash military outlays by withdrawing troops from Europe and cutting nuclear stockpiles, and give him added leverage in persuading Ukraine to forswear the nuclear capability it had inherited from the Soviet Union.[32]

If the strategy was reform, though, there was some confusion as to the tactics. With ex-communists, radical nationalists, and pseudodemocrats of various flavors competing for power in Russia, few observers were certain which faction would triumph. Some quarters urged Clinton to support Yeltsin. Yeltsin's democratic credentials were spotty, however, and he faced a hostile parliament. Unsure of which horse to pick, Clinton turned to Richard Nixon for advice. Nixon agreed that Yeltsin was not an ideal partner but pointed out that the alternatives—ex-communists and demagogues—were unattractive. "It's a risk to support Yeltsin," he told Clinton, "but if he goes down without U.S. support, it will be far worse."[33]

With Nixon covering his right flank, Clinton gave Yeltsin his endorsement, pledging to stand by the Russian leader in his country's "new hour of challenge." Just as important, he approved roughly $2 billion in aid to Russia. American contributions increased in April 1993, after the World Bank and the Group of Seven matched U.S. dollars with gifts of their own. As critics pointed out, the amount of aid was small given the enormity of Russia's needs. Clinton's caution was due largely to the difficulty of selling even a modest assistance package to Congress. Opposed by conservative Republicans, who charged that the new president was being too soft on a country that still had thousands of nuclear weapons targeted against the United States, Clinton sent Strobe Talbott to the Hill to campaign for the package. If the United States appeared reluctant to back Yeltsin, Talbott stated, the Russian leader's credibility would be undermined, and one of his principal advantages over his conservative opponents would be lost. "We want the Russian people to understand that the world stands with them as they make the transition from communism to free markets," Talbott said. After several weeks of debate, the aid bill passed.[34]

Despite Clinton's support, Yeltsin appeared weak by late 1993. Political instability persisted, and the First Russian Republic soon verged on collapse. When the Russian parliament rebelled and hastily impeached him, Yeltsin ordered tanks to shell the legislative building, an act that revived memories of past repression. Elections in late 1993 also hurt Yeltsin, as ultranationalist Vladimir Zhirinovsky's Liberal Democratic Party (a misnomer, to be sure) easily bested the reform ticket. Clinton's advisers were concerned, and political aide George Stephanopoulos advised the president to distance himself from a leader "who may be going fascist on us." For Clinton, however, Zhirinovsky's strong showing underscored the rationale for supporting Yeltsin: whatever his flaws, Yeltsin was far less frightening than any realistic alternative. "Knock it off," Clinton told Stephanopolous. "We're in this thing for keeps." The administration reaffirmed its support for Yeltsin, who rode out his immediate difficulties.[35]

Just as Clinton committed to a firm policy toward Russia, his blossoming interest in other European issues threatened to complicate this strategy. The revival of U.S.-NATO relations posed an especially serious obstacle to warmer ties with Russia. Since 1990, U.S. officials had recognized that good relations with Moscow required sensitivity in building friendships in the Kremlin's former domain in Eastern Europe. As the price of German reunification, James Baker had conceded in 1990 that NATO would not expand to the east. In an attempt not to prejudice the survival prospects of Moscow's liberals, the administration adhered to this pledge early on. In 1993, Christopher affirmed that eastward expansion of the alliance was "not on the agenda." Furthermore, with the Cold War over and the long-standing military rationale for the alliance thus bankrupt, the administration initially showed little interest in NATO.[36]

Clinton and his advisers reconsidered this position in late 1993, however, and soon the president favored expansion. There were a number of strategic and political reasons for the initiative: to promote stability in the area between Russia and Germany, to provide a security climate that would allow the nations of Eastern Europe to focus on economic and political reform, to keep an eye on newly reunified Germany by strengthening the bonds between Berlin and its eastern neighbors, and to promote the East-West integration of the continent as a whole. For Clinton, however, the issues at stake were not strategic but moral. According to the best available history of NATO expansion, Clinton's interest in the project was piqued by the emotional pleas of Czech Republic president Vaclav Havel and Polish leader Lech Walesa at an Oval Office meeting in early 1993. Moved by these countries' tragic pasts, Clinton developed an attachment to the idea of extending NATO's protection to Eastern Europe. Motivated mainly by an ethical imperative, Clinton joined the expansionists.[37]

As other officials realized, NATO expansion would complicate Clinton's established objectives in Europe. The central drawback to the plan was that it would undermine U.S. attempts to help Yeltsin beat back the scary cast of characters menacing the Russian political scene. When rumors of expansion spread in late 1993, the reaction by the Russian armed forces and intelligence services—institutions still manned largely by Cold War holdovers—was swift and strong. Yevgeny Primakov, now the head of Russian intelligence, said that expansion "would bring the biggest military grouping in the world, with its colossal offensive potential, directly to the borders of Russia." Primakov also alluded to the gains that Zhirinovsky and those who warned of Western "encirclement" would score from expansion. If NATO grew, he cautioned, "irritation in military circles might emerge that is not in the interests of the political or military leadership of Russia or the country in general." Under intense pressure from the armed services, Yeltsin authored a letter to Clinton and several European leaders stating his objections to expansion.[38]

As expansion's downsides came into focus, opposition to the initiative grew within the administration. The State Department's Russian desk, led by Talbott, argued that expansion would antagonize Moscow, strengthen the hard-liners, and generally make life difficult for Yeltsin. The Pentagon was equally unenthusiastic, dreading the prospect of working with the outdated militaries of potential new members (most likely Poland, the Czech Republic, and Hungary).[39]

Indeed, the best diplomatic arguments seemed to be on the anti side of the expansion issue. As many of Clinton's advisers realized, Russia was the most important question mark in U.S. foreign policy in the early 1990s. Washington's ability to relax its posture in Europe and deal with threats elsewhere was contingent on the viability of a relatively liberal government in Moscow. In the same vein, it was the need to keep an eye on Russia that drove up the U.S. defense budget. "The success of Russian reform is the largest single factor affecting the demand for U.S. defense dollars," explained Undersecretary of Defense Walter Slocombe. Expansion of NATO, which, Slocombe noted, "began historically as an alliance against the Soviet Union," was likely to spook the Kremlin and imperil the reform program.[40]

By late 1993, the administration had divided over these questions, with pro- and antiexpansionists arguing contentiously. As a NATO summit approached in early 1994, Clinton needed a policy. What emerged was the Partnership for Peace (PFP), an awkward compromise between the administration's competing factions. The PFP conceded ground to the Pentagon by encouraging the countries of Eastern Europe and the former Soviet Union to upgrade their military capabilities, and it appeased Talbott by allowing Moscow to participate in an endeavor perceived as less threatening than NATO expansion. Secretary of Defense Les Aspin made this intent of the PFP clear when he asserted publicly that "the partnership is not an enlargement" of NATO. Yeltsin was so relieved that Clinton appeared to be turning away from expansion that he called the PFP "a stroke of genius."[41]

This very appearance caused Clinton problems at home. Republicans and Polish, Hungarian, and Czech commentators condemned the PFP as a sellout to Moscow. Others rolled their eyes at what seemed to be another example of Clinton's inability to take a strong stand on foreign policy. Stung by such criticism, Clinton stunned many of his own advisers by pushing forward with expansion, announcing at the NATO summit in Brussels in January 1994 that the PFP was simply a pit stop en route to NATO membership. "The question is no longer whether NATO will take on new members," Clinton declared, "but when and how."[42]

Bold as it was, Clinton's statement was not the catalyst for expansion that he had hoped. The basic problem was that Clinton's contradictory objectives in Europe and lack of an overall strategy for the region left his advisers unsure of how much emphasis the president placed on expanding NATO versus conciliating Russia. The more opportunistic administration officials used this uncertainty to interpret the president's conflicting goals as they saw fit. Through 1994 and 1995, the Pentagon and State Department were cold to expansion. Even after Clinton's speech in Brussels, Talbott publicly implied that expansion would not happen anytime soon, saying that the process would commence only after "the mission for NATO in the post–cold war era is decided." Slocombe insisted that "expansion must not mean the dilution of the military effectiveness of the Alliance." With no firm policy driving the bureaucracy, Clinton's plans languished.[43]

Outside commentators also opposed expansion. Michael Brown of Harvard wrote that expansion "will probably lead Russia to adopt a more aggressive policy in Eastern Europe" and might cause Yeltsin to lose power.[44] The pessimists looked vindicated when Yeltsin warned in late 1994 that NATO expansion threatened to plunge Europe into a "cold peace." Domestic observers also questioned why NATO should grow when it had proved so ineffective in ending the Bosnian war, which even expansion enthusiast Holbrooke admitted was "the greatest collective security failure of the West since 1938." With these concerns in the background, expansion proceeded leisurely over the next two years.[45]

In mid-1995, the worsening situation in Bosnia added another element to Clinton's NATO-Russia balancing act. Serb forces shelled Sarajevo, and after NATO retaliated with air strikes, the Serbs took 350 UN peacekeepers hostage. In July, Serb troops shelled Srebrenica and massacred its inhabitants. The atrocities sparked an outcry in the United States. "Where is the supposed leader of the free world?" asked the *Philadelphia Inquirer*. Even the normally anti-interventionist *Chi-*

cago Tribune deemed it "a matter of national honor" to punish the Serbs and protect the Muslims. Clinton soon found himself trailing the Republican Congress on Bosnia policy. "If we don't have an interest in this fight, what are we?" asked Dole. In midsummer, Congress unilaterally terminated the UN arms embargo in the hope that this would allow the Bosnian Muslims to better defend themselves.[46]

Two years after the failure of lift-and-strike, this mounting domestic pressure spurred Clinton into action. The president's political advisers feared that continuing bloodshed would wreck Washington's diplomatic credibility and perhaps cost Clinton reelection. "Bosnia is destroying our foreign policy domestically and internationally," Madeleine Albright said; the current "muddle through" strategy "makes the President appear weak." Clinton agreed. If the administration did not find a solution, he believed, "We are history." Embarrassed by his failure to end the fighting in 1993, and driven by the outpouring of domestic anger following Srebrenica, Clinton could no longer defer intervention. "The status quo is not acceptable," he told aides in July. In early August, urged on by the hawk faction of Anthony Lake, Albright, and Al Gore, Clinton dispatched diplomats to Europe for a last-ditch effort at negotiating a settlement. It was time to "explore all alternatives, roll every die," Clinton said privately. Days later, when Serb shelling resumed, special envoy Holbrooke asked for and received sustained NATO strikes.[47]

NATO intervention in Bosnia was central to U.S. relations with both the alliance and Russia. After the Bosnia fiasco of 1993, observers questioned whether NATO was relevant to the new Europe. This question hung over the expansion initiative, allowing opponents to cast doubt on the efficacy of an alliance of any size. Forceful action in Bosnia could redeem NATO's credibility, but it could also sour relations with Moscow. If NATO proceeded too forcefully in Bosnia, Russian ultranationalists might benefit.

It was the latter of these issues that became salient as NATO struck. The attacks enraged Moscow, which favored the Serbs and resented NATO's presence in the Balkans. Russian legislators condemned the attacks as "terrorism," and public opinion lurched toward the position of the hard-liners. The threat of NATO retaliation was crucial to forcing Milosevic to negotiate, however, and the bombing continued despite Russian denouncements. Over the next month, NATO planes struck Serb artillery positions and troop concentrations. The attacks bore fruit in early October. Combined with the fact that a Croatian counteroffensive had recently established a stable front on the battlefield, the NATO strikes allowed Holbrooke to secure a cease-fire and a pledge from Milosevic, Croatia's Tudjman, and Bosnia's Izetbegovic to negotiate a final settlement at an air force base in Dayton, Ohio. After tense talks, the three leaders struck a deal dividing Bosnia into several ethnic and multiethnic cantons, and Clinton committed 20,000 troops to the UN-sponsored NATO peacekeeping force. The administration made it clear, however, that intervention did not herald a return to peace enforcement. Christopher told nervous senators, "The president will not put our troops in a situation where there is no peace to keep," and promised to withdraw U.S. forces after one year. Despite some misgivings, Congress acquiesced.[48]

Of course, NATO troops were even more offensive than NATO planes in the eyes of the Kremlin, and Clinton next tackled the task of persuading Yeltsin to accept the alliance's presence in the Balkans. Expectations were low as Yeltsin arrived at a summit in Hyde Park, New York. Many observers believed that Clinton had pushed too hard with the combination of NATO expansion and intervention in Bosnia. Clinton, whose skills as a politician were more easily transferable to personal diplomacy than strategy making, used this tension as an opening, suggesting to Yeltsin that they "prove the pundits wrong." "They want to write about a big blowup," Clinton said. "Let's disappoint them." Clinton's close personal relationship with Yeltsin paid off, and the Russian leader agreed to the heretofore unprecedented arrangement of putting two battalions of Russian troops under NATO's command as part of the implementation force. The agreement was a winner for both sides. Yeltsin could claim that Russia was participating in the settlement of the Balkan dispute, and Clinton removed the last serious obstacle to the NATO deployment.[49]

Intervention in Bosnia gave momentum to both NATO expansion and the policy toward Russia. The Hyde Park agreement built on another deal cut in 1995, which cemented Russian participation in the PFP and outlined the basics of a pact meant to win Russian acceptance of NATO expansion by making as yet undefined concessions regarding the stationing of foreign troops and nuclear weapons on the territory of new members. Expansionists also took heart from the brief war, claiming that NATO had proved its post–Cold War relevance. After two years of hesitation and conflict, U.S.-Europe relations finally seemed to be on track.

Skill or Luck?

By late 1995, however, Clinton's assertiveness on Bosnia and NATO threatened to undo his Russia policy. In parliamentary elections, ex-communists and neonationalists gained ground on Yeltsin, casting serious doubt on his prospects for reelection in 1996. Zhirinovsky's party finished second in the balloting, which was troubling enough, until one considered that the communists placed first. Furthermore, Clinton's reliance on Yeltsin forced him to turn a blind eye to the Russian leader's efforts to flex his country's remaining political and military muscle. This became evident when Russian forces invaded Chechnya, a convulsive province hoping for autonomy. Fearing that Chechen independence would give rise to ethnic unrest within Russia, Yeltsin ordered the military to bomb Grozny and attack separatist forces in the province in late 1994 and early 1995.[50] Clinton's unwillingness to go beyond mild disapproval of the war angered U.S. commentators and led to denunciations of the president's ties to Yeltsin. "Don't we care that Russia has returned to naked gangsterism?" a *Boston Globe* columnist inquired. When Clinton traveled to Moscow for a summit in 1995, Republicans roundly denounced the president for refusing to rebuke the Russian leader. "Whatever Yeltsin wants Yeltsin gets," grumbled Senator Mitch McConnell (R-Ky.).[51]

As controversial as Yeltsin was, Clinton had little choice but to back the Russian president. The strongest candidates other than Yeltsin were Zhirinovsky and other frightening characters. As the election approached, U.S. officials strongly implied that a Yeltsin victory would be a boon for relations with the United States. "All elections involve choices and have consequences," Talbott told a public audience in June. "That notably includes consequences for Russia's relations with the rest of the world. And this certainly applies to any Russian leader who would attempt to reconstitute the USSR, renationalize the economy, or abandon the democratic process." Buoyed by U.S. support and his own surprisingly energetic campaign, Yeltsin won the election and a subsequent runoff.[52]

Nonetheless, by 1996, there were serious doubts as to the status of Russian reform. After the invasion of Chechnya and his assault on the Russian parliament, Yeltsin's own commitment to liberalism was open to question. Crime and corruption were on the rise. Mafia-style organizations held more power than state authorities in many areas, and Russian businessmen complained that the real obstacle to economic reform was the pervasive corruption of government officials. Widespread poverty remained a problem, and what economic growth there was benefited mainly the wealthiest segments of the population.[53]

Watching these developments, U.S. observers grew pessimistic about the situation in Russia. CIA director John Deutch estimated that between 70 and 80 percent of Russian businesses suffered from extortion and warned that "organized crime and corruption pose an increasing threat to political and economic reform in Russia." At the end of Clinton's first term, Russia's future remained far from certain.[54]

Progress on Clinton's other European objectives also came slowly. Even with the Bosnian peace process under way and Russian opposition diminishing, NATO expansion struggled along. One obstacle was the Pentagon's continuing reluctance to embrace the initiative, which ensured that the process of vetting applicants occurred at a glacial pace. A second stumbling block reflected the contradictory nature of U.S. aims in Europe. During Yeltsin's reelection campaign, Clinton had to tread softly on NATO expansion to avoid endangering the Russian president's prospects. At home, Clinton's deliberate approach angered Republicans and conservative Democrats who hoped to wrap Eastern Europe in NATO's embrace. Expansion "needs a decision, not a study," Henry Kissinger told the Senate Armed Services Committee. During the 1996 campaign, Republican standard-bearer Dole alleged that Clinton was "missing an opportunity that may never come again." In response, Clinton made a rare campaign foray into foreign affairs, declaring that expansion would take place by 1999.[55]

Still, the fact that Clinton had been compelled to delay the process pointed to a fundamental problem in his dealings with Europe.

Despite being tightly connected, the administration's three top priorities often contradicted one another. Near though it was to Clinton's heart, NATO expansion threatened to shorten Yeltsin's political life span or, at the very least, complicate relations with Russia. Intervention in Bosnia offered a chance to rejuvenate NATO and put an end to a problem that had dogged Clinton for three years; it also gave Russian right-wingers an issue on which to pound Yeltsin. A conciliatory approach to Russia seemed wise in certain respects, but it would impede NATO expansion and complicate attempts to end the Bosnian war.

The tensions among these objectives had certain pernicious effects on U.S. policy. Perhaps the most obvious of these was that Clinton created sufficient friction among his various goals to retard the progress of each. Fear of alienating Moscow consistently slowed NATO expansion, first in late 1993 and again during the 1996 Russian presidential campaign. Alliance relations and the Bosnian intervention similarly complicated support for Yeltsin and Russian reform. The problems inherent in operating without a firm plan for regional affairs were also apparent in the administration's internal deliberations. Bureaucratic confusion and obstructionism prevailed in an atmosphere of uncertainty regarding U.S. priorities and the relative weight attached to each.

Equally troubling for Clinton, the halting appearance of U.S. diplomacy left him vulnerable at home. The complexity of U.S.-NATO and U.S.-Russia relations meant that Washington often found it necessary to take measures that partisans of the various issues considered less than satisfactory. Some observers contended that Clinton's relative stinginess in doling out aid to Russia would doom Yeltsin, while others criticized the administration for aiding the Russian president at all. The slow pace of NATO expansion appalled Kissinger and Zbigniew Brzezinski, whereas the mere fact of the process provoked others. From 1993 to 1995, Clinton faced attacks over his inaction in Bosnia; by 1996 and 1997, he was under fire for considering extending the intervention past the originally prescribed one year.[56]

Criticism such as this aside, one could argue that the president had handled a set of difficult and often divergent goals with relative dexterity. Despite Russian bluster, intervention in Bosnia and NATO expansion did not restart the Cold War or cause Yeltsin to fall. His questionable commitment to democracy notwithstanding, Yeltsin's reelection in 1996 was the best realistic outcome for the United States. After its lethargic start, NATO expansion was undoubtedly on track by 1997. And, though slow to come and just as slow to implement, NATO bombs and U.S. diplomacy helped establish a framework for peace in Bosnia.

Of course, it was not clear at the time whether the president's avoidance of the potential train wrecks accompanying his European diplomacy owed to shrewdness or luck. Had Clinton succeeded because he adeptly reconciled his goals, or had he simply been fortunate that his inconsistent policies did not destroy U.S.-Russia relations, allow NATO expansion to lapse, or leave Bosnia in the throes of civil war? To put the question more broadly, was the European balancing act attempted by Clinton a prerequisite for diplomatic success in the post–Cold War era, or was it an excessively risky maneuver necessitated by a contradictory strategy? On the one hand, Clinton's use of moral rather than diplomatic logic in pushing NATO expansion makes it hard to give the president full credit for the outcomes of his policy in Europe. On the other hand, that Clinton managed to avoid a number of potential pitfalls perhaps justifies a more sympathetic view of his efforts. In any event, although the answers to these questions were not yet clear in 1996, the mere fact that they needed asking indicated that the overall coherence of foreign policy would be a contentious issue as Clinton wrestled with the challenges of global strategy.

Clinton and the Middle East

In contrast to his experiences in Europe and East Asia, Clinton's involvement in the Middle East started auspiciously. Here, a concatenation of circumstances gave rise to a comprehensive strategy for managing regional affairs. The first factor influencing Clinton's Middle East policy was the fact that in 1993, the peace process involving Israel, the Palestinians, and the surrounding Arab states looked more promising than at any time since the signing of the Camp David accords fifteen years earlier. The Madrid Conference of 1991, a direct by-product of the Gulf War, had opened a dialogue between Israel and Yasir Arafat's Palestine Liberation Organization. The process matured, and in mid-1993, Israelis and Palestinians meeting in Oslo agreed on a "Declaration of Principles on Interim Self-Government" that provided for Palestinian civil control of Gaza and Jericho and raised the prospect of even greater Palestinian self-rule. When Israeli and Palestinian officials sought U.S. endorsement of the Oslo agreement, Clinton seized the opportunity. Eager to encourage the peace process and desperate for a diplomatic victory after Bosnia and Somalia, Clinton pledged to act as a "full and active partner" in subsequent negotiations.[57]

The second key to U.S. involvement in the Middle East was Iraq. Three years after Bush had altered the regional balance by invading Iraq but leaving Saddam Hussein in power, Clinton found himself dealing with the aftermath of that upheaval. Although there had been some talk early in Clinton's presidency about the United States doing business with a reformed Hussein, that possibility soon disappeared. In April 1993, Iraqi agents attempted to assassinate former president Bush during a trip to Kuwait. Hussein's role in the plot against Bush, in addition to his noncompliance with UN sanctions remaining from the Gulf War, proved to Clinton that there could be no reconciliation with the Iraqi leader. In June 1993, U.S. forces bombed the Iraqi intelligence ministry (believed to be responsible for the assassination scheme), intending to weaken Hussein's hold on power. The strikes, noted Aspin, aimed to demonstrate to Iraqi officials that "following this man is not good for your health." Clinton used strong language in announcing the bombing, telling Hussein, "Don't tread on us."[58]

Clinton's third major consideration involved Iran. After Tehran adopted a more aggressive anti-U.S. foreign policy in the early 1990s, the president's top advisers—Lake especially—concluded that workable relations with Iran were out of the question. Iran's support for Hezbollah and other terrorist groups, its opposition to the peace process and long-standing animus toward Israel, and its suspected pursuit of nuclear weapons led to a hardening of U.S. policy. The State Department called Iran "the most dangerous state sponsor of terrorism," and the Pentagon labeled the regime "both a serious immediate and an important long-term threat to the security of the Gulf."[59]

This combination of threats and opportunities allowed Clinton to develop a fairly cohesive strategy for Middle Eastern affairs. Beginning with Oslo, the administration gave priority to the Israel-Palestine and Arab-Israeli peace processes. This issue would dominate Clinton's Middle East policy over the next seven years, resulting in intensive efforts to move the negotiations along and exerting a determining influence on policy toward Iraq and Iran. For the United States and Israel to have the leeway necessary to forge a regional peace, Clinton believed, it was necessary to keep the two Gulf states subdued. Only if Iran and Iraq remained quiet, he reasoned, would Israel feel secure enough to negotiate. At the same time, progress in the peace process would further isolate Iraq and Iran from the Middle Eastern mainstream, facilitating U.S. efforts to restrain these two powers. Conversely, a crisis with Tehran or Baghdad would detract from U.S. involvement in the peace process and complicate efforts to maintain Arab support for the negotiations. The key to the Middle East, explained NSC adviser (later assistant secretary of state) Martin Indyk, was for Washington to "focus its energies on peacemaking, while containing the radical opponents of peace."[60]

This imperative of stability led to a departure in U.S. policy toward the Gulf. Washington had traditionally played Iraq and Iran off each other as a means of ensuring that neither could dominate the region, but Clinton rejected this balancing strategy. In early 1994, Lake unveiled Clinton's new policy, termed *dual containment*. Under this approach, the United States would no longer curry favor with Iran or Iraq, seeking instead to curb the aspirations of both. With the Cold War over, Lake reasoned, Washington could confront Iran and Iraq in a way that had not been possible during the superpower conflict. The demise of the Soviet Union, he wrote, "eliminated a major strategic consideration from our calculus." No longer worried that a disaffected Iran or Iraq might seek accommodation with Moscow, the United States could assume a stern posture toward both Gulf states. "Without the backing of an alternate superpower," Lake contended, Iraq and Iran "now confront serious difficulties in challenging U.S. power." The United States, Lake implied, could now dominate the Gulf and impose the tranquility needed to foster a regional peace.[61]

Clinton's Middle East policy may have been coherent in theory, but it encountered numerous obstacles in practice. From the start, relations with Iraq were considerably more turbulent than the president had hoped. In 1994, Hussein massed 80,000 troops on the Kuwaiti border, threatening a replay of the 1990 invasion. Clinton ordered reinforcements to the region and threatened air strikes if Iraqi forces did not withdraw to the north, and the crisis passed. Despite this success, flaws in the containment strategy soon became apparent. The policy entailed a continuing, costly presence in the Gulf and made Washington increasingly dependent on corrupt, authoritarian regimes in Kuwait and Saudi Arabia. By 1995 and 1996, NSC officials realized that the strategy was probably not sustainable in the long run. "How long can the U.S. hold containment of Iraq in place?" asked the NSC at one point. Given the expense involved in containing the Iraqi president, as well as the decreasing enthusiasm of other Gulf states for Washington's posture, a number of Clinton's advisers argued for aggressive efforts to topple, rather than simply restrain, Hussein's regime.[62]

Containment was also vulnerable politically. Following the 1994 elections, Dole repeatedly criticized the White House for its "timidity" in dealing with Hussein. This pressure and the weaknesses of dual containment gradually led Clinton to adopt a policy designed to force Hussein from power. After a trip abroad by Albright in early 1995 revealed solid Security Council support for a strong stance, Clinton approved an increase in covert anti-Hussein programs. U.S. operatives cultivated internal resistance and exile groups such as the Iraqi National Congress, and CIA agents in northern Iraq aided Kurdish factions opposed to Hussein's rule. Deutch affirmed that "there will be no stability in the region or improved circumstances for the Iraqi people until Saddam Hussein and his regime is replaced."[63]

Covert action was little more effective than containment. During 1994 and 1995, the CIA and the White House poured money and agents into northern Iraq, developing a two-track strategy aimed at either a quick coup by dissident army officers or a rebellion by Kurdish forces. Both plans fell apart in 1995, as Clinton grew nervous about an all-out effort to topple the Iraqi leader, and the Kurdish groups involved began to bicker with one another. The covert program collapsed in 1996, when Iraqi forces killed or detained more than a hundred leaders of the Iraqi National Congress. Dealing with Hussein was difficult, but getting rid of him seemed more challenging still.[64]

Iraq policy deteriorated again in 1996 when Hussein cracked down on Kurdish rebels in the north, despite Clinton's warnings not to do so. Clinton retaliated by blasting Iraqi air defense sites in south and central Iraq and extending the no-fly zone in the south, but the crisis proved to be both a diplomatic and a political setback for the president. Fear of becoming embroiled in the Kurdish issue, which had powerful implications for U.S.-Turkey affairs, had prevented Clinton from directly intervening in the fighting in northern Iraq. NSC aide Kenneth Pollack admitted that the episode was "a disaster," as Hussein had destroyed the Kurdish opposition and consolidated his own power. Deutch concurred. "Saddam Hussein's position has been strengthened in the region recently," he told the Senate Intelligence Committee. Just as bad, Clinton absorbed a domestic drubbing over the incident. Although the 1996 air strikes won overwhelming congressional support, observers and even U.S. officials questioned whether Clinton was sufficiently resolute to match wits with the Iraqi leader. Pentagon advisers grumbled that the 1996 attack "was a pinprick, not the sledgehammer needed." Others wondered why Clinton had attacked southern Iraq when the Kurds were being massacred hundreds of miles to the north. "We responded to this fight among Kurdish partisans in a way that could not possibly help the victims of that Iraqi aggression," groused a senator. By the end of Clinton's first term, Iraq had become a full-blown headache.[65]

The Iranian prong of U.S. policy ran into similar challenges. From the outset, containment of Iran had been more understated than the Iraqi variant of that policy. "Iran today does not present the threat that Iraq did to our interests some five years ago," explained Indyk. The administration thus did not "oppose [Iran's] Islamic government" or "seek the regime's overthrow." Instead, as one former official put it, Clinton's aim was "merely to constrain Iran's ability to make trouble in the Middle East through a rather modest series of measures"—namely, economic sanctions and diplomatic isolation—in the hope of being able to devote primary attention to the peace process.[66]

The policy did not run smoothly. The State and Commerce departments argued over how tight U.S. sanctions should be, and Christopher found little European support for a harsh policy. Conversely, Clinton's approach was too weak for the Republican majority that swept into power after the 1994 elections. Republican legislators called for a broadening of economic sanctions and sought to forbid U.S. companies to do business with Iran (a policy Christopher eventually endorsed). House Speaker Newt Gingrich pressed Clinton to add a covert element to his Iran policy, calling for "a serious, sophisticated campaign . . . designed to isolate, and frankly, in the long run, eliminate" the regime. Given the GOP hold on Congress and the proposal's appeal to the Israel lobby, Clinton had little choice but to agree. The CIA devoted $18 million to covert anti-Iran activities, the only proviso being that the money could not be expressly earmarked for overthrowing the Tehran regime (official U.S. policy did not sanction that purpose).[67]

As it turned out, containment was sufficient to neither satisfy Gingrich nor modify Iran's behavior. After Lake outlined dual containment in 1994, and especially after Gingrich publicly proposed an anti-Tehran campaign in 1995, Iran commenced its own attempts to confound the strategy. Iranian officials announced a $20 million program to counter Gingrich's "unpleasant and disgusting policy," and they called the Clinton administration "a renegade Government whose logic was no different from Genghis Khan or Hitler." From the start, the CIA conceded that there was almost no chance that such a meager U.S. effort would bring down the Tehran government. In 1994 and 1995, U.S. officials noticed an increase in Iranian support for Hezbollah and other terrorist groups and attempts to disrupt the Arab-Israeli negotiations. The fact that containment had failed to subdue Tehran became painfully clear in 1996, when Iranian-sponsored agents blew up the Khobar Towers in Riyadh, killing nineteen U.S. soldiers.[68]

The Khobar incident brought U.S.-Iran relations to the breaking point. Aside from costing American lives, the bombing had a chilling effect on Israel's willingness to proceed with the peace process. Clinton wanted a strong military response. "I don't want any pissant half-measures," he told advisers. As the NSC attempted to implement Clinton's wishes, however, it found the options unattractive. Limited air strikes seemed out of the question, given Clinton's directive, but more extreme measures (such as the massive invasion scenario laid out in Pentagon war plans) had little chance of winning public support. U.S. officials considered attacking Iranian naval bases, seaports, and air defense sites but feared that these actions would merely incite additional terrorist attacks. "What I personally think happens next," predicted JCS chairman John Shalikashvili, "is that they attack us again, with hidden missiles, with little boats, with terrorist cells going against us and the Saudis and the Bahrainis." Compounding Clinton's difficulties, Saudi authorities refused to turn over the evidence needed to establish conclusively that Iran had been behind the Khobar bombing. This left U.S. intelligence analysts in the awkward position of being sure that Tehran was responsible but lacking the proof to make the case publicly. Unable to overcome these obstacles, Clinton shelved his plans for a stern response. Although the administration eventually implemented a covert program to expose the identities of Iranian agents working abroad, as of the end of 1996, Iran policy proved to be just as frustrating as U.S. dealings with Iraq. Rather than minimizing Iran's impact on U.S. and Israeli policy, Clinton now found himself in a deep and unsatisfying confrontation with Tehran.[69]

By comparison, Clinton's attempts to mediate the peace process began more favorably. Having made this initiative the keystone of his Middle Eastern diplomacy, the president scored a major victory in the summer of 1994 with the conclusion of an Israel-Jordan peace treaty. U.S. support was crucial to the pact. During the 1980s and early 1990s, Jordan's economic situation had steadily deteriorated, with the country amassing billions of dollars in foreign debt. In addition, owing to King Hussein's pro-Iraq stance during the Gulf War, Amman had been one of the few Middle Eastern capitals not to benefit from U.S. largesse in 1990 and 1991. During early and mid-1994, special envoy Dennis Ross used the prospect of financial assistance to coax Jordan's Hussein into taking a bold step in the peace process. When Jordanian officials were reluctant to agree to a meeting between the king and Israeli prime minister Yitzhak Rabin, Ross made it clear that if Amman wanted economic aid, it would require "something dramatic." "For debt forgiveness," Ross said, King Hussein "has to pull a Sadat." In late July, Jordanian and Israeli negotiators concluded the peace treaty. Months later, Jordan received $700 million in debt relief from the United States.[70]

By the time Hussein and Rabin signed the accord, though, the peace process had lost momentum. Negotiations over control of Hebron and the creation of the Palestinian Authority took considerably longer than expected, exposing the difficulties attached to creating even a limited measure of Palestinian self-rule. Within both Israel and the Palestinian territories, there remained strong opposition to further compromise. Rabin's opponents in the Knesset were sufficiently strong to make him cautious about ceding additional territory. Meanwhile, even after Oslo, a debate raged among Palestinian leaders as to whether violence or negotiation was the wisest course. Beset by these obstacles, the peace process moved slowly when it moved at all. Although the Oslo schedule called for Israel to turn over jurisdiction in Hebron by December 13, 1993, the talks did not bear fruit until May 1994, and then only after continual involvement by Ross and Christopher.[71]

The problems involved in this negotiation were minor compared with those encountered in the Israel-Syria peace talks. Clinton considered an agreement between Rabin and Syrian president Hafiz al-Assad "key to the achievement of enduring and comprehensive peace," believing that only after Syria came to terms with Israel would Lebanon and the Palestinians follow suit. Although Assad agreed to negotiate in early 1994, the talks soon foundered. Assad demanded that Israel return the Golan Heights and agree to parity of security arrangements on both sides of the Israel-Syria border as preconditions to substantive discussions. For his part, Rabin insisted on an Israeli early-warning system on the Golan Heights. Damascus rejected the proposal, and the talks broke down. Despite perpetual exhortation and more than two dozen trips to the region by Christopher, no settlement emerged, and by 1996, the parties had hardly budged from their 1993 positions. "The negotiations proved tedious, to put it mildly," Ross later wrote.[72]

The peace process suffered another setback in 1995 when an Israeli extremist assassinated Rabin. The killing was devastating to Clinton personally and robbed the process of the foremost Israeli dove. Rabin's successor, Shimon Peres, struggled to keep the Oslo agreement alive, but he fell victim to Israeli politics. Despite strong U.S. support, Peres lost the 1996 election to the hawkish Benjamin Netanyahu. Ross believed (perhaps optimistically) that had Peres won, an Israel-Syria treaty would have been in the offing, but after Netanyahu's election, a series of suicide bombings in Israel only strengthened the security-first mentality of the new prime minister. Netanyahu formed a coalition consisting of groups that explicitly opposed the Oslo accords and, over the next two years, repudiated them. By 1996, the peace process had stalled.[73]

To be fair, even with these reversals, the balance sheet on Clinton's first-term involvement in the peace process was positive. Breakthroughs in the Jordan-Israel and Israel-Palestine talks represented the first substantive progress in the area since the Israel-Egypt peace treaty. But to the administration's dismay, domestic discussion of the Middle East focused not on these achievements but on the degree to which its intensive involvement in the region distracted it from other issues. In particular, critics cited Christopher's frequent (and ultimately fruitless) visits to Syria and Israel as evidence that the administration had been sucked into a diplomatic black hole. Even those familiar with the peace process contended that Clinton had allowed the Israel-Palestine conflict to become too prominent an aspect of foreign policy. "There is only so much time and energy for the president and his top aides to devote to foreign policy," wrote Richard Haass, one of the architects of the Madrid Conference, "and it is impossible to argue that two dozen more visits to Syria would be more useful to U.S. national security than spending that time consulting with leaders in Japan, China, Russia, and India."[74]

There was some truth to this charge. The State Department occasionally seemed distracted by Christopher's absences, which also left Clinton without a secretary of state for long periods. Christopher later acknowledged, "Pursuit of Middle East peace can easily become an all-consuming endeavor." The distribution of diplomatic authority in the Clinton administration increased this tendency toward overinvolvement. Lake and his deputy, Sandy Berger, who should have been responsible for integrating Middle East diplomacy into the overall framework of foreign policy, did not involve themselves in issues pertaining to the peace process. They instead left the subject to Ross and Christopher, each of whom had a substantial personal stake in the issue.[75]

Overall, Clinton's first-term experience in the Middle East fell short of his expectations. Although Ross and Christopher made progress in the peace negotiations, they did not cover the distance they had expected, and by 1996, the process had nearly come apart. Iran and Iraq did not remain quiet; instead, they caused Clinton problems both abroad and at home. More broadly, Clinton's Middle East policy underscored certain points relevant to the postcontainment conduct of foreign affairs. The perception and reality of the administration's distraction with Arab-Israeli affairs indicated the degree to which the absence of an overall foreign policy strategy could complicate attempts to prioritize among more important and less important goals. The drawbacks of dual containment similarly raised questions about how best to organize U.S. diplomacy in the post–Cold War era and exposed Clinton to criticism from domestic observers. Through 1996, Clinton was unable to resolve the considerable complexity of Middle Eastern politics or the attendant political minefields at home.

Paradigm Lost

For students of foreign policy, the years between 1993 and 1996 offered two plausible—but opposite—lessons. The first drew on the changing nature of the international landscape, the diversity of U.S. interests in Europe, the emergence of new issues in the Middle East, and the nuances of East Asian affairs, and led to the conclusion that one-word foreign policies were relics of a bygone era. Geopolitics was far more complicated in 1996 than in 1986, proponents of this view contended, and U.S. objectives diverged accordingly. The wise statesman would therefore discard the long-standing American attachment to simplicity, accede to the diversity of U.S. interests, and deal with each crisis or issue as effectively as possible.

Advocates of the second lesson saw the same global arena but arrived at a much different conclusion. Certainly, diplomacy was complicated, they conceded, but this simply underscored the need for a firm strategy driving U.S. interaction with the world. Without a strong overall framework, foreign policy would stray from its intended course, resulting in overcommitment to peripheral issues or situations in which interests collided dangerously. Prioritization and coherence were the keys to diplomatic success in the 1990s, they argued. Lacking these virtues, policy would drift according to the vicissitudes of a chaotic international order.

Characteristically, Clinton came down in the middle of this argument. In one sense, the administration accepted the notion that post–Cold War foreign policy required greater flexibility than Americans were accustomed to. As early as late 1994, planning documents showed a fluid conception of U.S. policy. PDD 29, though specifically geared toward reorganizing bureaucratic responsibility for foreign affairs, outlined Clinton's view of the world in the 1990s. A half decade into the post–Cold War period, the document stated, "our understanding of the range of issues that affect our national security continues to evolve."

> Economic issues are of increasing concern and are competing with traditional political and military issues for resources and attention. Technologies, from those used to create weapons of mass destruction to those that interconnect our computers are evolving and proliferating. With this greater diversity of threats, there is wide recognition that the security policies, practices and procedures developed during the Cold War must be reexamined and changed. We require a new security process based on sound threat analysis and management practices. A process which can adapt our security policies, practices and procedures as the economic, political, and military challenges to our national interests continue to evolve.[76]

The document's emphasis on evolution and adaptation signaled the administration's disinclination to attempt a newly comprehensive definition of U.S. security interests. A key passage stated, "Our security policies and [security practices] must match the threats we face and must be sufficiently flexible to facilitate change as the threats evolve."[77]

The administration's wariness of single-phrase foreign policy stemmed from its assessment of the volatile nature of international politics. The world was still plenty dangerous, Clinton's advisers believed, but it lacked the type of overriding threat that would give singular coherence to U.S. policy. "We still call this the post–cold war world," said Deutch in 1996. "Among the opportunities and challenges of our time, there is not yet one dominant enough to define the era on its own terms and give it a name." In these circumstances, it would be wise to avoid oversimplifying U.S. objectives.[78]

By 1996, Clinton's public statements on foreign policy reflected this belief. The president dropped his insistence on nominating a successor to containment, abandoning efforts to provide a catchy summation of U.S. strategy. *Enlargement, assertive multilateralism,* and other pithy phrases faded from public discourse as Clinton and his advisers instead stressed the need for vigilance on a range of issues. Having begun his presidency by trumpeting such notions, Clinton ended his first four years noticeably allergic to blanket labels. Americans should not fall prey to reductionism, Albright argued in early 1997; they should mind a number of potential challenges that could eventually mature into something scarier. "Today, the greatest danger to America is not some foreign enemy," she said. "It is the possibility . . . that problems abroad, if left unattended, will all-too often come home to America."[79]

Yet Clinton's rejection of catchphrase diplomacy did not signal that he had thrown up his hands at the complexity of post–Cold War geopolitics. Beginning late in his first term, Clinton moved toward a strategy that, though flexible, had an overall goal. The administration started from the premise that Sovietism's demise had not necessarily made the international environment any less dangerous. "At the macro level, the world has surely become much safer for Americans," said Assistant Secretary of State Toby Gati, but "at the level where individual citizens and corporations face the world the threats have become more varied, more pernicious, and more difficult to address."[80]

Moreover, the administration feared that U.S. indifference to these threats could eventually prove disastrous. "No one challenge today is yet as formidable as the threat from the former Soviet Union," Deutch argued, but "if nurtured by neglect on our part, these new challenges could expand to threaten the growth of democracy and free markets." The key to U.S. security, then, was not to pursue a single objective with utmost vigor but to diversify policy by concurrently focusing on a number of smaller threats. The United States' stance would essentially be a preventive one, aimed at averting the emergence of a new menace on the level of the former Soviet Union. "We must lead in two ways," Clinton stated in late 1996: "first, by meeting the immediate challenges to our interests from rogue regimes, from short-term crises; and, second, by making long-term investments in security, prosperity, peace, and freedom that can prevent these problems from arising in the first place."[81]

Of course, this approach was considerably more complicated than anything Americans had known for the last fifty years. In practical terms, it meant having to constantly shift among objectives. This seemed potentially problematic, because it might prove difficult to determine which aims trumped others or how Clinton would resolve the conflicting interpretations of policy that would inevitably arise from such a loose definition of interests. On a rhetorical level, the problems were similar. However firm the strategy was in Clinton's mind, he would have difficulty expressing it in a comprehensible fashion. A "foreign policy overview" by Christopher in 1996 touched on both these issues: "First, we must effectively manage our relations with the world's greatest powers, both our allies and former adversaries. Second, we must continue promoting peace and stability in regions of vital interest. Third, we must sustain the remarkable momentum we have achieved in creating jobs at home by opening markets abroad. Finally, we must intensify our efforts to confront an array of global challenges that no one nation can meet on our own."[82] This was a mouthful, far less clear and simple than containment or even enlargement. The president's policies, recalled aide Sidney Blumenthal, "lacked a larger, easily graspable explanation." And if Clinton had a hierarchy of objectives, he was not saying so. In both pragmatic and political terms, the new approach had potential liabilities.[83]

In 1996, though, these shortcomings were merely hypothetical. The practical problems were still in the future, and even the rhetorical issues were not immediately pressing. In fact, Clinton's decision to reject catchphrase diplomacy was made easier by the diminishing domestic importance of foreign policy. Although the 1994 elections had given congressional Republicans a strengthened voice in U.S. diplomacy and thus exposed Clinton to much criticism on the issue, for most Americans, foreign policy was what political scientists would call a "low-intensity" issue. Having come into office convinced that the public face of his diplomacy would be crucial to sustaining support for U.S. involvement abroad, Clinton now acknowledged the declining political significance of foreign affairs. "Foreign policy is not a matter of great interest in the debates in the barber shops and the cafés of America, on the plant floors and at the bowling alleys," he said in August 1996. With domestic concerns such as interest rates, health care, and gun control dominating the political agenda, the president was no longer obliged to take such a strong stance on diplomatic matters.[84]

This is not to say that Clinton's stance was uncontroversial in elite circles; quite the opposite was true. The foreign policy intelligentsia damned Clinton for his seemingly indifferent approach to foreign affairs. The intricacies of the post–Cold War world, they argued, made it imperative that the president clearly define U.S. interests abroad. Indeed, intellectuals and ex-officials were as upset by Clinton's reluctance to articulate a guiding tenet of foreign policy as they were by his various diplomatic initiatives. Former *Foreign Affairs* editor William Hyland claimed that U.S. policy was "vague and unpersuasive," and as a result, "American credibility and influence have declined at a time when this country's power is unmatched." A number of academics and former diplomatic practitioners at the John F. Kennedy School of Government were so troubled by the continuing lack of a successor to containment that they formed a group called the Commission on America's National Interests. "After four decades of unusual single-mindedness in containing Soviet communist expansion," they wrote, "we have seen five years of ad hoc fits and starts. If it continues, this drift will threaten our values, our fortunes, and indeed our lives." Believing that the United States owed its "victory" in the Cold War to the forceful simplicity and consistency of containment, these observers had little patience for a strategy that centered on the complexity of global affairs and the corresponding difficulty of defining U.S. interests.[85]

Seizing on these arguments, Republicans cast foreign policy as a crucial issue during the 1996 campaign. To great fanfare, Colin Powell joined the Republican ranks, declaring that Dole could provide "greater conviction and coherence to our foreign policy."[86] The charges fell flat. Clinton kept his head down, minimizing diplomatic questions just as he had done in 1992, and the Republican attacks failed to stick. With the domestic economy booming, most voters could not have cared less about foreign policy. The comeback kid confounded the predictions of two years earlier by winning reelection handily.

Aside from annoying the denizens of think tanks, Clinton's move away from a firmly structured foreign policy represented an important change in the U.S. approach to post–Cold War geopolitics. By stressing adaptability and implicitly conceding the inefficacy of catchphrase foreign policy, Clinton deviated from the still-prevalent notion that single-mindedness was the hallmark of effective diplomacy (subsequently, I refer to this idea as the *coherence paradigm*). Having come into office stressing the practical and political benefits of simplicity, Clinton now espoused a foreign policy style that was considerably more fluid. Although his strategy was not without an overall theme, the clear organizational prioritization and rhetorical forcefulness that had characterized enlargement had largely vanished, giving way to an altogether different approach.

This development marked a potentially momentous turning point in the evolution of foreign policy. In practical terms, Clinton's move appeared to herald a shift in the long-standing American style of international conduct. Instead of pursuing a specific goal or combating a dominant enemy with singular effort and resolve, the United States would now diversify its diplomacy. Depth would give way to breadth as numerous issues competed for the attention of U.S. policy makers.

The possible rhetorical ramifications of this decision were equally important. By repudiating his own dictum regarding the necessity to crystallize foreign policy, Clinton essentially conceded that the political justifications for U.S. diplomacy would mirror the growing complexity of the international environment. Rather than being able to point to a widely accepted theme as the be-all and end-all of American efforts abroad, U.S. officials would have to provide more nuanced rationales for bearing the costs of diplomacy and defense.

On a broader plane, Clinton's departure hinted that the lessons of the Cold War had ceded pride of place to those of the post–Cold War era. Whereas the older era had demonstrated the benefits of coherence, the newer, still maturing age placed a higher premium on flexibility. Beyond reshaping the structure and political defense of foreign policy, Clinton's new approach thus represented a dissent from the intellectual verities of the early 1990s. At the close of his first term, Clinton had broken not only with his own inclinations of years past but also with the conventional wisdom among informed observers of foreign policy. Would Clinton's dissent become the new received wisdom? In 1996, it was too early to tell. The president seemed to be vindicated by the election of that year, which apparently confirmed the public's lack of interest in the international scene, but the longer-term ramifications of his approach to foreign policy were still unclear. The practical consequences of the shift were not yet obvious; likewise, it was unknown to what degree the domestic audience would be receptive to a strategy that lacked an easily identifiable moral or strategic reference point. As Clinton's second term began, it remained to be seen whether this style represented a firm break with the past or merely a digression from the quest for a cohesive foreign policy.

7

Post–Bumper Sticker Diplomacy

What Clinton resolved toward the end of his first term he remained faithful to for the balance of his presidency. Despite the departure of some of the old cast and the appearance of new faces in the National Security Council, Clinton's second administration hewed closely to the strategic formulation arrived at in the latter part of the first. As Strobe Talbott and new national security adviser Sandy Berger liked to say, foreign policy could no longer be expressed on a bumper sticker. Discarded after the fall of enlargement, one-word encapsulations of national security strategy were nowhere to be found during Clinton's second term in the Oval Office.

As a result, the geopolitical landscape of the late 1990s served as the proving ground for the administration's new conception of foreign policy. Clinton's approach worked well in certain instances, such as when the president consummated NATO expansion and prosecuted a victorious war in the Balkans. During the next four years, however, the liabilities of a nuanced (and, to Clinton's critics, inconsistent) strategy were exposed. In practical terms, there were four basic problems with Clinton's vision of foreign policy.[1] The first was essentially an amplification of trends that had emerged during the first term, when the lack of a guiding paradigm had caused U.S. objectives to conflict with one another. To be sure, this was probably inevitable, given the diversity of U.S. interests in the late 1990s. Yet when pursued with sufficient vigor, contradictory policies could intersect perilously, impairing important aspects of American diplomacy or creating crises that threatened to spiral beyond Washington's control.

The second drawback of Clinton's approach was a tendency to lose sight of the connections between specific objectives and the overall strategic picture. As the president moved assertively in Europe, for instance, his actions produced adverse consequences elsewhere. Although Clinton focused his second-term diplomacy on preventing the emergence of new dangers to the United States, his efforts therefore sometimes encouraged just such an outcome. When the administration ignored the larger geopolitical ramifications of a particular regional policy, it opened the door to pernicious developments that might eventually pose a far greater menace to U.S. security than a smoldering conflict in the Balkans.

The third problem Clinton encountered was less strategic than organizational. Attempting to shift among a host of problems of varying import, Clinton and Albright struggled to prioritize their time and energy. They tended to get bogged down in certain issues and thus overlook other opportunities to better the U.S. position abroad. This quandary grew apparent as Clinton plunged into the Middle East peace process and became so consumed by the negotiations that he neglected other important matters and perhaps missed a chance to negotiate an end to U.S.–North Korean hostilities.

The fourth liability was also an internal one, and it involved Clinton's efforts to reform the U.S. military to better suit the contingencies of the post–Cold War world. Although Clinton had come into office committed to altering both the size and the composition of the armed forces, the uncertainty of international affairs and the president's failure to identify a central mission for defense policy allowed the Pentagon to resist many of his proposed changes. With no defining purpose for national security policy, the bureaucracies reigned supreme.

Overall, these difficulties illustrated the perils of a flexible approach to foreign policy and went to the heart of the United States' postcontainment dilemma. By 2000, it was clear that Clinton had failed to provide a sustainable basis for post–Cold War foreign policy—and that the coherence paradigm was not bankrupt yet.

Beyond Catchphrases

The fact that Clinton had largely gotten a pass on the foreign policy failures of his first term during the 1996 election did not ameliorate his displeasure with many of his top advisers. Having initially taken a backseat to Anthony Lake in foreign affairs, Clinton regretted that decision when he found himself marginalized in internal debates. Dick Morris, a calculating political operator who got on poorly with Lake, prodded Clinton to make a change. "I'm beginning to see how Lake runs foreign policy around here," he said to Clinton in 1995. "There's a regency. You're too young now to run your own foreign policy, so Lake and Christopher have to do it. But when you turn twenty-one they'll let you take it over." Clinton unhappily agreed with this characterization of the NSC, complaining that Lake restricted his sources of information.[2]

Immediately after the election, Clinton cleaned house. Secretary of Defense William Perry resigned amid the fallout from the Khobar Towers bombing. Lake had hoped to stay on but was booted upstairs to run the CIA in the wake of the Aldrich Ames scandal. Warren Christopher's departure was no surprise, as the secretary of state had been unpopular with Clinton, Congress, and almost everyone else since 1993 and had been on the brink of resignation at least once during the first term. The reshuffling of the NSC prompted some observers to predict that Clinton would steer a new course in foreign policy, but the changes were less significant than they initially appeared. That Clinton did not plan a thorough reevaluation of foreign policy was evident from the fact that Lake's and Christopher's replacements came from within the administration. Sandy Berger, Lake's former deputy, took over as national security adviser, and Madeleine Albright assumed control at the State Department.

If not for political concerns, the changes might have been greater. Clinton pondered a departure from his first-term diplomacy, considering Colin Powell and Republican senator Richard Lugar as potential secretaries of state. Al Gore scotched both candidates, however, fearing that four years at Foggy Bottom might give Powell or Lugar an advantage if either ran for president in 2000. As in 1992, Clinton turned cautious following an early misstep, opting for safe choices. Hoping to reduce the infighting that had led to leaks and perpetual bickering during the first term, Clinton sought advisers who would work well with one another. Clinton, related one administration official, saw the foreign policy team as "a puzzle that has to move together."[3]

Minimizing contentiousness was central to the search for a new secretary of state. Bosnia hand Richard Holbrooke was an early front-runner, but his prospects faded when it appeared that his abrasiveness might be objectionable to the Senate and to career officers at the State Department. Albright, in contrast, was popular with the Foreign Relations Committee due to her reputation as a forceful proponent of U.S. views in the United Nations, and she enjoyed strong support from women's groups. Seeking a secretary who could defend large foreign affairs budgets to a skeptical Congress, Clinton tapped the well-liked Albright. Maine senator William Cohen became secretary of defense for similar reasons. As a Republican, Cohen enjoyed solid congressional backing; as a moderate, his views would not be too out of sync in an administration seeking consensus.[4]

Clinton's choice of Berger as national security adviser exemplified the president's emphasis on agreement and cooperation over strategic vision. Unlike Lake, who had participated vocally in policy debates and contributed materially to the creation of enlargement, Berger took a more traditional view of his post. The new national security adviser acted as an enforcer of presidential decisions and an arbitrator in internal disputes. Talbott called Berger "the ultimate honest broker." Berger himself embraced this role, defining his task largely in administrative terms. "Our job here," he explained, "is to both try to make sure that the President gets the best, sharpest information he can to make decisions, and that once he does that they're carried out."[5]

Yet consensus came at the expense of intellectual firepower. The major drawback to Clinton's choices for the NSC was that their organizational, diplomatic, and political skills were greater than their strategic foresight. Albright was primarily a negotiator and the public face of Clinton's diplomacy; Cohen was a bureaucratic manager and conciliator of a hostile Congress; Berger was the internal peacemaker. By all accounts, none had the type of geopolitical vision considered by foreign policy observers to be crucial to forming an effective approach to post–Cold War diplomacy. "The biggest thing that these appointments tell you about the direction of U.S. foreign policy," groused one commentator, "is that there is no direction."[6]

If the composition of Clinton's staff was one reason that the second administration adhered closely to the foreign policy of the first, its view of the international environment was another. As Clinton's second term commenced, U.S. intelligence agencies warned that global perils had diversified greatly over the past five years. "Core threats which dominated our national security for fifty years have ended or receded," explained acting CIA director (later director) George Tenet. "In their place, however, is a far more complex situation that holds at least five challenges as we bring this century to a close and usher in the next." Actually, as Tenet's subsequent presentation made clear, the five challenges were actually categories of challenges encompassing roughly fifteen current and potential threats to U.S. security. Administration spokesmen explained that Clinton aimed to minimize each of these menaces, but Tenet hinted that it might be difficult for the president to prioritize them. "We do have a set of priorities that have been established by Presidential Decision Directive that basically looks at the world and says that there are 10 or 15 things that matter most to American security," he told the Senate Intelligence Committee. For observers awaiting a clear definition of U.S. interests, this was not a reassuring sign; having fifteen top priorities was probably equivalent to having zero top priorities.[7]

Other officials seconded Tenet's assessment. Defense Intelligence Agency director Patrick Hughes cited "significant uncertainty surrounding today's international security environment" and warned that "the nature of potential and actual conflict and the dimensions of it will vary broadly from place to place and circumstance to circumstance." Moreover, the situation would not revert to Cold War–era simplicity anytime soon: "The world is in the midst of an extended post–Cold War transition that will last at least another decade." Cohen made the same point, noting that with the rise in ethnic conflict and terrorism and the perils posed by "rogue states" such as Iraq, Iran, and North Korea, the administration must remain aware that "dangerous threats can arise suddenly and unpredictably." At a time when "the world is changing at an unprecedented and sometimes alarming pace," a static conception of foreign policy was impracticable.[8]

Accordingly, Clinton's advisers were unwilling in 1997 to attempt a concise statement of U.S. strategy. Talbott often asserted that the nation had entered the "post bumper sticker world," in that international relations had grown "more complicated" and would thus confound any simplistic foreign policy. When Albright detailed the administration's stance on foreign affairs in January 1997, she stressed the need for a nuanced strategy that would allow the United States to confront the complex threats of the day and prevent any of them from reaching a Soviet-level challenge. What this meant for the present was that the United States had to get over the long-held belief that foreign policy could be explained in simple terms. Americans needed "to stop thinking of our foreign policy in terms of the cold war that we all got used to for 50 years," she said. "The labels are not the same anymore. The problems are different. . . . It is a totally new ball game."[9]

Granted, a policy aimed at dealing with these new and diverse challenges would not be rhetorically cohesive and would therefore be significantly less comprehensible to the general public than its predecessors had been. The new threats, Albright conceded, "are much harder to explain to people. I think we all had 50 years of dividing life into the Communists and us, and it was much easier to explain."[10]

Undaunted by the challenge, Albright laid out the areas of greatest concern: preserving and strengthening NATO, encouraging Russian democratization and integration into Europe, staying on China's good side, preventing the spread of weapons of mass destruction, implementing strategic arms control, promoting stability in the Persian Gulf and East Asia, and expanding free trade and democracy, among other things. The list was long and expansive and encompassed multiple themes, some of which might contradict others (expanding NATO and conciliating Russia, to cite a familiar example). As such, it defied clear characterization. Albright conspicuously avoided slogans that reporters or critics might use to describe the administration's strategy. Asked about Clinton's slogan-happy first two years in office, Albright replied, "I am not going to use words any longer that have a lot of syllables and end in an 'ism.'"[11]

This general conception of U.S. interests remained much the same for the duration of Clinton's presidency. In strategy documents released in 1998 and 1999, the administration reiterated that U.S. priorities now lay in a number of different directions and could not be expressed in a single phrase. No new term emerged to fill the vacancy left by enlargement's demise five years earlier, and Clinton's and Albright's public statements generally focused on specific issues or the "dynamic and uncertain" nature of the threats facing the nation, rather than on any overall paradigm for foreign affairs.[12]

Contrary to his critics' contentions, Clinton was not wholly without ideas regarding American purpose at the end of the twentieth century. He had a relatively clear image of the global environment and crafted a security strategy to match. The United States was the dominant power of the mid-1990s, the administration assumed, and should therefore aim to prevent any new enemy from challenging this preeminence. (In a sense, this strategy was a toned-down version of the Pentagon's 1992 plan.) What was absent from Clinton's attempt to manage the situation was less strategic awareness than logical consistency, a structured conception of how to pursue numerous goals that had little in common and often contradicted one another. As Clinton's first term had showed, this state of affairs was rife with the potential for internal conflict. Despite his best efforts, Clinton had defined a diplomatic framework of questionable efficacy. The effectiveness of this strategy would only become more dubious as his second term unfolded.

European Insecurity

As it turned out, the problem of conflicting objectives was prominent in one of the most important diplomatic arenas of the late 1990s. In European affairs, Clinton's second-term goals were nearly identical to those of his first: stabilize the Balkans, revitalize NATO, and conciliate Russia. Early on, Clinton enjoyed modest success, juggling his objectives with relative facility. When a conflict in Kosovo became the nexus for Clinton's policies, however, the latent friction between his aims burst into view, propelling the United States and Russia on a collision course that resulted in perhaps the most dangerous moment for U.S. foreign policy in the late 1990s.

The first European issue to arise in 1997 was Bosnia, which was still being patrolled by a NATO force with a sizable U.S. contingent. So far, Bosnia had occupied a strange niche in Clinton's diplomacy. Although the president had favored intervening there in 1993, his eventual decision to do so two and a half years later had involved domestic politics and diplomatic credibility rather than humanitarianism. Trying to strike a balance between inaction and recklessness, Clinton had initially pledged to withdraw U.S. troops from the region by the end of 1996; once in, however, the president found that getting out was no easy matter. Disentangling Serb, Croat, and Bosnian Muslim forces from one another proved to be a difficult process, exacerbated by the fact that Serbian president Slobodan Milosevic was in no hurry to relinquish conquered territory. At one point, Serb troops threatened to fire on U.S. helicopters overseeing the cease-fire, and in late 1996, Milosevic's forces destroyed the homes of Muslims who were set to return under the Dayton agreement. Muslim leaders contributed to the problems as well, interfering in Dayton-mandated elections by detaining members of the Bosnian opposition. The slow process of implementing the Dayton accords precluded a punctual exit by U.S. forces. "Real peace has not yet taken root in Bosnia," Perry conceded in December 1996. "There's a real danger that if NATO were to completely withdraw, that those [outstanding] disputes would ignite into another general war." Accordingly, it came as little surprise when Clinton announced in December (after the 1996 elections, of course) that U.S. forces would remain in Bosnia until June 1998.[13]

This determination did little to speed implementation. The basic problem was that setting a timeline for withdrawal encouraged recalcitrant Serbs, Croats, and Muslims to ignore Dayton in the hope of simply waiting out the U.S. presence. Making the situation more difficult was the fact that the administration was divided on the question of how vigorously to enforce the accords. Whereas Albright favored a more active role for U.S. troops in making Dayton work, Cohen opposed expanding the mission. In January, he publicly stated that U.S. troops would come home by June 1998. "Setting a timeline is important," he declared, "because it is telling our European friends that we are not going to make an unlimited commitment to that region." At times, Cohen's stance bordered on callousness. "Are [Serbs, Muslims, and Croats] going to go back to slaughtering each other [after a U.S. withdrawal]?" he asked. "It's going to be up to them."[14]

With Washington wavering, the peace process came unhinged. Radovan Karadzic, a notorious Serb war criminal, flouted an agreement to stay out of political life, and overall compliance with the

Dayton accords dropped dramatically. Croat militias attacked Muslims in early February and revived memories of ethnic cleansing by evicting roughly a hundred Muslims from their homes. By February 1997, Dayton (and Bosnia) was coming apart.[15]

Under increasing criticism at home for his passivity, Clinton commissioned Berger to conduct a policy review in March. Holbrooke, now a private adviser to the president, urged an increased U.S. role. "Bosnia has gone nowhere since Dayton," he told Clinton. "People out there are not even sure we still support Dayton, or if we still care what happens in Bosnia." Berger's study returned similar findings, and despite Cohen's opposition, Clinton gradually moved toward a restatement of the U.S. commitment. In May, after British prime minister Tony Blair also counseled firmness, Clinton hinted that he might extend the U.S. presence. "We can't play around with this," he concluded. "We can't just sort of hang around and then disappear in a year."[16]

Conditions in Bosnia added impetus to the implementation process. General Wesley Clark, an aggressive proponent of enforcing the Dayton agreement, assumed control of the NATO contingent, and in July 1997, U.S. troops arrested their first suspected war criminals. In August, Clark took another long-delayed step, disarming Serb paramilitary forces. Still, the operative question remained whether Clinton would remove the June 1998 deadline on the U.S. presence in Bosnia. If he did not, certain advisers feared, Karadzic and others would simply go to ground until that time. Cohen and the Joint Chiefs of Staff opposed any extension of the U.S. mission, and the House of Representatives had previously resolved to terminate funding for the project at the June deadline.

By the late summer of 1997, however, Albright, Berger, and Holbrooke had convinced Clinton that the Dayton accords would collapse without a new U.S. commitment. In September, Berger gave a speech that all but confirmed the decision to discard the June 1998 deadline. Consolidating the gains made under Dayton "will require that the international community stay involved in Bosnia in some fashion for a good while to come," he stated. Berger's speech left the House with the politically dangerous option of refusing to fund U.S. troops in the field. The representatives wisely declined to shorten their careers, passing a resolution two days later that provided continued funding for the mission. As expected, Clinton made the decision official in December, lifting the June deadline and stating that U.S. efforts would now focus on objectives rather than dates.[17]

In the meantime, other issues from the first term resurfaced. The most prominent was NATO expansion, which by early 1997 was on track, with invitations to prospective members scheduled to be issued from the alliance's summer summit. The basic outlines of an agreement between NATO and Russia to minimize Moscow's apprehensions had been evident since 1995, but a final pact had not yet been concluded. Hoping to wring concessions from NATO, Moscow made oblique threats as the July summit approached. Prime Minister Victor Chernomyrdin hinted that Russia might rearm and, in an allusion to Yeltsin's precarious domestic situation, warned that "developments in Russia could take an ominous turn" if NATO expansion proceeded. U.S. officials downplayed these possibilities in public. Albright authored an article for the *Economist* that helpfully informed the Russians of their true feelings on the subject. "The Russian people know that their future will be written in Moscow, in Perm, in Irkutsk—and certainly not in Brussels," she wrote. Privately, however, Clinton feared that the pessimists were correct. After George Kennan argued in early February that expansion would endanger Russian democracy, Clinton asked Talbott, "Why isn't Kennan right?" Even while forging ahead, Clinton realized that an assertive NATO policy might detract from other U.S. objectives.[18]

Despite their alarmist rhetoric, Russian officials took a conciliatory tone in private. Meeting with Gore in early February 1997, Chernomyrdin backed away from his hard line. "I understand that the decision has been made, and we know you can't reverse it," he told Gore, "but we need help on managing our own domestic politics on the issue." Encouraged by Chernomyrdin's comments, Clinton scheduled a March summit with Yeltsin in Helsinki, where he hoped to finalize the NATO-Russia pact.[19]

Yeltsin arrived in Helsinki willing to conclude a pact on the basis of the "three no's": that the alliance currently had no reason, no intention, and no plan to station foreign troops or nuclear weapons in Eastern Europe. Complicating matters, Yeltsin also demanded a private assurance that NATO expansion would not include former Soviet republics (a reference to Latvia, Lithuania, and Estonia). Clinton stood firm, telling Yeltsin that even a secret agreement to that effect would leak and incite a congressional revolt. Faced with the prospect that expansion might go ahead without him, Yeltsin gave in. As a consolation prize, Clinton promised to support Russia's entry into the Group of Seven and offered Yeltsin an observer's seat at the group's upcoming meeting in Denver.[20]

Predictably, the outcome at Helsinki raised hackles in Russia. The Duma called enlargement "the largest military threat to our country over the last 50 years." The leader of the Russian Communist Party took a similar tone. "The Helsinki agreements were effectively a Treaty of Versailles for Russia," he declared. Yeltsin maintained his support for the agreement, however, and the accord held. Expansion hurt Yeltsin domestically, but the injury was not as grave as a breach with Clinton might have been.[21]

Emboldened by his success in Helsinki, Clinton continued to play his strong hand following the July announcement that Poland, Hungary, and the Czech Republic would receive invitations to join NATO. In early 1998, Clinton entered into an agreement with Latvia, Lithuania, and Estonia, reaffirming U.S. support for their independence and stating that these nations would eventually become members of the alliance. Despite Russian fears of foreign involvement in the Baltic, the administration accompanied its move with blunt talk. "The Russians need to get over their neuralgia on this subject," Talbott said. "They need to stop looking at the Baltic region as a pathway for foreign armies or as a buffer zone." At the same time, Clinton's behind-the-scenes balancing act continued. American diplomats briefed their Kremlin counterparts on the U.S.-Baltic pact before going public, Clinton urged Baltic leaders to seek normalized relations with Moscow, and U.S. officials made it clear that these nations would achieve NATO membership only after both Clinton and Yeltsin had left office. The administration was pleased with the restrained Russian reaction, which encouraged the notion that Clinton was correct to make bold moves in Eastern Europe while Russia was weak and its president friendly.[22]

Clinton's exploitation of the Russian position created an undercurrent of tension between Moscow and Washington, however, and gradually put the two countries on a diplomatic collision course. The trouble began in a familiar spot in early 1998, when Milosevic cracked down on rebels in the Serbian province of Kosovo. The origins of the Kosovo conflict, which pitted ethnic Albanians against Serbs, went back roughly a decade. After enjoying semiautonomy under Tito, the Kosovar legislature capitulated to Serb pressure in 1989 and suspended its privileged status. Kosovo's Albanian population soon rued this decision, as Milosevic treated the province as conquered territory. He undertook the "Serbianization" of Kosovo, replacing Albanian officeholders with Serbs and stationing 60,000 police and soldiers in the province. Kosovar nationalists initially responded with peaceful resistance, but they turned to violence after Kosovo was not included in the Dayton accords. In 1996 and 1997, the separatists attacked Serb troops and officials in Kosovo. Confronted with this challenge, Milosevic authorized a military response, and in January and February 1998, Serb forces struck against Kosovar separatists in the province.[23]

Washington had long seen Kosovo as the most explosive area in the Balkans due to its proximity to Albania and Macedonia, two other states that were also experiencing considerable unrest. For this reason, Bush had warned Milosevic in late 1992 that conflict in Kosovo would bring about a U.S. response "against Serbians in Kosovo and in Serbia proper." The Clinton administration took the same view of the conflict's incendiary quality. State Department adviser Robert Gelbard contended that the conflict could "spiral out of control," imperiling the stability of "the region as a whole."[24]

As usual, Albright took the lead in pushing for a military response to Serb outrages. In April 1998, she and Gelbard recommended that NATO begin planning for air strikes against Serb forces. Berger was hesitant. "What would you do the day after?" he asked, alluding to the problem of crafting a political settlement in Kosovo. The Pentagon was also reluctant to join the fray, fearing that Clinton would insert U.S. troops into Kosovo without defining an exit strategy. Even if the administration had been united in its desire to act, there were external obstacles to intervention. Moscow desired to preserve its own influence in the Balkans and was wary of U.S. involvement in the crisis. "Russia has been present in the Balkans for two hundred years, maybe more," Yevgeny Primakov told Albright. "It's beyond me why the Americans want to force their recommendations on the Balkans without consulting us." Russian officials demanded that NATO obtain UN consent before taking action, but because Moscow was sure to veto any such resolution, the process stalled. Instead of launching air strikes, NATO conducted a flyover of Serb positions in June 1998, an ineffectual action widely ridiculed as the "Balkans Air Show."[25]

Yet, as in Bosnia in 1995, the continuing violence in Kosovo was impossible to ignore. In July, Gelbard cited "the potential for spillover into neighboring countries" when he stated that "all options, including robust military intervention in Kosovo, remain on the table." In September, the UN Security Council passed a new resolution demanding that Milosevic withdraw from Kosovo (but not authorizing military action if he did not). When Milosevic refused, NATO prepared for air strikes. Cohen, though personally skeptical of intervention, called Milosevic's latest actions "a challenge I don't think NATO can afford to walk away from." In late September, Clinton opted to begin air strikes in the next two weeks, but the initiative foundered on domestic and international opposition. Clinton's war plan failed to impress congressional leaders, who argued that the administration lacked a political strategy to end the conflict. Moscow was also vehemently opposed to NATO action. Foreign Minister Igor Ivanov told U.S. officials that Yeltsin could "not countenance" air strikes, words that Talbott took to mean that Moscow might consider reprisals if NATO went ahead.[26]

Clinton was in a bind, urged on by his advisers but restrained by domestic opinion and growing hostility from Russia. In an ironic turn, Milosevic temporarily extricated the president from his predicament, agreeing to a cease-fire in late 1998 and beginning to withdraw Serb forces from Kosovo. The situation was momentarily stabilized, it appeared—a double NATO-Serb and U.S.-Russian confrontation averted.

War for the Alliance

The appearance of stability was misleading, however, for Milosevic's retreat merely postponed these clashes. Tensions in Kosovo once again exploded in early 1999, when Serb forces massacred the inhabitants of Racek. Milosevic's latest flouting of NATO's warnings introduced a new element into Clinton's calculations. With NATO's fiftieth anniversary approaching, the alliance's inability to stop the slaughter in Kosovo had become an embarrassment. If NATO could not end the Balkan war in eight years, critics asked, what was it good for? Walter Slocombe argued that the alliance could no longer tolerate such flagrant nose-thumbing. "We have a broad interest going beyond the immediate issues in Kosovo or even in the Balkans in maintaining the capability and credibility of NATO and American leadership in it," he contended. Clinton resolved in late January to issue an ultimatum to Milosevic and to commit peacekeepers to Kosovo after a settlement was reached.[27]

Aware of domestic and international apprehension about NATO involvement in Kosovo, the administration made a final diplomatic effort. In February, Albright brought Serb and Kosovar negotiators to Rambouillet, France, in the hope of reaching a deal. Clinton rejected the idea of Kosovar independence, fearing that further division of the Balkans would fuel instability. Instead, he demanded that Milosevic permit the province a higher degree of autonomy. The negotiations failed, in part because Albright was eager for a showdown with Milosevic, and in part because of Russia's refusal to back the U.S. position. Not eager to see NATO peacekeepers in Kosovo, Moscow kept Milosevic's hopes of splitting the Western coalition alive by remaining aloof from the alliance's stance. The negotiations reached an impasse, and at a March 19 meeting, Clinton approved air strikes if Milosevic refused a last-ditch appeal by Holbrooke. Five days later, NATO attacks commenced without UN sanction.[28]

Announcing the attacks to the nation, Clinton cited his desire to avoid regional instability as one motive for the war. "Let a fire burn here in this area, and the flames will spread," he said. By this point, though, it was obvious that intervention was as much about NATO as it was about the Balkans. Clinton briefly alluded to this factor in his speech, framing the issue as one of credibility. "Imagine what would happen if we and our allies instead decided just to look the other way, as these people were massacred on NATO's doorstep," he mused. "That would discredit NATO, the cornerstone on which our security has rested for 50 years now." No less than humanitarian or regional concerns, intervention in Kosovo reflected an attempt to save the centerpiece of Clinton's diplomacy.[29]

The fact that the United States had entered an armed conflict for NATO's sake must have been perplexing to certain of the president's advisers. After all, Clinton's original attachment to expanding the alliance had been moral rather than strategic. Now, however, Clinton had plunged into a war with potentially serious ramifications for U.S.-Russia relations in defense of an initiative that had originated with little grounding in diplomatic logic.

Beginning in late March, NATO planes targeted Serb forces in Kosovo, as well as government and military posts in Serbia proper. Damage was initially light as U.S. commanders, preoccupied with avoiding casualties, refrained from more effective low-level attacks in favor of safer (but less accurate) high-altitude bombing. The strategy was better suited to mollifying the U.S. public than forcing Milosevic to capitulate. No American planes were lost, but Milosevic showed few signs of retreating.[30]

Clinton soon encountered other problems as well, as the conduct of the war was immediately complicated by the lack of international and domestic consensus on intervention. In a nod to war-wariness at home, Clinton ruled out the use of ground forces in Kosovo until a settlement was in place. This restriction undermined NATO's claim that it would do everything necessary to save Kosovo, and it may have encouraged Milosevic to believe that he could outlast the air war. The fact that U.S.-Russia relations had deteriorated to their lowest point since the Cold War made matters worse for Clinton. The air strikes provoked a virulent Russian response that featured calls to aid the Serbs with materiel or "volunteers." The gravity of the situation became clear when Yeltsin, normally the voice of moderation, issued what nearly amounted to a threat of war. "Don't force us to take military action," he warned in April, "since that will certainly lead to a European war or even a world war, which is inadmissible." In rhetoric reminiscent of the 1956 Suez crisis, other officials threatened to retarget Russian missiles "against those countries that are carrying out military action against Yugoslavia." Although many U.S. officials dismissed this talk as mere domestic posturing, Russian hostility had an undeniable effect on NATO's attempts to end the war. With Moscow hedging its support for the alliance's peace plan, Milosevic was able to exploit the distance between NATO's and Russia's stances.[31]

By late May, the air war had dragged on for two months, with little end in sight. Congressional support for the mission, which had never been strong, waned as it appeared that Clinton had found his way into another open-ended engagement. As happened so often during the 1990s, domestic unease over a military intervention gave rise to the Vietnam analogy. Republicans talked of "the Kosovo quagmire," and Representative Dennis Kucinich (D-Ohio) called the war "a debacle that rivals Vietnam itself."[32]

Desperate to end the conflict, Clinton considered invading Kosovo through Macedonia. To up the pressure on Milosevic, Clinton hinted that he might use ground troops. "We intend to see our objectives achieved," he declared, "and . . . we have not and will not take any option off the table." In May and early June, NATO began a buildup of "peacekeepers" in Macedonia, rumored to be the main body of an invasion force. Certain members of the Joint Chiefs of Staff opposed the idea, but Clark and Army Chief of Staff Dennis Reimer believed that an invasion was the logical and necessary next step. "If you're going to use military force," Reimer argued, "using the total military force available is the right way to go." Berger too took a hard line, detailing "four irreducible facts" about the war: "One, we will win. There is no alternative. Second, winning means what we said it means. Third, the air campaign is having a serious impact. Four, the president has said he has not ruled out any option. So go back to one. We will win." The planning eventually came to naught, as Milosevic agreed in early June to give Kosovo increased autonomy.[33]

As the war ended, however, the real danger began. Hoping to win Russian approval of the peace plan, Clinton allowed Moscow to participate in the peacekeeping mission to Kosovo. After Milosevic initiated the Serb withdrawal, Talbott met with Russian officials to discuss command arrangements for the joint occupation. The talks broke down, however, when the Russians demanded their own sector in Kosovo. Talbott refused, fearing that such an arrangement might lead to partition. In response, a Russian general threatened to deploy into

Kosovo unilaterally (Moscow still had troops in the region from the 1995 intervention). The volatile situation nearly exploded on June 12, when Russian troops preempted NATO's entry and "accidentally" crossed the Serbia-Kosovo border. Within hours, Russian soldiers seized the airport in the capital, Pristina. In Washington, Clinton and his advisers feared that Yeltsin had lost control of the military, as there was some confusion about whether Yeltsin had authorized the move. Sources in Moscow insisted that he had known of the plan, and Cohen suspected that Yeltsin was the real culprit. Other advisers were not so certain, hypothesizing that a renegade field commander was at fault.[34]

Although Clinton accepted Yeltsin's explanation that the intrusion had been a mistake, the two nations came perilously close to a military confrontation. Upon learning of the Russian move to take Pristina, Clark ordered NATO troops to seize the airport. It was a reckless decision and, given the Russian head start, more likely to cause a battle than to prevent Russian control of Pristina. Fortunately, cooler heads prevailed. "I'm not starting World War III for you," protested British commander Michael Jackson. Clark's higher-ups agreed and countermanded the order. Still, the situation remained dangerous, as the White House received word that Moscow planned to airlift reinforcements to Pristina. Clinton and his advisers insisted that Eastern European countries close their airspace to the transports, and they considered overpowering Russian soldiers at the Pristina airport or even shooting the planes down. The situation reached yet another critical point on June 13, when British troops arriving in their assigned occupation zone demanded access to the airport. Luckily for all involved, the commanders on the scene kept calm, and the tension gradually decreased.[35]

Even so, the crisis had been fraught with danger. Had any of several events turned out differently, NATO and Russian troops might well have crossed swords. As it was, Kosovo seriously impaired the relationship between the United States and Russia. A poll conducted in June showed that 72 percent of Russians viewed the United States unfavorably. Chernomyrdin remarked that the confrontation "set [U.S.-Russia relations] back by several decades," and high-level Soviet officials denounced the U.S. role in the war. As the 1990s ended, the

United States and Russia were less "strategic partners" (as Clinton was fond of saying) than strategic competitors. Between 1998 and 2003, the cooperation that had marked the early post–Cold War era evaporated, with Moscow opposing U.S. initiatives in the UN Security Council and cultivating "rogue states" such as Iraq and Iran in an effort to counterbalance American power.[36]

The Kosovo crisis and resultant fallout marked the culmination of a process that had begun in 1993, when the Clinton administration first set its sights on resolving the Balkan conflict and revitalizing NATO. In the debates over expansion, Bosnia in 1995, and finally the Kosovo crisis in 1998–1999, Clinton's pursuit of European security hampered his efforts at a stable relationship with Russia. NATO expansion and the victories in Bosnia and Kosovo were the successes of Clinton's European policy; U.S.-Russian hostility and the near disaster at Pristina were the price of these achievements.

The ill effects of Clinton's European policy were not limited to Europe. Another problem with the president's diplomatic style was that it complicated the links between regional policies and larger geopolitical concerns. By focusing on local events without a firm understanding of their global ramifications, Clinton undermined his own efforts to preserve the status quo. NATO expansion might (or might not) have made sense in European terms, but by increasing Russian hostility toward the United States, the initiative encouraged a strategic backlash. As Russian leaders grew disenchanted with the West, they looked to the East for a counterweight to U.S. influence, seeking an alliance with China that would produce a more equitable balance of world power. In April 1997, shortly after Yeltsin's embarrassing retreat in Helsinki, the Russian president hosted Jiang Zemin in Moscow. The two leaders pledged to reduce tensions between their countries, considered the possibility of Russian arms sales to China, and explicitly stated their desire to counteract U.S. domination of the international scene. "Some are pulling the world toward a unipolar order," said Yeltsin. "We want a multipolar world. . . . These poles constitute the foundation of a new world order." By 2001, Sino-Russian cooperation was at its post-1968 high, with Beijing often joining Moscow in opposing U.S. proposals in the Security Council. Though Clinton's stated desire to include Moscow in the new Europe and his conciliatory policy toward Beijing decreased the likelihood of a full partnership between the two nations, the late 1990s were still a time of increased collaboration between Russia and China. As Clinton prepared to leave office in early 2001, Moscow and Beijing announced another joint venture, a "strategic partnership" unvarnished in its anti-U.S. orientation.[37]

These unintended effects of Clinton's European diplomacy reflected larger problems inherent in the administration's foreign policy scheme. Although they perceived the complexity of the international order, Clinton and his advisers sometimes failed to reconcile specific initiatives with one another or to account for the broader consequences of individual policies. With no obvious guidepost for U.S. diplomacy, it was too easy for Washington to pursue contradictory aims or to focus on the regional at the expense of the global. This problem was apparent in the friction between Clinton's European objectives, as well as when NATO expansion and intervention in Kosovo encouraged adverse strategic shifts in the eastern half of Eurasia. In the end, Clinton's Europe policy was racked by internal inconsistencies and eventually fostered a potential challenge to the United States' geopolitical position that threatened to outweigh the strategy's positive effects. As Clinton's diplomacy illustrated, policies undertaken without reference to one another or to the global picture risked being counterproductive.

Peacemaker in Chief

Facing a daunting reelection challenge in 1995 and 1996, Clinton and his advisers considered various methods of putting a positive spin on his diplomatic efforts thus far. With Rwanda having exposed the limits of humanitarianism, the White House looked elsewhere for a suitable theme. Clinton's efforts to negotiate an end to the conflict in Northern Ireland, along with the recent conclusion of the Dayton accords and progress in the Middle East peace process, provided a useful alternative. Prior to the 1996 election, Clinton recast himself as "Peacemaker in Chief."[38]

Though originally formulated as an electoral catchphrase, the label stuck during Clinton's second term. In fact, Clinton's most visible and time-intensive foreign policy initiatives occurred in this realm.[39] Between 1996 and 2000, the Middle East peace process dominated the agenda. Clinton's second-term involvement in the region did not start auspiciously, however. By early 1997, the NSC recognized that the process had reached a crisis point. Benjamin Netanyahu's election as Israeli prime minister and a series of Palestinian attacks and Israeli reprisals had stalled the talks, with neither party willing to move toward implementing the Oslo agreement. Clinton arranged a summit between Palestine Liberation Organization (PLO) chairman Yasir Arafat and Netanyahu in late 1996 in a bid to restore momentum, but the meeting ended in a deadlock. Following the summit, Assistant Secretary of State Robert Pelletreau acknowledged that the peace process "has slowed during 1996" and admitted to "some genuine frustration on our part." Privately, Clinton and Gore worried that another terrorist attack would kill Oslo once and for all.[40]

Hoping to salvage the situation, the president took two important steps. First, he attempted to place a steadying hand on the negotiations by increasing his own role in the peace process. In January 1997, Clinton pledged that the United States (specifically, Albright and Dennis Ross) would assume the role of full-time arbiter, prodding both sides to live up to their Oslo commitments. Second, to elicit greater cooperation from the hawkish Netanyahu, Clinton sent the prime minister a letter affirming an "ironclad" U.S. commitment to Israeli security and, going beyond this familiar promise, allowing Netanyahu to determine what constituted Israeli security. Clinton's intensified involvement in the talks and his pledge to Netanyahu paid dividends, as Arafat and the Israeli leader agreed in early 1997 to restore Palestinian control of Hebron, a long-delayed milestone in the Oslo process.[41]

Even after this breakthrough, though, Clinton and Ross feared that the Oslo agreement would never come to fruition with Netanyahu in power. Netanyahu's conservative coalition partners left him little flexibility to negotiate with Arafat, and the prime minister's own behavior was not conducive to progress. Netanyahu placated his political allies by demanding far-reaching concessions from the Palestinian Authority before reciprocating even modestly. He also took a number of steps that severely disrupted Arab-Israeli ties, such as announcing the construction of new settlements in Gaza and attempting to assassinate a Hamas agent in Amman. Ross worried that Netanyahu's "impulsiveness" was "destroying confidence step by step," and Albright even considered a public declaration that the administration would no longer work with the prime minister. After some deliberation in February and March 1997, Clinton decided that the peace process would fail unless he proposed a bold initiative to both reenergize the negotiations and provide an alternative to the tedious Oslo discussions. Clinton's solution was to persevere with Oslo and at the same time start talks on "permanent status," or the creation of a Palestinian state. In August, Albright announced that the administration would now pursue Oslo as well as an expedited final settlement.[42]

Over the next three years, Clinton, Albright, and Ross devoted an enormous amount of time and energy to both these tracks. In 1997 and 1998, Ross and Albright oversaw painstaking negotiations on the amount of land to be turned over to the Palestinians in accord with the Oslo agreement. During this period, both officials made repeated trips to the Middle East and hosted summits in the United States and elsewhere. The talks stalled at various junctures, with either Arafat or Netanyahu proving reluctant to take the next step. At one point, Albright issued a virtual ultimatum to the Israeli leader, resolving to tell him that "we have to get something done or this is over." In 1998, these tactics produced the Wye River accords, which provided for the release of Palestinian prisoners, fewer restrictions on Palestinian travel, the collection of Palestinian weapons by U.S. intermediaries, and the transfer of an additional 13 percent of the occupied territory to Palestinian jurisdiction. Soon thereafter, however, Netanyahu responded to Palestinian demonstrations and resistance from his own conservative allies by suspending implementation of the Wye River accords. For Berger and Ross, this about-face was the last straw. "We need a new government," they told Clinton.[43]

As it happened, the near collapse of the peace process caused by Netanyahu's decision led to a political crisis in Israel and, eventually, the election of the more dovish Ehud Barak in May 1999. The development was a welcome one for Clinton. Barak soon announced that he desired to strike a deal on permanent status by April 2000, and he agreed in September 1999 to restart implementation of the Wye River accords. The new prime minister first focused on concluding a peace treaty with Syria, which, he believed, would facilitate a settlement with Lebanon and ultimately the Palestinians. Barak's overtures were productive at the outset, as Syrian president Assad agreed to restart negotiations in December 1999. At a summit in early 2000, Clinton personally intervened in the talks, outlining a Syrian-Israeli peace treaty that would resolve outstanding disagreements over the border between the two states, the issue of Jewish settlements on the Golan Heights, and water rights. Just as a breakthrough appeared imminent, however, both Assad and Barak came under domestic pressure not to bend in the negotiations. Knesset conservatives objected to Barak's eagerness for a final settlement, while Assad worried that making concessions might complicate succession arrangements in Syria. Assad objected to Clinton's proposed placement of the border along Lake Tiberias, and the discussions broke down in what Ross later termed a "high-visibility failure."[44]

The Israeli-Palestinian negotiations followed a similar trajectory. Intensive talks began only in early 2000 (Barak was reluctant to negotiate with Assad and Arafat simultaneously) and focused on the percentage of Palestinian land to be annexed by Israel for security purposes, the ultimate disposition of Jerusalem, and the rights of Palestinian refugees. The discussions progressed slowly, foundering on the issue of Jerusalem, and by July, Clinton felt a sense of urgency with regard to the prospects for a permanent settlement. The "lack of progress," he believed, was "spinning out of control." With the end of Clinton's presidency fast approaching, Berger and Albright argued for a concerted effort to broker a deal. Clinton all but coerced Arafat into attending a summit at Camp David, ignoring the chairman's assertions that the Palestinian political climate was not conducive to an agreement at this juncture. In mid-July, Clinton, Arafat, and Barak met for a marathon fifteen-day summit. Despite Clinton's mediation, the Palestinian leader held out for additional concessions on Jerusalem, and the meeting ended in a deadlock. The result was in some sense Clinton's fault because of his insistence on holding the summit over Arafat's protestations, but the president blamed the PLO chairman for the impasse. In Clinton's words, Arafat had become "the skunk at the party," putting the entire peace process in jeopardy by rejecting offers made by Barak at the risk of incurring the wrath of the Israeli Right. The situation subsequently unraveled after inflammatory Israeli politician Ariel Sharon visited the Temple Mount in Jerusalem, touching off an uprising in the Palestinian territories and provoking a spiral of violence.[45]

This latest failure convinced several of Clinton's advisers that Arafat himself was the main obstacle to a settlement. Both Ross and Albright were pessimistic about the chances of reaching an agreement, believing that the opportunity had been lost with the collapse of the Camp David summit. Clinton desperately wanted to achieve a historic agreement before his term was out, however, and after Arafat assured him that "we will follow any move you want to take," the president made a last-ditch effort to broker a deal. In late December, Clinton brought Arafat and Barak to Washington and presented a set of proposals in take-it-or-leave-it fashion. He offered a division of jurisdiction in Jerusalem, compensation for Palestinian refugees, and the return of roughly 95 percent of traditionally Palestinian land to Palestinian control. "We are running out of time and cannot afford to lose this opportunity," he told his two counterparts. "If theses ideas are not accepted by either side, they will be off the table and have no standing in the future." Barak accepted the proposal, but Arafat remained noncommittal, killing any hope for an agreement. Having spent so much of his second term seeking a treaty, Clinton was crushed. When Arafat congratulated Clinton on his efforts, the president replied, "Mr. Chairman, I am not a great man. I am a failure, and you have made me one."[46]

This comment reveals how much importance Clinton placed on finding a settlement and the degree to which the peace process dominated his diplomatic program during his second term. That Clinton saw the Middle East peace process as his most significant foreign policy initiative is confirmed by his memoirs, which devote far more pages to this subject than to any other international issue. The depth of Clinton's immersion in the process is also evidenced by the extent to which it distracted him from other diplomatic issues. In 2000, for instance, Clinton missed part of the G-8 summit in Okinawa to keep the ultimately fruitless Camp David talks alive. At another point, the president's desire to attend to the negotiations forced him to postpone a trip to India scheduled as part of a diplomatic opening to New Delhi.[47]

Another example of Clinton's preoccupation with the Middle East concerned his policy toward North Korea. Since the nuclear crisis of 1994, Clinton and Albright had quietly looked for ways to reduce tensions on the Korean peninsula. The issue became more pressing in 1998, when the North test-fired a missile over Japan. The incident raised concerns that Kim intended to develop intercontinental ballistic missiles (ICBMs) and might at some point repudiate the agreement reached in 1994. Given Pyongyang's proclivity for erratic behavior, this prospect raised considerable alarm in Washington. Deputy Assistant Secretary of Defense Kurt Campbell called the test "dangerous and provocative" and termed Kim's regime "deeply unpredictable and very dangerous to the maintenance of peace and stability" in the Far East. Seeking answers to the North Korean riddle, Clinton commissioned William Perry (now retired) to conduct a study of U.S.-Korea relations.[48]

In late 1999, Perry delivered a report advocating sharp departures in U.S.–North Korean affairs. Although Pyongyang had held to the bargain reached in 1994, Perry wrote, there was no guarantee that the framework would hold in the future. In light of recent events, it also seemed likely that Kim aimed for an ICBM capability. Perry laid out a series of options for averting these developments. Attempting to remove Kim from power or waiting for the regime to collapse was unrealistic, he believed. Abhorrent as it was, Kim's government appeared to be stable, at least in the short term, so U.S. policy would have to deal with that regime "as it is, not as we might wish it to be." Confronting Kim was also out of the question. "The intensity of combat in another war on the Peninsula would be unparalleled in U.S. experience since the Korean War," Perry wrote, and neither South Korea nor Japan desired a showdown with Pyongyang.[49]

Conciliation seemed the only workable course. Perry rejected assessments that labeled Kim as intransigent, describing him instead as a pragmatist working in a "profoundly different landscape than existed in 1994." Kim's people were starving, and his closest ally (China) was eager to reduce the possibility of conflict in Korea. In these circumstances, Perry believed, "the DPRK appears to value improved relations with [the] U.S., especially including relief from the extensive economic sanctions the U.S. has long imposed." Productive negotiations were therefore possible. If Kim agreed to end his nuclear and missile programs, Perry wrote, Washington should offer the regime security guarantees, economic aid, and diplomatic recognition.[50]

The idea of reversing fifty years of policy toward North Korea was controversial, but in 1999 and 2000, Perry's suggestions seemed to be the only viable option for averting an eventual showdown over Kim's advanced weapons and eliminating a recurring security problem. The administration endorsed Perry's policy, calling it "the best opportunity to change the stalemated situation on the Korean Peninsula in a fundamental and positive way." Concrete steps followed. In 2000, Clinton relaxed the U.S. economic headlock on North Korea to permit more humanitarian aid. Kim reciprocated with a moratorium on missile tests, and the two sides pledged to exchange envoys. Talks on an agreement to eliminate the North's nuclear and missile programs came next. In October 2000, the prospects for the grand bargain outlined by Perry improved further. Kim sent the second-ranking North Korean army official to Washington to explore the possibility of an agreement, a move that Albright and Clinton interpreted to mean that Pyongyang's military would support reconciliation.[51]

Later that month, Albright went to Pyongyang to speed the negotiations and to gauge the outlook for a visit by Clinton. Given Kim's personal control of foreign policy and his unwillingness to negotiate with subordinates, Albright and Clinton believed that a summit would be necessary to conclude the deal. The secretary's meetings with Kim and other North Korean officials went fairly well. Albright, normally an outspoken advocate of human rights, put those concerns aside in her dealings with the world's most repressive regime. "America's immediate interest is to make gains on core security issues," she said. "There are, after all, few human rights imperatives more meaningful than preventing war." Kim was cooperative as well. Enticed by the possibility of economic aid and diplomatic recognition, Kim sought to remove obstacles to better relations between the two countries. He agreed in principle to cease missile technology exports and pledged to refrain from conducting additional missile tests. Clinton should come to Pyongyang to finalize a deal on nuclear weapons, missiles, and a revision of the relationship, he told Albright.[52]

Leaving Pyongyang, Albright was optimistic about the prospects for reconciliation. She judged that, above all else, Kim wanted normalized relations with Washington. Economic aid and an end to the embargo, she believed, represented Kim's only chance to sustain his regime over the long term. Kim was fundamentally a realist, Albright told a Russian official, "practical, decisive, and seemingly non-ideological." Although there might not be sufficient time to conclude a treaty before the end of Clinton's term, Albright and Berger thought that a summit "might well" produce a "joint statement of mutual obligations" that could be formalized by Clinton's successor. South Korean president Kim Dae Jung, pursuing his own policy of reconciliation with the North, also encouraged Clinton to go to Pyongyang. By November, U.S. and North Korean officials meeting in Kuala Lumpur, Malaysia, were in the midst of intensive negotiations on Kim's weapons programs.[53]

In the end, though, Clinton declined Kim's summit invitation. George W. Bush, set to assume the presidency in early 2001, was cool to the initiative. More important to Clinton's decision, however, was his deep involvement in the Middle East negotiations. Even though Clinton thought that a deal with North Korea was at hand, he could not tear himself away from his last-minute effort to broker an agreement between Arafat and Barak. Believing that Arafat would seriously consider a settlement, Clinton "simply couldn't risk being halfway around the world when we were so close to peace." Albright's description of the episode, though less charitable, confirmed that the "scheduling chaos created by crisis-driven negotiations on the Middle East" killed the North Korea initiative. Clinton left the North Korea issue hanging as Bush took office, and Washington-Pyongyang relations gradually deteriorated.[54]

In fairness to Clinton, it is impossible to know whether a trip to North Korea would have produced the comprehensive agreement he sought. The negotiations would have been hurried, with little room for error. Additionally, the incoming administration had staked out a hawkish position on North Korea, and Clinton might have feared that Bush would disavow rapprochement (though his memoirs state that this was not the case). Still, in retrospect, it is hard to escape the impression that Clinton would have been better off pursuing reconciliation with North Korea in December 2000 than continuing his already struggling quest for peace in the Middle East. And at the time, Clinton's advisers advocated just that course. The president's top aides on the peace process concluded prior to the Washington summit that an Arab-Israeli deal was unlikely (Ross, the expert on the subject, had "grave doubts" that a settlement remained feasible), whereas Berger and Albright were considerably more optimistic about a breakthrough with Kim. Clinton later conceded that he had chosen poorly, telling Albright that he "wished he had taken the chance of going to North Korea."[55]

The missed chance with Pyongyang demonstrated a problem underlying much of Clinton's second-term diplomacy. The president never established clearly delineated hierarchies of importance with regard to his various goals; instead, he simply listed a number of objectives without indicating the relative weight attached to each. Thus, there was little organizational structure to Clinton's foreign policy. The president had no overall strategy to guide his expenditure of time, energy, and resources, and the direction of U.S. policy ended up reflecting the president's personal inclinations rather than a systematic assessment of means and ends. (Political adviser Sidney Blumenthal attributed Clinton's fascination with the peace process to the president's belief that he was "a legatee, a political son, of the murdered Yitzhak Rabin, whom he revered above all other leaders," and he noted that Clinton kept a number of private shrines to Rabin following the Israeli leader's death in 1995.)[56] In this particular instance, Clinton's own optimism and attachment to the peace process overrode the counsel of his top aides and their assessment that reconciliation with North Korea, however tenuous the prospect, was more likely than an Arafat-Barak deal. Despite the obviously fading possibility of an agreement and the fact that events elsewhere demanded presidential attention, the Middle East remained Clinton's primary focus.

In a sense, this preoccupation with the Middle East seems reasonable. The Arab-Israeli conflict undoubtedly complicated U.S. diplomacy in the Middle East, and in the light of later events, Clinton's efforts to extinguish a major source of tension between Washington and the Muslim world appear almost prescient. On the other side of this argument, the connection between terrorism and the Arab-Israeli conflict was not nearly as clear in the 1990s as it has become in the aftermath of 9/11. Even now, there is considerable debate over what effect the resolution of this dispute—as opposed to rethinking the U.S. relationship to Saudi Arabia, Kuwait, and other repressive Middle Eastern regimes, for instance—would have on jihadism. One Clinton-era official has argued that the president's depth of engagement in the peace process actually prevented him from attacking the source of Middle Eastern terrorism—the unwillingness of U.S. allies in the region to permit political and social liberalization.[57]

Whatever the importance of easing Arab-Israeli tensions, the fundamental fact remains that Clinton's immersion in the peace process was detrimental to his overall foreign policy. The issue was not so much his involvement in the negotiations but rather the extent of his involvement and the degree to which it undermined other initiatives. With U.S.-Russia relations at their post–Cold War nadir, the Balkans a mess, China's role in U.S. policy uncertain, fast track languishing in Congress, and trouble continually brewing in the Persian Gulf, Clinton's devotion to the peace process meant a lack of top-level involvement in matters that were arguably just as important.

Albright had recognized this dilemma early on, discussing with Clinton "how much time Middle Eastern negotiations consume" and the resulting potential for distraction. During her intensive mediation of the Oslo process in 1997 and 1998, in fact, Albright realized that shuttling back and forth between Washington and the Middle East and poring over the details of the discussions were not necessarily conducive to the effective management of a foreign policy that comprised a wide range of pressing issues. Being the arbiter of an Arab-Israeli peace was a worthy task, she said in 1997, but one that threatened to dominate her agenda to the exclusion of equally significant questions. "The United States's responsibilities are so large," she said in exasperation after a particularly unproductive trip to the region. "I can't be occupied with this full time."[58]

Yet it was precisely this unwillingness to impose limits on the U.S. commitment to Middle East peace that characterized Clinton's second term. Looking back, Albright conceded as much and noted that this tendency was an unfortunate by-product of the administration's approach to foreign policy. Clinton and his advisers tackled a broad range of issues without attempting a firm conception of commitments and resources, and U.S. diplomacy grew discombobulated and, in the case of North Korea, ineffective as a result. "Because I was interested in so much," Albright later wrote, "I was.insufficiently ruthless in setting priorities." Not wanting "any part of the world to feel that America was indifferent," the administration was prone to overcommitting in certain areas at the expense of others. In the case of North Korea, this characteristic of Clinton's diplomacy compromised his efforts to maintain and extend a stable international status quo.[59]

Doing Everything

A less visible consequence of this approach to foreign affairs occurred in the realm of defense management. Touted as reformers when they took power in 1993, Clinton and his secretary of defense, Les Aspin, had promised to cut the defense budget and remake the military to better fit the post–Cold War environment. In early 1993, the two called on the services to cut spending by $60 billion over the next four years and pledged to make the military more efficient by slicing its overall size by 400,000 troops and eliminating "redundancies" in defense systems. Clinton encountered resistance early on, however, as his attempt to reform military policy on homosexuals and his clashes with Colin Powell over Somalia and Bosnia undermined presidential prestige at the Pentagon and stalled the reform program.[60]

The situation did not change noticeably for the rest of Clinton's presidency. Although the defense budget fell somewhat, the cutbacks were not as drastic as the reformers had hoped. In 1999, Clinton actually increased military spending by $112 billion, a hike that was to take effect over the next five years.[61]

There were several reasons why the budget did not shrink as much as Clinton and Aspin had planned. In a sense, the fault was less the president's than the world's. With the international security landscape having diversified considerably since 1989, it was difficult to identify expendable weapons programs. Russia and China were still potential rivals, so the United States had to retain a healthy nuclear force. Regional conflicts such as the Gulf War loomed large in Pentagon planning, so tanks and troops remained essential. With Clinton sporadically authorizing peacekeeping missions, capabilities for this type of intervention were also imperative. And, with all these roles so prominent, the armed forces could not part with the expensive airlift and sealift equipment that was vital to its forward presence and speed of deployment. As General John Shalikashvili, chairman of the Joint Chiefs of Staff, explained in 1995, "We are, in fact, in an era in which we are going to have to retain a very powerful and very ready military force."[62]

The unpredictability of the international environment was also an argument against dramatic cutbacks. Pentagon officials were quick to point out that they could not possibly foresee all the challenges of a volatile world. Accordingly, the United States had to prepare not only for present threats but also for those that had not yet arisen. For the first time, "uncertainty" became a factor in the defense budget. "We are going to have to remain ready for the unexpected," Shalikashvili argued at one budget hearing. The notion rankled reformers, and one spendthrift congressman asked, "And how many tanks does uncertainty have?"[63]

Yet the difficulty of reforming the military was not due solely to conditions in the international arena. Clinton's failure to prioritize among objectives proved equally pernicious to the process. Because the president did not define a clear mission for U.S. defense forces, the Pentagon was in the both enviable and unenviable position of having to prepare to meet a variety of threats without being able to center its efforts on a single one. This was problematic because it magnified the complexity of training and strategic planning. It was beneficial for the services because they could point to any number of contingencies to justify budget requests. As Perry said when defending the budget in 1995, "Our strategy calls for a force structure that will be capable of fighting two nearly simultaneous major regional conflicts, *and conducting a wide range of other military operations*." Cohen took the same view. Military outlays, he said, must be sufficient to allow the United States to "respond to the full spectrum of crises." The 1990s had seen a broadening of the defense mission, he argued in 2000. "Our soldiers can't simply be peacekeepers, because you can go from peacekeeping very quickly up to peace enforcement to a major conflict in a very short period of time. So our soldiers, sailors, airmen, Marines, all of our services, must be trained to do everything."[64]

Doing everything also meant getting everything, and military spending remained high throughout the 1990s. The overall numbers dropped somewhat from the profligacy of the Cold War era, but this was attributable to reforms in acquisition techniques and development procedures rather than a diminishment of purchases. Perry's innovative management tactics, which exploited the greater efficiency of commercial producers on a wide range of defense-related goods, saved billions of dollars that the Department of Defense used to offset what budget cuts there were. Far from retrenching, the Pentagon simply became more efficient.[65]

The president's lack of a defining defense policy also hampered efforts to remake the structure of U.S. forces. With Clinton largely abandoning his efforts to give the military a new mission for the twenty-first century, the composition of the armed forces remained much the same as it had been at the outset of the decade. "What's wrong with this picture?" Cohen asked late in Clinton's presidency. In 1999, the U.S. military "drove M-1 tanks, flew F-15 and F-16 fighters and F-117 bombers, and sailed Nimitz-class carriers. They were organized into unified and specified commands, governed primarily by the Goldwater-Nichols Department of Defense Reorganization Act of 1986." In 1989, by comparison, "with the Soviet Union still standing and the Gulf War soon to begin—the picture was strangely similar." American soldiers "drove M-1 tanks, flew F-15 and F-16 fighters and F-117 bombers, and sailed Nimitz-class carriers. They too were organized into unified and specified commands, governed primarily by the Goldwater-Nichols act." In other words, the post–Cold War military differed little from the Cold War military. When U.S. policy lacked a singular purpose to drive bureaucratic change, institutional inertia and power went unchallenged.[66]

The dangers and disappointments of relations with Russia and North Korea, the Middle East peace process, and defense reform reflected an emergent truth of the post–Cold War era. For American diplomats, it was not sufficient to simply identify the goals of U.S. policy. This was necessary, to be sure, but when Washington's objectives spanned the globe and the diplomatic spectrum, there had to be a solid rationale for how the various issues fit together in the larger conception of U.S. statecraft. Clinton was not entirely unsuccessful in providing this connecting logic—his status quo strategy was, in theory, well matched to the post–Cold War world—but his answer to the problem was incomplete. Preventing new threats was clear enough as an overall principle, but as Clinton's experience showed, the outlook grew murkier when one delved into the relationships among specific policies and the relationships between those policies and the broader picture. Without some scheme of organization and prioritization, the management and practice of foreign policy became disjointed.

Clinton's struggles in this regard did not condemn his entire foreign policy to failure, contrary to what some of his critics asserted. In individual cases, Clinton did quite well. Steering NATO expansion through four years of roadblocks took great skill, as did holding that alliance and a domestic consensus together long enough to end the wars in Bosnia and Kosovo. Clinton's progress on international commerce was also notable (see chapter 5), and he came closer to a comprehensive peace in the Middle East than any president before or since.

The problem with Clinton's foreign policy was not his specific initiatives but his inability to manage their intersection. Like the president's foreign policy team, American statecraft was a puzzle that had to fit together. At a time when Washington's interests were so broad and numerous, it was inevitable that these goals would rub against one another. The administration occasionally seemed close to grasping this reality, such as when Albright objected to devoting so much attention to the peace process, but it ultimately failed to resolve this dilemma. Flexibility turned to contradiction, diversity to distraction. In the end, these problems undermined Clinton's achievements, leaving important issues unsettled and lessening the overall efficacy of his diplomacy.[67]

This failure touched on one of the essential difficulties of conducting foreign policy in the 1990s, one that neither Clinton nor the coherence devotees seemed to fully comprehend. The sheer complexity of the world defied attempts to define a new bumper-sticker strategy, yet the United States still needed the logical and practical guidance that such a policy would provide. (Clinton was right about the first part of that statement; his critics had the second part correct.) Though misleading and prone to oversimplification, bumper stickers could still be useful in offering a strategic reference point and a means of internal prioritization that might allow U.S. leaders to avoid the type of problems that plagued Clinton. The converse was also true, of course (containment had created as many problems as it had solved), but in the late 1990s, the benefits of simplicity seemed most apparent—and most lacking. Clinton may have thought that the coherence paradigm had been discredited, but at times, his approach looked little more efficacious. Having perceived the need to diversify his foreign policy efforts, Clinton had allowed the pendulum to swing too far from its Cold War position. Surely there was some midpoint between the current and former settings, but as of 2000, the balance had yet to be found. At the end of Clinton's presidency, he was no closer to cracking the riddle that had now defined U.S. policy for a decade.

8

The Politics of Foreign Policy

In late 1997, Strobe Talbott addressed the question of whether the lack of a rhetorical paradigm in foreign policy might complicate the administration's attempts to justify its individual diplomatic initiatives. If not motivated by a clear threat or compelling goal, he acknowledged, Americans tended to lose interest in foreign affairs. "Without doubt, there is, in the American body politic, a nerve of isolationism," he conceded. Many of Clinton's advisers worried "that the nation would have trouble making the transition from an era in which the main purpose of American foreign policy could be expressed, literally, on a bumper sticker—'Contain Communism' or 'Deter Soviet Aggression'—to one in which it takes at least a paragraph to explain the purpose of American foreign policy." "The more we thought about how that paragraph should read," he said, "the more we worried that it would lose readers—and support—out in the heartland." Talbott downplayed this concern in public, but it was hard to escape the impression that the mere act of addressing the possibility meant that he feared it to be true.[1]

Talbott did not want to be a prophet, but he ended up as one nonetheless. During Clinton's second term, while the complexity of international affairs was giving the president's statecraft one beating, the realities of American politics were handing it another. Indeed, if the diplomatic consequences of Clinton's approach to foreign policy had been troubling to the president, the political ramifications must have been downright scary. By failing to enunciate an easily understandable expression of U.S. policy, Clinton forfeited the benefits of moral and rhetorical clarity. This absence of a persuasive rhetorical frame encouraged dissent and noncompliance from domestic observers and eventually proved subversive to both the particulars and the generalities of Clinton's diplomacy.

Between 1997 and 2000, the political effects of incoherence were twofold. First, a policy as variegated as Clinton's was bound to lack an easily identifiable moral center. Although Clinton made no pretense of abandoning the moral high ground perpetually claimed by U.S. officials, his diplomacy as a whole was missing the sort of obvious moral component that had made containment so attractive. Certain of Clinton's goals seemed ethically sound, but others entailed subjugating moral concerns to international realities. By 1997, the overall moral tenor of U.S. policy that had prevailed for fifty years had weakened, and it had been replaced by a largely amoral pragmatism that, in some cases, made little pretense of serving ideals such as human rights.[2] The result was a growing public discontent with certain tenets of presidential diplomacy. When strong enough, these grievances intruded on Clinton's policy, forcing him to compromise his own objectives for the sake of ethical purity and public approval.

Second, as Talbott had predicted, the absence of an apparent rationale for U.S. involvement abroad left the administration's individual policies vulnerable to challenge. With Clinton unable to claim convincingly that his efforts were in support of some greater good, opponents of the president's worldview successfully attacked many of his more controversial policies. Judged solely on their individual merits, rather than by their service to an overall goal, Clinton's initiatives were unable to withstand sustained assault from conservative critics determined to reverse what they saw as the soft-headed multilateralism of the 1990s. With increasing frequency, Clinton discovered that his foreign policy program was open to question.

Combined, the rhetorical shortcomings of Clinton's strategy brought about a significant diminution of his power in foreign affairs. Moral clarity and an agreed-on end point had been the wellsprings of Cold War consensus; as these virtues disappeared, so did the consensus. New disagreement emerged over the direction of U.S. diplomacy, and Clinton often found himself on the losing end of the battles that resulted. Senator Jesse Helms (R-N.C.) and like-minded conservatives capitalized on the lack of a foreign policy consensus to defeat many of Clinton's diplomatic efforts and weaken White House control of foreign policy. In the process, they repudiated the internationalist trend established by Clinton and, before him, Bush, forging a new direction in U.S. involvement abroad. When added to the emergence of a new global threat environment, the resultant impulse gave the United States' international posture a distinctly unilateral look at the end of the twentieth century.

Rights and Wrongs

In early 1997, Madeleine Albright addressed the rhetorical conundrum of the post–Cold War era. The threats of the present "are much harder to explain to people," she said. "I think we all had 50 years of dividing life into the Communists and us, and it was much easier to explain." Clarity had been abundant during the Cold War but was no longer so plentiful.[3]

As Albright hinted, the job of justifying particular policies had grown decidedly more difficult since the end of the superpower conflict. This was especially true in areas where moral principles were at stake. After 1995, Clinton dropped some of the moralistic rhetoric that had characterized the 1992 campaign and his strategy of enlargement. His second-term "framework for American leadership" contained the requisite references to democracy and the rule of law, to be sure, and conceded little in terms of moral righteousness (Albright regularly referred to the United States as the "indispensable nation"), but the strategy also recognized that the complexity of the international environment precluded judging nations or policies solely on ethical grounds. In other words, dictators who abused their citizens might be abhorrent, but they might also be necessary partners in protecting against the new threats of the 1990s.

The most prominent example of this mix of strategic necessity and moral discomfiture was Clinton's relationship with China. In 1997, Clinton continued his efforts to engage the Asian power. China was at a crossroads between full participation in the international community and a return to isolation, the administration believed. "China is at an important point in its rich history," argued Undersecretary of State Roy Tarnoff, "with some forces pulling inward toward nationalism and some forces pulling outward toward integration." To ensure that China made the right choice, the United States needed to promote an expanded economic and political dialogue with Beijing and avoid hostile actions that would evoke suspicion. Cooperation with China was also vital to U.S. security interests in the Pacific. The Chinese government had recently taken an active role in four-party talks with North Korea, a process that Clinton termed the "only realistic avenue to a lasting peace." Finally, trade with Beijing was crucial. As Bush and Clinton had previously discovered, restricting economic relations would hurt the United States as much as China.[4]

At the outset of his second term, Clinton had a firm agenda for U.S.-China relations. He hoped to support China's entry into the World Trade Organization in return for Beijing's help in lowering barriers to U.S. trade and ending missile and nuclear exports to Iran and Pakistan. As in 1994, pursuing this "strategic partnership" entailed limiting criticism of Beijing's human rights practices. According to Albright, the relationship with China was "multifaceted" and would not be contingent on progress (or the lack thereof) in any one aspect of Sino-American intercourse. "For years, the debate in Washington linking trade to human rights in China has raged," she said in April 1997, "and for years, it has failed to produce progress in China." To forge better relations with China, Albright believed, it was necessary to highlight areas of common interest and minimize divisive issues.[5]

This aspect of engagement drew fire from human rights advocates, who claimed that Clinton had forsaken America's moral heritage in his search for profit. Gary Bauer, head of the Family Research Council and future presidential candidate, was appalled by Clinton's emphasis on trade over human rights. China policy, he declared, was "about whether America's most deeply held values will be at the center of our foreign policy or whether the Chinese are right when they refer to us as a money bags democracy." Helms, chair of the Senate Foreign Relations Committee and a frequent Clinton antagonist, caustically predicted a "cave-in" to Chinese obstinacy on human rights. Public sentiment accorded with the views of these critics; 59 percent of Americans thought that taking a strong stand on human rights was more important than maintaining good relations with China.[6]

Although Clinton had no desire for a confrontation with Beijing, domestic disapproval of engagement was sufficient to give him pause. Facing intense criticism from conservatives, Clinton reluctantly elevated human rights to the forefront of China policy. In early 1997, U.S. diplomats introduced a UN resolution condemning China's human rights practices. "With others if possible, but alone if we must, the United States will continue to shine the spotlight on human rights violations in China," Albright declared.[7] Alone was how it turned out; the initiative died when Italy, Germany, France, and Japan refused to cooperate. Aside from isolating the United States, the resolution put U.S.-China relations on hold for several months, with no real progress made on North Korea, WTO accession, or military exports to Iran and Pakistan.

Fortunately for Clinton, these other issues were too important to both Washington and Beijing to permit human rights—a subject that neither side wanted to talk about—to chill the relationship for long. Jiang Zemin saw an economic partnership with the United States as integral to the growth of the Chinese economy, and he viewed diplomatic cooperation as a means of elevating China to great power status in the eyes of international observers. China's increasingly influential business community was desirous of WTO membership and vocally lobbied for strong relations with the United States. In late 1997, Jiang visited Washington, agreeing to halt nuclear exports to Iran in return for Clinton's pledge to allow U.S. firms to sell reactor technology to China. In 1998, Clinton withstood domestic criticism and chose not to introduce another anti-China resolution at the United Nations, reflecting both the improved state of relations and the reality of U.S. isolation on the human rights issue. Traveling to Beijing in mid-1998, Clinton made only modest progress on the WTO issue but salvaged the appearance of a successful summit when Jiang agreed to debate the president on human rights issues on live television. In early 1999, Foreign Minister Zhu Rongji came to Washington for discussions with Clinton, and the administration was optimistic about a deal on WTO entry. After stalling in his first term, U.S.-China relations appeared to be progressing in Clinton's second.[8]

As Zhu arrived, however, domestic factors again intruded on China policy. In early 1999, a House investigation uncovered evidence that Chinese agents had penetrated the U.S. nuclear program, gaining knowledge of "every currently deployed thermonuclear warhead in the U.S. intercontinental ballistic missile arsenal." Coming on the heels of allegations that Clinton had accepted large campaign donations from Chinese contributors in 1996, the revelations created an intensely anti-China mood on the eve of the summit.[9]

Faced with such damning critiques, Clinton had little choice but to reject a Chinese offer that would have resolved (as one official estimated) 95 percent of outstanding U.S. grievances against Beijing's import and investment practices. National Security Adviser Sandy Berger supported the deal, but Treasury Secretary Robert Rubin warned that, given the high level of anti-China sentiment, Congress might reject the agreement. Bowing to this concern, Clinton rejected Zhu's proposal. Speaking to reporters, Zhu bluntly explained why the two sides had failed to reach an agreement despite their overwhelming common interest in cooperation. "If you want to hear some honest words," he said, "then I should say that now the problem does not lie with this big difference or big gap but lies with the political atmosphere." The failure of the negotiations was a serious blow to Clinton's hope for progress in the Sino-American relationship, which suffered another setback when U.S. bombers accidentally struck the Chinese embassy in Belgrade in May 1999.[10]

Once again, however, the commonality of interests between the two countries was too great to ignore, and in late 1999, Chinese and U.S. negotiators finalized the WTO deal. The pact allowed increased foreign ownership of Chinese companies and significantly reduced agricultural and industrial tariffs in return for U.S. support of China's WTO bid. Despite the economic benefits of the arrangement, Clinton faced a serious challenge in defending the pact at home. Congressional approval was necessary to give China the permanent normal trade status (PNTS) required for WTO entry, and many legislators were still upset about the nuclear espionage and Clinton's refusal to hammer Beijing on human rights. In a concession to the hawks, Clinton reintroduced in early 2000 a UN resolution condemning Beijing's human rights practices. Clinton's trade initiative received a boost when Republican presidential candidate George W. Bush supported PNTS, and the House and Senate eventually approved the measure.[11]

Yet the success of the WTO deal obscured the fact that U.S.-

China relations were on no firmer footing than at the outset of Clinton's presidency. The president's repeated concessions to human rights advocates, necessary to enact his trade program, ensured that this issue remained a sticking point. Criticism of engagement forced Clinton to emphasize issues that were sure to antagonize Beijing and delay the WTO deal he had sought since the beginning of his second term. Arms sales to Taiwan, another problem that Clinton had long hoped to minimize, also hampered Washington-Beijing cooperation, and the embassy incident had incited anti-U.S. protests in several Chinese cities. Chinese officials viewed U.S. military action in Kosovo and the Middle East suspiciously, worrying that Washington sought to impose its will on the world. All told, Clinton's talk of engagement and his ability to find common ground on trade issues could not hide the reality that China remained a strategic question mark in U.S. policy. Perhaps more important, engagement was a domestic loser. In the 2000 election, Al Gore refrained from discussing China, and Bush labeled Beijing a "strategic competitor." Despite Clinton's strides on trade, U.S. views of China (and China policy) remained largely negative.[12]

For the most part, this hostility stemmed from a perception that China policy no longer embodied American moral principles. A *Washington Post* editorial showed that not even progress in Sino-American relations could mollify this discomfort. Though generally supportive of engagement, the editors were ambivalent about the WTO deal, terming it a "vote for greed in which the nightmare of lost sales mattered more than the crushing of rights and lives in a country far away." On the other side of the political spectrum, conservative William Buckley agreed. Clinton's China policy, he wrote, made Americans feel as though they were "abandoning [their] ethical reserves."[13]

As these critiques suggest, opposition to Clinton's China policy was often based less on a calculation of its costs and benefits than on the uneasy feeling that engagement equated to condoning Beijing's repressive policies. And this fact pointed to a gaping rhetorical hole in Clinton's second-term diplomacy. In dealing with the economic and geopolitical realities of the 1990s, the administration occasionally went in the company of brutes. There was nothing new about this fact of diplomatic life; the United States had supported dictators and other distasteful characters during World War II and the Cold War. In these instances, however, the ultimate end of U.S. policy enjoyed such great moral clarity that unsavory means were acceptable to the public audience. China policy from 1972 to 1989 was a good example of this phenomenon. During these years, U.S. presidents created consensus on the need to engage a morally repugnant regime in Beijing by claiming that good relations with China were the key to containing the Soviet Union. By 1996, however, there was no longer a greater strategic or moral end to cite as justification for treating with tyrants. With this moral counterweight gone, public commentators became ambivalent about cooperation with repressive governments. As shown by the reaction to Clinton's stance on China, Americans needed to feel good about their foreign policy; when they could not, they rebelled. Until a president could identify a greater moral good to make up for his inevitable dealings with unlikable regimes, foreign policy would remain vulnerable at home.

The Post–Post–Cold War World

Even as relations with China illustrated the difficulties of conducting foreign policy in the post–Cold War era, there were signs that this period was drawing to a close. It had never been quite clear what the post–Cold War era was, as its name was drawn from a negative characteristic rather than a positive one. Nonetheless, there had been certain prominent hallmarks. If the Gulf War, which inaugurated the period, was any clue, the post–Cold War world featured increased multilateral cooperation made possible by the depolarization of international politics. Between 1990 and 1995, Bush and Clinton used this new multilateralism to win UN approval for intervention in the Persian Gulf, Somalia, Bosnia, and Haiti. By 1997, however, the original international coalition of the 1990s had begun to fray over developments in the very region where the post–Cold War era had been born. A year later, the United States was nearly isolated in Gulf affairs, signaling that the age of multilateralism was at an end.

As Clinton's second term commenced, there were already signs of discord among the Gulf War allies. The trouble started after the 1996 Kurdish crisis embarrassed Clinton and prompted calls for tougher action against Saddam Hussein. Reviewing the crisis, CIA director

John Deutch predicted that "Saddam will continue to challenge the coalition" in coming years and warned that only a change of government would stabilize the region. Clinton initiated a policy review at the end of the year. A more hawkish viewpoint emerged, in no small part because Berger and Albright, recently elevated to national security adviser and secretary of state, respectively, were considerably keener to overthrow Hussein than their predecessors had been. Encouraged by a group of senators, congressmen, academics, and former officials, the administration resolved to make a concerted effort at "regime change." In March 1997, Albright, citing "overwhelming" evidence that "Saddam Hussein's intentions will never be peaceful," openly called for a "change in Iraq's government" and affirmed that the United States would keep Iraq "trapped in a strategic box" until this happened.[14]

As in 1995, though, there were limitations to this strategy. There was little domestic enthusiasm for the strong measures required to depose the Iraqi leader, so Clinton confined his efforts to modest support for opposition groups inside and outside Iraq. The president himself was lukewarm to regime change, fearing after his first-term experience that Iraq might again become a political and diplomatic liability. A third problem was that, by 1997, international support for a stronger stance against Hussein was almost nonexistent. Iraq owed billions of dollars to French and Russian companies, which made Paris and Moscow eager to do away with the sanctions that prevented Iraq from selling oil and paying up. In addition, as NATO expansion proceeded, Boris Yeltsin sought closer ties with Iraq, hoping to win influence in the Middle East that would counteract U.S. assertiveness elsewhere.[15]

Consequently, France and Russia moved repeatedly to soften the UN stance toward Iraq. When Clinton sought to punish Iraqi interference with UN weapons inspections in October 1997, Moscow and Paris refused to follow the U.S. line. The Russian delegation blocked a resolution that would have authorized the coalition to use force if Iraq failed to comply with UN demands. The U.S. position had deteriorated substantially, and the October crisis passed only when Russian negotiators brokered a deal allowing UN inspectors to reenter the country. When Hussein again crossed the United Nations in January 1998, the Clinton administration found itself isolated once more. Most Arab states refused to publicly back Clinton's threat to initiate air strikes, and Saudi Arabia would not allow its bases to be used as a staging ground for the bombing. This time, it took the mediation of UN Secretary-General Kofi Annan to resolve the deadlock. All told, it was another discouraging episode for Washington. "The [Gulf War] consensus has broken down," admitted one official.[16]

Hoping to rebuild support for an anti-Hussein policy, the administration took a circumspect position toward Baghdad in 1998. After another policy review found that a full invasion would be necessary to topple the Iraqi president, Clinton de-emphasized regime change and took a low profile on Iraq, waiting for a grievous sanctions violation that would demonstrate Hussein's intractability. Albright also downplayed the idea of overthrowing Hussein, arguing that this "would require a far greater commitment of military force, and a far greater risk to American lives, than is currently needed to contain the threat Saddam poses." When Hussein again obstructed UN inspectors in August 1998, Clinton chose not to respond, hoping that the Iraqi leader would blunder into a larger violation.[17] The strategy paid dividends in October and November 1998, when Hussein challenged inspections once again. This time, France and Russia backed Clinton's threat of military action, and the Iraqi president retreated at the last minute.

This instance of cooperation was in fact the last gasp of the Gulf War coalition. When Hussein committed further outrages in December 1998, the National Security Council unanimously opted for air strikes, and Clinton did not bother to go to the UN Security Council for approval.[18] Operation Desert Fox, which entailed four days of attacks against Iraqi targets, went forward with only British assistance and elicited disapproval from other Security Council members. "You can't do anything you want against any country," Yevgeny Primakov told Gore. "It's this approach that leads to global destabilization." As the coalition crumbled, it became clear that any further action against Hussein would represent collaboration between Washington and London rather than a truly multilateral project.[19]

Hussein's December challenge also pushed many domestic observers toward a revival of support for regime change. In early 1998,

Iraqi exiles and neoconservative foreign policy experts had testified before the Senate Foreign Relations Committee in support of more aggressive efforts. Ahmed Chalabi, an Iraqi National Congress leader, made an impassioned plea for U.S. assistance. "Give the Iraqi National Congress a base, protected from Saddam's tanks, give us the temporary support we need to feed and house and care for the liberated population, and we will give you a free Iraq, an Iraq free of weapons of mass destruction and a free market Iraq," he promised. Rand analyst (and future Bush administration adviser) Zalmay Khalilzad was bluntly optimistic about ousting Hussein: "He can be overthrown." Tempted by these assessments, Congress passed the Iraqi Liberation Act, which committed the United States to regime change and required the president to increase support to seven anti-Hussein groups.[20]

Clinton was reluctant to support the bill. Regime change was impracticable and would further alienate the Europeans, he feared. Such a policy "cannot be done by imposing a new regime by military force from without," warned Undersecretary of Defense Walter Slocombe. "Nor, in our judgment, can it be done by encouraging an internal insurrection before the conditions exist that would make it possible for such an uprising to succeed." After debacles in 1995 and 1996, the CIA was reluctant to propose any but the most cautious operations in Iraq. The Iraqi opposition was in bad shape; NSC adviser Kenneth Pollack termed the situation "a mess." Through 1998, Clinton advocated keeping the containment policy in place. The process of destroying the regime through quiet but consistent pressure would be long, his advisers conceded, but it was the least costly method of removing Hussein. "Containment doesn't bring about a decisive resolution quickly," said one official. "It's unsatisfying and ungratifying by its nature. But 40 years of containing the Soviets in the cold war paid off. You've got to be patient."[21]

Americans were in no mood to wait forty years. In 1999 and 2000, George W. Bush campaigned on a platform urging regime change, and a number of midlevel advisers within the administration also moved toward a more hawkish position. In early 1999, Clinton halfheartedly endorsed the Iraqi Liberation Act. Although the president had no real enthusiasm for regime change, fearing that a serious confrontation with Iraq would detract from his efforts to mediate the Arab-Israeli peace process, he publicly backed Congress's stance. In March, administration officials explicitly acknowledged regime change as a goal. Clinton made no meaningful attempt to topple Hussein, but the mere perception that the U.S. position had hardened hastened the collapse of the Gulf War coalition. French officials proposed to end the sanctions, charging that "the embargo has become the wrong tool to achieve the goals of the Security Council." Days later, Moscow joined Paris in calling for termination of the sanctions.[22]

The multilateral mood of the Gulf War was gone, and the United States now confronted Hussein without significant European or Arab support. In part, this isolation resulted from an honest clash of interests over Iraq; in part, it stemmed from the efforts of American hawks to reorient U.S. strategy (if only superficially) in a manner that was sure to annoy the allies. Combined, these factors destroyed international consensus on Iraq and left the United States largely alone in its standoff with Saddam Hussein.

A War on Terrorism?

Iraq policy was only one manifestation of this tendency to go it alone. In 1998, Clinton also took unilateral military action against Afghanistan and Sudan in response to the bombings of U.S. embassies in Kenya and Tanzania.

The evolution of counterterrorism policy under Clinton had been a long and disjointed process. In June 1995, Clinton signed PDD 39, which focused on the danger that terrorists might acquire weapons of mass destruction (WMD). The directive assigned "highest priority" to denying advanced weapons capabilities to terrorist groups, stating that such an outcome would be "unacceptable" to the United States. After the Khobar Towers bombing in 1996, preventing attacks against U.S. interests became one of several priorities of Clinton's second term. State-sponsored terrorism "poses an enormous danger" to American lives, property, and security, warned Toby Gati in 1997.[23]

In mid-1998, at the urging of Berger and NSC staffer Richard Clarke, Clinton considered centralizing counterterrorism operations under a "national coordinator." In the absence of an obvious threat, however, the bureaucracy was slow to mobilize. The involved agencies resisted this proposed dilution of their powers, and by the time Clinton approved the measure, it had been substantially weakened. During this same period, the CIA considered kidnapping known terrorist organizer Osama bin Laden from his sanctuary in Afghanistan. The Saudi construction heir, U.S. intelligence believed, was a chief source of "financial support to militants actively opposed to moderate Islamic governments and the West." "Sooner or later," warned one NSC report, "bin Ladin will attack U.S. interests, perhaps using WMD." In the end, though, the administration rejected the CIA plan, fearing that it would cause extensive "collateral damage" and might expose the White House to criticism if it failed. Terrorism was a rising threat, but its profile was not yet high enough to convince Clinton to take stronger measures.[24]

The missing sense of urgency was provided in early August when terrorists bombed U.S. embassies in Kenya and Tanzania, killing hundreds. Clinton immediately suspected that bin Laden was the culprit. George Tenet at the CIA and Albright pushed for a military response, agreeing that the situation presented "a real occasion for decisive action" against terrorists and their state sponsors. On August 12, Tenet told Clinton that there was no question that al Qaeda (bin Laden's group) was behind the bombings. "This one is a slam dunk," he said. Upon learning that bin Laden planned to meet with several lieutenants at a camp in Afghanistan on August 20, Clinton tentatively approved plans for an attack.[25]

Clinton ruled out using ground troops or manned planes for the assault because of the risk to U.S. pilots and soldiers, and he settled on cruise missiles as the weapon of choice. He also declined to work through the Security Council in executing the reprisals. "When there's an imminent threat, you don't call the judge," explained one official. After hurried diplomatic efforts failed to convince Afghan leaders to expel bin Laden, the attacks went forward on August 20, with Clinton consulting only Britain and Pakistan (from which overflight rights were needed) in advance.[26]

Despite U.S. efforts to portray the attacks as a response to a new type of global threat, it was this turn away from multilateralism that international leaders seized on as the most salient aspect of the incident. Clinton's decision not to involve the United Nations elicited much foreign criticism, which only mounted when a "chemical weapons factory" in Sudan, added to the target list at the last moment, turned out to be a pharmaceutical plant. Yeltsin called the attacks "indecent," Italy's prime minister called for fighting terrorism with "political solutions" rather than military action, and the Chinese Foreign Ministry released a statement that declaimed U.S. unilateralism and advocated handling the matter through the United Nations.[27]

Ignoring this adverse reaction, the administration unequivocally defended its actions. The attacks against Afghanistan and Sudan "should not be seen simply as a response to the Aug. 7 bombings in Kenya and Tanzania, but as the long-term, fundamental way in which the United States intends to fight the forces of terror," Secretary of Defense William Cohen stated. "As always, we will work with our friends around the world when we can, but we are also ready to act unilaterally when circumstances require." Clinton too warned that "our efforts against terrorism cannot and will not end with this strike," and he promised to take "extraordinary steps" if necessary to protect U.S. security. The fight against terrorism, Clinton made clear, would not be impeded by the diplomatic trappings that had complicated Iraq policy.[28]

The growth of the terrorist threat led some officials to recommend reprioritizing U.S. diplomatic and military efforts around this rising challenge. Clarke, the White House's top terrorism adviser, envisioned a series of strikes against bin Laden's Afghan training network. The goal, Clarke wrote, was to "immediately eliminate any significant threat to Americans" from bin Laden. Even after the embassy bombings, though, there was little official support for such costly measures. Deputy National Security Adviser James Steinberg argued that the plan entailed "little benefit, lots of blowback against bomb-happy U.S." Clinton's military advisers also consistently opposed the plan, fearing that a campaign against bin Laden would be ineffective and expose U.S. forces to substantial risk. The administration rejected other initiatives as well. In December 1998, after U.S. intelligence pinpointed bin Laden's whereabouts, the NSC opted against a strike, fearing high civilian casualties.[29]

These concerns defeated Clarke's efforts to raise counterterrorism's prominence in U.S. policy. Although bin Laden presented a danger to American interests, the challenge did not seem so great as to necessitate the broad refocusing of foreign policy that some officials had recommended. There would be costs to a muscular effort to eradicate al Qaeda, and until the threat was more immediate and mortal, policy makers hesitated to pay them.

Even if Clinton had been inclined to make antiterrorism the new central theme of U.S. policy, he would have been hard-pressed to do so. The strikes against Afghanistan and Sudan coincided with the publication of Clinton's grand jury testimony regarding Paula Jones and Monica Lewinsky. This latest "bimbo eruption" dominated news coverage between August 1998 and February 1999, when the Senate failed to convict Clinton of perjury and obstruction of justice, the two charges for which he had been impeached. When Clinton called for the air strikes in August, in fact, more than a few commentators alleged that he was merely trying to distract public attention from his own licentiousness. Sensitive to these attacks, Clinton could hardly launch a new crusade in foreign policy when he was already under suspicion of insincerity. Moreover, with the hostility between Clinton and the Republican opposition at a historic high, the political capital needed for such an endeavor was in short supply. Counterterrorism remained simply one aspect of an exceedingly diverse foreign policy.[30]

Even so, Clinton's response did have ramifications for the basic orientation of U.S. policy. Combined with the decision to intervene in Kosovo without UN approval in early 1999, Clinton's reaction to the embassy bombings signaled a degree of disenchantment with multilateral institutions and an increased willingness to use force independently. The frustrations of coalition diplomacy toward Iraq set Clinton on the path toward unilateralism, and the emergence of a new threat in the form of state-sponsored terrorism promoted the idea that U.S. policy could no longer accommodate lengthy deliberation in the Security Council. Confronted by the liabilities of multilateralism and tempted by the attractions of unilateral action, the administration distanced itself from the international cooperation of the early post–Cold War period.

The entire embassy bombing episode was also indicative of broader trends in the global threat landscape of the late 1990s. The ability of small, relatively weak groups to target their enemies in locales around the world was an unforeseen outcome of the global openness movement that Clinton championed. During the 1990s, globalization had fostered the anger underlying international terrorism. The process exacerbated inequalities in wealth between and within societies, giving rise to frustration in the underdeveloped world.[31] Within many Muslim countries, the diffusion of cultural and social values brought about by globalization had become another source of discontent with the West. Globalization brought Internet pornography and U.S. movies to the Middle East, challenging the values and social norms of devout Muslims and eventually provoking a sharp reaction from jihadist groups such as al Qaeda.[32]

Globalization and terrorism were linked in more immediate ways, too. The same openness and technological advancement that allowed U.S. firms to do business in other countries facilitated the work of groups like al Qaeda as well. The money laundering and drug trafficking that often financed terrorism became easier in an open system, while the international travel and communication needed to carry out these strikes grew less difficult as well.[33]

In 1999 and 2000, Clinton came to perceive this trade-off to globalization. "Globalization . . . brings risks," one planning document acknowledged. "Avenues of international trade provide a highway for the tools and weapons of international terrorists," the 2000 *National Security Strategy* stated. "Globalization and electronic commerce transcend conventional borders, fast rendering traditional border security measures at air, land, and sea ports of entry ineffective or obsolete." If globalization brought benefits, it also brought challenges. As borders disappeared, new dangers emerged.[34]

Unilateralism Ascendant

Clinton's counterterrorism policy indicated that the president was, in some instances, willing to align with the unilateralists. In most cases, though, he remained true to his multilateral inclinations, especially in matters of arms control and international law. Yet to an increasing degree, Clinton no longer controlled U.S. policy. In several episodes, domestic concern about the internationalist tilt of Clinton's diplomacy was sufficient to override the president's initiatives, and by 2000, multilateralism was dead. The lack of a defining purpose of U.S. diplomacy not only discombobulated Clinton's efforts abroad but also allowed for greater debate on the means and ends of foreign policy at home. In the absence of a broadly accepted framework for foreign affairs, there was new room for domestic interference in the management of American statecraft.

The debate over the Comprehensive Test Ban Treaty (CTBT) was one manifestation of the unilateralist revolt. U.S. diplomats negotiated the accord, which banned nuclear tests of all types, to little fanfare between 1994 and 1996. Clinton, who personally signed the treaty at the United Nations, hailed it as an example of international cooperation and a barrier to proliferation. Clinton delivered the agreement to Congress in 1997, but the GOP leadership kept it from reaching the floor for more than two years.

The linked issues of nuclear testing and nonproliferation gained a higher profile in May 1998, when India and Pakistan each tested several nuclear devices. The Indian tests on May 12 caught the administration flat-footed. Having been assured by Indian defense minister George Fernandes that there would be "no surprises" on testing, Clinton's advisers were stunned by the detonations. Clinton attempted to halt the nascent arms race in South Asia, offering to waive federally mandated sanctions against India if the nationalist government froze its nuclear program, but New Delhi refused. Pakistan also rebuffed U.S. appeals to refrain from responding to the Indian tests. Pakistani officials demanded security guarantees or protection under the U.S. or Chinese nuclear umbrella, conditions to which neither Clinton nor Jiang could agree.[35]

Events on the subcontinent energized the CTBT debate. Optimists hoped that prompt action on the treaty might restrain further testing and argued that the recent detonations made ratification of the pact all the more urgent. Pessimists arrived at an altogether different conclusion, believing that the tests illustrated the bankruptcy of arms control agreements in general.[36]

Proponents and opponents of the treaty developed these arguments more fully as the ratification debate unfolded in 1998 and 1999. Clinton stressed the nonproliferation value of the treaty. The agreement, he contended, was a strong moral disincentive to proliferation. Global norms were important, and the CTBT was a forceful statement against proliferation. The treaty, Clinton maintained, would "increase the pressure on and isolation of other nations that may be considering their own nuclear test explosions." "Global standards matter," seconded Albright. "Why else . . . did South Africa, Brazil, and Argentina abandon their nuclear programs? Why else did China agree to halt its own nuclear tests and sign the CTBT? Why else have India and Pakistan agreed, in principle, to do the same?" From this perspective, the CTBT would discourage proliferation by threatening to bring down moral opprobrium on governments outside the nontesting regime.[37]

Doubtful, answered critics of the accord. Some opponents took a technical tack, charging that the CTBT was unverifiable and might detract from the effectiveness of the U.S. arsenal. Other commentators mounted a broader assault on the treaty's premises and on international agreements in general. In many instances, critics rejected the administration's contention about international norms. "Kim Jong Il, Saddam Hussein, Moammar Qaddafi will not be affected in their quest for nuclear weapons by whether or not the United States tests," explained James Schlesinger. "Other nations will refrain from or pursue nuclear capabilities based upon their own assessment of their national interests, not by whether or not the United States sets an example." Henry Kissinger too marveled at Clinton's credulity, arguing that "restraint by the major powers has never been a significant factor in the decisions of other nuclear aspirants."[38]

These critiques were representative of a common complaint against Clinton's diplomacy: that the president naively believed that the end of the Cold War had somehow replaced old-fashioned strategic calculus with a kinder, gentler international order. This tendency to believe that international legal action could influence the behavior of great powers and rogue states, conservatives alleged, was a persistent problem of U.S. policy. Clinton's insistence on the treaty, charged Caspar Weinberger, illustrated "a degree of naivety that is extremely dangerous."[39]

Going further down the antinorms path, some treaty opponents attacked the idea of limiting U.S. security capabilities through international agreements of any sort. Treaties, they argued, restricted U.S.

defense options without meaningfully decreasing the external threat. From this perspective, the CTBT represented the soft-minded approach to national security that had hindered U.S. diplomacy for the past decade. For the unilateralists, defeating the treaty became a virtual crusade. "U.S. national security cannot be based upon pieces of paper," contended one writer. "It must, instead, be rooted in the Reagan philosophy of 'peace through strength.'" Archunilateralist Charles Krauthammer was positively exultant when the CTBT eventually went down to defeat:

> This was more than the defeat of a treaty. It was the defeat of an idea, indeed a series of ideas about nuclear weapons, about arms control, and even more generally, about the international order of parchment barriers and paper treaties that [the] Clinton administration has set about trying to construct during the 1990s. . . . Inspectors, bureaucracies, governing boards, lofty goals, and professed norms—these are supposed to protect us from the ambitions of unappeasable rogue states. With these phony safeguards in place, the urgency to take real and often unilateral measures . . . is blunted.[40]

Krauthammer's basic message was that U.S. policy was most effective when leaders ignored the temptation to compromise for the sake of compromise and instead exercised U.S. strength to its full potential. The United States, he contended, possessed the power to get its way in most situations. The only question was whether American officials would fulfill the promise of U.S. strength or undermine that power by binding the nation to restrictive treaties.

In October 1999, the CTBT came up for a vote. The antitreaty forces, combining the unilateralist argument with doubts about the treaty's verifiability and its effect on U.S. nuclear stockpiles, routed the CTBT supporters. The pact failed to gain even a simple majority. Aside from illustrating concerns about the provisions of the treaty, the vote demonstrated that the themes of strength and freedom of action had moved to the forefront of the debate over foreign policy.

The importance of such concerns was nowhere more evident than in the growth of quasi-imperial sentiment in neoconservative quarters during the late 1990s. Reviving ideas that had surfaced at the outset of the post–Cold War era, several prominent writers argued that the establishment of a liberal American empire was vital to national—and international—security. Multilateralism had failed, William Kristol and Robert Kagan argued, and if the United States wanted order, it would have to create it itself. Rogue states, terrorists, and international drug dealers menaced the world scene, and the "international community" was powerless to intercede. In these circumstances, Washington should aim for "benevolent global hegemony," a policy of "military supremacy and moral confidence" through which the United States would spread its values and protect its interests. At a time when the United States enjoyed "strategic and ideological predominance," forging a comparatively gentle imperium was the "only reliable defense against a breakdown of peace and international order." A neoimperial strategy—or, as Kristol and Kagan termed it, a "neo-Reaganite foreign policy"—would be "good for America, and good for the world."[41]

This notion received a warm reception from other neoconservatives. Irving Kristol argued that the current international anarchy cried out for what he called "the emerging American imperium." Another Republican commentator stated that Americans should "reconceive their global role from one of traditional nation-state to an imperial power," establishing the "informal" empire needed to ward off the dangers of the day. Thomas Donnelly, executive director of Project for a New American Century, put it plainly: "I think Americans have to become used to running the world."[42]

To be sure, this imperial sentiment never gained a majority public adherence or a foothold within the councils of power in Washington. Berger maintained in 1999 that "we are the first global power in history that is not an imperial power." Irving Kristol conceded that "public opinion and all of our political traditions are hostile to the idea" of empire.[43] Empire advocacy may not have been a dominant influence in the late 1990s, yet it demonstrated the same faith in American power, concern with encroaching international disorder, and impatience with multilateralism that were so typical of the unilateralist worldview. Whatever opposition it provoked, the pro-empire viewpoint was a noteworthy indication of themes that had grown increasingly prominent in public discussions of Clinton's diplomacy.

Unmaking Foreign Policy

Clinton's emphasis on cooperation with the United Nations was another area of conflict between the president and the unilateralists. Between 1990 and 1996, Bush and Clinton had both consciously attempted to involve the United Nations in pursuing U.S. aims abroad. At the time, conservatives grumbled about the growing power of the world body. The issue exploded after the debacle in Somalia, which many observers blamed on UNISOM's repeated enlargement of its mandate. Legislators wondered why the United States was using its prestige and soldiers in the service of an institution that was unwieldy, inefficient, and sometimes unfriendly to the United States.

Beginning in 1996, conservatives began a concerted attack on U.S. participation in the United Nations. They complained that the organization demanded too large a U.S. contribution for overall expenses and peacekeeping missions (by 1996, the U.S. government owed more than $1 billion to the UN). More broadly, Helms and many of his colleagues raised fundamental objections to U.S.-UN cooperation. In its current state, Helms argued, the "power hungry and dysfunctional organization" impinged on American sovereignty and restricted the exercise of U.S. power. The senator called for sweeping changes in the world body, including a restructuring of national financial commitments and elimination of many supporting agencies. He sharply criticized Secretary-General Boutros Boutros-Ghali, who in the early 1990s had published a book labeling national sovereignty an anachronism. "UN reform is about much more than saving money," Helms declared. "It is about restoring the legitimacy of the nation-state." Reform the organization or leave it, Helms demanded of Clinton.[44]

Clinton had little choice but to comply. As head of the Foreign Relations Committee, Helms could (and did) withhold U.S. dues to the United Nations, and Clinton needed his support to ensure continued U.S. membership in the world body. The president and his advisers believed that the United Nations played a vital role in legitimizing the use of U.S. power and argued that full participation in the organization was necessary to establish international norms of cooperation and legality. The failure to pay UN dues, lamented Albright, "undermines a basic goal of U.S. foreign policy—to convince others to play by the rules of the international system." At Helms's insistence, Clinton withdrew his support for a second term for Boutros-Ghali, singlehandedly confounding the wishes of the other fourteen members of the Security Council. Clinton also introduced a reform agenda calling for expansion of the Security Council and a lower cap on U.S. financial obligations. Appeased, Helms supported a bill authorizing payment of the delinquent dues. The outlook improved again in mid-1997, when media mogul Ted Turner pledged $1 billion to alleviate the existing shortfall. Clinton soon discovered, however, that Senate conservatives were still eager to cause him trouble on the UN issue. The dues authorization included a provision stating that U.S. money could not be used to fund UN programs that promoted abortions. As a right-to-chooser, Clinton was in a difficult spot. Ultimately, domestic politics trumped his desire to reestablish the U.S. commitment to the United Nations, and Clinton torpedoed the payment package.[45]

Combined with the heavy-handed manner in which Clinton had fired Boutros-Ghali, this refusal to pay infuriated much of the General Assembly. "They have poisoned the well," fumed one foreign diplomat. In this climate, the U.S. reform package died, further alienating conservatives. By mid-1998, the United Nations was virtually bankrupt, and new Secretary-General Kofi Annan was reduced to pleading for support on the op-ed page of the *New York Times*. "Fiji has done its part," Annan scolded. "What about the U.S.?"[46]

In 1999, the relationship continued to deteriorate. As the U.S. debt grew, foreign delegations threatened punitive action. By summer, Washington risked losing its General Assembly seat if it did not make good on its debts. When the Senate again passed an authorization bill that included an antiabortion rider, Clinton caved and signed the measure. The United States paid a large percentage of its UN debt in 1999 and 2000.

Even after this limited reconciliation, the U.S.-UN relationship hardly returned to its post–Cold War state of bliss. Visiting the Security Council in 2000, Helms chastised a group of astonished diplomats for their "lack of gratitude" for U.S. global leadership. Speaking for many conservatives, Helms made clear his continued distrust of the organization: "A United Nations that seeks to impose its presumed authority on the American people without their consent begs for confrontation and, I want to be candid, eventual U.S. withdrawal." Determined to preserve U.S. sovereignty and independence of action, Helms and his allies had reversed the emphasis on U.S.-UN cooperation that characterized much of 1990s American diplomacy.[47]

The debate over the United Nations bore striking similarities to a concurrent clash over the International Criminal Court (ICC), a body charged with prosecuting war criminals across international borders. The proposal was rooted in the notion of international cooperation to uphold human rights and was built on many of the principles of the New World Order and enlargement. For this reason, the ICC had a certain intellectual appeal for Clinton. At first, he supported the initiative, but the ICC immediately encountered resistance from within the administration. The Pentagon demanded assurances that U.S. soldiers accused of crimes could be tried in American courts rather than those of their accusers. This opposition forced Clinton to modify his position, and by late 1997, U.S. officials wanted a Security Council veto (that is, a U.S. veto) on prosecutions related to peacekeeping missions.[48]

Pentagon opposition was only the beginning, as conservatives wanted no part of the ICC. John Bolton, a Republican foreign policy spokesman, mocked the "fanciful" idea that such an entity could deter genocide. Here was another instance in which Clinton was willing to compromise American freedom of action in exchange for a meaningless treaty. Helms made it clear that the United States had no intention of recognizing the jurisdiction of the court and issued a declaration of hostility toward those countries that did. The ICC, he stated, "is an outrage that will have grave consequences for our bilateral relations with every one of the countries that signs and ratifies the treaty, and they better understand this at the outset."[49]

Attempting to save U.S. participation in the ICC, the administration demanded a provision exempting American soldiers from prosecution. The measure would have made a mockery of the idea of universal jurisdiction and was rejected overwhelmingly. The United States sat on the sidelines as more than 140 nations, including all the NATO allies except France, signed the accord in July 1998. The U.S. abstention heightened negative international perceptions of the United States and produced condemnations of the administration's claim to impunity. Clinton's refusal to sign the accord put the United States on the "wrong side of history," opined one international newspaper.[50]

Far from chastening opponents of the ICC, such foreign responses only strengthened their determination to kill the treaty. In 2000, Helms sponsored the American Servicemen's Protection Act, which cut off aid to nonallied nations that were party to the ICC, prohibited U.S. cooperation with the court, and required the president to take "all appropriate measures" to rescue members of the U.S. armed forces held by the court. "Our aim with this bill is to isolate the ICC and then to kill it," a Helms spokesman declared.[51]

Helms's bill was an added insult to ICC participants, as it implied that the United States not only was unwilling to compromise its own sovereignty but also objected to other nations exercising their sovereignty by joining the court. For the next several years, the ICC was a sticking point in U.S.-European relations. Clinton belatedly signed the ICC charter in December 2000, but this action did little more than symbolize the outgoing president's disappointment. The Senate made clear its intention to reject the treaty if it ever came up for a vote, and George W. Bush showed no enthusiasm for the ICC. By the end of Clinton's presidency, domestic opposition had bankrupted much of his international agenda. Added to Clinton's difficulty in creating a consensus on trade and globalization (see chapter 5), these setbacks were all the more notable.

Underlying this conservative hostility to the United Nations, as well as the defeat of the CTBT and the ICC, was an emergent unilateralist worldview. Protective of American freedom of action and fearful of an uncertain world, commentators aligned with this perspective objected to any measures that might limit the expression of U.S. power. In a unipolar world, they believed, the greatest danger to U.S. security was not the existence of any single threat but rather the possibility that the nation's leaders might lack the will to take strong—and, if need be, unilateral—measures. In many cases, this impulse was a rejection, implicit or explicit, of the premises of Bush's and Clinton's foreign policies. The setbacks of the early 1990s and the growing danger of international affairs, they argued, had exploded the false promise of multilateralism. Multilateralism had failed to prevent the emergence of the perils that now confronted the nation; how could it be expected to deal with these threats? By the late 1990s, this sentiment was a popular one among foreign policy observers. Partisans of this view became assertive enough to derail the CTBT and the ICC and to damage the U.S.-UN relationship, and to a noticeable degree, they succeeded in reorienting U.S. policy toward a more independent path.[52]

The growing effectiveness of the conservative opposition, in turn, fed on the jumbled state of both the international scene and Clinton's foreign policy. The links between incoherence and unilateralism were not obvious at the time, but in retrospect, they seem clear enough. In the absence of a dominant danger to the territory, prosperity, or citizens of the United States, Americans simply lost interest in foreign affairs.[53] Polls taken at the end of Clinton's presidency revealed that most Americans were apathetic and uninformed about diplomatic issues. When surveys asked respondents to identify "two or three foreign policy problems facing the nation," the most common answer was "don't know." Only one in nine respondents followed the war in Kosovo "very closely," and a clear majority was unable to identify or describe the CTBT just after its widely publicized defeat. Perhaps most telling, only 2 to 3 percent identified foreign policy issues as the most important facing the country. Public apathy became painfully tangible for the administration in the summer of 1999, when Albright failed to arouse public opposition to a House bill that gutted the foreign affairs budget by 15 percent.[54]

This lack of interest proved disastrous for Clinton's foreign policy. When ordinary Americans did not care about international affairs, a political vacuum emerged that invited opponents of Clinton's program to exert greater influence on the policy process. In the case of the CTBT, for instance, more than 80 percent of those who knew about the treaty favored ratification, but the general lack of concern with foreign policy allowed a group of conservative spokespersons and senators to defeat this cornerstone of Clinton's arms control efforts. Without an easily understandable conception of foreign policy, the administration was unable to make a convincing case for its specific policies. In other words, Clinton's opponents could challenge his proposals without fear of being labeled a liability in the fight for some greater good. At several points between 1997 and 2000, domestic groups exploited the deterioration of public interest and consensus regarding diplomatic issues to oppose the president on matters that went to the very heart of foreign policy. Their efforts contributed to the end of the post–Cold War mood, killed significant aspects of Clinton's agenda, and went far in giving foreign policy its unilateralist appearance at the end of the twentieth century.

The Shrinking President

The degree to which the basic principles and control of foreign policy were now at stake was most evident in the debate over national missile defense (NMD) and the Anti-Ballistic Missile (ABM) Treaty. This episode amplified the trends apparent in domestic discussions of Iraq, the CTBT, the ICC, and the United Nations, as a strengthened conservative insurgency and perceptions of a growing foreign threat aroused resistance to Clinton's policy. As in so many other cases during his second term, the president's program proved unsustainable under this attack. When Clinton's opponents triumphed in 2000, it was clear that the White House no longer controlled the direction of U.S. policy.

For much of Clinton's presidency, it seemed unlikely that he would pursue NMD in any meaningful sense. For the most part, the idea had died after Reagan and Bush left office. In 1993, Clinton, eager to remove an irritant in U.S.-Russian relations, terminated the already languishing Strategic Defense Initiative of Reagan's day. The idea of a more limited form of missile defense remained attractive, though, since the Gulf War of 1991 had suggested that U.S. military forces and allies in certain regions remained vulnerable to missile attack. Clinton's solution was theater missile defense (TMD), a limited variant of an antimissile program. The administration planned to develop TMD in conjunction with allies such as Japan and Israel to decrease the threat from short- and medium-range missile attacks while avoiding the diplomatic headaches associated with NMD. In 1996 and 1997, the administration reached an understanding with Yeltsin that permitted the United States to develop TMD without violating the ABM Treaty.[55]

Soon, however, domestic pressure built for a more expansive conception of missile defense. In 1995, Clinton had attempted to restrain enthusiasm for NMD by releasing a national intelligence estimate stating that the continental United States would not face a ballistic missile threat from "rogue states" (Iran, Iraq, North Korea, Syria, and others) for at least a decade. But shortly thereafter, evidence surfaced that the White House had encouraged the CIA to downplay the threat. Senate conservatives bemoaned Clinton's alleged irresponsibility on defense affairs and urged the construction of NMD, relations with Russia be damned. Helms called withdrawal from the ABM Treaty "an absolute necessity." Clinton, he charged, would "leave the American people strategically naked as hostile nations rush forward in their relentless pursuit of nuclear, chemical, and biological-tipped missiles." This minor furor galvanized NMD proponents, and Congress initiated funding for research and deployment of a missile shield.[56]

The administration resisted this momentum, making multiple arguments against NMD. The Pentagon maintained that a real missile threat to the United States was years, if not decades, away. Other officials cast doubt on the effectiveness of NMD. Albright cited a danger "that we will rush to deploy systems that don't work or that cost so much that they hurt other defense priorities." Moreover, NMD would complicate important aspects of Clinton's foreign policy. Attempting to salvage a relationship with Russia amid NATO expansion and later Kosovo, the president was not eager to undertake another initiative that was sure to strengthen the position of Kremlin hard-liners. "We didn't want an anti-missile program intended to deal with non-Russian threats to provoke nationalistic fervor in Moscow during a period when the very survival of Russian democracy was in doubt," Talbott later wrote. Finally, the administration feared that NMD would sink the already struggling U.S. arms control agenda. The Pentagon warned that NMD would be a clear violation of the ABM Treaty and would likely increase Russian reluctance to ratify START II, which had already been sitting in the Duma for years. In 1997 and 1998, Clinton therefore threatened to veto any bill mandating deployment of NMD.[57]

White House and Pentagon opposition had only a temporary effect on the push for NMD. In 1997, the Senate commissioned a committee led by former secretary of defense Donald Rumsfeld to study the missile threat. Rumsfeld and his colleagues took a far more pessimistic view of the situation than had Clinton and the CIA. Rumsfeld believed that North Korea and Iran would soon have both the motive and the capability to strike the United States. "Each could pose a threat to the United States within 5 years of a decision to do so," he concluded, "and . . . the United States might not know for several years whether such a decision had been made." As if to dramatize Rumsfeld's findings, North Korea tested a new class of ballistic missile in 1998, heightening fears that Kim might soon be able to target Hawaii, Alaska, or the West Coast. Rumsfeld did not explicitly address the question of NMD, but he certainly implied that the United States needed a means of defending itself from ballistic missiles. Defense policy should be revised "to reflect the reality of an environment in which there might be little or no warning" of a missile attack, he recommended.[58]

Rumsfeld's report set off renewed debate over NMD and the ABM Treaty. NMD supporters claimed that the development of ballistic missiles by Iran, Iraq, or North Korea would fundamentally alter regional balances. These states, they claimed, would use WMD-armed missiles to force the United States to ignore acts of local aggression. Saddam Hussein, for instance, might use a ballistic missile capability to deter the United States from responding to an invasion of Kuwait. The United States, contended conservative spokesman Stephen Hadley, must retain the power to shape events in the Middle East and elsewhere. "The principal threat to this ability," he argued, "is WMD directed against U.S. military forces and allies in the region—and against the U.S. homeland." The best way to counter this threat, in Hadley's view, was to make the U.S. homeland invulnerable to ICBM attack.[59]

Yet for many NMD advocates, the issue was less Hussein's missiles than Clinton's devotion to the ABM Treaty. When Clinton attempted to lessen the effects of NMD on U.S.-Russia relations by negotiating a permissive add-on to the ABM Treaty, the missile defense hawks attacked. So what if Russia objected to NMD? they asked. Former CIA director James Woolsey professed to be mystified by Clinton's desire to clear NMD with Moscow. "We are dealing from a position of strength here," he told the Senate Foreign Relations Committee. "It was their political and economic system that was cast onto the ash heap of history, not ours." For Helms, the NMD debate was simply another instance of Clinton placing international consensus ahead of national security. "The Clinton administration wants to negotiate permission from Russia over whether the U.S. can protect itself from ballistic missile attack by North Korea," he stated, appalled. Seeking to outflank Clinton, NMD advocates tried various maneuvers to free the United States from the ABM Treaty. Their most creative argument was that the agreement was no longer valid because the Soviet Union, an original party to the pact, had ceased to exist.[60]

Coming as the ICC and CTBT debates reached a crescendo, Clinton's display of loyalty to the ABM Treaty seemed to many conservatives to be just another illustration of the folly of international cooperation. The president, they feared, naively believed that legal agreements could mitigate the dangers of an anarchic world order. The only effect of treaties such as the ABM pact, they contended, was to restrict the United States' ability to defend itself from a host of scary characters. Krauthammer summed up the conservative critique of Clinton's diplomacy in words that easily could have been recycled from the CTBT episode. "It is hard to think of an administration in American history with a greater mania for writing, signing, ratifying, and producing international agreements than the Clinton administration," he wrote. This method of foreign policy was fine in terms of improving friendships with states that posed no threat to the United States, Krauthammer argued, but it was "hopelessly utopian" as a means of protecting Americans from the "rogue" nations that were left out of arms control pacts.[61] For Krauthammer, Helms, and many of the chief GOP foreign policy voices, the NMD debate boiled down to a now-familiar proposition: Clinton should concentrate less on the niceties of international consensus and more on the hard realities of protecting the United States from foreign threats. If this meant alienating other nations and pursuing U.S. security unilaterally, so be it.

Clinton stood firm. The ABM Treaty was crucial to maintaining the nuclear balance with Moscow, administration officials contended. "To the extent that there is no ABM treaty, then certainly Russia or other countries would feel free to develop as many offensive weapons as they wanted," warned Cohen. Clinton argued that U.S. defense dollars would be better spent elsewhere, such as in preventing terrorist attacks. A missile strike, he reasonably claimed, was perhaps the least likely tactic for an assault on the United States. "Any country with any sense, if they wanted to attack us, would try to do it through a terrorist network," Clinton said in 1999, "because if they did it with a missile we'd know who did it, and then they'd be sunk." Clinton was fighting a losing battle. When the Pentagon reversed its earlier position on NMD and endorsed Rumsfeld's report, Clinton was cornered. He dropped his threat to veto NMD in early 1999. Later that year, Clinton signed the National Missile Defense Act, which pledged $6.6 billion to research and development and required deployment of NMD by 2003.[62]

Still hoping to salvage both the ABM Treaty and some vestige of control over foreign policy, Clinton looked for a compromise. Berger coordinated internal agreement to go forward on a version of NMD that might be permissible under the ABM pact. The administration tried to balance congressional and Russian concerns, conceding the basic argument of NMD while making conciliatory noises toward Moscow. The goal, in Clinton's eyes, was to modify both parties' stances, convincing the Russians to alter the ABM Treaty and Congress to settle for something less than the fullest conception of NMD. Even this softened position failed to impress Yeltsin and his successor, Vladimir Putin. Moscow had relatively warm ties with Iraq and Iran, two states high on Washington's list of potential ICBM proliferators, and Putin simply did not believe that the missile threat was as grave as U.S. commentators made out. The Russian military, a constituency that Putin felt compelled to court early in his presidency, strenuously objected to NMD in any form. When Clinton made a last-ditch effort to convince Putin to amend the ABM Treaty in 2000, the Russian president replied that he would wait until after the U.S. presidential election to negotiate. With George W. Bush staking out a hawkish position on NMD, Putin would not risk reaching an agreement with one president only to see it repudiated under the next.[63]

The failure of Clinton's middle-ground strategy strengthened the

NMD advocates and sealed the fate of the ABM Treaty. In late 2000 and early 2001, House and Senate conservatives urged a more aggressive approach to NMD, arguing for quick deployment with or without Russian consent. Bush campaigned on a similar platform, and it came as no surprise in 2001 when the new administration abrogated the ABM Treaty.

Coming in the wake of congressional revolts against Clinton's policy toward Iraq, the CTBT, the United Nations, and the ICC, the president's inability to keep the NMD debate on his own terms indicated a significant diminution of executive influence in foreign policy. By the end of his second term, the president often found that his policies were hostage to the consent of an unfriendly legislature, as the Republican Congress exploited the lack of domestic consensus on foreign affairs to assert its own agenda. In short, Clinton had lost control of basic aspects of foreign policy to a degree not seen since the 1970s. As his presidency ended, congressional influence in foreign policy was at a twenty-five-year high. Clinton's failure to articulate a coherent vision of foreign affairs left his initiatives open to domestic assault and ultimately subverted his authority in diplomacy and defense.[64]

More pungently than the subtle contradictions of his diplomacy, Clinton's inability to maintain control of U.S. policy indicated a failure to overcome the post–Cold War dilemma he had inherited. Like Bush, Clinton was unsuccessful in restoring order to public debate on foreign policy. This ineffectiveness was clear even when measured by Clinton's own standards. During his time as president, Clinton was unable to live up to the dictum with which he had begun his foreign policy odyssey. "You've still got to be able to crystallize complexity in a way people get right away," he had told Talbott early on. "The operative problem of the moment is that a bunch of smart people haven't been able to come up with a new slogan, and saying that there aren't any good slogans isn't a slogan either."[65] As it turned out, this statement was absolutely correct. Clinton never provided the compelling narrative that would give rhetorical coherence and political durability to his foreign policy, and eventually, he paid the price. As the rhetorical void in U.S. diplomacy remained, domestic consensus eroded, and

Clinton's authority suffered. By the end of his second term, Clinton's continuing lack of a new slogan had become a marker of his shortcomings as a foreign policy leader.

These political troubles confirmed what Clinton's strategic difficulties had hinted at. Just as incoherence had been problematic from a diplomatic standpoint, it undermined the selling of foreign policy as well. If the early 1990s demonstrated the dangers of rigidity, the second half of the decade suggested the advantages of the coherence paradigm. Even though rhetorical simplicity could be dangerously misleading, Clinton's second-term experience illustrated that the absence of clarity could be equally damaging. The first circumstance blinded policy makers to nuance; the second robbed them of the consensus needed to sustain presidential diplomacy. By the end of the twentieth century, this latter effect was most salient in the politics of diplomacy. For those who would follow him in the Oval Office, Clinton's was a cautionary example.

In a broader sense, Clinton's difficulties showed that U.S. leaders remained unsuccessful in setting the nation on a stable post–Cold War course. Attempts to restore the simplicity of the superpower struggle had failed, and efforts to depart from the coherence paradigm had fared no better. Neither end of the spectrum offered an attractive solution, it seemed. The failure of the New World Order, enlargement, and Clinton's ill-defined "framework for American leadership" were all testaments to this quandary. American strategic vision was still incomplete; domestic consensus was no more evident. A full decade after the end of the Cold War, the United States had yet to find a durable conception of its role abroad.

9

Full Circle

The next administration was keenly aware of both the continuing uncertainty of U.S. policy and the unsettling precedent of the Clinton years. Condoleezza Rice, a National Security Council official under George H. W. Bush and a campaign adviser to his son, was particularly troubled by the course of events over the last decade. During this period, she asserted in 2000, the United States had failed to accustom itself to the new shape of international affairs. One telling indication of this failure was that the period was still referred to as the post–Cold War era. Defining the times according to what they were not, rather than what they were, was a clear sign of perplexity. This state of affairs, Rice alleged, was Clinton's fault (she was polite enough not to implicate her former boss in the indictment). Over the last eight years, she wrote, Clinton had failed to "separate the important from the trivial" and "assiduously avoided" outlining a coherent foreign policy. The result, according to Rice, was confusion abroad and disagreement at home. "The problem today . . . is the existence of a vacuum," she concluded. "In the absence of a compelling vision, parochial interests are filling the void."[1]

For the incoming administration, the task was essentially the same as it had been for the elder Bush in 1991 and Clinton in 1993: to articulate a doctrine that would give cohesiveness to U.S. policy and restore basic public agreement on foreign affairs. At the start, Rice (who became national security adviser) and George W. Bush seemed no more likely to succeed than their predecessors. For all their talk of defining a new national interest, the president and his aides stumbled on the same obstacles that had confounded George H. W. Bush and Bill Clinton. With the international environment no less fluid than during the 1990s, vision and consensus initially remained out of reach.

Bush's contribution to the post–Cold War evolution of foreign policy soon became clear, however, as a national tragedy served as an apparent blessing in terms of the management, conception, and rhetoric of U.S. diplomacy. The attacks of September 11, 2001, gave the administration a new view of the nation's international priorities and a single-minded—and highly attractive—conception of its mission. Within days of the attacks, Bush identified the next great American crusade, and in subsequent months, the president and his advisers enunciated a cohesive and compelling scheme of U.S. diplomacy. The terrorist attacks of 9/11 provided policy makers with the dominant threat and overriding purpose that had been absent for the past ten years, giving rise to a strategy more coherent than any since the end of the Cold War. At the same time that this "war on terror" gave form to foreign policy, it restored public agreement on international affairs. September 11 and Bush's response made international relations relevant and concrete for Americans in a manner reminiscent of past hours of peril, and the nation once again perceived its world role with great moral clarity and logical simplicity. In both strategic and political terms, the war on terror seemed to resolve the long-standing post–Cold War dilemmas of doctrine making.

As the nation embarked on this new course, however, these dilemmas were rarely far from the surface. The Bush administration drew directly on the lessons of the 1990s in framing an expansive response to 9/11. In particular, Bush took care to avoid Clinton's error of failing to articulate a persuasive, overarching conception of the United States' international role. Bush fashioned a narrative so attractive, all-encompassing, and moralistic that it left Americans no choice but to subscribe to his worldview. As the nation returned to a foreign policy no less clear or straightforward than containment, the themes of the post–Cold War experience were close at hand.

New President, Same Problems

If Bush planned to remake U.S. foreign policy, the early results were inauspicious. After famously flunking a pop quiz on diplomatic issues in late 1999 (Bush referred to Pakistan's president Pervez Musharraf as "General. I can't name the general. General"),[2] Bush largely avoided the subject during the campaign, giving only two major speeches on foreign policy. Running against Clinton, rather than Al Gore, his putative opponent, Bush blasted the outgoing president for failing to define a post–Cold War policy. "Unless a president sets his own priorities," Bush stated in November 1999, "his priorities will be set by others—by adversaries or the crisis of the moment, live on CNN." Diplomacy "must have a great and guiding goal to turn this time of American influence into generations of democratic peace."

> This is accomplished by concentrating on enduring national interests. And these are my priorities. An American president should work with our strong democratic allies in Europe and Asia to extend the peace. He should promote a fully democratic Western Hemisphere bound together by free trade. He should defend America's interests in the Persian Gulf and advance peace in the Middle East based on a secure Israel. He must check the contagious spread of weapons of mass destruction and the means to deliver them. He must lead toward a world that trades in freedom.[3]

Yet if these particular interests were clear, how Bush planned to pursue them in a coherent fashion was considerably less so. As Clinton had discovered, identifying a number of important goals did not necessarily add up to a rhetorically or practically cohesive foreign policy.

When Bush delved into specific issues, in fact, his stance was convoluted. At times, he adhered to the unilateralist school. On arms control, Bush had little patience for Clinton's policies. The Comprehensive Test Ban Treaty offered "only words and false hopes and high intentions with no guarantees whatsoever," he contended. The Anti-Ballistic Missile Treaty also earned Bush's scorn. If Moscow would not modify the outdated pact, Bush promised, he would abandon the treaty in order to develop national missile defense.[4]

Rice, Bush's top adviser during the campaign, agreed with those who believed that Clinton's diplomacy had not been sufficiently assertive. The age of multilateralism was over, Rice believed; we "should not find ourselves looking to the United Nations to sanction the use of American military power." Clinton came under criticism for his arms control methods and his pursuit of "illusory 'norms' of international behavior." China was referred to not as a strategic partner but as a "strategic competitor." Iraq was due for regime change; Iran required continued isolation. According to Rice, the United States was at the pinnacle of the global order and should not hesitate to act like it.[5]

Bush endorsed some of these recommendations during the campaign but rejected others. Running as a conservative and attempting to distance himself from Clinton, Bush took a less activist stance than Rice. Bush tempered her unilateralism, for instance, pledging to eschew adventurism and avoid "arrogant" displays of U.S. power. "I just don't think it's the role of the United States to walk into a country, say, 'We do it this way, so should you,'" he said in one debate. "I don't think our troops should be used for what's called nation-building." The United States needed a subdued approach to world affairs in order to retain its moral leadership, Bush argued. The nation's reputation abroad "really depends upon how our nation conducts itself in foreign policy. If we're an arrogant nation, they'll resent us. If we're a humble nation but strong, they'll welcome us." Bush's quasi- dovish stance on defense further belied his reputation as an advocate of unleashing U.S. might. A fiscal conservative, he supported only a $45 billion increase in defense spending over the next decade. This amount was barely enough to match inflation, less than half that called for by Gore, and nowhere near what the Joint Chiefs of Staff deemed desirable. Accordingly, in 2000, it was difficult to gauge Bush's intentions.[6]

Luckily for Bush, the electorate was not looking for a diplomatic sage. In a campaign that centered on tax cuts, a budget surplus, Social Security, prescription benefits for senior citizens, and education, Bush (like Clinton before him) largely avoided a discussion of international matters. Normally, a domestic-oriented election should not have played to Bush's advantage; with the economy strong, a Gore victory seemed likely. In the end, though, the vice president was unable to distance himself from Clinton's moral lapses or establish a likable persona, and Bush squeaked into the White House.

Once in power, Bush did little to alter the impression that his interests lay elsewhere than foreign affairs. The composition of the NSC certainly implied that the president-elect intended to delegate responsibility for foreign policy. Bush's highest-profile selection was Colin Powell as secretary of state. Though Powell was a good soldier, he was also a political force in his own right, and it seemed unlikely that he had been enlisted simply to act as a glorified negotiator. Defense Secretary Donald Rumsfeld was also an old hand, having run the Pentagon for Gerald Ford. Rice had a similarly solid pedigree, and Vice President Dick Cheney had honed his skills under George H. W. Bush as well. Expectations for Bush himself were therefore low; the *New York Times* commented that the star-studded cast would likely "help compensate for Mr. Bush's own inexperience."[7]

During his first eight months in office, Bush both pleased and disappointed those who had hoped for a vigorously unilateralist foreign policy. He hewed to an ambiguous strategy, taking assertive, go-it-alone stances on some issues but playing the conciliator on others. Establishing his neoconservative credentials, Bush moved toward abrogating the ABM Treaty. The pact, he announced, "prohibits us from exploring all options for defending against the threats that face us, our allies, and other countries." Bush halfheartedly engaged Russian president Vladimir Putin in an attempt to amend the ABM Treaty, but it came as no surprise when Bush later withdrew from the accord.[8] The Kyoto Protocol on global warming elicited similar disdain, with Bush explaining that its carbon dioxide emissions caps did not make "economic sense for America."[9]

In substance, Bush's stance on the ABM and Kyoto agreements (as well as the Comprehensive Test Ban Treaty and the International Criminal Court, to which Bush was also hostile) did little to alter U.S. policy. Although Clinton had supported the treaties, Senate ratification had never been likely (the upper house had once voted 95 to 0 against Kyoto). Still, Bush's approach marked an important tactical departure from the policies of his predecessor. Because Clinton knew that his stance was unpopular in Congress, he had withheld the Kyoto and International Criminal Court pacts to save them from certain rejection. These maneuvers, along with his efforts to sustain the ABM regime, had preserved at least a semblance of international cooperation. Bush reversed this trend, taking more aggressive positions on all these issues. This shift in methods alarmed internationalists and Atlanticists on both sides of the ocean, with one commentator remarking that "the specter of unilateralism" had replaced the fear of isolationism as Europe's chief concern regarding the United States.[10]

For all the consternation that Bush's early diplomacy produced among multilateralists, however, the new president was hardly the gunslinging cowboy some Europeans—and not a few Americans—presumed him to be. In fact, Bush confounded both supporters and detractors by taking understated positions on some potentially incendiary issues. For example, in early April, a U.S. electronic surveillance plane was forced to land on China's Hainan Island after colliding with a Chinese fighter. Given Bush's campaign rhetoric, the incident seemed to present a natural opportunity for a strong response. Beijing demanded an apology, Bush demanded the release of the interned Americans, and a crisis loomed.

As the standoff played out, though, the administration found itself with few effective means of expressing its displeasure. "There aren't a lot of good options," one official admitted. Recalling the U.S. ambassador would "deprive us of our point man." Punishing Beijing with economic sanctions would strangle commerce and be "counterproductive at best, stupid at worst." Compounding the difficulty was the fact that there was little domestic enthusiasm for a confrontation. Although the crisis emboldened a few anti-China congressmen, most public observers greeted the incident with a yawn. Bush took a conciliatory posture, expressing "regret" and stating his desire for productive relations with China. "The message to the Chinese is, we should not let this incident destabilize our relations," he said. With Bush's concession, tempers gradually cooled, and the crisis ended when Beijing released the crew in mid-April. Far from the assertive unilateralist, Bush had been the patient diplomat during the confrontation.[11]

In mid-2001, it was difficult to know what to make of Bush's foreign policy. The president was bold at times, circumspect at others. He had given mixed signals about his overall intentions and provided few indications of how he planned to fill the void that he and Rice accused Clinton of creating. Diplomacy had not been an especially visible aspect of Bush's presidency early on, as tax cuts and a controversial education bill captured the attention of the media. At this point, Bush's contribution to the decade-long debate on foreign policy was far from obvious.

Bush thereby confirmed by experience what his predecessors knew well: that articulating a workable diplomatic vision was easier said than done. Despite his exaltation of the "national interest," Bush was confounded by the same basic dilemmas that had plagued his father and Clinton. The nation still faced no overriding menace that would give coherence to its foreign policy. Moreover, as the lack of enthusiasm for a confrontation with China indicated, there was no consensus behind conservative calls for a more assertive expression of U.S. power. With no great threat or purpose apparent, the United States' mission for the new century remained unclear. If Bush recognized the perils of Clinton's approach to foreign policy, he was, as yet, unable to overcome them.

Watershed

First impressions notwithstanding, Bush was not destined to replicate Clinton's experience. On September 11, al Qaeda operatives turned four planes into flying bombs. They felled both World Trade Center towers in New York City and damaged the Pentagon, and the fourth crashed en route to Washington. The death toll, initially feared to number in the tens of thousands, was later fixed at roughly 3,000, enough to qualify as the deadliest peacetime attack on U.S. soil.

The threat from al Qaeda specifically, and from anti-U.S. jihadism more generally, had developed over the two decades prior to 9/11. Al Qaeda had its origins in the Afghan war of the 1980s, where Osama bin Laden and other foreign fighters had combined with indigenous mujahideen to break the Soviet occupation of the country. Emboldened by victory, bin Laden and several associates created al Qaeda as a guerrilla army dedicated to aiding Muslims who were coming under pressure from outside, "infidel" forces.[12]

During the 1990s, the United States assumed the role of this outside force. Bin Laden objected vehemently to the stationing of U.S. troops in Saudi Arabia during and after the Gulf War. He saw U.S. efforts to secure cheap oil in the Middle East as the "biggest theft ever witnessed by mankind in the history of the world." The infiltration of Western culture into the Middle East was no less disturbing to many of bin Laden's followers, who saw this penetration as a threat to Muslim piety. Bin Laden further charged that the United States propped up corrupt governments in Egypt and Saudi Arabia, and he labeled U.S.-sponsored sanctions against Iraq a design of the "Crusader-Zionist alliance" to "annihilate what is left of this people." Finally, many jihadists saw U.S. support for Israel—which top al Qaeda strategist Ayman al-Zawahiri called "a developed American military base in the heart of the Islamic world"—as a plot to establish pro-Western regimes in the Middle East and a cause of the Arab states' military impotence.[13]

In 1996, bin Laden declared war on Washington. Although there is some confusion as to his aims in this struggle, scholars largely agree that bin Laden sought to end U.S. influence in the Middle East (particularly Saudi Arabia), support for Israel, and pressure on Iraq. As he put it in 1999, "We are seeking to drive them out of our Islamic nations and prevent them from dominating us." If the United States was forced out of the region, bin Laden believed, the "apostate regimes" in Egypt, Saudi Arabia, and elsewhere would collapse, paving the way for the rise of an Islamist state.[14]

To this end, al Qaeda carried out several strikes on U.S. targets beginning in the late 1990s, including the 1998 embassy bombings in Africa and the attack on the USS *Cole* in Yemen in 2000. Planning for the 9/11 attacks began in 1996. The al Qaeda leadership apparently believed that a strike of this magnitude would cause Washington to retrench its involvement in the Middle East, as had the Lebanon bombing in 1983 and the battle of Mogadishu ten years later. With this oppressive presence lifted, Muslims would rally to al Qaeda's cause, toppling corrupt regimes and ending the "severe oppression, suffering, excessive iniquity, humiliation, and poverty" caused by the U.S. presence. Although American intelligence received a number of vague warnings about al Qaeda's plan to strike U.S. targets, Washington was unable to uncover the plot, and the operation went forward on September 11 with stunning success.[15]

In the United States, the psychological and emotional impact of the attacks was every bit as tremendous as bin Laden had intended.

"There are no measures yet for the anger and apprehension," wrote the *Miami Herald*. "The horror transcends calculation."[16] On September 11 and the days thereafter, Americans could not escape the catastrophe. The TV networks, as well as a host of cable news stations, replayed video of the attacks and kept constant watch on New York and Washington. Bush himself was not immune to the shock that registered following the strikes. He learned of the attacks while reading to some schoolchildren, and it took him several minutes to find the wherewithal to respond.

On September 12, public commentators struggled to comprehend what the attacks meant for the United States and the world. Few disputed that there had been a profound change in Americans' thinking about national security. This was no longer an issue that Americans could approach at their discretion, as had been the case during recent years. As the *Chicago Tribune* put it, "An America that, of late, had worried most about a declining stock market and rising gasoline prices was suddenly confronted by death and destruction on an unprecedented scale."[17] Whatever course events took after 9/11, most assumed that the effect would be revolutionary.

For policy makers, the impact was all the more transformative because few top-level advisers had expected antiterrorism to be a central aim of Bush's presidency. Although George Tenet had warned in February 2001 that "the threat from terrorism is real, it is immediate, and it is evolving," the administration had not gone much beyond Clinton's efforts to fight the phenomenon. Richard Clarke had warned that "decision makers should imagine themselves on a future day when the [U.S. government] has not succeeded in stopping al Qida [*sic*] attacks and hundreds of Americans lay dead in several countries, including the US," but his alarum had little influence. Rice and the NSC opted for a gradual, indirect approach to deal with the terrorist threat, which focused on combating al Qaeda by ending Taliban rule in Afghanistan within three years.[18]

After September 11, both antiterrorism specifically and foreign policy in general were given an urgency that had long been lacking. Bush's reaction to the attacks was immediate and visceral. "We're at war," he declared to the NSC hours after the strikes. "We'll clean up the mess," he told Rumsfeld, "and then the ball will be in your court."[19]

Before the night was over, the NSC Deputies Committee commenced work on a directive governing the diplomatic and military aspects of the U.S. response. Bush's post-9/11 policy had begun to take shape.[20]

Any Terrorist, Any Place

Given the shock of 9/11 and Bush's initial decisions thereafter, it was clear that counterterrorism would dominate U.S. policy in the near term. In the early planning phase, the NSC refocused its foreign policy efforts around this issue. For Bush, the threat of terrorism was global and provided a convenient point on which to center relations with Russia and China. Powell was of a like mind, believing that 9/11 marked a watershed in U.S. ties with Pakistan, whose intelligence service had sponsored the Taliban during the 1990s. On September 12, Powell and Deputy Secretary of State Richard Armitage drew up a broad list of demands to make of Musharraf, including overflight rights for the coming war and intelligence on the Taliban. "Speaking candidly," Powell told Musharraf, "the American people would not understand if Pakistan was not in this fight with the United States."[21]

Looking beyond the short term, though, the extent to which counterterrorism would characterize U.S. policy was not entirely certain. The issue hinged on how Bush defined his objectives at the outset. Was the endgame the destruction of al Qaeda and the Taliban, the two groups directly involved in the attacks, or did the plan involve something grander—namely, a war against terrorism more broadly? If Bush took the former course, there might be a foreseeable end to the coming conflict, after which U.S. policy would look something like it had on September 10. If he opted for the latter, antiterrorism would be a more expansive struggle and would surely dominate foreign policy for the long term.

On September 12, the administration addressed this issue. Bush initially worried that a war against terrorism itself would be too nebulous to sell to the public. "We don't want to define [it] too broadly for the average man to understand," he told advisers. From a practical standpoint, moreover, "terrorism" seemed an amorphous enemy. Most experts thought of terrorism as a tool, not an entity. How did one target a tool? And what complications might arise from a broader definition? If the U.S. response reached beyond Afghanistan, would it fracture the anti–al Qaeda coalition currently taking shape? In this sense, a war on terrorism, rather than a war on al Qaeda, seemed dangerously vague and impractical.[22]

Conversely, there was little doubt within the NSC that the threat from Islamism went beyond al Qaeda. From this perspective, 9/11 had been merely one manifestation of a broader confrontation between jihadism and the West. To Powell, it therefore made sense to take a wider view of the problem. "The goal is terrorism in its broadest sense," he said, "focusing first on the organization that acted yesterday." Citing tactical reasons, Cheney sided with the secretary of state. Terrorist groups were hard to target, he argued, as they shifted from one host nation to another and faded into deserted locales or urban populations. Attacking their national sponsors, in contrast, was far less complicated. "To the extent we define our task broadly, including those who support terrorism, then we get at states," he told Bush. "And it's easier to find them than it is to find bin Laden." Deputy Secretary of Defense Paul Wolfowitz also favored thinking big, because he believed that a broader war would inevitably include Iraq. Wolfowitz had long favored regime change in Baghdad and, as Powell remembered, saw 9/11 "as a way to deal with the Iraq problem." With his top advisers in agreement, Bush tentatively approved Powell's formulation. "Start with bin Laden, which Americans expect," he said. "And then if we succeed, we've struck a huge blow and can move forward." Bush's decision was a limited affirmation of the broader conception of antiterrorism, and initially, the president apparently intended to unveil the full scope of his mission only after the first phase was complete.[23]

Over the next few days, however, Bush warmed to framing the issue in global terms from the outset. As Cheney had hinted, the larger definition of aims made sense from a political standpoint. Destroying al Qaeda and apprehending or conclusively killing its leaders would be a difficult task. If Bush laid out his aims narrowly, he might be accused of failure if bin Laden or Taliban leader Mullah Omar escaped the American net. If he took a more expansive view of antiterrorism, however, the president could pitch the campaign against al Qaeda as part of a larger "war on terror."

Even more important to Bush and his advisers was a growing conviction that Powell was right: the conflict that had begun on September 11 was a global struggle. The secretary of state thought that the attacks heralded a dramatic shift in the international environment, from the post–Cold War era to the "post–post–Cold War era," in which the advance of globalization and the erosion of national sovereignty made it imperative that the United States forge a new approach to foreign affairs. Powell's colleagues largely agreed with this sentiment. Rumsfeld believed that the danger posed by al Qaeda and other such groups was on par with the Cold War–era Soviet threat. "There's always been terrorism," he stated at one point, "but there's never really been worldwide terrorism at a time when the weapons have been as powerful as they are today, with chemical and biological and nuclear weapons spreading to countries that harbor terrorists." Fighting al Qaeda, he said, was "not a one-country problem." In the days after the attacks, Bush endorsed this conclusion and embraced the notion of reorganizing foreign policy around an encompassing assault on terrorism. "Now is an opportunity to do generations a favor, by coming together and whipping terrorism," he stated at an Oval Office meeting.[24]

There was also a secondary rationale for the wider approach, one that went to the heart of the nation's post–Cold War experience. This reasoning reflected the domestic imperatives of policy making as much as it did the practicalities of foreign affairs. Rice and Rumsfeld believed that the 1990s had witnessed a dilution of public interest in and support for foreign policy. In Rumsfeld's view, Americans had ceased to think of international issues as long-term problems. The lack of an overriding national interest, he felt, had disposed the public to lose patience with military and diplomatic initiatives. The result was that Americans had ceased to see the necessity of making sacrifices on behalf of their international objectives, instead fixating on exit strategies and other means of minimizing the costs of superpowerdom. Following 9/11, Rumsfeld worried that a similar scenario could play out in the coming war. Americans might lose enthusiasm for antiterrorism if Washington seemed to accomplish its immediate objectives or incurred heavy losses early on, deflating enthusiasm for the longer-term measures needed to prevent a recurrence of 9/11.

"Forget about 'exit strategies,'" he declared. "We're looking at a sustained engagement that carries no deadlines."[25]

What the current situation called for, from Rumsfeld's perspective, was a definition of aims that would persuade Americans that the struggle ahead would be long, arduous, and worthwhile. Asked to define victory in what was already becoming known as the "war on terror," he replied, "I say that victory is persuading the American people and the rest of the world that this is not a quick matter that is going to be over in a month or a year or even five years." Rumsfeld was drawn to analogies between the emerging struggle and the Cold War. The latter conflict, he said in a display of less-than-stellar mathematical facility, "was not won in a year or two. It was fifty-plus years we were engaged in that." A similar commitment would be needed to triumph in the current clash. In this sense, a narrow view of U.S. objectives was unlikely to inspire the necessary level of public dedication.[26]

Rice shared this concern. Having observed domestic interference in diplomacy during the 1990s, Rice was convinced that the political stability of foreign policy demanded that the president enunciate a widely accepted strategic vision. If he failed to do so, Rice feared, Bush would be vulnerable to the same pitfalls that had plagued Clinton. "In a democracy as pluralistic as ours," she wrote in 2000, "the absence of an articulated 'national interest' either produces a fertile ground for those wishing to withdraw from the world or creates a vacuum to be filled by parochial groups and transitory pressures." For Rice, a broad notion of the war on terror could be a useful tool with which to combat the apathy and disagreement that had surfaced in the previous decade.[27]

In the end, the more ambitious viewpoint carried the day. On September 12, the Deputies Committee commenced work on National Security Presidential Directive (NSPD) 9, which elaborated the response to 9/11. An early draft had focused on al Qaeda, but the final version took a far broader view of antiterrorism. Now titled "Defeating the Terrorist Threat to the United States," it contained sections dealing with numerous groups other than al Qaeda. Under NSPD 9, the United States would aim to destroy all terrorist networks "of global reach." The goal was no longer simply defeating al Qaeda but rather "the elimination of terrorism as a threat to our way of life." This wording was significant, in that it defined the object to be defended not as the American homeland but as the American "way of life." This, presumably, was a greater goal, one that would give the president increased latitude in determining where and how to wage the fight. Indeed, NSPD 9 opened the door to a virtually unbounded notion of antiterrorism. Bush stated without equivocation on September 27, "This is a nation that's determined to defend freedom from any terrorist, anyplace in the world."[28]

Following the completion of NSPD 9, Bush left little doubt that he intended antiterrorism to be the hallmark of his presidency. As he told a journalist, the fight against terrorism "is the primary focus of this administration." In the month following 9/11, Bush used this focus to frame a wide range of policy proposals. "The question in meetings is, 'How is this helping or hurting our effort to fight global terrorism,'" noted White House communications director Dan Bartlett. The members of Bush's inner circle were of like mind and reshuffled bureaucratic arrangements to reflect the new ordering of priorities. Outlining a covert action plan, Tenet called for an "absolute seamlessness" of policy and called for an "unrelenting focus" on defeating al Qaeda.[29]

One month after 9/11, antiterrorism in its broadest sense had emerged as the dominant long-term concern of Bush's foreign policy. With an overriding, easily identifiable purpose in sight for the first time in more than a decade, the administration prepared to restructure its approach to foreign affairs around this new threat.

Selling the War on Terror

Making this shift entailed two basic tasks. First, Bush had to convince Americans that a war on terror was an appropriate bedrock for U.S. involvement abroad. After all, a pertinent lesson of the 1990s had been that any foreign policy scheme would be tenuous if the public did not accept its premises. Second, and just as important, Bush needed to craft a strategy that would take antiterrorism beyond the generalities offered following 9/11 and integrate this new, dominant concern into the overall framework of U.S. policy.

Within days of the attacks, Bush turned to the first of these challenges. From the start, he frankly acknowledged the scope of his program and the manner in which it would dominate the diplomatic landscape. "Our war on terror," Bush said on September 20, "will not stop until every terrorist group of global reach has been found, stopped, and defeated." The struggle would be all-pervasive, requiring "every resource at our command—every means of diplomacy, every tool of intelligence, every instrument of law enforcement, every financial influence, and every necessary weapon of war."[30]

Bush offered a number of reasons for undertaking this worldwide struggle, but two were most prominent in his post-9/11 rhetoric: threat and mission. Terrorism posed a fundamental danger to Americans and their way of life, he argued, and a crusade against this peril would allow the nation to once again assume its historical mission of defending freedom and liberty.

Given that al Qaeda had leveled two thousand-foot buildings in New York, Bush probably did not have to convince Americans of the immediacy of the terrorist threat. Still, in the days after the attacks, Bush left little doubt that a new era of danger had begun, an era in which the country's traditional immunity from assault no longer applied. Addressing a joint session of Congress on September 20, Bush stressed the uniqueness of the emerging security environment. "Americans have known wars, but for the past 136 years, they have been wars on foreign soil, except for one Sunday in 1941," he stated. "Americans have known the casualties of war, but not at the center of a great city on a peaceful morning. Americans have known surprise attacks, but never before on thousands of civilians." The United States was no longer invulnerable, Bush declared, and Americans ignored this reality at their peril.[31]

To Bush, the danger went beyond the physical. The September 11 attacks had been against not only American lives, he argued, but also the American way of life. What the American way of life was, Bush left largely to the imagination, but the notion apparently centered on liberty and good governance. "America was targeted for attack because we're the brightest beacon for freedom and opportunity in the world," he said just hours after the strikes. The terrorists intended not to accomplish a set of political objectives but to destroy liberty and representative government. The goal of al Qaeda, Bush declared on September 20, "is remaking the world and imposing its radical beliefs on people everywhere." At stake was not just the physical security of the United States but also the principles of government and human interaction that formed the American "way of life."[32]

Describing the threat was only half of Bush's rhetorical campaign. The president also provided a positive rationale for action, one that drew liberally on moral and historical themes. From the start, the moral connotations of the war on terror were prominent. If al Qaeda and its jihadist brethren were the assaulters of freedom, Bush stated, the United States was its defender. In off-the-cuff remarks, Bush gave a no-frills explication of this idea. Jihadists "are evil people," he said. "They don't represent an ideology; they don't represent a legitimate group of people. They're flat evil. That's all they can think about, is evil. And as a nation of good folks, we're going to hunt them down, and we're going to find them, and we will bring them to justice." In Bush's view, the United States would be the avenger of freedom and the scourge of evil, as it had been during previous struggles against fascism and communism.[33]

Indeed, the president's language drew directly on World War II and the Cold War, depicting the war on terror as not simply a moral imperative but a historical imperative as well. Bush described the coming fight as part of a continuing struggle between good and evil. Bin Laden and his followers were legatees to a pattern of tyranny, "heirs of all the murderous ideologies of the 20th century." They followed "in the path of fascism and Nazism and totalitarianism," he explained, and would be no more successful than these antecedents. Like communism and Nazism, jihadism would end up "in history's unmarked grave of discarded lies."[34]

This resurgence of evil presented an opportunity for Americans to resume their role as history's heroes. Bush was already talking in these terms on September 14, describing a historical cycle of good versus evil that was now making another pass through the American experience. "Our responsibility to history is already clear," he declared, "to answer these attacks and rid the world of evil." This was not a new task, Bush assured his listeners, but rather a new incarnation of the special responsibility that Americans bore as members of freedom's elect. "In every generation, the world has produced enemies of human freedom," he said. "They have attacked America because we are freedom's home and defender. And the commitment of our fathers is now the calling of our time." Once more, it was America's turn to rout the "evil-doers" and illuminate the path to freedom and justice.[35]

Addressing Congress on September 20, Bush gave a rhetorically brilliant articulation of this idea. The war on terror was not just a response to 9/11, he said, but also a means of channeling U.S. efforts to the greater good of humanity. "In our grief and anger, we have found our mission and our moment," he said. "Freedom and fear are at war. The advance of human freedom, the great achievement of our time and the great hope of every time, now depends on us. Our Nation—this generation—will lift a dark threat of violence from our people and our future. We will rally the world to this cause by our efforts, by our courage. We will not tire; we will not falter; and we will not fail."[36] In every sense, this was to be the great national mission of the twenty-first century, or, as Bush said in a comment that was as revealing as it was unfortunate, the American "crusade."[37]

This slip notwithstanding, Bush's post-9/11 rhetoric was masterful. He crafted a message so morally, logically, and historically powerful that it seemingly left Americans with little choice but to subscribe to the war on terror. Indeed, the nation approved overwhelmingly of Bush's joint session speech and foreign policy leadership in the weeks following 9/11.[38] In no small part, this popularity stemmed from Bush's ability to reduce complex issues to simple propositions. Terrorists were not rational actors pursuing political goals and perhaps open to a modus vivendi; they were zealots driven only by animus for freedom and human life. "Why do they hate us?" Bush asked. "They hate our freedoms—our freedom of religion, our freedom of speech, our freedom to vote and assemble and disagree with each other." That quickly, Bush had demonized the enemy and delegitimized its purposes.[39]

Bush's rhetoric also had the distinct advantage of logical clarity, in that it divided the world into two irreconcilable camps. "Every nation, in every region, now has a decision to make," he stated. "Either you are with us, or you are with the terrorists." The intricacies of international politics that had bedeviled U.S. officials and confused the public during the 1990s thus disappeared, replaced by a more understandable formula. As policy makers had done throughout the Cold

War, Bush promoted a simplified view of geopolitics that lent logical consistency to U.S. policy. Like anticommunism, the war on terror offered a mental shortcut that made diplomacy comprehensible.[40]

From an objective perspective, Bush's approach was full of liabilities. By reducing the origins of terrorism to false piety and hatred of freedom, the president discouraged Americans from attempting to understand the phenomenon. U.S. support for Israel and for repressive Middle Eastern regimes was unimportant, it seemed, because terrorists were merely irrational democracy haters. With this more comforting version of 9/11's sources established, Americans could avoid the troubling questions about Middle Eastern society, U.S. policy, and the links between them. Dichotomizing the world was equally perilous. The world had not grown significantly less complicated since 9/11, but Bush's statements gave exactly that impression. By oversimplifying foreign affairs, Bush threatened to blind Americans to the considerable complexity of the global environment. In sum, the strengths of Bush's rhetoric were the weaknesses of the U.S. worldview. At the time, though, the former were more salient than the latter in public debate. Whatever the drawbacks to Bush's stance, he simply made it easy for Americans to agree.

The effectiveness of Bush's public campaign was evident in the months after 9/11. The shock of the attacks and the strength of Bush's appeals ended the disagreement, divisiveness, and disinterest of the last decade. The war on terror was nearly sacrosanct in domestic discussion, providing the foreign policy consensus that had been absent since the end of the Cold War.

Perhaps the most basic post-9/11 change in the domestic views of foreign policy was the public's skyrocketing interest in world affairs. Whereas many Americans had snoozed through Bosnia in 1995, shrugged at Afghanistan and Sudan in 1998, and yawned during Kosovo in 1999, post-9/11 policy inspired rapt attention. When U.S. forces attacked Afghanistan in October 2001, CNN, MSNBC, Fox News, and other television outlets carried around-the-clock coverage of the action. In the process, the news stations popularized the phrase *war on terror* by scrolling colored banners emblazoned with the words across the bottom of the screen. By the end of 2001, the phrase had entered the public lexicon as a concise, easily comprehensible expression of both intervention in Afghanistan and the larger scheme of foreign policy.[41]

Public observers who subscribed to the war on terror were no less receptive to the idea that its conduct should be left to the commander in chief. On September 14, Congress approved by a near-unanimous vote (98 to 0 in the Senate, 420 to 1 in the House) a resolution authorizing Bush to "use all necessary and appropriate force against those nations, organizations or persons he determines planned, authorized, committed or aided the terrorist attacks that occurred on September 11, 2001, or harbored such organizations or persons." The bill, which gave Bush the authority to determine which groups fit this description, was a blank check in terms of waging the initial phase of the war on terror. This was not an unforeseen consequence of the vote—legislators across the political spectrum agreed that the executive should be dominant in foreign policy in times of crisis. "I'm not for putting a lot of strings on it," said Senator John Kyl (R-Ariz.) of the bill. Maxine Waters (D-Calif.), one of the most liberal members of the House, included herself when she said, "Right now, the president has approval to do almost anything he wants." This was a sea change from the 1990s, when the House and Senate had regularly hamstrung Clinton's handling of foreign affairs. With a clear threat at hand, Congress now returned to the White House much of the diplomatic authority it had wrested during the Clinton years.[42]

Beginning in late 2001, in fact, Congress essentially ceded control of the entire foreign policy agenda. Carl Levin (D-Mich.), head of the Senate Foreign Relations Committee, quietly ended his fight against national missile defense. After withholding funding from the project for several months, Levin acceded to Bush's definition of diplomatic priorities. The current crisis, he explained, was not the time to "create dissent where we need unity." There were other examples of this new deference, as well. When legislators questioned restoring aid to Pakistan and other countries that Bush deemed vital allies, Senator Mitch McConnell (R-Ky.) was quick to reframe the issue. "All of the legislation has to be viewed through the prism of the situation we find ourselves in," he said. "We need to reward those countries that cooperate with us in fighting terrorism and punish those countries that don't." The aid bill soon passed.[43]

Nor did the public object to the notion that the war on terror would be a prolonged conflict requiring patience, sacrifice, and determination. With Bush framing the struggle as the next American crusade, observers looked to the last such mission for lessons. The war on terror, argued one writer, would be "Cold War II," a long struggle that would be won only if Americans showed sufficient resolve. In an uncharacteristically supportive editorial, the *New York Times* echoed the president's call for Americans to dedicate themselves to the task at hand. The nation needed to get over its "short attention span" and aversion to casualties, argued the editors. The coming conflict would be neither brief nor bloodless, but it offered a chance at a better world and a stronger national character. "We are in this for the long haul," they wrote.[44]

As they accepted the need for sustained action, Americans also embraced Bush's calls for a grand crusade. "America exists to defend freedom, overcome adversity, and right wrongs," declared conservative radio host Rush Limbaugh in words that Bush might have spoken himself. Another writer remarked that the joint session speech was "perfectly pitched to the mood of America."[45]

Many commentators found the president's summons especially appropriate in light of the experience of the prior decade. Having lacked a cause around which to rally during the 1990s, they eagerly accepted the notion that the United States again had something worth fighting for. *Weekly Standard* senior editor David Brooks, who had long bemoaned the absence of a great purpose in foreign affairs, was exultant at the prospect: "Now we remember that America is a cause and not just a free trade zone." Senator Pat Roberts (R-Kans.) thought that, with his joint session speech, Bush had become "the first president to articulate the post–Cold War policy." Such sentiment was not limited to conservatives. "Tonight the president has again called us to greatness, and tonight we answer that call," declared Senate Majority Leader Tom Daschle (D-S.D.). After the uninspiring 1990s, the idea of reclaiming a clear national purpose was a welcome one.[46]

This was especially the case in neoconservative quarters. For those who had proposed the creation of an American empire during the 1990s, Bush's "liberty and security" program meshed well with existing beliefs. Following 9/11, these advocates drew on Bush's rhetoric, citing the presence of rogue regimes and terrorists and the need to spread liberty as arguments in favor of an American imperium. Foreign policy analyst Max Boot called for the United States "to embrace its imperial role." The nation must answer 9/11 by liberating Afghanistan and Iraq, turning the latter state "into a beacon of hope for the oppressed peoples of the Middle East." Bush should create an empire of liberty in the region and emulate America's World War II–era leaders by remaking the globe along the lines of a "liberal world order based on peace and national self-determination." Confronted with new challenges and opportunities, Boot wrote, the United States must enlarge its political and ideological influence in the fashion of "a liberal and humanitarian imperialism."[47]

All in all, the idea of an ambitious war on terror was a winner at home. Most Americans endorsed recentering U.S. policy around this new theme and accepted the costs of doing so. Polls from late 2001 revealed hearty accordance with Bush's aims. Eighty-seven percent of respondents labeled his joint session speech as either excellent or good, and 89 percent approved of his handling of post-9/11 foreign policy. Perhaps more revealingly, Americans adopted the president's language. When Bush quoted Todd Beamer, one of the civilian heroes of 9/11, in announcing the initiation of military action in Afghanistan, the phrase "Let's roll" became a national rallying cry. Even U.S. casualties in Afghanistan failed to significantly dent public enthusiasm; in 2002, more than three-quarters of Americans favored continuing the fight in other countries, and Bush's approval rating stayed at or above 70 percent. As an answer to the political dilemmas of post–Cold War foreign policy, the war on terror looked quite promising.[48]

Shaping a Strategy

Bush simultaneously tackled the second requirement of reorienting U.S. diplomacy: integrating the concerns and priorities illuminated by 9/11 into the broader framework of foreign policy. The resulting strategy, drawn together in the year following the attacks, found its clearest expression in three official statements: the 2002 *National Security Strategy (NSS)*, Bush's State of the Union address in January 2002, and his speech at West Point in June of that year. Taken together and in the context of the administration's response to 9/11, these documents represented a conception of foreign policy that was more structured and (in theory, at least) more cohesive than any devised during the post–Cold War era.

At the heart of this strategy was an awareness of American power. "The United States possesses unprecedented—and unequaled—strength and influence in the world," the *NSS* stated. This position of preeminence presented "a time of opportunity for America," in that it allowed Washington both to provide for the immediate physical safety of the United States and its domestic institutions and to shape an international environment conducive to maintaining this security over the long run. The overall goal of U.S. policy, the *NSS* explained, would be to "translate this moment of influence into decades of peace, prosperity, and liberty."[49]

Although this overall goal was rather bland and, indeed, hardly different from that of the Clinton administration (or most Cold War–era administrations, for that matter),[50] Bush's view of potential threats to this goal was decidedly more focused than that of his predecessor. The United States, Bush's advisers believed, now faced a strategic situation vastly different from that of the 1990s. The period of "flux" that followed the "collapse of Soviet power," Rice asserted, "is coming to an end." Out of the geopolitical fluidity of the last decade, the administration believed, had arisen a confluence of threats more direct and imminent than any in the post–Cold War era. "The gravest danger our nation faces lies at the crossroads of radicalism and technology," wrote Bush in a concise summation of these perils. Whereas similar pronouncements during the Clinton years had often listed up to a dozen issues as the most pressing threats to U.S. security, Bush now focused on two: terrorism and weapons of mass destruction. The challenge posed by the first was, after 9/11, quite obvious. The attacks demonstrated that the dictates of national defense had "changed dramatically," with relatively weak actors now able to inflict catastrophic damage on the United States. "Enemies in the past needed great armies and great industrial capabilities to endanger America," Bush explained. "Now shadowy networks can bring great chaos and suffering to our shores for less than it costs to purchase a single tank." In an age in which it had become all too easy for terrorists to "penetrate open societies and to turn the power of modernized technology against us," defeating this threat must command primary attention.[51]

This danger was compounded by the proliferation of WMD among "rogue states." To be sure, Bush's concern over this issue predated 9/11. The president and Rice had long cited Saddam Hussein's weapons programs as cause for seeking regime change in Iraq, and the WMD aspirations of North Korea and Iran had elicited hostility from Bush as well. After 9/11, however, the WMD problem seemed all the more urgent. Primarily, the attacks raised the danger of a linkup between terrorists and states pursuing WMD. Many of the nations believed to have active weapons programs were also listed as state sponsors of terrorism by the State Department, and U.S. officials warned that the arming of al Qaeda or other groups with WMD would allow these organizations to take tens of thousands of American lives. "Mass civilian casualties is the specific objective of terrorists," the *NSS* stated, "and these losses would be exponentially more severe if terrorists acquired and used weapons of mass destruction."[52]

Even if Iran, Iraq, North Korea, or other enemies did not transfer WMD to terrorists, the administration believed, the United States could not tolerate the spread of these weapons in the post-9/11 security environment. Within Bush's inner circle, September 11 caused a fundamental rethinking of the nature and intentions of rogue regimes, resulting in a more aggressive stance against WMD proliferation. Before the attacks, Rice had argued that deterrence was sufficient to restrain rogue states. In this view, the United States could contain Iran and Iraq with its conventional presence in the Gulf and dissuade them from using whatever weapons they had through the threat of immediate and overwhelming retaliation. "If they [the Iraqis] do acquire WMD," she wrote in 2000, "their weapons will be unusable because any attempt to use them will bring national obliteration."[53]

The events of September 2001 caused the administration to rethink this assumption. The attacks had an immense psychological impact on Bush; he termed 9/11 "the Pearl Harbor of the twenty-first century." The realization that the United States' massive military strength had failed to dissuade an enemy from attacking prompted Bush to discard long-held concepts of defense. "Deterrence . . . means nothing against shadowy terrorist networks with no nation or citizens to defend," he declared in June 2002. "Containment is not possible when unbalanced dictators with weapons of mass destruction can deliver those weapons on missiles or secretly provide them to terrorist allies." Rumsfeld made the same point. The United States had entered "a new era of vulnerability; one in which new enemies strike our cities and our people in novel and surprising ways." In this new era, the only sure path to security lay in denying one's enemies the ability to attack. From Bush's perspective, combating terrorism and WMD proliferation were therefore overriding concerns.[54]

Bush's determination to emphasize these issues was obvious from any number of official statements in the year following 9/11. In most cases, Bush lumped antiterrorism and anti-WMD together under some variation of the "war on terror" label. In the *NSS,* he left little doubt that this vaguely designated struggle would command primary attention. "The war against terrorists of global reach is a global enterprise of uncertain duration," he explained. As a struggle of "uncertain duration," the conflict would characterize U.S. policy for the foreseeable future; as a "global enterprise," it would span the spectrum of U.S. initiatives abroad.[55]

Bush had priorities beyond the war on terror, of course, but the *NSS* left no doubt that these concerns were secondary. Regional conflicts, such as those between Israel and Palestine or India and Pakistan, had the potential to cause trouble insofar as they might spread or intensify, but in the eyes of the Bush administration, they were far less worrying than the terrorism-WMD nexus.[56]

Great power relations occupied a similar position in Bush's worldview. Like Clinton, Bush had no intention of surrendering the U.S. position of global preeminence. As a hedge against the resurgence of tensions between Washington and major powers such as China, Russia, or India, the *NSS* stated, the nation would maintain "military strengths beyond challenge," dissuading potential competitors from confronting the United States and channeling "rivalries to trade and other pursuits of peace."[57]

This hegemonic approach to great power relations was controversial, but Bush and his advisers did not think that it would detract from efforts to wage the war on terror. Primarily, they did not see great power relations as a source of major difficulty. Although there remained points of friction between the "centers of global power" (Europe, the United States, Russia, India, and China), the administration also perceived a commonality of interests between the United States and each of its counterparts. NATO kept the United States tied to Europe, and "a truly global consensus about basic principles" was "slowly taking shape" in relations between Washington and Beijing, New Delhi, and Moscow. With the United States and Russia "no longer strategic adversaries," U.S.-Russian affairs would move away from military issues and toward areas where there were strong common interests: Russian accession to the World Trade Organization, Russia's integration into Europe, and the forging of greater bonds between Russia and NATO. Although Washington and New Delhi disagreed about India's nuclear program, their shared desires for free passage through the Indian Ocean and India's growing interest in economic liberalization were conducive to warm relations. China's military buildup was a source of concern, but here too, Bush planned to emphasize areas of agreement, such as trade and the need for stability on the Korean peninsula.[58]

Moreover, as Bush focused on fighting terrorism and WMD, the likelihood of serious tensions arising among the great powers would decrease. According to the *NSS,* 9/11 "fundamentally changed the context" of great power relations. Catastrophic terrorism threatened not just the United States but Europe, Russia, India, and China as well. The major powers thus had greater incentive to cooperate with one another and to avoid conflicts that might hinder the antiterrorist effort. After 9/11, the *NSS* asserted, "the world's great powers find ourselves on the same side—united by common dangers of terrorist violence and chaos."[59]

With respect to tactics, Bush outlined a wide array of measures for fighting the war on terror. Defending against terrorism and WMD, the *NSS* made clear, required comprehensive efforts in the military, diplomatic, and economic realms. In many ways, the most striking aspect of Bush's strategy was its reliance on the military component of national power. To a degree not seen during the post–Cold War era, Bush's approach to foreign policy rested on the threat and use of force. With terrorists operating "in 60 or more countries," the United States would intervene militarily "to disrupt and destroy terrorist organizations of global reach and attack their leadership; command, control, and communications." The *NSS* emphasized "direct and continuous action using all the elements of national and international power," including covert operations, military assistance to friendly nations, and, in certain cases, direct U.S. intervention. Bush pledged to seek international support and sanction for this effort to destroy "the threat before it reaches our borders," but at the same time, he warned that if cooperation was not forthcoming, "we will not hesitate to act alone."[60]

Indeed, preemptive action was crucial to U.S. policy.[61] In speeches and planning documents, Bush and his advisers stated repeatedly that the United States would not permit rogue nations or terrorists to acquire WMD. Given the obsolescence of deterrence and the catastrophic potential of attacks using WMD, the United States must retain the option to strike before being attacked or even before a threat had fully matured.[62] If actors deemed hostile by Washington even attempted to develop WMD, they made themselves subject to preemptive assault.

The administration's post-9/11 approach to foreign policy brought about other departures as well. During the 2000 election, Bush had criticized nation building as a drain on U.S. resources and moral standing. The fact that al Qaeda had used Afghanistan, a state with no effective government for much of the 1990s, as a training ground led him to reconsider. September 11 "taught us that weak states . . . can pose as great a danger to our national interest as strong states," Bush wrote. States lacking a capable government and working civil society might become terrorist sanctuaries. Accordingly, the United States must help reconstruct and strengthen these states so as to deny al Qaeda and other terrorist groups space to operate. Nation building was back.[63]

American diplomacy should be similarly proactive in addressing the threat. As mentioned earlier, Bush planned to emphasize antiterrorism in U.S. relations with the major powers. Beyond providing for stronger ties with these nations, this approach would promote burden sharing and a more effective conduct of the war on terror. Foreign assistance was crucial to forming the type of "shifting coalitions" that, in Rumsfeld's view, would prosecute the conflict. Washington would need foreign help in shutting down terrorists' sources of revenue, tracking enemy operatives, and gathering intelligence. Measures such as the Proliferation Security Initiative, a multinational effort to restrict the movement of WMD components, were similarly dependent on international assistance.[64]

In addition, Bush planned to thoroughly review U.S. relations with those nations that had links to terrorist organizations or WMD proliferation or that occupied strategic positions in the fight against these threats. Although Bush's much-discussed statement that "either you are with us, or you are with the terrorists" was in part a threat to states such as Iraq and Iran, it also raised the possibility of improved ties to those countries that were "with us." If diplomatic pressure, moral opprobrium, and even military action awaited those nations that refused to aid the United States, various rewards would be available to those that were more forthcoming. In particular, the administration would consider offering economic and security assistance, as well as political support, to capitals that allied themselves with Washington. In one way or another, Bush would restructure important relationships around the new preoccupations of U.S. policy.[65]

The problem of which states to support and which to confront was especially pertinent with respect to U.S.–Middle East relations. In this region, Bush's emphasis on simultaneously pursuing terrorists and pressuring rogue regimes produced a conflict in U.S. policy. In order to fight a war in Afghanistan and take a strong stance against Iraq, the United States needed the support of Egypt, Saudi Arabia, and the smaller Gulf countries. Yet in many ways, these "moderate" states were breeding grounds for the very terrorists Bush proposed to fight. Fifteen of the nineteen 9/11 hijackers were from Saudi Arabia, and experts on terrorism contended that authoritarian governance in Riyadh, Cairo, and elsewhere contributed to the dissatisfaction and frustration informing jihadism. In the long run, defeating international terrorism might require the United States to push for political and social reform in the Middle East.

In the aftermath of 9/11, though, Bush rejected this argument and instead committed to supporting "modern and moderate" (that is, pro-American) regimes in the region. To some degree, his decision stemmed from the fact that, with war on the horizon, it seemed unwise to alienate those governments amenable to working with Washington. In addition, Riyadh controlled one-third of the world's proven oil reserves, and Bush saw Saudi cooperation as crucial to avoiding supply disruptions. At a deeper level, in the months after 9/11, the administration simply did not accept the idea that terrorism could be defeated by addressing the "root causes" identified by academics and other commentators. Echoing Bush's characterization of al Qaeda as "flat evil," one official argued, "There's no point in addressing the so-called root causes of bin Laden's despair with us." Terrorism did not stem from legitimate grievances but rather from the evil and twisted nature of its practitioners. "Short of the United States going out of existence," said L. Paul Bremer, an adviser to Clinton and later Bush, "there's no way to deal with the root cause of [bin Laden's] terrorism."[66] In 2002, well after the initial shock of 9/11 had faded, the State Department gave an official explication of this position. "Al-Qaeda is a movement defined by hatred," a department report stated. "They hate progress, and freedom, and choice, and culture, and music, and laughter, and women, and Christians, and Jews, and all Muslims who reject their distorted doctrines. They love and worship only one thing, and that is power—power they use without mercy to kill the innocent." From this perspective, confrontation was the only viable option for defeating terrorism, and forcing Middle Eastern reform to the detriment of support in that confrontation was unwise. Although the United States would gladly back liberalization movements that did not endanger the stability of friendly regimes in the region, that would be the limit of its exertions. At the outset, the military and diplomatic exigencies of the war on terror took precedence over more distant concerns.[67]

All told, the strategy formulated in the year after 9/11 represented an attempt to craft a coherent foreign policy centering on the threat of terrorism and proliferation. In shaping this approach, Bush's advisers placed great emphasis on cohesiveness; Powell stressed the "establishment of priorities" that would be "unified by a strategy," while Rice boasted that the *NSS* represented a doctrine "as coherent as any since the end of World War II." If the phraseology (war on terror) was vague, the strategic conception underlying the words was in fact quite focused. It was, in Bush's view, a policy meant to "make use of every tool in our arsenal," reaching across the range of U.S. diplomatic and military activities.[68]

Bush's personal determination to make fighting this war on terror his overriding priority was evident in the evolution of his thoughts on foreign policy. Prior to 9/11, Bush had adhered to a conservative, anti-interventionist view of the United States' world role. He portrayed excessive adventurism as corrosive to U.S. defense readiness and diplomatic standing, stressed the need for "humble" behavior, and warned against assuming that U.S. values were universally applicable. The nation should not allow fuzzy moral concerns to distract it from the hard realities of foreign affairs, he argued. "My guiding question," Bush promised in 2000, would be, "Is it in our nation's interests?"[69]

After the attacks, Bush's worldview changed dramatically. Given mission and purpose by 9/11, he now took a far different view of the United States' international task. "Different circumstances require different methods, but not different moralities," declared the same president who had once warned against such universalism. "Moral truth is the same in every culture, in every time, and in every place." Having earlier cautioned against excessive moralism, Bush now considered foreign affairs "a conflict between good and evil." The search for an understated foreign policy had been replaced by a Manichaean worldview and a militarized approach to international affairs. Winning this battle between freedom and terror, Bush repeatedly averred, would be the "primary focus" of his presidency.[70]

To be sure, the war on terror was not the be-all and end-all of U.S. policy. Several objectives enumerated in the *NSS*, such as maintaining the world's strongest military and promoting free trade, had long been characteristic of American statecraft.[71] There were, moreover, several conceptual gaps in the strategy. The phrasing was awkward, as the administration hesitated to make clear which terrorist groups were "of global reach" and thus enemies in the war on terror. The term *war on terror* was itself problematic. Although it served as a convenient encapsulation of U.S. strategy, it also tended to treat antiterrorism and anti-WMD as the same, but in practice, they could be very different. This problem was already evident in certain official statements. The administration generally conflated its two dominant concerns, treating the behavior of terrorist groups and "rogue states" as essentially identical. Finally, for a policy geared toward combating the threat of terrorism, Bush's approach initially offered little in the way of long-term solutions, focusing instead on the more immediate situation.

These issues notwithstanding, Bush's was a more coherent strategy than any that had been laid out since the end of the Cold War. Rather than encompassing a broad range of interests and dangers without prioritizing them, the *NSS* was clear on which questions were most important and which were secondary. Equally notable, the administration planned to adapt its diplomatic and military practices to conform to this conception of threats and priorities. Finally, unlike enlargement and the New World Order, Bush's strategy benefited from the unreserved enthusiasm and determination of the chief executive. On a conceptual plane, at least, Bush's strategy represented a return to the focus and clarity that had been absent for more than a decade.

The War on Terror Unfolds

During the roughly one year following 9/11, the same preoccupations that shaped Bush's formal strategy exerted a determinative influence on a number of U.S. policies abroad. In various instances, U.S. officials reworked existing policies to account for the new centrality of terrorism and WMD, altering American diplomacy in ways that had not been foreseen before 9/11 changed the context for Washington's interaction with the world.

The most obvious departure was in U.S. relations with Afghanistan. Whereas Clinton had been unwilling to take strong measures to deprive al Qaeda of its sanctuary, and Rice had initially opted for a gradualist approach to the problem, just four weeks after the 9/11 attacks, the United States was embroiled in a war in that country. The countdown commenced in the days after 9/11, as Bush told Rumsfeld and JCS Chairman Hugh Shelton to be ready to attack within one month. After the Taliban refused to turn over bin Laden and allow U.S. inspectors virtually unlimited access to the country, Bush put his war plan into action. CIA and special-forces operatives infiltrated Afghan territory, linking up with a loose confederation of anti-Taliban groups known as the Northern Alliance. They plied Northern Alliance commanders with money and supplies, urging them to take the offensive. On October 7, the air war began as U.S. planes attacked al Qaeda camps and the Taliban's front lines. The effort progressed slowly at first, and certain commentators, recalling Afghanistan's past as the graveyard of empires, whispered about a quagmire. The Pentagon soon unleashed the full might of the U.S. air arsenal, including the much-talked-about "daisy cutter" bombs, and the CIA prodded the Northern Alliance into action. Opposition forces captured the strategic city of Mazar-e-Sharif and then the capital, Kabul, in late 2001. By year's end, the Northern Alliance had fractured the Taliban's hold on the country, and major combat operations concluded in early 2002.[72]

In some respects, Operation Enduring Freedom bore a strong resemblance to Clinton's wars. U.S. ground troops played a minimal role, with much of the fighting being done by Afghan proxies. American involvement and American casualties were kept to a minimum. This strategy was popular politically and made sense in view of Moscow's bloody experience in Afghanistan during the 1980s. It backfired in December 2001, however, when Northern Alliance forces allowed a cornered bin Laden to slip away.[73] Still, the fact of prolonged U.S. military involvement in Afghanistan was a break with the recent past. Although they had realized that bin Laden posed a threat to the United States, neither Clinton nor Bush would have seriously contemplated such an initiative pre–September 11. As Madeleine Albright acknowledged, before this "megashock," measures along the lines of Operation Enduring Freedom had been out of the question.[74]

An equally impressive reversal of U.S. policy came in the aftermath of the fighting. Working from the new calculus of the war on terror, the Bush administration pledged to oversee Afghanistan's reconstruction. Assistant Secretary of State Christina Rocca acknowledged that the Afghan war "will be followed by a longer, internationally supported process that aims to rebuild and bring lasting stability to the war-torn country to prevent it from being a safe haven for terrorists in the future." Over the next four years, U.S. soldiers built roads, supervised elections, and trained police, among other activities. U.S. assistance to Afghanistan climbed to $1.6 billion in 2004, with no exit in sight, and the State Department confirmed that the United States would "remain engaged for the long haul." In 2000, Bush had considered nation building a waste of money and lives; after 9/11, he saw it as crucial to national security.[75]

The diplomacy surrounding the Afghan war was no less indicative of Bush's new priorities. Before 9/11, Pakistan had been veering toward enemy status in the eyes of both the Bush and the Clinton administrations. Nuclear tests in 1998, a military coup a year later, infiltration into the disputed province of Kashmir, and Pakistani support for the Taliban soured the relationship in the late 1990s. Within hours of the terrorist attacks, this trend reversed itself. Perceiving that it would not be beneficial to be accused of sponsoring terrorism after 9/11, Musharraf made an abrupt about-face. He agreed to allow U.S. planes to use Pakistani airspace and landing facilities in the coming war in Afghanistan and pledged his "unstinted cooperation in the fight against terrorism."[76]

Musharraf's turnaround, combined with the fact that Pakistan occupied valuable real estate next to landlocked Afghanistan, opened a new phase in U.S.-Pakistan relations. On September 14, U.S. diplomats in Islamabad urged Washington to give complete backing to Musharraf's government. The Pakistani leader would incur significant political risk by cooperating with Washington, they reported, and would therefore "need full U.S. support." In response, Bush approved an economic and diplomatic assistance package. He lifted sanctions remaining from the 1998 nuclear tests, and the money flowed. All told, Pakistan received cash and debt forgiveness totaling roughly $1 billion. "Pakistan is a strong ally," Bush declared in November, praising his new friend Musharraf's "courage, vision, and leadership." Within weeks of 9/11, U.S. military officials were operating in Pakistan, coordinating the use of Pakistani airspace and territory for the assault on Afghanistan. In the coming months, Pakistan assumed the role of full (if tacit) military ally, stationing thousands of troops on the Afghan border to prevent al Qaeda soldiers from escaping the U.S. noose.[77]

More quietly, Bush pursued other avenues of cooperation that previously would have seemed improbable. Prior to 9/11, U.S. officials had little patience with the central Asian republic of Uzbekistan, owing mainly to its blatant disregard for civil liberties. In 2000, the State Department called Uzbekistan "an authoritarian state with limited civil rights," and through mid-2001, U.S.-Uzbek relations were cold at best. Yet if Tashkent abused its citizens, it also occupied strategic territory near Afghanistan, a fact that exerted a profound influence on the relationship after 9/11. The Pentagon needed bases from which to conduct search-and-rescue missions during Operation Enduring Freedom, and Uzbekistan seemed an ideal candidate. In relatively short order, Bush obtained landing and overflight rights for U.S. pilots. In return, Washington toned down its criticism of Uzbek security practices, guaranteed Uzbek territorial integrity, and gave Tashkent $500 million in security assistance. In October, the two nations signed an agreement looking forward to "a qualitatively new relationship based on a long-term agreement to advance security and regional stability."[78]

The changes in the U.S.-Uzbek relationship outlasted major combat in Afghanistan. In 2002 and 2003, the United States went from scorning Uzbekistan's human rights violations to taking advantage of those less-than-admirable qualities. In a process known as "extraordinary rendition," the CIA shipped suspected al Qaeda operatives to Tashkent for interrogation. Given Uzbekistan's sorry human rights record and propensity for torture, certain diplomats criticized the policy. "We should cease all cooperation with the Uzbek security services," one British official complained. "They are beyond the pale." The appeal was ineffective. Rendition was reputed to be a valuable source of intelligence, and with minor operations ongoing in Afghanistan, Uzbek bases remained precious commodities. The United States had "benefited greatly from our partnership and strategic relationship with Uzbekistan," averred new JCS Chairman Richard Myers. State Department officials also affirmed U.S. ties to Tashkent. Assistant Secretary Elizabeth Jones stated without a hint of irony, "Our country is now linked with [Uzbekistan] in ways we could never have imagined before September 11."[79]

Even enemies received a fresh look after 9/11. Bush considered approaching Iran in late 2001, believing that the two countries' mutual antagonism toward the Taliban (Iran and Afghanistan had previously been on the brink of war after Taliban forces killed a number of Shiite Muslims) outweighed twenty years of hostility between Tehran and Washington. Given Bush's harsh stance on Iran during the 2000 campaign and his continuing concern over Tehran's nuclear activities, this potential shift was all the more notable. After 9/11, Bush subtly explored the possibility of rapprochement. The State Department opened a back channel to Tehran, and British foreign secretary Jack Straw examined areas of collaboration during a visit to Iran. Iranian officials reciprocated these gestures, offering to conduct search-and-rescue missions for U.S. pilots downed over Afghanistan, pledging to help rebuild that nation after the war, and supporting the formation of a new Afghan government. The overtures eventually came to naught, and Iran ended up an enemy in Bush's war on terror. Even so, the administration's willingness to seriously consider a change in U.S.-Iran relations showed how 9/11 had tinted Washington's worldview.[80]

This tendency to rethink old relationships manifested itself even more clearly in the case of Libya. Like Pakistan, Libya had been the subject of considerable U.S. hostility before 2001. Muammar Qaddafi's involvement in international terrorism, most notably his government's suspected complicity in the 1988 Lockerbie bombing, and his pursuit of WMD were areas of particular concern, and both the first Bush and Clinton had sought to isolate the regime. At the outset of the younger Bush's presidency, U.S.-Libya ties remained strained. The State Department cited Qaddafi's terrorist ties as the chief reason why "the United States remains dedicated to maintaining pressure on the Libyan Government." In April 2001, Bush professed "no intention" of easing the economic and diplomatic sanctions long in place against Tripoli.[81]

At first, it looked as though U.S.-Libyan affairs might go from simmering hostility to open confrontation following 9/11. With Bush now viewing WMD proliferation as a top-level threat, Qaddafi's weapons programs were all the more offensive to Washington. The CIA reported that Qaddafi's nuclear and chemical programs continued apace, and Defense Department advisers urged Bush to force a showdown on the issue. Ultimately, however, Bush sided with State

Department officials, who recommended a more understated approach. With a war in Afghanistan already in progress and a clash with Iraq on the horizon, U.S. military and diplomatic resources were stretched too thin to sustain another confrontation. Perhaps more important was the fact that Qaddafi was quick to see the writing on the wall after 9/11. Deducing that being tarred as a state sponsor of terrorism and a WMD aspirant would be a distinct liability in the post-9/11 era, the Libyan leader took a conciliatory tone in his dealings with Bush. Already pursuing reconciliation with Britain in the fall of 2001, Qaddafi offered the olive branch to the United States as well. He called the 9/11 attacks "horrible," pledged to cooperate with Washington to "eliminate the common dangers of international extremism and terrorism," and supported the war in Afghanistan. Shortly thereafter, Qaddafi announced his willingness to sign the Chemical Weapons Convention and to share intelligence on al Qaeda with Western officials.[82]

Beginning in 2002, Bush reciprocated these feelers, pursuing a dialogue with Qaddafi in the hope of negotiating an end to Libya's WMD programs and suspected terrorist links. In early 2003, Libyan officials offered to make restitution for the Lockerbie bombing and to terminate Tripoli's weapons programs in return for an end to U.S. and UN sanctions. After Libya took responsibility for Lockerbie and pledged to pay compensation to the families of the victims, Bush promised that regime change was not on the agenda with respect to Libya. In late 2003, the negotiations concluded, with Qaddafi pledging to provide U.S. inspectors with access to Libya's weapons facilities "immediately and unconditionally." He also forswore building missiles with a range greater than 150 miles and acceded to the Non-Proliferation Treaty. The Bush administration promised "tangible improvements" in Libya's "relations with the world community" (a reference to lifting sanctions) and even referred to Tripoli as a potential "source of stability in Africa and the Middle East." U.S. officials soon dismantled Qaddafi's chemical and nuclear programs, and the normalization of relations proceeded shortly thereafter. To the surprise of most observers, U.S.-Libya relations became more congenial than they had been in decades.[83]

Bush's preoccupation with terrorism-related issues also produced subtle changes in U.S. diplomacy toward some of the major powers. During 2000 and 2001, U.S.-Russia relations were strained as the United States moved toward deploying national missile defense. September 11 momentarily shifted the focus of that relationship, and a common interest in fighting terrorism led Bush and Putin to emphasize areas of agreement between the two powers. Having pursued what one writer called an "anti-hegemonic" foreign policy during the late 1990s, Moscow reversed recent practice by not opposing a UN resolution authorizing the United States to use force in Afghanistan, and during the opening months of the antiterrorist campaign, it provided Washington with intelligence on al Qaeda and the Taliban. Putin also overruled advisers who sought to trade this assistance for an explicit quid pro quo on national missile defense and the future expansion of NATO, and he further established his bona fides by urging Uzbekistan to grant the United States basing rights.[84]

These steps led to a temporary upswing in U.S.-Russia relations. Bush did not retreat from his stance on national missile defense, but he took other conciliatory steps. The Moscow Treaty of 2002 took some of the sting out of ABM abrogation, as Bush and Putin pledged to further slash their nuclear arsenals over the next ten years, a step long advocated by the Russian leader. Putin's war in Chechnya, which before 9/11 had elicited only scorn from the White House, now garnered grudging support, as Bush refrained from objecting to a conflict against an enemy suspected of carrying out terrorist attacks in Russia. Having previously condemned "Russian brutality" in Chechnya, Bush now demanded that Chechen leaders "immediately and unconditionally cut all contacts with international terrorist groups." On the economic front, Bush backed Moscow's bid for WTO accession, and the Commerce Department certified Russia as a "market economy," facilitating freer trade between the countries. Although the war on terror failed to erase the sources of U.S.-Russian tension, it did provide something of a palliative for the relationship. As one Russian observer noted, 9/11 was "so advantageous to the Russian government, you might think they did it themselves."[85]

The logistics of post-9/11 diplomacy were no less revelatory of Bush's adapted thinking. In the Middle East, for instance, a new view of priorities and resources greatly affected the U.S. approach to the

Israel-Palestine peace process. Having distanced himself from Clinton by disengaging from the negotiations at the start of 2001, Bush had been preparing for a new foray into the process in the weeks before 9/11. He had planned, as a symbolic gesture, to meet Yasir Arafat at the United Nations and, much as Clinton had, to assume the role of "honest broker" in the talks. Following the attacks, however, Bush decided that he could no longer afford the type of intensive involvement demanded by the peace process. Nor could he consort with a leader with ties to Hamas and other Palestinian groups that were deemed terrorist organizations by the State Department. Bush postponed the peace proposal, temporarily shelving what had only recently been seen as a major diplomatic initiative. When Bush was able to devote attention to Israel-Palestine issues, his view of the conflict showed the effects of the emerging war on terror. Having already been strongly pro-Israel, Bush tilted further in this direction. He labeled Hamas and other Palestinian groups as enemies in the war on terror and subsequently moved to restrict their foreign funding.[86]

Even in areas in which U.S. interests did not change after 9/11, the omnipresence of the war on terror shifted the relevance of long-standing goals. Bush's call to "ignite a new era of global economic growth through free markets and free trade" could just as easily have come from Clinton, but the influence of the administration's new focus was still evident. International commerce, explained U.S. trade representative Robert Zoellick, was about more than domestic prosperity. Economic openness promoted "the values at the heart of this protracted struggle." Trade fostered prosperity and political liberty in developing countries, Zoellick argued, and it served as an antidote to the poverty and isolation that bred terrorism. Accordingly, commerce was no less integral to the war on terror than military force. In this respect, post-9/11 policy was less a change in direction than a reframing of old issues.[87] Whether it caused shifts in policy or merely shifts in focus, the war on terror thus emerged as the lodestar of U.S. diplomacy.

In the roughly one year after 9/11, U.S. policy came full circle, back to the coherence and simplicity of the Cold War. Following the attacks, the Bush administration crafted a strategy that, though hardly seamless, showed a concerted effort to prioritize objectives and threats and to restore internal consistency to U.S. policy. This is not to say that Bush's approach was the optimal one to achieve the ends he outlined, but merely to note that his worldview was a good deal more focused than that of his predecessors. By forging a strategy that encompassed a broad range of issues but centered on combating the dangers posed by terrorism and WMD, Bush, for better or worse, provided a clear organizational structure to the conception of foreign policy.

In practice, too, these concerns were central to numerous elements of post-9/11 diplomacy. In several instances, Bush's policies illustrated the new dictates of antiterrorism and antiproliferation, as he tailored individual initiatives to reflect the centrality of these issues. Even when objectives did not change following 9/11, the attacks left an imprint on official characterizations of U.S. aims. There were, no doubt, aspects of national security strategy that stood apart from the war on terror, but given Bush's words and actions after 9/11, it is clear that the president saw this conflict as the centerpiece of his international agenda. It served as the heuristic that had been missing for more than a decade, the logic that connected various policies and provided a greater overall uniformity to U.S. interaction with the world than had existed since the close of the Cold War.

Just as important were the domestic effects of the war on terror. After struggling for twelve years to find a formula that could hold the attention and interest of the public, U.S. officials at last crafted a message powerful enough to create a solid domestic consensus. Bush packaged his strategy into an easily understandable, emotionally appealing, and logically attractive whole, giving him the political leverage his predecessors had lacked. U.S. officials could once again compel domestic cooperation, minimize dissent, and ensure public support for costly endeavors abroad—all things that the senior Bush and Clinton had failed to do. Finally, it appeared, an administration had solved the strategic-political dilemma of the post–Cold War era, reformulating American policy in a largely coherent fashion and doing so in a way that satisfied the domestic audience.

Indeed, the political legacy of 1990s diplomacy likely contributed to Bush's portrayal of post-9/11 foreign policy as an all-encompassing crusade. There is little doubt that the strategy that emerged after 9/11 was primarily a factor of strategic and security issues, but political and rhetorical concerns complemented this principal motivation. If Rice's and Rumsfeld's comments are any indication, the rationale for framing the war on terror in so grandiose a manner drew on the lessons gleaned from Clinton's experience during the 1990s. Bush's broad definition of policy was important both as a means of guaranteeing U.S. security and as a way of escaping the political quandaries of the post–Cold War era. As the United States emerged from the disorienting diplomatic odyssey of the 1990s, the legacy of that decade remained relevant.

Underlying the United States' return to coherence, however, was yet another potent dilemma. In weaving so compelling a narrative about the national purpose, the administration greatly oversimplified U.S. aims and world realities. Contrary to Bush's "with us or against us" rhetoric, the world was not dichotomized between terror and freedom. Contrary to his assertions, al Qaeda was not driven solely by an antipathy for democracy. And contrary to his lofty language, U.S. policy often acted as a drag on liberty by shoring up repressive Middle Eastern regimes. However well-intentioned it may have been, Bush's rhetoric was more effective as a domestic political tool than as a description of foreign affairs. Given the expansiveness of the war on terror, this approach seemed likely to court disappointment—or worse. Even as Americans reclaimed the holy grail of simplicity, it remained to be seen whether the effects would be for good or ill.

10

Waging the War on Terror

As it turned out, the drawbacks to the moral and logical reductionism of the war on terror were not long to appear. By 2006, the simplicity offered by Bush's strategy had proved to be less than the cure-all that so many observers had predicted or hoped. In some cases, the moralistic nature of the president's diplomacy served as a hindrance rather than an aid to the conduct of foreign policy. At other points, U.S. officials succumbed to the temptation to make matters "clearer than truth," using the war on terror as singular justification for initiatives whose origins were in fact quite complex.

As the war on terror unfolded, moreover, it became clear that the Bush administration's strategy was not nearly as well integrated as it had originally appeared. In certain instances, the supposed coherence of foreign policy was illusory, and the contradictions of diplomacy were no less vexing in 2004 than in 1994. Indeed, between 2002 and 2006, Bush's top priorities increasingly came into conflict with one another. Policies conducive to antiterrorism were not necessarily compatible with a strong stand against the proliferation of weapons of mass destruction, while confronting rogue regimes with WMD aspirations could impede, rather than further, the struggle against jihadism.

On the domestic scene, the war on terror took a similar turn. Antiterrorism remained a powerful rhetorical tool—perhaps too powerful. The war on terror quickly evolved into a political lever, an implement of electoral warfare, and an illiberal influence on domestic society. After a decade in which there had been little agreement on foreign policy, the political strength of the new consensus was sufficient to cause concern.

In the end, the return to coherence brought about by 9/11 had mixed results for the practice and politics of U.S. diplomacy. The apparent intellectual consistency of the war on terror eased the making and selling of foreign policy, which U.S. officials likely considered all to the good. But these virtues of the new paradigm were also its flaws. At the beginning of the twenty-first century, simplicity's upside had been more prominent; as U.S. policy developed over the next four years, the disadvantages came into view.

Morality and Myopia

When Bush took office in 2001, U.S.–North Korea relations were at their highest point in fifty years. Clinton's engagement policy had restored direct diplomacy between Washington and Pyongyang, and an agreement to end Kim Jong Il's nuclear and missile programs remained a possibility. After some initial diffidence, Bush signed on to this policy, pledging to take a "comprehensive approach" to better ties. If Kim acted in good faith, he promised, "we will expand our efforts to help the North Korean people, ease sanctions, and take other political steps."[1] Maintaining another facet of Clinton's policy, Bush's advisers downplayed the odiousness of Kim's regime. The Pyongyang government had proved surprisingly resilient over the past decade, noted North Korea policy coordinator Charles Pritchard. "There is a degree of stability within instability here." Kim was not going anywhere, and the United States would have to deal with him.[2]

As with so many other aspects of foreign policy, however, 9/11 altered this approach. Bush's growing preoccupation with WMD, displayed most prominently in his dealings with Iraq, disposed the president toward a sterner stance. After 9/11, Bush declared, he could not "permit the world's most dangerous regimes to threaten us with the world's most dangerous weapons."[3]

The moral certitude of the war on terror also figured in Bush's move toward confrontation. Whereas Bush chose conciliation over conflict with respect to Libya, he was far less inclined to negotiate with North Korea, a "despotic regime" that "starves its people." After 9/11, Bush came to view the morally abhorrent aspects of Kim's rule as a primary reason for confronting the North. "I loathe Kim Jong Il," he said. "I've got a visceral reaction to this guy, because he's starving his people." Bush became decidedly undiplomatic in discussing North Korea, calling Kim a "pygmy." Having come into office pledging to think only of "interests" when determining foreign policy, Bush now took a decidedly moralistic perspective on international affairs. In early 2002, he grouped Pyongyang with Tehran and Baghdad under the label "axis of evil" and subsequently moved toward a showdown with the North. In March, the administration alleged that Pyongyang had violated the 1994 framework, and four months later, U.S. officials revoked an offer to meet with Kim's negotiators.[4]

As the White House sought to isolate North Korea, relations with Kim unraveled. The fragile ties established during the 1990s broke conclusively in October 2002, when Pyongyang declared that it possessed nuclear weapons and planned to withdraw from the Non-Proliferation Treaty. The revelation both stunned and angered the Bush administration. One official called the announcement a "jaw-dropper," and Richard Armitage allowed that it "threw us into a bit of a tizzy."[5]

The crisis deepened in late 2002 and early 2003, and Washington soon found itself with few appealing options. Military action against Pyongyang's nuclear facilities would likely lead to a war of immense destruction. "Nobody . . . is talking about attacking North Korea," Condoleezza Rice promised. Hawks such as Undersecretary of State John Bolton wanted to take a hard diplomatic line, including possible economic sanctions, but this course was problematic as well. U.S. allies in the region, most notably South Korea, denounced Bush's recent actions as unnecessarily provocative. When engagement advocate Roh Moo Hyun, a persistent critic of Bush's "hard-line" policy, won the South Korean presidency in late 2002, the estrangement increased.[6]

The remaining options seemed no more palatable. China, South Korea, Japan, and Russia all favored a conciliatory approach, but for Bush, negotiation was anathema. After 9/11, the ethical view of foreign affairs had become ubiquitous in Bush's policies, and it proved difficult to untangle U.S.–North Korea relations from this paradigm. In contrast to mid-2001, when Kim's style of government had been troublesome but not diplomatically salient, in 2003 and 2004, it dominated U.S. policy. Citing the iniquities of Kim's rule, Bush refused to negotiate directly with the North. "I just can't respect anybody that would really let his people starve, and shrink in size as a result of malnutrition," he explained in 2003.[7]

Forced to choose between unattractive options, Bush eventually—and rather halfheartedly—accepted six-party negotiations with North and South Korea, Russia, Japan, and China. Through 2004, the talks made little progress. Washington disagreed fundamentally with the other parties over the proper mix of sticks and carrots to be used in negotiating with Kim, and U.S. proposals therefore remained vague and unattractive to the North. By early 2005, U.S. policy was in crisis. Attempts to isolate Pyongyang were ineffective, with China continuing to provide fuel and food to North Korea. The six-party talks repeatedly broke down amidst recriminations from one side or the other, and they bore little resemblance to the quiet diplomacy of the late 1990s. After Rice labeled North Korea one of several "outposts of tyranny" in early 2005, Pyongyang again broke off negotiations. By spring, U.S.–North Korea diplomacy had devolved into name-calling. Bush described Kim as a "tyrant," and adviser Andrew Card called him a "bad person"; Kim labeled Bush a "hooligan" and a "philistine." The relationship remained frozen, with North Korea using the halt to further its weapons programs. The CIA now believed that Pyongyang might have as many as eight nuclear weapons, and in April 2005, Defense Intelligence Agency director Lowell Jacoby reported that North Korea had the technological know-how to mount its warheads on missiles that could reach the West Coast.[8]

The strident rhetoric and lack of progress in the six-party talks provoked concern among U.S. allies in East Asia. In May and June, South Korean officials criticized a plan to enforce an economic "quarantine" on the North and stated their intention to bring Kim back to the table by means of energy and diplomatic concessions. Seoul also broke openly with Bush over U.S. public diplomacy. "Leaders should be providing solutions rather than slogans," said South Korea's deputy foreign minister. "These public exchanges are not going to solve anything."[9]

Confronted with growing opposition, the Bush administration altered its negotiating strategy. After an interagency review and a summit with Roh in early June, Bush approved a less confrontational approach. Deviating from their earlier refusal to negotiate directly with Pyongyang, U.S. officials agreed to "direct contacts" within the framework of the six-party talks. Bush subsequently supported a South Korean offer of energy and financial assistance to Kim and toned down his previously heated language. "We can't have dueling speeches," argued chief U.S. negotiator Christopher Hill. During June and July, Bush refrained from the type of accusatory exchanges that had earlier impeded the discussions. The president referred to the North Korean leader in more respectful tones as "Mr. Kim," while Rice affirmed U.S. recognition of the North's territorial and political sovereignty.[10]

This policy bore fruit in the summer of 2005. The six-party talks reconvened in August and, after intensive negotiations, produced a statement of principles in which North Korea pledged to eventually give up its nuclear program. The statement had been a Chinese proposal; following North Korea's withdrawal from the Non-Proliferation Treaty in 2003, Beijing's desire to avoid a U.S.–North Korea confrontation near China's borders had led it to take an active role in the six-party talks. The agreement was also made possible by the efforts of both U.S. and North Korean officials to maintain a tone that was, in Hill's phrasing, "businesslike." A last-minute concession by Hill to provide Pyongyang with a light-water reactor in addition to security guarantees and economic aid was also crucial.[11]

After this encouraging development, however, U.S.–North Korea relations again took a turn for the worse in late 2005. One the eve of talks meant to formalize the loose deal reached two months earlier, Bush made an ill-timed reference to Kim as the "tyrant in North Korea." A new round of recriminations ensued, and the parties failed to set a schedule for implementing the statement of principles. The negotiations lapsed, and a year later, North Korea confirmed what U.S. analysts had long suspected when it staged its first nuclear test. U.S. diplomats tried to win UN approval of a series of harsh economic sanctions, but South Korean and Chinese resistance again resulted in a considerably more moderate stance. By this point, the White House looked largely powerless either to rein in Kim's nuclear program or to effectively isolate his regime.[12]

A final judgment of Bush's North Korea policy has yet to be rendered, but the trajectory of the relationship since 2001 underscores an important liability of the administration's approach to foreign affairs. Following 9/11, the moral impetus created by the launching of the war on terror pervaded Bush's dealings with North Korea. Often, this characteristic made the president rigid in his view of the North and proved incompatible with effective diplomacy. (In a sense, Bush's stance mirrored the U.S. approach to the third world during the early Cold War, when the inflexibility of the Truman and Eisenhower administrations impeded U.S. policy.)[13] Viewing Washington-Pyongyang relations through the moral prism that was so influential after 9/11, Bush had little interest in the distasteful—but, as Clinton had discovered, often necessary—business of negotiating with morally repugnant regimes. Although the moral simplicity of the war on terror had certain benefits for the making and selling of foreign policy, it was not without its drawbacks as well.

With Friends Like These . . .

Relations with Pyongyang exposed the liabilities of Bush's diplomatic paradigm; U.S.-Pakistan relations during 2003 and 2004 gave the lie to the notion that the war on terror represented a fully cohesive program for foreign policy. Since 9/11, Pakistan had been an ally of necessity. Although Bush had little sympathy for Islamabad's nuclear program or its Kashmir policy, Pakistan's Afghan frontage made its cooperation crucial. "Pakistan is probably more responsible for the arrests of and capture of al Qaeda personnel than perhaps any other country in the world," Rice acknowledged in 2003. Moreover, with Islamist sentiment potent in Pakistan (certain opposition parties openly supported the Taliban), Musharraf's dictatorial tendencies were less objectionable. Between 2001 and 2004, Pakistan offered a rare Muslim source of solidarity in the war in Afghanistan and against jihadism more broadly. Bush spoke glowingly of Musharraf, calling him "a courageous leader and a friend of the United States."[14]

In late 2003 and early 2004, though, Western intelligence agencies uncovered evidence that Pakistan and the United States continued to work at cross-purposes. In past decades and up to the present, it appeared, Pakistani scientist A. Q. Khan had run an extensive proliferation network, selling nuclear components to at least seven countries. The buyers included Libya, Syria, North Korea, and Iran—in short, nearly all the nations that Bush counted as enemies in the war on terror. Libya received a complete blueprint of a nuclear weapon; North Korea and Iran obtained much of the expertise needed to build a uranium bomb.[15]

Even more disconcerting to U.S. officials were signs that the Pakistani government had facilitated Khan's work. Because Khan had used air force jets as delivery vehicles, it seemed unlikely that he was merely a renegade agent. "Dr. Khan was not working alone," asserted International Atomic Energy Agency director Mohammad El Baradei. Speaking off the record, U.S. officials agreed. "This was not a rogue operation," said one. "The military has to be involved, at high levels." Doubts about Musharraf's cooperativeness were compounded by the fact that he had neutralized Khan only after a visit from Armitage.[16]

Given Bush's priorities after 9/11, Khan's actions might have provoked a strong response. As it happened, however, the U.S. reaction was quite tepid. Bush professed himself satisfied that Musharraf "has assured us that his country will never again be a source of proliferation" and took no diplomatic or economic action against Pakistan. In language that was more than a little ironic, given events in Afghanistan and Iraq (discussed later), U.S. officials declared that Pakistan's internal affairs were no business of Washington's. The Khan matter, including Musharraf's suspiciously lenient treatment of the scientist (he was pardoned almost immediately), was not "a matter for the United States to sit in judgment on," said State Department adviser Richard Boucher.[17]

The Khan episode illustrated Washington's dependence on Pakistan and, more generally, that the logic of the war on terror was far from straightforward. Despite the fact that Khan had undoubtedly undermined Bush's nonproliferation efforts, the United States simply could not prosecute the fight against al Qaeda without Musharraf's cooperation. Pakistani forces guarded the Afghan border, and Pakistani intelligence tracked al Qaeda operatives. Musharraf had "been a stand-up guy when it comes to dealing with the terrorists," Bush said. And as bad as Musharraf looked after the Khan scandal, his willingness to aid Washington and his ability to keep Pakistani hardliners at bay made him a valuable ally. Pakistanis considered Khan "a national hero" due to his role in developing the Pakistani nuclear deterrent, Colin Powell explained; pressuring Musharraf to take stronger action against the scientist would thus not be wise.[18]

Moreover, when revelations about the Khan network emerged in early 2004, U.S.-Pakistan relations were at a particularly crucial juncture. For two years, U.S. officials had struggled with the rules of engagement in Afghanistan. Al Qaeda operatives used Pakistan as a safe haven, escaping across the border, where U.S. forces could not pursue. This constraint hampered U.S. operations and frustrated the Bush administration. After months of quiet negotiations, Musharraf had finally agreed to allow U.S. forces the right of "hot pursuit" in an upcoming spring offensive aimed at capturing Osama bin Laden. A strong response to Khan's actions would likely undermine Musharraf's already tenuous position (he had recently survived two assassination attempts) and scuttle this tacit pact (which Pakistan denied publicly). "It's a quid pro quo," explained a U.S. official. "We're going to get our troops inside Pakistan in return for not forcing Musharraf to deal with Khan."[19] U.S.-Pakistan relations remained pleasant in public, and the administration had to acquiesce in this setback to nonproliferation as the price of furthering its antiterrorism campaign. In this case, at least, antiterrorism and antiproliferation proved not to be synonymous—or even compatible. Pakistan continued to straddle the administration's neat divide between "terror" and "freedom," illustrating that world politics was considerably more complex than Bush made out and debunking the notion that 9/11 had provided universal consistency to U.S. policy.

Shifting Priorities?

During the 2000 campaign, Bush had joined the conservative assault on Clinton's foreign policy by calling for the rapid development and deployment of national missile defense. He maintained this stance once in office, abrogating the Anti-Ballistic Missile Treaty in late 2001. As the war on terror unfolded, Bush placed even greater emphasis on NMD, increasing the project's funding and announcing plans to deploy by 2004. "As the events of September 11 made all too clear, the greatest threats [come] . . . from terrorists who strike without warning, or rogue states who seek weapons of mass destruction," Bush declared. "We know that the terrorists, and some of those who support them, seek the ability to deliver death and destruction to our doorstep via missile."[20]

In some ways, 9/11 certainly made NMD more attractive to the administration. As noted previously, Bush became increasingly sensitive to threats following 9/11, and missile defense promised (in theory, at least) to close one avenue of attack against the United States. Furthermore, 9/11 had promoted the idea that U.S. enemies were less rational than the Cold War–era Soviet Union and that deterrence must therefore give way to defense. "The probability that a missile with a weapon of mass destruction will be used against U.S. forces or interests is higher today than during most of the Cold War," the CIA predicted in 2002. In this sense, NMD comported well with Bush's post-9/11 policy.[21]

Yet in other regards, NMD (later referred to simply as "missile defense," to stress that the project would protect U.S. allies as well) did not fit squarely within the new policy framework. For one thing, a number of official statements raised questions as to how effective missile defense would be in protecting the United States in the "new era" to which Bush and his advisers so often referred. As the CIA recognized in late 2001, a missile strike was perhaps the least likely method of attack against the United States. After all, September 11 had shown that box cutters and airliners could be as dangerous as ballistic missiles. "U.S. territory is more likely to be attacked . . . from nonmissile delivery means—most likely from terrorists—than by missiles," the CIA concluded.[22]

Another argument in favor of rethinking missile defense was that there were a number of gaps in homeland security that seemed equally or more pressing. Port security was particularly lacking, receiving only $93 million in funding in 2002 (compared with $8 billion for NMD). Given that a cargo container, rather than a missile, was more likely to be the delivery vehicle for a chemical, biological, or radiological device, this paucity was especially significant. Border security was similarly bare; only 300 agents patrolled the U.S.-Canada frontier. The Coast Guard was struggling to stay afloat, being unable to afford even routine repairs for its vessels. The status of nuclear materials in Russia and the former Soviet republics, long a source of concern for U.S. officials, was especially worrisome to many observers in light of the fear that al Qaeda desired to manufacture "dirty bombs." Senator Joseph Biden (D-Del.) questioned whether it was wise to spend more than $100 billion over the next decade to protect against "the least likely threat we face" when more vulnerable areas of homeland security were being managed at or below subsistence levels.[23]

The practicality of missile defense was also a concern. Although Bush radiated confidence in the system, other officials acknowledged that the project faced substantial technological and design hurdles. Tests conducted in late 2002 failed to produce the desired results, and experts argued that missile defenses could be overcome by relatively inexpensive modifications to offensive weapons (such as using dummy warheads to confuse the interceptors). After these setbacks, Assistant Secretary of Defense J. D. Crouch stated that missile defense was only "a potential and partial solution to one" of the dangers confronting the United States. Rumsfeld was not much more optimistic, calling the system "better than nothing."[24]

Nonetheless, Bush pushed forward. In late 2002, he announced plans to deploy the system by 2004, and the administration continued to fund the project at levels exponentially higher than those for port security, border patrol, and other homeland defense measures.[25] If Bush's reasons for doing so stemmed partly from the issues highlighted by 9/11, they also reflected the fact that, in certain regards, U.S. policy had changed very little since the attacks.

In a strategic sense, the rationale for missile defense had been present well before 9/11. Asked at one point to describe how his view of missile defense had changed since the attacks, Rumsfeld replied, "I don't know that it has." Since assuming power, the administration had seen missile defense less as a tool designed solely to shelter the homeland and more as a means of shoring up U.S. power projection capabilities in the Persian Gulf and other vital regions. On the Arabian and Korean peninsulas, U.S. strength and credibility were based on Washington's ability to deploy forces with relative impunity. As Iraq, Iran, and North Korea deployed ICBMs, this ability would be imperiled. If Saddam Hussein, Ayatollah Khamenei, or Kim Jong Il possessed the capability to strike New York, a president might think twice about exerting U.S. power in the region in question. For these governments, one official document explained, missile programs were intended to "overcome our nation's advantages in conventional forces and to deter us from responding to aggression against our friends and allies in regions of vital importance." Accordingly, missile defense was important not simply to protect the United States but also to protect the U.S. position in strategically important areas.[26]

There was, additionally, a political aspect to Bush's persistent enthusiasm for the project. Missile defense had been a campaign promise in 2000, and, like any president, Bush was loath to reverse himself. In the same manner, the administration was understandably reluctant to jettison what had previously been the centerpiece of its defense policy. Doing so would be a tacit admission that Bush had been wrong about defense priorities and would cede a political victory to the anti-NMD forces, almost all of whom were Democrats.

Missile defense remained attractive in economic and bureaucratic terms as well. At $8 billion per annum, the system was the single largest defense item in the Pentagon's budget. If Bush delayed implementation of the project, this money would likely go to other agencies, in effect, slashing military outlays. Thus, in addition to keeping the United States safe from North Korea, missile defense promised to keep the Defense Department safe from the budget cutters.[27] The financial implications were no less relevant for aerospace contractors. Just as the Strategic Defense Initiative had been a windfall for these corporations, so was missile defense. Even when divided multiple ways, $8 billion was a substantial sum, and firms lined up for their share. Northrop-Grumman entered the missile defense game in 2004, seeking an entrée into the "global missile defense market." When the firm won a large contract, chairman Ronald Sugar gushed, "That award blows away all of our assumptions of revenue synergies." Economically lucrative and strategically attractive, missile defense benefited from the unqualified support of the aerospace community.[28]

To note these additional sources of enthusiasm for missile defense is not to allege some hegemonic-political-bureaucratic-economic conspiracy. Rather, it is merely to point out that, even after 9/11, original concerns existed alongside old issues and familiar internal factors that drove U.S. policy. It is also meant to underline that, as in the case of relations with Pakistan, antiterrorism did not always coexist easily with Bush's other objectives. In this case, the cost of missile defense hampered improvements in homeland security. The war on terror certainly provided a new sense of direction for foreign policy, but the change was not as all-pervasive or as seamless as the administration sometimes made out.

On to Baghdad

Even as combat continued in Afghanistan in early 2002, there were signs that there would soon be a second front in the war on terror. Although Iran, Syria, Libya, and North Korea were all mentioned as potential targets, Iraq seemed to be the most likely candidate. Since 9/11, rumors of war had swirled in Washington. Taken in the context of his support for regime change, Bush's inclusion of Iraq as part of the "axis of evil" mentioned in his 2002 State of the Union address did little to dispel these notions. By early 2002, war appeared probable, and even dove Colin Powell was telling senators that the president was "looking at a variety of options" for toppling Saddam Hussein. As the rhetoric intensified during 2002, it seemed that war against Iraq was only a question of when, how, and with whom.[29]

The "why" was complicated. The Iraq war sprang from a multitude of sources, some of which predated 9/11, and some of which came into focus only after the attacks. The strategic rationale had been in place long before Bush took office. For many of Bush's future advisers, regime change had been on the agenda since the mid-1990s. In 1998, members of the Project for a New American Century, including Rumsfeld, Wolfowitz, Armitage, Zoellick, and Bolton, authored a letter to Clinton deploring the deterioration of the U.S. position in the Gulf. Hussein's pursuit of WMD, they declared, had "a seriously destabilizing effect on the entire Middle East." Should these programs reach fruition, they wrote, "The safety of American troops in the region, of our friends and allies like Israel and the moderate Arab states, and a significant portion of the world's supply of oil will all be put at hazard." To protect these interests, the United States should seek to overthrow the Iraqi leader and, in the meantime, conduct sharp military responses to his periodic violations of the sanctions imposed against his regime. At roughly the same time, Bolton elaborated on the need for regime change. At the heart of the matter, he wrote, was "the accelerating decline of U.S. influence in the Gulf and the increasing likelihood that Saddam Hussein will break out of the ring so laboriously built around his regime." In short, maintaining Washington's primacy in the region entailed bringing down Hussein.[30]

This idea affected U.S. planning well before 9/11. Treasury Secretary Paul O'Neill recalled that, "from the start," Bush's advisers engaged in "building the case against Hussein and looking at how we could take him out." In this sense, 9/11 offered a chance to implement a long-desired policy. Shortly after 9/11, Rumsfeld told Bush that the attacks presented an "opportunity" to end Hussein's rule, an opening to "go massive, sweep it all up, things related and not." Wolfowitz was of like mind and "was always of the view that Iraq was a problem that had to be dealt with," Powell recalled. "And he saw this as one way of using this event as a way to deal with the Iraq problem."[31]

If the administration favored toppling Hussein before 9/11, the attacks made Bush even more receptive to using force to achieve this goal. September 11 "changed the nature of the presidency," Bush believed. The commander in chief had to be proactive in the new era, eliminating threats before they matured. The "lesson of September 11," Rice agreed in early 2002, was to "take care of threats early." This lesson seemed particularly relevant with respect to Iraq. Long convinced that Hussein had chemical and biological weapons and sought to obtain a nuclear capability, Bush felt that he could no longer tolerate the Iraqi leader's apparent prevarications on issues of WMD or rely on sanctions to keep him in check. Now skeptical of the efficacy of deterrence and increasingly alert to potential threats, Bush came to see war as an appropriate response to Iraq's transgressions. "September the 11th obviously changed my thinking a lot about my responsibility as president," he commented at one point. "Because September the 11th made the security of the American people . . . a sacred duty for the president." If the reasons for toppling Hussein were roughly the same, then, the urgency had grown. By invading Iraq, Bush and his top advisers reasoned, they could remove a danger to national security and at the same time warn other rogue regimes against pursuing WMD or harboring terrorists.[32]

The idea of democratizing Iraq also became more alluring after 9/11. In late 2002 and early 2003, democracy building began to take on greater importance in Bush's overall conception of the war on terror. In part, this new emphasis reflected the same moral-historical imperative that was so prominent in his rhetoric. After 9/11, it seems that Bush genuinely came to believe that eradicating terrorism and spreading freedom were the national heritage and duty of the United States. Warned by aides that this would be an arduous task, he was unperturbed. "At some point, we may be the only ones left," he conceded. "That's okay with me. We are America." Freeing Iraq from tyranny, Bush said in late 2002, was a matter of the United States' historical "responsibility of defending human liberty against violence and aggression."[33]

There was also a strategic aspect to creating democracy in Iraq. Implanting a liberal government in the heart of the Middle East would have a profound impact on the overall climate in the region, Bush believed, starting a sort of "domino effect" that would dramatically improve the U.S. security posture. "Clearly there will be a strategic implication to regime change in Iraq," he predicted privately. A democratic Iraq would undermine illiberal governments in Tehran and Damascus, removing other threats to U.S. interests. The mood in the White House was that "with American troops so close, the Iranian people would be emboldened to rise against the mullahs," adviser David Frum later recalled.[34]

If Bush's motives for invading Iraq were multiple, his rhetoric was in most cases misleadingly simple. When Bush's Iraq policy encountered opposition in mid-2002, the president chose to focus on what he knew would sell. Eschewing complex justifications, Bush and his advisers reduced the issues at hand in Iraq to fit more comfortably within the current foreign policy consensus. As one official later stated, the administration "needed something that inspired fear." Accordingly, Bush portrayed war with Iraq as a vital corollary to the war on terror, arguing that Hussein had WMD and ties to international terrorism and had perhaps been complicit in 9/11. This was quite an oversimplification of the actual motives for regime change, and Wolfowitz later admitted as much. "We settled on the one issue that everyone could agree on," he said, "which was weapons of mass destruction, as the core reason." The administration emphasized the conjunction of WMD and 9/11 at the expense of other factors influencing Bush's decision.[35]

In the run-up to war in late 2002 and early 2003, Bush's spokesmen unflinchingly insisted that toppling Hussein was crucial to the war on terror. "Iraq and terrorism go back decades," Powell told the United Nations in February 2003. The secretary described a "sinister nexus between Iraq and the al Qaeda terrorist network." After 9/11, Powell said, the United States could not wait for tedious inspections to work. "Should we take the risk that he will not someday use [WMD] at a time and place and in the manner of his choosing?" he asked dramatically. "Not in a post-9/11 world." Bush stressed the same themes. In his most important speech on Iraq in October 2002, Bush predicted that "Iraq could decide on any given day to provide a biological or chemical weapon to a terrorist group or individual terrorists." Given this possibility and the nuclear threat, he argued, "We cannot wait for the final proof—the smoking gun—that could come in the form of a mushroom cloud."[36]

Having committed to this line of argument, the administration felt compelled at times to overstate its case. In mid-2002, when intelligence on Hussein's WMD programs proved to be less concrete than expected, U.S. officials exaggerated Iraq's weapons capabilities. In July, advisers to Tony Blair warned that even though "the case [against Iraq] was thin," U.S. intelligence was "being fixed around the policy." "Bush wanted to remove Saddam, through military action," the report stated, "justified by the conjunction of terrorism and WMD." An example of this tendency came in October 2002. After receiving a highly hedged national intelligence estimate of Iraqi WMD programs, the administration removed the qualifications from a public version of the document. The State Department's Bureau of Intelligence and Research had concluded that there was no "compelling case that Iraq is currently pursuing . . . an integrated and comprehensive approach to acquire nuclear weapons," but this statement was omitted from the unclassified report. The strategy was not one of deliberate distortion but rather one of excessive zealousness. As one official said after the fact, "We were not lying [about WMD]. But it was just a matter of emphasis."[37]

Whatever its inaccuracies, the administration's public campaign was effective. By repeatedly linking Iraq to the issues that dominated public concern in the year following 9/11, Bush created a consensus for war. Polls from late 2002 and early 2003 revealed that 87 percent of respondents believed that Saddam Hussein had "certain" or "likely" ties to al Qaeda, and a clear majority accepted that war with Iraq was part of the war on terror. After Powell's UN speech, the *Washington Post* concluded, "It is hard to imagine how anyone could doubt that Iraq possesses weapons of mass destruction." Congress was no more inclined to challenge Bush; a war resolution passed easily.[38]

Preemption and Its Consequences

Even before the war began, however, there emerged serious questions of whether invading Iraq would be as beneficial to the antijihadist campaign as the administration claimed. Conquering and occupying Iraq promised to severely strain the operational capabilities of the military, impairing its ability to conduct missions in Afghanistan and elsewhere. General Eric Shinseki estimated that "something on the order of several hundred thousand troops" would be needed to stabilize postwar Iraq. "We are talking about post-hostilities control over a piece of geography that is fairly significant with the ethnic tensions that could lead to other problems," he warned.[39]

A preemptive war could be similarly deleterious for Bush's coalition-building efforts. Although the major NATO allies had rallied to the cause in the wake of 9/11, committing several thousand troops to the reconstruction of Afghanistan, they were, with the exception of Britain, unenthusiastic about attacking Iraq. Powell was well aware of this resistance, warning shortly after 9/11 that a unilateral strike would "wreck" coalition solidarity. After Bush resolved for war, Powell tried to ameliorate the effects of the decision by urging the president to work with the Security Council to obtain new resolutions calling on Hussein to disarm and authorizing military action if he did not. Cheney objected, arguing that new resolutions would "provide false comfort that Saddam was somehow 'back in his box,'" but Bush sided with Powell. U.S. diplomats spent much of late 2002 and early 2003 lobbying for UN support.[40]

Even so, relations with the other Security Council powers came under considerable strain as Bush moved toward war. Whereas Bush hoped that the United Nations would quickly declare Iraq in breach of sanctions and authorize the use of force, the Europeans favored a more deliberate approach. French, Russian, and German leaders doubted U.S. claims about Iraq's WMD programs and terrorist affiliations and believed that a revitalized inspection program was the best course. Germany's Gerhard Schroeder pledged to use "all my power" to avoid war, and Vladimir Putin warned against "unilateral action, outside of international law." French foreign minister Dominic de Villepin called the U.S. stance "impatient," and on the eve of the final Security Council vote, President Jacques Chirac pledged to veto the force resolution "whatever the circumstances." As Bush pushed forward in spite of this opposition, his policy risked fracturing the international consensus that had prevailed following 9/11.[41]

War with Iraq might prove counterproductive in other respects as well. If negative perceptions of the United States were at the root of anti-Americanism in the Middle East, observers warned, perhaps bombs and bullets were not the solution. Former Central Command head Joseph Hoar, whose experience in Somalia had given him some insight on the subject, argued that Iraq would merely distract the United States from the real war on terror. The United States had to go beyond military solutions and address the deeper causes of hatred for the West. "At the end of the day," he urged, "the war on terrorism will be won only when we convince one billion Muslims that we are, in fact, a just society, that we support peace, justice, and equality for all people."[42]

With multiple reasons impelling Washington toward war, these objections did not alter U.S. policy. After demanding in mid-March 2003 that Paris and Moscow "show their cards" in the United Nations, Bush concluded that the Security Council would not pass the resolution. Days later, a force of mainly U.S. and British units invaded Iraq. At first, the war went smoothly. Casualties were low as the coalition swept toward Baghdad and evicted the Baathist regime. After the initial rout, however, momentum dissipated rapidly, and the conflict's aftermath was hardly what Bush and his advisers had expected. Casualties steadily rose as an insurgency took root and a civil war broke out between Iraq's Shia and Sunni populations. Iraq's reputed ties to al Qaeda proved to have been exaggerated or untrue. The much-touted WMD stockpiles turned out to be mere phantoms, most likely destroyed by Hussein after the first Gulf War. A blue-ribbon panel created to study the issue concluded that the intelligence community had been "dead wrong in almost all of its pre-war judgments about Iraq's weapons of mass destruction."[43]

Over the next three years, the war had a number of negative consequences for U.S. policy. Sectarian and insurgent violence mounted, threatening to destroy Iraqi society and destabilize the Middle East as a whole. American forces soon found themselves party to a civil war, and the continuing occupation, requiring nearly 150,000 troops through 2006, became a serious drain on U.S. military resources. As early as May 2005, JCS chairman Richard Myers confided to Congress that the presence in Iraq had undermined U.S. capabilities worldwide. As a result of the protracted engagement, he stated, the military "may be unable to meet expectations for speed or precision as detailed in our current plans." Should America have to fight another conflict simultaneous to the Iraq war, he warned, this overstretch would result in higher casualties and lower efficiency for U.S. forces.[44]

Instead of reducing the terrorist threat, moreover, the invasion was actually a boon for jihadists and a blow to U.S. credibility in the Muslim world. The war produced a strong anti-U.S. reaction in the region, complicating Bush's efforts to cultivate ties with Middle Eastern states whose cooperation was needed to prosecute the fight against al Qaeda. The Arab League termed the attack "illegitimate," with Secretary-General Amr Moussa calling the event "a sad day for all Arabs." Riyadh refused to allow U.S. forces to use Saudi bases for the assault on Iraq, and there were riots in the smaller Gulf countries that had backed the invasion. In general, the war resulted in a marked upswing in anti-U.S. opinion in the Middle East, and whatever goodwill Washington had accumulated as a result of 9/11 largely vanished.[45]

From a military perspective, too, the war in Iraq brought benefits to al Qaeda and other jihadists. The al Qaeda leadership had long sought to draw Washington into a prolonged, guerrilla-style conflict in the Middle East that would allow jihadists to recruit new fighters and expose U.S. soldiers to repeated attacks. The war in Afghanistan in 2001–2002 had been disappointing on this count due to the relative scarcity of U.S. ground forces, but in the years following March 2003, the Iraq campaign provided precisely this opportunity. Jihadists from across the Middle East streamed into Iraq, in some cases joining the growing Sunni insurgency. Abu Musab al-Zarqawi, the leader of the newly constituted "al Qaeda in Iraq," pledged allegiance to bin Laden in 2004, giving the organization a presence in Iraq that, ironically, it had previously lacked. Combined, the insurgents and jihadists conducted thousands of attacks on U.S. troops and the new Iraqi government, bringing the stability of the nation very much into doubt. In 2005, a classified CIA report concluded that Iraq had become the terrorist nexus that Powell had described two years earlier, as insurgents and foreign jihadists gained experience and acquired valuable contacts while fighting the occupation forces. According to CIA director Porter Goss, the foreign fighters would leave Iraq "experienced in and focused on acts of urban terrorism," forming "a potential pool of contacts to build transnational terrorist cells." As an exercise in counterterrorism, the war in Iraq proved to be profoundly counterproductive.[46]

The diplomatic consequences were similar. After Bush went ahead with the invasion over the opposition of three-fifths of the UN Security Council, many foreign observers started to see the United States less as an aggrieved victim of 9/11 than as a hyperactive global hegemon. Having aligned more closely with Washington after 9/11 than at any time since the mid-1990s, Putin gradually returned to the antihegemonic stance that Yeltsin and Primakov had charted in years prior. Moscow continued to explore deeper ties with China, and during the run-up to the Iraq war, Putin considered including India in the partnership as a means of rounding out the anti-U.S. coalition. Relations with China suffered as well. Chinese leader Hu Jintao warned that Washington's "strategic eastward movement has accelerated," and he warmed to the idea of a countervailing alliance with Russia. In 2005, Moscow and Beijing pressured Uzbekistan to end its basing agreement with the United States, and when Tashkent abrogated the pact, an Uzbek-Russian alliance followed shortly thereafter. In Western Europe, relations with the United States followed a similar decline. Washington's "favorable rating" fell to 25 percent in Germany and 31 percent in France. Whereas *Le Monde* had proclaimed "we are all Americans" after 9/11, Chirac now pledged to "end unilateralism once and for all." The Iraq war rent NATO and the short-lived anti-terrorist coalition, returning the United States to the unilateralist course charted in the late 1990s.[47]

Issues involving Iraq eventually undermined Bush's standing at home as well. During the three years following the invasion, questions repeatedly arose whether Bush had been entirely forthcoming in his prewar presentation of intelligence. As U.S. casualties mounted, more and more Americans answered in the negative. A November 2005 poll showed that 57 percent believed that Bush had "deliberately misled" the country on the issue of Iraq's WMD programs. The inevitable comparisons to Vietnam, which had accompanied every major U.S. intervention in the post–Cold War era, also began to dog the president. With the situation in Iraq deteriorating, yet Bush claiming that there was no alternative but to stay the course, cartoonists and columnists likened the president's outlook to Lyndon Johnson's blinkered stance in 1967 and 1968. By refusing to consider a change in policy, critics alleged, Bush had led the nation into an all too familiar predicament. Bush's moral authority, so crucial in the earlier conduct and selling of post-9/11 foreign policy, waned as U.S. involvement in Iraq grew less popular. In November 2006, in an election that turned largely on public dissatisfaction with the president's handling of Iraq, the Democrats took control of both the House and the Senate.[48]

Beyond giving the United States its first truly disillusioning experience of the post-9/11 era, the Iraq war touched on several emergent realities of foreign policy. On a rhetorical level, it showed that, like their Cold War predecessors, U.S. policy makers had fallen prey to the temptation to make matters (as Dean Acheson liked to say) "clearer than truth." In the political climate of 2002 and early 2003, when memories of 9/11 were fresh, the notion of using the anxieties created by that event to sell Iraq policy was all too attractive to the Bush administration. Rather than presenting war with Iraq on its own complex merits, U.S. officials reduced the issues at hand to fit within the dominant rhetorical paradigm of the moment. Presented with broad agreement on the war on terror after a decade of discord, Bush put this consensus to full use in the run-up to war.

The episode also demonstrated that, during the approach to the conflict, at least, this reductionist approach remained effective. Although invading Iraq was a contentious issue, Bush successfully framed it in the attractive terms of the war on terror. His success in this regard was all the more notable given that, in the debate over Iraq since 1991, there had been little or no enthusiasm for a full-scale invasion. Public discussion in 2002 and 2003, by contrast, showed that 9/11 had shifted the range of acceptable policies to encompass the most assertive and costly of measures. As a means of inducing cooperation from a previously reticent public, the rhetoric of the war on terror could be powerful indeed.

Finally, more so than relations with Pakistan and the subtleties of the NMD debate, the United States' post-9/11 involvement in Iraq laid plain the disjunctures of the war on terror. The invasion succeeded in eliminating a rogue regime suspected of pursuing WMD and consorting with terrorists (although the allegations turned out to be false), but only at the cost of creating a jihadist haven, straining the U.S. military, rending the antiterror coalition, and tarnishing Bush's reputation as a foreign policy leader. In other words, whatever Bush achieved in Iraq came at a heavy cost in other important areas of his own national security strategy. Combating terrorism and confronting regimes that pursued WMD were compatible with the conceptual framework of the war on terror, but in practice, the fit was not nearly so seamless.

By late 2006, in fact, Iraq was seriously distorting Bush's foreign policy. The war drained U.S. diplomatic capital, making it increasingly difficult to organize even "shifting coalitions" with American allies and other nations. The growing turmoil in Iraq invited Iranian influence in the southern part of the country. The occupation stretched the U.S. military to the limit, detracting from Washington's credibility in other crises and generally handicapping American efforts abroad. And as the chaotic reality of events in Iraq increasingly consumed the attention and energy of top-level officials and the nation as a whole, it became difficult to keep the larger strategic picture in view. To Bush and his advisers, the war on terror may have remained a coherent program, but to many observers—American and international alike—it appeared that the president's strategy had begun to unravel.

The War on Recession

If U.S. diplomacy indicated the incongruities and contradictions of Bush's strategy, the domestic conduct of the war on terror had a like effect. Although the notion restored a foreign policy consensus, it also took on some pernicious aspects of a national crusade. At times, leaders exploited the post-9/11 climate for political gain, using the emotions sparked by the attacks to their own advantage. In other instances, an understandable concern with security predisposed U.S. officials to restrict the very freedoms and liberties that lay at the heart of the nation's cause.

Even in the immediate aftermath of 9/11, the war on terror carried important political connotations. If the fight against terrorism offered an opportunity to mobilize Americans for a foreign challenge, it was no less useful as an inducement to action on the domestic scene. This was especially so in terms of the national economy, which by September 2001 was already showing signs of sluggishness. Analysts predicted that the uncertainty engendered by the attacks would further slow consumer spending and economic growth. The travel industry was in particularly poor shape; several airlines were on the verge of bankruptcy, and a few slid over the precipice.[49]

With recession (and the dip in presidential popularity that accompanies such downturns) staring it in the face, the administration could not resist tweaking Americans' surging patriotism in an attempt to bolster the economy. Although restoring consumer confidence was surely a worthy goal following 9/11, Bush and other officials portrayed consumption as a national duty. "Get on board," he told skittish airline passengers. "Do your business around the country; fly and enjoy America's great destination spots; get down to Disney World in Florida; take your families and enjoy life the way we want it to be enjoyed." The attacks should not make Americans hesitant to spend, he argued, but rather made spending a patriotic duty. After 9/11, he stated, "We've got a fantastic opportunity to reinvigorate this economy." Cheney was even more direct, urging Americans to "stick their thumb in the eye of the terrorists and . . . not let what's happened here in any way throw off their normal level of economic activity."[50]

Whether these appeals had any meaningful effect is difficult to determine. The economy endured a predictable slippage after 9/11, but the damage was not as bad as some analysts had feared. To an indeterminate extent, Bush's encouragement probably helped limit consumer uneasiness. Still, it was not long before cynical observers took aim at his blandishments. A *New Yorker* cartoon depicted two corporate executives indulging in an expensive lunch, with one saying, "I figure if I don't have that third martini, then the terrorists win." Former Clinton adviser Robert Reich ridiculed the notion of "market patriotism." "Patriotism normally suggests a willingness to sacrifice for the good of the nation—if not lives, fortunes and sacred honor, at least normal creature comforts," he wrote. "But market patriotism suggests a strange kind of sacrifice: Continue the binge we've been on for years." Needless to say, Reich did not find this conception of sacrifice endearing.[51]

Condemnations such as Reich's eventually exposed the inanity of the "if we don't spend, the terrorists win" appeals, but in the aftermath of 9/11, these calls to action were commonplace. As the administration's rhetoric demonstrated, the war on terror brought with it political opportunity. Even on issues that bore little relevance to foreign policy, the emotional and psychological imperative of resistance could be used to advantage. As an early precedent, Bush's appeals demonstrated that the logic of the war on terror was not always resistant to exploitation.

Terror-Baiting

This trend continued in the three years following 9/11. Politicians looked to create electoral gains by touting their own security credentials or, more often, by impugning those of their opponents. Terror-baiting first emerged as an aspect of electoral politics in the 2002 midterm elections. In tightly contested races, Republicans allied themselves with a popular president and cast aspersions on the patriotism of their Democratic rivals. The mudslinging was most intense in Georgia, where GOP challenger Saxby Chambliss tarred incumbent Max Cleland as a foreign policy weakling. Chambliss ran television ads that portrayed Cleland alongside Hussein and bin Laden and castigated the senator for voting against certain of Bush's security proposals (the votes were actually procedural rather than substantive). "Max Cleland says he has the courage to lead, but the record proves that's just misleading," an announcer intoned ominously. Given that Cleland had lost three limbs in Vietnam, Democrats and even many conservatives expressed outrage at the tactics. Nonetheless, Chambliss's strategy paid dividends. Despite trailing until just before the election (when the ads appeared), Chambliss won a narrow victory.[52]

Outside Georgia, terrorism was a major issue in congressional races across the country. In polls, 82 percent of those surveyed considered a candidate's antiterrorist qualifications as "extremely important." With a Republican in the White House, the GOP enjoyed the fruits of this concern. Fifty-two percent of respondents thought that Republicans were better at fighting the war on terror, with only 23 percent favoring Democrats. The GOP gained seats in both the House and the Senate, bucking a historical trend of midterm setbacks for the ruling party. As one scholar put it, the outcome was the "undeniable, if unintended, gift of Osama bin Laden."[53]

The 2002 elections were a mere prelude to the 2004 presidential contest. The ability to lead the country in the war on terror became a central issue in the race, which never had a clear leader. Bush and Senator John Kerry blasted each other on the subject. Kerry made an issue of Iraq, faulting Bush for a "rush to war." "Facing reality is not necessarily this president's strong suit," Kerry charged; Bush's obsession with Saddam Hussein had led the United States into a quagmire. Bush supporters turned the tables on Kerry, accusing him of being soft on defense and diplomacy in a manner reminiscent of the Red-baiting of the 1950s. Conservative Democrat Zell Miller argued that a Kerry victory would mean a U.S. defeat in the war on terror. "This politician wants to be leader of the free world," Miller fumed. "Free for how long? For more than 20 years, on every one of the great issues of freedom and security John Kerry has been more wrong, more weak and more wobbly than any other national figure." As president, Miller concluded, Kerry would be a disaster, an irresolute politician who would merely "encourage our enemies and confuse our friends."[54]

Cheney painted an even starker picture of the ramifications of a Kerry win. If Kerry triumphed, Cheney contended, his weakness and vacillation would court disaster. "It's absolutely essential that eight weeks from today, on November 2nd, we make the right choice," Cheney warned. "Because if we make the wrong choice, then the danger is that we'll get hit again, that we'll be hit in a way that will be devastating." Electing Kerry, Cheney hinted, would invite a second 9/11.[55]

Although terrorism was surely an issue that needed to be argued in 2004, these exchanges were in many cases more spurious than substantive. Cheney's and Miller's comments aside, Kerry proposed a vigorous prosecution of the war against al Qaeda (discussed later). What these verbal attacks lacked in seriousness, though, they made up for in effectiveness. Eighty-five percent of voters saw the issue of terrorism as "extremely important" in determining their choice, and a poll in mid-October gave Bush a 21-point lead in this category. Equally important, terrorism allowed Bush to shift the debate away from his own difficulties in Iraq and with the domestic economy. In an election widely seen to turn on foreign policy, Bush won narrowly.[56]

If the superpower struggle had given rise to the label "soft on communism," twenty-first-century diplomacy now had an equivalent pejorative. The war on terror had quickly evolved from an expression of national purpose into a political bludgeon, and politicians used the emotions and fears of the domestic audience for electoral gain. As the rhetoric escalated between 2002 and 2004, the situation in many ways resembled the less savory aspects of the political Cold War.

Homeland Security and Civil Liberties

Beyond shedding much heat (and considerably less light) on electoral politics, the war on terror exerted an equally important effect on legal and judicial matters. After 9/11, Congress and the Bush administration cooperated to pass a raft of internal security provisions in the form of the Patriot Act. In the wake of the attacks, there was bipartisan agreement on the need for a law that gave the federal government increased power to delve into the lives of citizens and foreign nationals. A few isolated worries about the legislation's effect on civil liberties dissipated amid the fearful reaction to 9/11 and a subsequent anthrax scare. With Bush, Attorney General John Ashcroft, and prominent leaders of both parties claiming that the Patriot Act was crucial to homeland security, other concerns were relegated to the background.

By its nature, a growth in governmental authority requires a consequent reduction in individual freedom. However necessary the Patriot Act and other laws may have been to prevent future attacks, they had a corrosive effect on both civil liberties and open debate. Ashcroft was particularly vocal on the need for conformity and deference to the executive on matters of internal security. He stridently dismissed objections to antiterrorism legislation. "To those who scare peace-loving people with phantoms of lost liberty," he chided, "my message is this: Your tactics only aid terrorists." Congress and other critics should refrain from interfering in the presidential conduct of homeland security and "respect this President's authority to wage war on terrorism and defend our nation and its citizens with all the power vested in him." When the nation's fate hung in the balance, Ashcroft implied, dissent was inappropriate.[57]

Although such admonitions largely subdued congressional critics of the Patriot Act, a few skeptics railed against the law. The speed with which the Justice Department shepherded the Patriot Act through Congress after 9/11 raised eyebrows among civil liberties advocates. Because Justice had sought some of the more intrusive provisions of the act, such as expanded wiretapping authority, before 9/11, some suspected that the attacks were just a convenient pretext for introducing the legislation. The sheaf of new powers won through the Patriot Act was "something that's been on the wish list for a long time," according to one cynic. "They just used this to get it through."[58]

This was a dubious interpretation, given the level of concern within the White House about preventing future attacks, but Patriot Act critics were correct in noting that individual rights suffered as a result of the executive's enhanced authority. In the weeks after 9/11, federal officials detained more than 1,200 suspected terrorists or material witnesses, holding hundreds of them for months without ever charging them with a crime. Eight months later, more than 100 suspects were still in legal limbo, denied access to attorneys and their names withheld from the public. In November 2001, Bush announced that captured "enemy combatants" would be tried not in civilian courts but by military tribunals operating on lower standards of evidence and with no provision for appeal. Furthermore, the decision of who qualified as a terrorist would reside solely with the White House. Critics charged that the United States was adopting undemocratic tactics. "This is the kind of 'trial' we associate with the most lawless of totalitarian dictatorships," wrote one columnist. Nonetheless, Bush maintained that it was "not practicable" to extend the "principles of law and the rules of evidence" to suspected terrorists.[59]

Over the next four years, this approach to domestic security produced a number of instances in which civil liberties and due process were the casualties of an energetic prosecution of the internal war on terror. In some cases, owing to a lack of judicial oversight, suspects who were likely innocent remained in U.S. custody for extended periods. The Justice Department proved reluctant to comply with even the limited authority that Congress retained in matters pertaining to the Patriot Act, missing deadlines for reporting to the legislature on governmental activities. The Bush administration also went beyond the authority ceded by the Patriot Act, authorizing the National Security Agency to wiretap telephone conversations inside the United States without prior judicial consent.[60]

Although one could certainly make a case that these incidents were the cost of effective homeland security, the abuses and errors that came to light gradually undermined the nation's claim to moral supremacy in the contest between terror and freedom. For many foreign observers, American invocations of freedom, liberty, and democracy rang hollow in the face of policies that seemed to contradict these ideals. A report by the American Civil Liberties Union found that repressive governments around the world had taken to citing U.S. methods as justification for their own practices. To many observers, it began to appear that aggressive antiterrorism had its downsides. In the wake of the wiretapping controversy, Congress declined to extend the Patriot Act for the period sought by Bush, and in a poll, nearly half of those surveyed believed that the administration was "not doing enough to protect the rights of American citizens."[61]

At the four-year mark, the war on terror had thus taken on certain deleterious characteristics of a consuming national quest. On a diplomatic level, the coherence of U.S. policy proved misleading at times. September 11 or no, U.S. objectives remained too diverse—and, at times, too contradictory—to be encompassed within a strategy as single-minded as the president's. On the domestic scene, the war on terror had evolved into a political truncheon and, in some cases, challenged the very virtues that Americans proposed to defend. In these regards, the war on terror in 2005 bore a striking resemblance to the Cold War of the 1950s and early 1960s. The crusade had moved beyond the foreign policy sphere and now pervaded the domestic arena as well. Whether the effect was a positive one was open to debate.

The War on Terror Resilient

Whatever its drawbacks, the war on terror endured. It was still the catchphrase for U.S. involvement abroad, and it retained substantial support at home. Although growing dissatisfaction with the Iraq war produced intense disagreement about the tactics of the war on terror, the overall premise remained fairly strong. If one measure of a doctrine's currency is the degree to which the political opposition subscribes to the idea, then the war on terror emerged from the 2004 election nearly unscathed. Kerry harshly criticized Bush on Iraq, but he made no broader assault on the war on terror and, in fact, fundamentally agreed with the president on the underlying premises of U.S. policy. Kerry's attacks on the Iraq issue reflected not dissent from the accepted wisdom but a belief that the war was a "profound diversion" from the greater struggle against jihadism. When Kerry discussed the overall war on terror, his words could easily be mistaken for those of the president. "The terrorists are beyond reason," Kerry said. "We must destroy them."[62] Regardless of whether Kerry or Bush triumphed, it was all but certain that the war on terror would remain.

When Bush emerged the victor, he wasted little time reaffirming his commitment to the struggle. He did, however, alter the tactics of the war on terror, placing less emphasis on forcible regime change and more on nation building and the peaceful promotion of democracy in the Middle East. The administration revised its earlier view that there was no point in addressing terrorism's root causes and increasingly adhered to the idea that eliminating the threat from al Qaeda and other groups required reforming the repressive conditions that gave rise to jihadism. "Free societies are peaceful societies," Bush stated. As civil society and liberal government came to the region, the administration argued, the conditions underlying Muslim anger and resentment would disappear. "If the Middle East is to leave behind stagnation, tyranny, and violence for export, then freedom must flourish in every corner of the region," said Rice.[63]

In part, this shift was a result of the Iraq war, which left Americans less eager to bump off additional regimes in the Middle East or elsewhere. In part, it stemmed from the fact that, with Washington fully embroiled in Iraq and Afghanistan, nation building was necessarily central to foreign policy. It also reflected a rethinking of the nature of the war on terror. Having initially favored a military approach to fighting terrorism, the administration had gradually taken a broader view of the problem. "I'm a student of the Cold War," explained Rice. "The values of freedom and democracy, as much, if not more than economic power and military might, won the Cold War. And those same values will lead us to victory in the war on terror." Antiterrorism was not simply about defeating al Qaeda in battle but also about providing an alternative to its ideology. In this view, the war on terror was "as much a conflict of visions as a conflict of arms." By advancing a liberal option in the Middle East, Bush calculated, Washington would undermine the jihadists' ability to capitalize on grievances resulting from authoritarian rule in the region. The "only way to defeat the ideologies of hatred and fear, the only way to make sure our country is secure in the long run," he said in 2005, "is to advance the cause of freedom." Victory would come, Bush argued, when the U.S. "ideology of freedom" overcame the "dark vision of the terrorists."[64]

This change in focus notwithstanding, Bush's second-term agenda was still centered on the (now slightly adapted) war on terror. Although Bush placed less stress on preemption in his second term, his overall priorities remained the same. The nation's "worst nightmare," Rice reaffirmed in 2004, remained "the possibility of sudden, secret attack by chemical, biological, radiological, or nuclear weapons and the coming together of the terrorist threat with weapons of mass destruction." Bush's second inaugural address stayed squarely within the framework that had been dominant since 9/11. The combination of fighting terror and spreading freedom, he asserted, "is the urgent requirement of our nation's security and the calling of our time." The United States would continue the war on terror with the goal of protecting the nation and ultimately "ending tyranny in our world." In this formulation, the crusade had lost none of its relevance or necessity.[65]

There was some speculation during 2005 that the administration was moving away from the war on terror as the organizing principle of foreign policy, but Bush quickly quashed the idea. He continually proclaimed Iraq "the central front in the war on terror," declared that democratizing that nation was "a crucial part of our strategy to defeat the terrorists," and maintained that the United States would remain in the Gulf "until victory is achieved." Bush's personal devotion to waging the war on terror remained evident as well. When midlevel officials, hoping to provide a less militaristic description of U.S. policy, proposed changing the conflict's name to the "global struggle against violent extremism," Bush nixed the idea at once. "Make no mistake about it, we are at war," he declared.[66]

Rumsfeld seconded this assessment, giving an articulation of U.S. policy remarkably similar to that of the 2002 *National Security Strategy*. "Let there be no mistake about it," he said. "It's a war." Consequently, "The only way to defend against terrorism is to go on the attack." Indeed, a 2006 update of the 2002 *National Security Strategy* averred that the United States was "in the early years of a long struggle, similar to what our country faced in the early years of the Cold War," and it listed another rogue regime with suspected WMD aspirations, Iran, as the greatest threat to U.S. security. Whatever else had changed in U.S. policy, the war on terror, with its dichotomized worldview, freedom-versus-terror mentality, and characterization of threats to American safety, remained the operative paradigm for the administration's interaction with the world.[67]

That the war on terror showed such vitality in the wake of various disappointments and setbacks illustrates a number of themes pertaining to both U.S. perceptions of national security and the nation's post–Cold War experience. First, it must be noted that, whatever its drawbacks, Bush's foreign policy resulted in successes as well. The toppling of the Taliban and the destruction of al Qaeda's Afghan infrastructure were coups for Bush, as was rapprochement with Libya. Although U.S. invasion had brought nothing even remotely resembling stability to either Iraq or Afghanistan by late 2006, the holding of successful constitutional referenda and elections in both countries provided hopeful signs amid generally discouraging conditions.

One thing that figured prominently in the persistence of the post-9/11 mind-set was the fact that both the administration and the public still saw international terrorism as the greatest threat to the nation. The memories of September 11 were a piercing reminder of the nation's vulnerability, and the incessant attacks against U.S. soldiers in Iraq and Afghanistan showed the ability of jihadists and insurgents to do Americans harm. (In this latter sense, of course, the war on terror was self-perpetuating.) Moreover, due to the very nature of the war on terror, it was unknowable whether the struggle was nearing a close or even who was winning. Did the absence of attacks mean that the United States was ahead, or did it mean that the terrorists were gearing up for another 9/11? In these circumstances, there remained sufficient enthusiasm for a foreign policy such as the one Bush described. The president continually referenced "the lessons of September 11," described protecting the nation as his "sacred duty," and evinced a determination not to be struck again. Polls showed that, whatever their quarrels with Bush over Iraq, the public more or less agreed with his definition of priorities. Large majorities placed "top priority" on preventing terrorism and the spread of WMD, while 79 percent thought that the threat of terrorism was something the United States would "always live with." In this sense, continuing the fight seemed imperative.[68]

Yet we might speculate that the endurance of the war on terror could also be attributed to its arrival on the heels of the rather discombobulated 1990s. In policy-making terms, the notion of forging a single-minded foreign policy around a dominant issue was attractive to officials such as Rice and Rumsfeld, who had been so disturbed by Clinton's apparent distraction. The war on terror, whatever its effectiveness as the intellectual structure for U.S. policy, provided structure nonetheless. For U.S. officials, it was a means of prioritizing threats and interests, allocating resources and commitments. "What the war on terrorism has done," commented Rice, "is it's given us an organizing principle." From this perspective, the war on terror was an answer to the diplomatic dilemmas of the 1990s.[69]

The apparent moral clarity of the war on terror was similarly attractive. In a manner that must have been welcome after the confusion of the 1990s, the moral purpose of U.S. policy again seemed obvious after 9/11. Although revelations such as the torturing of Iraqi prisoners by U.S. military personnel at the infamous Abu Ghraib prison were no doubt disconcerting, in the four years after the attacks, there emerged no major challenge to the broader moral paradigm of the war on terror. As during the Cold War and World War II, Americans could conceive of themselves sallying forth under the menaced banner of freedom and beating back the onrushing forces of evil. Whereas the diplomatic experience of the 1990s had often appeared morally obtuse, after 9/11, it was easy for Americans to feel good about the object (if not the tactics) of their exertions. As a psychological and emotional impetus, this perceived morality was powerful indeed.

Just as important, the war on terror provided the United States with an easily identifiable, and presumably unredeemable, enemy. As they surveyed the international scene in the 1990s, Americans had been unable to find this type of villain. In some ways, the absence had been profoundly disconcerting. During the Cold War, Americans had at least known who and what they were fighting against; the post–Cold War era offered no such certainties. With the emergence of the terrorist threat, the United States once again had a foe against which to contrast its values and beliefs. Jihadism provided an alien ideology, and Osama bin Laden gave a face to the enemy. "Nations need enemies," Charles Krauthammer wrote of the Cold War.[70] This statement was no less true of the war on terror.

If the war on terror was a response to the threats of the early twenty-first century, it was also a conceptually simple and comfortable means of defining U.S. involvement in the world. After a decade of struggling with the intricacies of a changing global environment,

Americans once again had a comprehensible formula for understanding international relations. Offering coherence and clarity, the war on terror provided intellectual refuge from a world that was intractably complex and unfamiliar. The notion that the globe could be dichotomized between terrorists and freedom lovers was a welcome one, giving Americans an uncomplicated means of thinking about their international role. In contrast to the complexity of the 1990s, this subject could hardly have seemed clearer after 9/11. In this respect, the United States' attachment to the war on terror was an understandable reaction not only to 9/11 but also to the decade that preceded it. As a statement of national purpose, the war on terror was just too attractive to leave behind.

Conclusion

The present international scene . . . is about as much of a blank slate as history ever provides.
—George H. W. Bush, 1998

Sometimes I really miss the Cold War.
—Anthony Lake, circa 1994

In many ways, these two quotations encapsulate U.S. foreign policy during the long 1990s. Bush's statement touched on perceptions that the geopolitical rigidity of the Cold War had vanished and also (unconsciously, perhaps) hinted at the manner in which the legacy of the superpower conflict contributed to characterizations of the period that followed. The 1990s were such a "blank slate" to Bush and his colleagues largely because they came on the heels of an era in which structure was believed to be the rule. Lake's quip, in contrast, hinted that this declension created as many problems as it solved.

It would be a mistake, of course, to take either of these statements too literally. As the foregoing pages have demonstrated, the notion of the 1990s as a blank slate is misleading to the extent that it obscures the continuities between Cold War and post–Cold War foreign policy. These links were present on various planes. On an intellectual level, the common belief that the United States had "won" the Cold War informed American efforts to find a new grand strategy. In a geopolitical sense, the end of the Cold War and the collapse of the Soviet Union placed Washington in the position of uneasy preeminence that it retained throughout the 1990s and beyond. With respect to specific issues such as NATO expansion and U.S. relations with the Middle East, the legacies of the Cold War remained very much alive.[1]

Yet insofar as the notion of a blank slate indicates the conceptual, strategic, and political dilemmas that confronted U.S. policy makers after 1989, it accurately captures the mood of the United States' post–Cold War experience. Throughout the 1990s, U.S. officials wrestled with the challenges and opportunities of a new order. At times, they overcame the complexity that confronted them, managing crises successfully and devising policies that were well suited to a fluid international environment. More often, it seemed, the complexity overcame them. Even after a full decade, Americans had yet to identify a stable, efficacious basis for foreign policy, and domestic debate was no less fragmented than at the outset of the post–Cold War era. U.S. officials struggled amid the uncertainty of the post-bipolar world, ultimately leaving many of the practical and political imperatives of foreign policy unmet.

With the 1990s as a backdrop, the U.S. reaction to September 11, 2001, takes on broader meaning. Beyond illustrating the dictates of national defense in the twenty-first century, 9/11 offered a return to the certainty and consensus that had been so notably absent of late. After an unsettling stretch of confusion, the world scene and the United States' part therein appeared to have returned to a more straightforward (if profoundly dangerous) norm. Once more, international relations were comprehensible; U.S. policy was understandable and morally reassuring. As a means of resolving the conflicts and contradictions of foreign policy in the 1990s, the war on terror seemed quite promising.

After 1989, U.S. policy thus traversed a circular path, moving from simplicity to complexity and back. Beginning at the comfortable certitude of the Cold War, American diplomacy then traversed the often inchoate middle expanse of the post–Cold War era before returning to the logical simplicity and ethical assurance of the war on terror. In fact, the three segments of this period shared important conceptual and perceptual links. The post–Cold War era seemed all the more disjointed because of the constancy of the period that preceded it, while the war on terror seemed all the more attractive in light of the prior decade of unpredictability and distraction. As Americans entered and exited the post–Cold War era, they were influenced by the experience and intellectual residue of their previous worldviews.

Both the general unease of U.S. policy during the 1990s and the subsequent durability of the war on terror demonstrate one of the fundamental realities of policy making in the United States: in American politics, simplicity sells, and the best story wins. Enduring foreign policies arise not simply as a result of strategic foresight (or myopia, as the case may be) but also as a product of political cunning. As evidenced by both the war on terror and the Cold War before it, the most reliable method of creating domestic political consensus on foreign policy is to provide an attractive and intellectually facile conception of the U.S. role in international affairs. This was the case during the Cold War, when proposing a crusade for freedom seemed preferable to discussing the specific merits of aid to Turkey and Greece, when détente's extension of moral legitimacy to Moscow proved so discomfiting, when Ronald Reagan again fashioned a Cold War consensus with his confrontational rhetoric. It was no less so during the 1990s, when the absence of an obvious moral and intellectual be-all and end-all to U.S. policy disoriented and disturbed domestic observers. The notion was just as applicable after 9/11, when the oversimplified rhetoric of freedom versus terror restored public agreement on foreign policy and relegated meaningful discussion of terrorism's causes to the background. George W. Bush provided the compelling narrative that had been lacking since the end of the Cold War, linking the United States' international aims in a comprehensible and flattering manner. With its powerful themes of threat and mission, this was a better story than either Bill Clinton or George H. W. Bush had been able to weave. Reducing international issues and U.S. diplomacy to utmost simplicity, George W. Bush created the nation's first solid post–Cold War foreign policy consensus.

The rise of the war on terror (and the failure of its doctrinal predecessors) therefore confirms the dual nature of the dilemma that faced the United States from 1989 to 2001. In part, the problem was strategic and came as a matter of course for Washington (as it would for any global power, for that matter). Confronting myriad issues, great powers must seek some means of reconciling and prioritizing their objectives. They must determine how to shape and deploy intelligence, military, and diplomatic resources; how to determine which issues merit foremost consideration; in other words, how to manage the day-to-day conduct of foreign policy. Meeting each of these challenges demands a coherent view of world affairs. As the American experience suggests, this quest for an all-encompassing doctrine is probably quixotic; the very expansiveness of U.S. goals makes it unlikely that there is a single comprehensive thread binding all of Washington's aims. Nonetheless, the necessity of comprehensibility remains, as strategists must identify some method of organizing and structuring foreign policy.

During the Cold War, containment served as this mental shortcut for the United States. In an objective sense, anticommunism did not encompass the entirety of U.S. policy abroad, but it was sufficiently integral to U.S. goals to serve as the needed heuristic.[2] After the superpower showdown, the United States remained a great power, in that its international commitments and capabilities were still vast, but U.S. policy had lost its connecting logic. (Critics might prefer to say that the American empire lost its moral and strategic justification. In the sense in which I refer to it, the difference between these formulations is not so great.) Until American strategists could restore intellectual stability to the conception and implementation of foreign policy, managing the nation's objectives seemed a far more complicated task. In this regard, the challenge that faced the United States during the 1990s afflicts only world powers; one does not imagine that Brussels's interests are so sprawling as to require great soul-searching regarding the ultimate meaning of Belgian diplomacy.

If the dilemma is unique to the powerful, though, it is also the peculiar province of pluralistic democracies. American policy makers have to manage foreign policy in a manner that captures the attention and support of the domestic audience. Indeed, diplomacy in the 1990s was as much about domestic politics as geopolitics; in some cases, the former concern seemed more consequential than the latter. Bad policy led to adverse developments abroad, but bad politics entailed pernicious consequences where it really hurt—at home. As a result, the blurring of the line between the domestic and the international that had characterized so much of U.S. foreign policy in the twentieth century continued. In 2005, these issues were no less intertwined than before.[3]

As the war on terror illustrated, however, this linkage created significant tension. The global and political dictates of foreign policy were not always complementary. Although simplicity was a virtue in political debate, it had mixed results for the conduct of foreign affairs. Like his Cold War predecessors, George W. Bush fell prey to the temptation to make the international situation and American aims clearer than they were in reality. In domestic politics, the moral absolutes and the "us versus them" mentality of the war on terror were pure genius, but when put into practice, these black-and-white conceptions were hardly conducive to the successful negotiation of world affairs that came in several shades of gray. At the same time that it solidified domestic consensus, the freedom-versus-tyranny mind-set blinded Americans to the complexities of local affairs and caused them to not ask difficult questions about the sources of anti-Americanism. As a rhetorical portrait, the war on terror worked quite well; as a worldview, it was seriously deficient.

In the end, we are left with troubling conclusions regarding the development of U.S. policy between the end of the Cold War and George W. Bush's second term. The unsettled state of affairs that prevailed from 1990 until 2001 was utterly unsatisfying from a rhetorical standpoint and was, at times, ineffective on a practical level. But if incoherence had been problematic, by 2005, an oversimplified coherence appeared little less so. The rigidity and morality of the war on terror worked better in domestic politics than had Clinton's freewheeling approach, but the strategy left U.S. policy makers and public commentators blind to nuance and lent itself to abuses of the new foreign policy consensus. Although it resolved many of the issues of the 1990s, the war on terror simply introduced a new set of problems to the practice and politics of diplomacy.

Is there an answer to the coherence conundrum? In certain regards, Bill Clinton and his advisers had it right: as long as American aims are global and the globe remains a complicated place, any simplistic characterization of U.S. policy will mislead as often as it informs. In another sense, his critics were correct: without some intellectual architecture, the complexity of the world and the variegation of U.S. interests will overwhelm policy makers. That both flexibility and parsimony offer some virtue but are thoroughly imperfect suggests that there may be geopolitical middle ground between the two.

Perhaps what is needed is something akin to a more structured variant of Clinton's second-term strategy, a policy that eschews thematic rigidity yet recognizes the interconnections between various initiatives and the need for the prioritization of objectives. A strategy of this type would not erase all the perplexities encountered during the 1990s, and the potential for friction between goals would remain, but it might offer some solution to the more avoidable of these difficulties (how best to allocate time and resources, for instance).

Devising such a scheme would be only half the battle, though, for while the strategists must shape policy, the politicians must defend it. Flexibility might be desirable from a geopolitical standpoint, but if Clinton's experience is any clue, it is likely a loser in American politics. In this case, the domestic aspects of foreign policy seem the more intractable. As long as politicians seek to make trouble for the president, and as long as there are dueling conceptions of national interest —in essence, as long as the United States remains a democracy—the rhetorical and political imperatives of foreign policy may remain quite vexing.

At a basic level, the foreign policy dilemmas of the 1990s are thus entwined in the practical and political fabric of American diplomacy. After the close of the Cold War, Americans confronted these dilemmas and struggled to resolve their contradictions. If the events of this period are any indication, they will be forced to do so again.

Notes

Introduction

1. Bush in *Public Papers, 2001,* 1144.

2. Studies of humanitarian intervention, NATO enlargement, free trade, and other pressing matters of the period are too numerous to cite here and are referred to as relevant in subsequent notes. Broader accounts of certain aspects of U.S. policy during the 1990s include Hyland, *Clinton's World,* a highly critical and incomplete treatment of the first five years of Clinton's diplomacy. For shorter (and similarly harsh) treatments of Clinton's diplomacy, consult Haass, "The Squandered Presidency," and Goldman and Berman, "Engaging the World," in Campbell and Rockman, eds., *The Clinton Legacy.* On civil-military relations, there is Halberstam, *War in a Time of Peace,* and Feaver and Gelpi, *Choosing Your Battles.* Brands, *What America Owes the World,* 297–319, provides a brief summary of certain intellectual issues in the early 1990s. Von Hippel's *Democracy by Force* offers an introduction to interventionism. McCrisken's *American Exceptionalism and the Legacy of Vietnam* is also helpful in discussing the attempts of George H. W. Bush and Bill Clinton to propagate the notion mentioned in the title. Another notable title is Mead's *Power, Terror, Peace, and War,* which places certain of the intellectual roots of the George W. Bush administration's security policy in the context of the 1990s.

3. Bacevich's *American Empire* discusses many of the same issues presented here but arrives at a far different conclusion. Melanson's *American Foreign Policy since the Vietnam War* discusses some of the political aspects of foreign policy during this period but relies predominantly on secondary sources and leaves large segments of Bush's and Clinton's foreign policy untreated. Stein, ed., *U.S. Foreign Policy since the End of the Cold War,* provides a topical, pre–September 11 look at several important issues but is far from comprehensive and contains no dominant analytical thread.

4. I make no claims about the comprehensiveness of this volume; certain events receive less attention than some readers may think appropriate. Policy

toward Africa figures minimally, for instance. For the most part, though, this volume covers the major developments in American diplomacy during this period.

5. See Haley, *Strategies of Dominance.*

6. The most cogent statements are Bacevich's *American Empire* and *The New American Militarism.* For a more understated argument along similar lines, see Leffler, "9/11 and American Foreign Policy."

7. The Cold War consensus hardly went unchallenged between 1945 and 1989, of course. Disagreements about tactics aside, however, American policy makers and public commentators largely agreed that managing the U.S.-Soviet confrontation should be the defining aspect of Washington's diplomacy. Gaddis, *Strategies of Containment* (2005).

8. Remarks to the American Enterprise Institute, Federal News Service transcript, December 3, 1991. Unless otherwise noted, all transcripts were retrieved from www.lexis-nexis.com.

9. Thomas Friedman, "Clinton's Foreign Policy: Top Adviser Speaks Up," *New York Times,* October 31, 1993.

10. Bush remarks at the Reagan Presidential Library, Federal News Service transcript, November 19, 1999.

Chapter 1. Beyond the Cold War?

1. Gaddis, *Strategies of Containment* (2005).

2. The controversy over whether Reagan or Gorbachev drove this reconciliation continues. See Gaddis, *Strategies of Containment* (2005), 342–79; Garthoff, *The Great Transition;* Fitzgerald, *Way Out There in the Blue;* and Fischer, *The Reagan Reversal.*

3. Kennan, "Obituary for the Cold War," 50–51.

4. Kirkpatrick, "The Withering Away of the State?" 36.

5. Fukuyama, "The End of History?" 3–18.

6. Charles Krauthammer, "Beyond the Cold War," *New Republic,* December 19, 1988, 14–19.

7. On Gorbachev's motives, see Wallander, "Western Policy and the Demise of the Soviet Union," 136–77; Stokes, *The Walls Came Tumbling Down,* 75–77; Odom, *The Collapse of the Soviet Military,* especially 49–64; and Chernyaev, *My Six Years with Gorbachev.*

8. Matlock, *Autopsy on an Empire,* 178; Ross to Baker, December 16, 1988, Box 1, Rice-Zelikow Papers, Hoover Institution.

9. Scowcroft to Rice and Zelikow, February 27, 1995, Box 1, Zelikow-Rice Papers, Hoover Institution; Scowcroft quoted in David Hoffman, "Gorbachev Seen as Trying to Buy Time for Reform," *Washington Post,* January 23, 1989; "Mary Finch Notes of Interview," January 18, 1995, Box 1, Zelikow-Rice Papers. Finch used shorthand in taking these notes, which I have reconverted to standard language.

10. Bush in *Public Papers, 1989,* 79. See also National Security Review 12, March 3, 1989, National Security Reviews File, Bush Library.

11. Ross to Baker, February 21, 1989, Box 1, Zelikow-Rice Papers.

12. CIA Intelligence Estimate, "Rising Political Instability under Gorbachev: Understanding the Problem and Prospects for Resolution," April 1989, Soviet Estimate Collection, National Security Archive (NSA). All NSA documents were accessed at the archive reading room in Washington, through the NSA Web site (http://nsarchive.chadwyck.com/), or through the various published microfilm collections.

13. NSD 23, September 22, 1989, National Security Directives File, Bush Library. Although Bush did not officially sign the document until September, it was in final form in May.

14. Bush in *Public Papers, 1989,* 540–43.

15. State Department official Curtis Kamman in House Committee on Foreign Affairs, *Developments in Europe, July 1989,* July 27, 1989, 54.

16. Bush and Scowcroft, *A World Transformed,* 564; Matlock, *Autopsy on an Empire,* 591; NSR 12, March 3, 1989, NSR Files, Bush Library; Baker and de Frank, *The Politics of Diplomacy,* 40.

17. Bush and Scowcroft, *A World Transformed,* 564.

18. Baum, *Burying Mao,* 242–74; Gwertzman and Kaufman, *The Collapse of Communism,* 52.

19. "Ballistic Missiles/Arms Sales by PRC," February 14, 1989; Department of Defense to various offices, March 28, 1989, China Collection, NSA.

20. State Department Bureau of Intelligence and Research Report, May 15, 1989; and Lilley to Baker, April 18, 1989, China Collection, NSA; memorandum for Brent Scowcroft (Talking Points for Meeting with Wan), May 13, 1989, China Collection, NSA.

21. Beijing to State Department, May 20, 1989, Box 1, National Security Council (NSC) Situation Room Files, Bush Library; William Webster Oral History Interview, August 21, 2002, 49–50, Reagan Oral Histories Project, Miller Center.

22. Baum, *Burying Mao,* 275–310; Scobell, "Why the People's Army Fired on the People," 196–98; Manion, "Reluctant Duelists," xxxiii–xl; Li quoted in Dutt and Dutt, *China after Mao,* 7. It also appears that Beijing may not have foreseen the extent to which Tiananmen would outrage the West. Nathan and Ross, *The Great Wall and the Empty Fortress,* 48–50, 72; Wang, "China's Perception of the Post–Cold War International Environment," in Li, Hu, and Zhong, *Interpreting U.S.-China-Taiwan Relations,* 260–61.

23. Claudia Rosett, "Miss Liberty Lights Her Lamp in Beijing," *Wall Street Journal,* May 31, 1989; James Barron, "One Man Can Make a Difference: This One Jousted Briefly with Goliath," *New York Times,* June 6, 1989; Tom Shales, "Television's Global Drama," *Washington Post,* June 5, 1989.

24. Bush Diary entries, June 5 and 24, 1989, in Bush and Scowcroft, *A World Transformed,* 98, 104.

25. Bush in *Public Papers, 1989,* 669–70.

26. Lilley to State Department, June 7 and 14, 1989, China Collection, NSA; Bush to Deng, June 20, 1989, reprinted in Bush, *All the Best, George Bush,* 428–31; Lilley to Baker, December 8, 1989, China Collection, NSA.

27. On Chinese interests and views of cooperation with Washington, see Ross, *Negotiating Cooperation,* 238–43, 260–62; Wang, "China's Perception of the Post–Cold War International Environment," 264; Nathan and Ross, *The Great Wall and the Empty Fortress,* 160–71.

28. Charles Krauthammer, "The Communist Imperative," *Washington Post,* June 23, 1989; U.S. House of Representatives, *Congressional Record,* 101st Cong., 2nd sess., vol. 136, 1:H22.

29. Michael Dobbs, "The Global Shake-up," *Washington Post,* June 11, 1989.

30. "Soviet Deeds and American Words," *New York Times,* May 14, 1989.

31. Fitzwater quoted in David Hoffman, "Gorbachev 'Gambits' Challenged," *Washington Post,* May 17, 1989.

32. Baker in Senate Foreign Relations Committee, *The Future of U.S.-Soviet Relations,* 911; Bush in *Public Papers, 1989,* 602–3.

33. Telephone Conversation (TelCon) between Bush and Kohl, June 15, 1989, Box 3, Presidential TelCons, NSC Files, Bush Library; Bush to Gorbachev, July 21, 1989, in Bush, *All the Best,* 433.

34. Kamman in House Committee on Foreign Affairs, *Developments in Eastern Europe,* 3–4; see also Embassy in Warsaw to the Secretary of State, June 2, 1989, Solidarity Collection, NSA; CIA Intelligence Estimate, "Gorbachev's Domestic Gambles and Instability in the USSR," September 1989, Soviet Estimate Collection, NSA; Rice notes, undated (summer 1989), Box 1, Files of Condoleezza Rice, NSC Files, Bush Library.

35. Kramer, "The Collapse of East European Communism (Part I)," 178–204; Stokes, *The Walls Came Tumbling Down,* chs. 3–5; Garton Ash, *The Magic Lantern,* 25–129.

36. Although U.S. officials did not know it, the Brezhnev Doctrine had actually been dead for years. After intervening in Czechoslovakia in 1968 and Afghanistan in 1979, Soviet officials had concluded that the costs of "socialist internationalism" were too high, because any future intervention would certainly bring moral opprobrium and economic sanctions from the West. Ouimet, *The Rise and Fall of the Brezhnev Doctrine.*

37. Chernyaev Diary, October 5, 1989, End of the Cold War Collection, Cold War International History Project (CWIHP). See also Chernyaev Diary, November 10, 1989, ibid.; Embassy in Prague to Secretary of State, November 20, 1989, Vaclev Havel Collection, NSA; and memorandum of

conversation between Matlock and I. P. Aboimov, December 25, 1989, End of the Cold War Collection, CWIHP.

38. "Beyond the Berlin Wall," *St. Louis Post-Dispatch,* November 12, 1989; "The End of the War to End Wars," *New York Times,* November 11, 1989.

39. Meetings between Gorbachev and Bush, December 2 and 3, 1989, End of the Cold War Collection, CWIHP; TelCon between Bush and Kohl, December 3, 1989, Box 1, Presidential MemCons and TelCons, NSC Files, Bush Library.

40. Soviet draft, "Directives for the Ministers of Foreign Affairs of the USSR and the United States," undated [December 2 or 3, 1989], Box 1, Wilson Files, NSC Files, Bush Library; "Excerpts from Bush's News Conference after NATO Meeting," *New York Times,* December 5, 1989.

41. TelCon between Bush and Kohl, November 10, 1989, Box 3, Presidential TelCons, NSC Files, Bush Library; Maier, *Dissolution,* 3–145; Stent, *Russia and Germany Reborn,* 18–108.

42. Gorbachev to Bush, Margaret Thatcher, and François Mitterand, November 10, 1989, End of the Cold War Collection, CWIHP; Matlock, *Autopsy on an Empire,* 383.

43. "Mitterand, in Kiev, Warns Bonn Not to Press Reunification Issue," *New York Times,* December 7, 1989; Thatcher, *Downing Street Years,* 792–99; Glenn Frankel, "Cautious Voice Amid Euphoria," *Washington Post,* December 26, 1989; Robert Keatly, Glynn Mapes, and Barbara Toman, "Thatcher Sees Eastern Europe Progress as More Urgent than Germans' Unity," *Wall Street Journal,* January 26, 1990.

44. See "Poll Finds Wide Support for German Reunification," *Boston Globe,* November 23, 1989; William Safire, "Kohl at Camp David," *New York Times,* February 23, 1990; "One Germany: Not Likely Now," *New York Times,* November 19, 1989.

45. TelCon between Bush and Kohl, October 23, 1989, Box 3, Presidential TelCons, NSC Files, Bush Library; State Department Chronology of Movement toward German Unification, Box 2, Zelikow-Rice Files, Hoover Institution.

46. TelCon between Bush and Kohl, November 17, 1989, Box 3, Presidential TelCons, NSC Files, Bush Library.

47. TelCon between Bush and Kohl, December 3, 1989, Box 1, Presidential MemCons and TelCons, NSC Files, Bush Library.

48. Bush in *Public Papers, 1989,* 1644.

49. Gorbachev, *Memoirs,* 529–33; TelCon between Bush and Kohl, March 20, 1990, Box 3, Presidential TelCons, NSC Files, Bush Library.

50. TelCons between Bush and Kohl, February 13 and March 15, 1990, Box 3, Presidential TelCons, NSC Files, Bush Library; Maier, *Dissolution,* 169–243.

51. "Directives for the Negotiations of the USSR Foreign Minister with the U.S. President G. Bush and State Secretary J. Baker," April 4–6, 1990, translated document found in Box 3, Zelikow-Rice Papers. See also Thomson to various officials in the State and Defense Departments, CIA, and NSC, May 24, 1990, Box 5, FOIA request 00–0233, Bush Library; TelCon between Bush and Kohl, March 20, 1990, Box 3, Presidential TelCons, NSC Files, Bush Library.

52. Rice background briefing, May 29, 1990, Box 1, Rice Files, NSC Files, Bush Library.

53. Bush and Scowcroft, *A World Transformed,* 282–83; Zelikow to Scowcroft (Bush Talking Points for June 5), June 4, 1990, Box 1, Wilson Files, NSC Files, Bush Library.

54. See Gorbachev, *Memoirs,* 529–33; Maier, *Dissolution,* 215–83; and Stent, *Russia and Germany Reborn,* 109–49.

55. "2 + 4 Minutes," June 22, 1990, Box 1, Zelikow-Rice Papers.

56. TelCon between Bush and Kohl, July 17, 1990, Box 4, Presidential TelCons, NSC Files, Bush Library.

57. George Kennan, "The Wall Falls," *Washington Post,* November 12, 1989.

58. Zoellick in Senate Foreign Relations Committee, *Treaty on the Final Settlement with Respect of Germany,* September 28, 1990, 27. As Marc Trachtenberg has pointed out, there was actually a great deal of concern about the German question underlying U.S.-NATO and East-West diplomacy during the Cold War. My point here is merely that the end of the Cold War forced these questions to the forefront of public debate and ensured that the dominant U.S.-Soviet confrontation no longer overshadowed these issues. Trachtenberg, *A Constructed Peace.*

59. Bush in *Public Papers, 1990,* 1348. A more extensive treatment of German reunification can be found in Rice and Zelikow's insider account, *Germany Unified and Europe Transformed.*

60. State Department opinion poll, March 15, 1990, Box 1, Zelikow-Rice Papers; Gallup poll, August 25, 1991, Gallup Database.

61. "Excerpts from Clinton's Speech on Foreign Policy Leadership," *New York Times,* August 14, 1992.

62. "Gorbachev at Stanford: Excepts from Address," *New York Times,* June 5, 1990.

63. David Wilson, "A Decade in Which the Good Guys Won," *Boston Globe,* December 16, 1990. Rehnquist is quoted in the same editorial. Various incarnations of Cold War triumphalism are detailed in Schrecker, ed., *Cold War Triumphalism.*

64. Horner, "America the Victorious," 39–42.

65. A. M. Rosenthal, "Victors in the Cold War," *New York Times,* June 10, 1990.

66. Puddington, "The Anti–Cold War Brigade," 38.

67. George Kennan, "The G.O.P Won the Cold War? Ridiculous," *New York Times,* October 28, 1992.

68. Muravchik, "Losing the Peace," 39.

Chapter 2. Peace Elusive

1. Michael Gordon, "Pentagon Drafts Strategy for Post–Cold War World," *New York Times,* August 2, 1990.

2. Maureen Dowd, "Backing Pentagon, Bush Says Military Can Be Cut 25% in 5 Years," *New York Times,* August 3, 1990.

3. Oliver North to John Poindexter, August 23, 1986; Poindexter to Noriega, August 23, 1986; North to Poindexter, September 20, 1989, in The Contras, Cocaine, and Covert Operations Collection, NSA; National Security Decision Directive 221, April 8, 1986, http://www.fas.org/irp/offdocs/nsdd/; William Webster Oral History Interview, August 21, 2002, 27–29, Reagan Oral Histories Collection, Miller Center. On Noriega's relations with the United States during the Reagan years, see Scranton, *The Noriega Years,* 105–65; Conniff, *Panama and the United States*, 154–58.

4. U.S. Southern Command Fact Sheet, February 8, 1989, El Salvador Collection, NSA; and Directorate of Intelligence Report, December 2, 1987, ibid.

5. NSD 18, August 21, 1989, National Security Directives File, Bush Library; NSD 12, June 7, 1989, ibid.; Frank Carlucci Oral History Interview, August 28, 2001, 45, Reagan Oral Histories Collection, Miller Center.

6. Donnelly, Roth, and Baker, *Operation Just Cause*, 46; Baker and de Frank, *The Politics of Diplomacy,* 181.

7. Office of the Chairman of the Joint Chiefs of Staff, *Operation Just Cause: The Planning and Execution of Joint Operations in Panama*, 12–14; Embassy in Guatemala to the Secretary of State, June 20, 1989, Guatemala Collection, NSA; NSD 21, September 1, 1989, National Security Directives File, Bush Library.

8. Office of the Chairman of the JCS, *Operation Just Cause,* 12–15; William Webster Oral History Interview, 42–43; Powell with Persico, *My American Journey*, 405.

9. U.S. Army Center for Military History, *Operation Just Cause: The Incursion into Panama*, 9; Baker and de Frank, *The Politics of Diplomacy,* 186–87; Joe Pichirallo and Patrick Tyler, "Long Road to the Invasion of Panama," *Washington Post,* January 14, 1990.

10. Powell quoted in Donnelly, Roth, and Baker, *Operation Just Cause,* 96. Bush's credibility concerns are discussed in Hathaway, "The Role of Drugs in the U.S.-Panamanian Relationship," in Watson and Tsouras, *Operation Just Cause*, 42; and Conniff, *Panama and the United States*, 161. Powell's stance on intervention is discussed in greater detail in the next chap-

ter. On Bush's concerns about appearing weak, see also William Webster Oral History Interview, 27–28.

11. "Transcript of President Bush's News Conference," *Washington Post,* December 22, 1989; R. W. Apple Jr., "Bush's Obsession," *New York Times,* December 26, 1989; Scowcroft quoted in Donnelly, Roth, and Baker, *Operation Just Cause,* 99; Powell quoted in Office of the Chairman of the JCS, *Operation Just Cause: The Planning and Execution of Joint Operations in Panama,* 14; U.S. Army Center for Military History, *Operation Just Cause: The Incursion into Panama,* 10.

12. NSD 34, January 24, 1990, NSD Files, Bush Library.

13. Richard Boudreaux, "Top Latin American Leaders Roundly Condemn U.S. Military Attack," *Los Angeles Times,* December 21, 1989; Jack Nelson, "For Bush, Panama Seen as Major 'Political Bonanza,'" *Los Angeles Times,* January 6, 1990; Richard Morin, "Poll Shows Rising Support for Bush, Republicans," *Washington Post,* January 18, 1990.

14. Jentleson, *With Friends Like These*; also National Security Decision Directive 114, November 26, 1983, http://www.fas.org/irp/offdocs/nsdd/nsdd-114.pdf.

15. Baghdad to Secretary of State and other posts, September 12, 1989, Iraqgate Collection, NSA; NSD 26, October 2, 1989, National Security Directives File, Bush Library; Parnell to Brady, November 8, 1989, Box 10, FOIA 99-0461, ibid.

16. "Thinking about a Policy for Iraq," January 12, 1990, Iraqgate Collection, NSA.

17. Kelly in Senate Foreign Relations Committee, *United States Policy toward Iraq*, June 15, 1990, 5.

18. Baker to Baghdad and other posts, July 24, 1990, Box 41, FOIA 98-0099, Bush Library; minutes of meeting between Glaspie and Saddam Hussein, July 25, 1990, Iraqgate Collection, NSA; Glaspie to State Department, July 26, 1990, Box 41, FOIA 98-0099, Bush Library.

19. Hussein quoted in Khadduri and Ghareeb, *War in the Gulf, 1990–1991*; embassy quoted in Freedman and Karsh, *The Gulf Crisis, 1990–1991,* 47. See also Musallam, *The Iraqi Invasion of Kuwait,* especially 93–96; Rahman, *The Making of the Gulf War,* 293–300; and Hassan, *The Iraqi Invasion of Kuwait.*

20. William Webster Oral History Interview, 50; NSC Meeting, August 3, 1990, Box 42, FOIA 98-0099, Bush Library.

21. Meetings of the NSC, August 3 and 6, 1990, Box 42, FOIA 98-0099, Bush Library.

22. Minutes of the NSC, August 3, 1990, Box 42, FOIA 98-0099, Bush Library.

23. Baker and de Frank, *The Politics of Diplomacy,* 3–16.

24. Primakov, *Russian Crossroads*; Gow, "The Soviet Involvement," in

Gow, ed., *Iraq, the Gulf Conflict, and the World Community,* 124–26; Baker and de Frank, *The Politics of Diplomacy,* 13–16.

25. Meetings of the NSC, August 3 and 5, 1990, Box 42, FOIA 98-0099, Bush Library.

26. Meetings of the NSC, August 3 and 5, 1990, Box 42, FOIA 98-0099, Bush Library; *Public Papers, 1990,* 1102. Saudi concerns are detailed in Unger, *House of Bush, House of Saud*, 132–35.

27. Robson to Scowcroft, August 14, 1990, Box 81, John Sununu Chief of Staff Files, Bush Library; NSD 45, August 20, 1990, National Security Directives File, ibid.

28. "Press Conference with President Bush," Federal News Service transcript, August 30, 1990.

29. Ehteshami, "The Arab States and the Middle Eastern Balance of Power," in Gow, ed., *Iraq, the Gulf Conflict, and the World Community,* 60–73; Haseeb and Rouchdy, "Egypt's Speculation in the Gulf Crisis," in Bresheeth and Yuval-Davis, eds., *The Gulf War and the New World Order;* Heisbourg, "France and the Gulf Crisis," and Kaiser and Becter, "Germany and the Iraq Conflict," in Gnesotto and Roper, eds., *Western Europe and the Gulf*, 17–69; Baker to Bush, November 8 and 10, 1990, Box 43, FOIA 98-0099, Bush Library.

30. Conaghan, "Allied Contributions in Support of Operations Desert Shield and Desert Storm," 1–13; Friedman, *Desert Victory*, 43–108, 261–324.

31. Baker in Senate Foreign Relations Committee, *U.S. Policy in the Persian Gulf,* September 5, 1990, 9; Bush in *Public Papers, 1990,* 1218–22. I discuss the evolution of the New World Order in chapter 3.

32. Pickering to Baker, August 30, 1990, Box 42, FOIA 98-0099, Bush Library.

33. Riyadh to Secretary of State, October 29, 1990, Box 43, FOIA 98-0099, Bush Library.

34. Powell, *My American Journey*, 474–76.

35. Baker and de Frank, *The Politics of Diplomacy,* 289; Baker to Bush, November 6, 8, and 10, 1990, Box 43, FOIA 98-0099, Bush Library; Primakov, *Russian Crossroads,* 43–56.

36. Burns to Eagleburger, undated, Box 43, FOIA 98-0099, Bush Library.

37. Defense Intelligence Agency memorandum, "Iraq's Armed Forces after the Gulf Crisis: Implications of a Major Conflict," January 1991, Box 44, FOIA 98-0099, Bush Library; untitled NSC analysis, January 11, 1991, ibid.

38. "Responding to Saddam's Pre–January 15 Initiatives," December 31, 1990, Box 44, FOIA 98-0099, Bush Library; "Points to Be Made with Ambassador Bessmertnykh," January 1991, ibid.

39. MemCon between Bush and Shamir, December 11, 1990, Box 44, FOIA 98-0099, Bush Library.

40. Pell in Senate Foreign Relations Committee, *U.S. Policy in the Persian Gulf,* January 8, 1991, 1.

41. *Congressional Record,* 102nd Cong., 1st sess., vol. 137, 1:S11; ibid., 5:H101; Gordon Black/*USA Today* poll, December 2, 1990, USGBUSA.903227.R007, iPoll Database.

42. Bush and Scowcroft, *A World Transformed,* 354, 484; C. Boyden Gray to Bush, August 7, 1990, Box 81, Sununu Chief of Staff Files, Bush Library; Rademaker to Scowcroft, December 11, 1990, Box 51, FOIA 98-0099, ibid.; "Points for Cabinet Room Meeting with Congressional Leaders," undated [early January], Box 44, ibid.; Haass and Virginia Lampley to Scowcroft, "Talking Points for December 19 Meeting with Senators Returning from the Gulf," December 18, 1990, Box 50, ibid.

43. "Points for Cabinet Room Meeting with Congressional Leaders," undated [early January], Box 44, FOIA 98-0099, Bush Library.

44. Baker to Haass, January 11, 1991, Box 44, FOIA 98-0099, Bush Library.

45. NSD 54, January 15, 1991, National Security Directives File, Bush Library.

46. Friedman, *Desert Victory,* 147–96, 297–309, 353–60.

47. Postal, "Lessons of the Gulf War Experience with Patriot," 119–71.

48. MemCon between Bush and Arens, February 11, 1991, Box 45, FOIA 98-0099, Bush Library.

49. Bush and Scowcroft, *A World Transformed,* 473. Primakov describes Soviet peace overtures in *Russian Crossroads,* 49–70.

50. Bush and Scowcroft, *A World Transformed,* 473; Primakov, *Russian Crossroads,* 49–70; Bush to London, Paris, and other capitals, February 19, 1991, Box 45, FOIA 98-0099, Bush Library.

51. TelCon between Bush and Gorbachev, February 23, 1991, Box 45, FOIA 98-0099, Bush Library.

52. Bush to Gorbachev, undated [February 24 or 25, 1991], Box 81, Sununu Chief of Staff Files, Bush Library; Bush and Scowcroft, *A World Transformed,* 477.

53. Friedman, *Desert Victory,* 108–46, 197–235, 261–96.

54. Powell, *My American Journey,* 505–8; Bush and Scowcroft, *A World Transformed,* 485–88; Oral History Interview with Bush and Scowcroft, October 9, 1998, tape II, p. 4, in author's possession.

55. One poll showed Bush's approval rating at 89 percent. Gallup poll, March 3, 1991, Gallup Database.

56. *Public Papers, 1991,* 201.

57. *National Security Strategy,* August 1991, 2.

58. *Public Papers, 1991,* 1200; Pickering in Senate Foreign Relations

Committee, *Relations in a Multipolar World,* November 13, 1991, 63; Baker in Senate Foreign Relations Committee, *Foreign Policy Overview,* February 5, 1992, 4.

59. Kotkin, *Armageddon Averted*, especially 1–3, 28–44, 58–85; Remnick, *Lenin's Tomb*, 38–51; Pryce-Jones, *The War That Never Was*, 6; Kramer, "The Collapse of East European Communism, Part II," 3–64; Watson, *The Collapse of Communism in the Soviet Union*, 33; Tuminez, "Nationalism, Ethnic Pressure, and the Breakup of the Soviet Union."

60. Directorate of Intelligence, "Gorbachev's Future," May 23, 1991, Soviet Estimate Collection, NSA.

61. NIE 11-18-90, "The Deepening Crisis in the USSR: Prospects for the Next Year," November 1990, in Fischer, ed., *At Cold War's End,* 87; NIE 11-18-91, "Implications of Alternate Soviet Futures," June 1991, in ibid., 124. See also Office of Soviet Analysis, "The Soviet Cauldron," April 1990, in ibid., 111–20.

62. Matlock, *Autopsy on an Empire,* 251; Zlotnick, "Yeltsin and Gorbachev," 128–64.

63. Bush remarks to Ukrainian Parliament, August 1, 1991, Federal News Service transcript; Matlock, *Autopsy on an Empire,* 565.

64. William Safire, "After the Fall," *New York Times,* August 29, 1991.

65. Remnick, *Lenin's Tomb,* especially 418–21; Vienna to Situation Room, August 19, 1991; Belgrade to Situation Room, August 20, 1991; and Leningrad to Situation Room, August 19 and 22, 1991, Box 1, White House Situation Room Files, NSC Files, Bush Library; Beschloss and Talbott, *At the Highest Levels*, 422–23; Dunlop, "The August 1991 Coup," 94–127; Tuminez, "Nationalism, Ethnic Pressure, and the Breakup of the Soviet Union."

66. Robert Gates, testimony before the House Committee on Foreign Affairs, Federal News Service transcript; "New Age of Exploration," *San Francisco Chronicle,* January 5, 1992.

67. "President George Bush at the NATO Summit Conference in Rome, Italy," Federal News Service transcript, November 8, 1991; Cheney in Senate Armed Services Committee, *Department of Defense Authorizations for Fiscal Years 1992 and 1993*, 13–14.

68. Cheney in Senate Armed Services Committee, *Department of Defense Authorization for Fiscal Year 1993*, 11.

69. Powell in Senate Armed Services Committee, *Department of Defense Authorization for Fiscal Years 1992 and 1993,* 42.

70. Cheney in House Committee on Foreign Affairs, *The Future of U.S. Foreign Policy in the Post–Cold War Era,* March 24, 1992, 291, 293.

71. Michael Putzel, "U.S. Searches for Stability in New World's Disorder," *Boston Globe,* September 29, 1991; Andrew Rosenthal, "Farewell, Red Menace," *New York Times,* September 1, 1991.

72. Quoted in Thomas Friedman, "Rethinking Foreign Affairs," *New York Times,* February 7, 1992.

73. R. W. Apple, "The Sense of Triumph Fades, Uncertainty and Unease Grow," *New York Times,* December 29, 1991.

Chapter 3. The Search for Order

1. One might consider Jimmy Carter's foreign policy a brief exception to this rule.

2. See Fousek, *To Lead the Free World.*

3. Cheney remarks to the National Press Club, Federal News Service transcript, March 22, 1990; Bush and Scowcroft, *A World Transformed,* 355.

4. Testimony before the House Committee on Foreign Affairs, Federal News Service transcript, February 25, 1992.

5. Cheney remarks to the Foreign Policy Association, Federal News Service transcript, January 27, 1992; Bush remarks to the American Enterprise Institute, Federal News Service transcript, December 3, 1991.

6. Russett and Sutterlin, "The UN in a New World Order," 82.

7. Krauthammer, "The Unipolar Moment," 23–32.

8. Kennedy, *The Rise and Fall of the Great Powers;* Kirkpatrick, "A Normal Country in a Normal Time," 40–44.

9. Buchanan, "America First—and Second, and Third," 77–82.

10. Perot, *United We Stand,* 99.

11. *National Security Strategy,* 1991, 2; Bush in *Public Papers, 1991,* 1378, 1574.

12. Bush and Scowcroft, *A World Transformed,* 317.

13. *Congressional Record,* 101st Cong., 2nd sess., vol. 136, 116:S13406; ABC News poll, August 20, 1990, USABC.082190.R10, iPoll Database; Brands, "George Bush and the Gulf War of 1991," 128–29; Freedman and Karsh, *The Gulf Crisis, 1990–1991,* 224.

14. Robin Wright, "World View," *Los Angeles Times,* June 25, 1991; Bush remarks, April 13, 1991, in Jahn to Snow, "Presidential References to New World Order," June 26, 1991, Box 3, Alpha File, Speech Backup Files, Speechwriting Office Files, Bush Library.

15. Don Oberdorfer, "Bush's Talk of a 'New World Order,'" *Washington Post,* May 26, 1991.

16. Card note, undated, and RGD outline, "Potential Joint Session Address on Iraq and the Economy," August 31, 1990, Box 77, Sununu Chief of Staff Files, Bush Library.

17. Bush in *Public Papers, 1990,* 1218–22.

18. Gordon Black/*USA Today* poll, December 2, 1990, USGBUSA.903227.R007, iPoll Database; *Congressional Record,* 102nd Cong., 1st sess., vol. 137, 6:S107, E107.

19. Michael Jackson to Cabinet and Agency Contacts, December 4, 1991, Box 10, Files of Stephanie Dance, Cabinet Affairs Office, Bush Library; "Gulf Policy Themes," December 14, 1990, Box 17, Subject File, Marlin Fitzwater Files, White House Press Office, ibid.

20. Haass to Hall, March 2, 1991, Box 1, Robert Gates Files, NSC Files, Bush Library; research materials for March 6, 1991, address, Box 94, Chron File, Speech File Backup File, ibid.; Bush remarks, March 6, 1991, in Jahn to Snow, "Presidential References to New World Order," June 26, 1991, Box 3, Alpha File, Speech Backup Files, ibid.

21. Bush remarks, February 6, 1991, in Jahn to Snow, "Presidential References to New World Order," June 26, 1991, Box 3, Alpha File, Speech Backup Files, Speechwriting Office Files, Bush Library; Wright, "World View."

22. Joshua Muravchik, "At Last, Pax Americana," *New York Times,* September 24, 1991; Bush in *Public Papers, 1991,* 366–68.

23. Bush in *Public Papers, 1991,* 1201–3.

24. Gallup poll, November 15, 1990, Gallup Database; "The New World Order So Far," *New York Times,* January 20, 1991.

25. John Yemma, "Building the World's 'New Order,'" *Boston Globe,* March 3, 1991; Tom Wicker, "What Kind of Order," *New York Times,* June 8, 1991.

26. Wright, "World View."

27. Senate Foreign Relations Committee, *Foreign Policy Overview,* February 5, 1992.

28. House Committee on Foreign Affairs, *The Future of UN Peacekeeping Operations,* March 25, 1992, 12.

29. Senate Armed Services Committee, *Threat Assessment, Military Strategy, and Defense Planning,* March 20, 1992, 466.

30. Powell, *My American Journey,* 451; Colin Powell, "Why Generals Get Nervous," *New York Times,* October 8, 1992; House Committee on Foreign Affairs, *The Future of U.S. Foreign Policy,* March 24, 1992, 351. Powell's education and the development of the anti–small wars doctrine are covered in Boot, *The Savage Wars of Peace,* 308–24.

31. Powell, "U.S. Forces: Challenges Ahead," 32–45.

32. Rogel, *The Breakup of Yugoslavia,* 16–24; Bennett, *Yugoslavia's Bloody Collapse,* 141–67; Bookman, "Economic Aspects of Yugoslavia's Disintegration," in Thomas, ed., *Yugoslavia Unraveled,* 120–21; Liotta, "Religion and War," in ibid., 91–106.

33. Hutchings to Gantt and Uhl, January 24, 1991, "Yugoslavia—General, 1991," Hutchings Files, NSC Files, Bush Library; "Serbia vs. the New World Order," *New York Times,* August 14, 1991.

34. Bush Diary, July 1, 1991, in Bush, *All the Best,* 527–28; Baker and de Frank, *The Politics of Diplomacy,* 636.

35. Burg and Shoup, *The War in Bosnia-Herzegovina,* 70–74; Rogel, *The Breakup of Yugoslavia,* 31; Bennett, *Yugoslavia's Bloody Collapse,* 180–85.

36. Quoted in Thomas Friedman, "It's Harder Now to Figure Out Compelling National Interests," *New York Times,* May 31, 1992; *Public Papers, 1992,* 1799.

37. *Public Papers, 1992,* 1799, 1931.

38. Dupuy, *Haiti in the New World Order,* 71–139.

39. Thomas Friedman, "Haiti's Coup," *New York Times,* October 3, 1991.

40. Bush in *Public Papers, 1991,* 1263.

41. Aronson in House Committee on Foreign Affairs, *Update on the Situation in Haiti,* October 31, 1991, 23, 29.

42. Joel Dreyfuss, "Don't Forget Haiti," *Washington Post,* November 12, 1991.

43. For instance, "The Hell Called Somalia," *New York Times,* July 23, 1992; Liz Sly, "For Somali Town, Too Little, Too Late," *Chicago Tribune,* November 22, 1992.

44. See Don Oberdorfer, "U.S. Took Slow Approach to Somali Crisis," *Washington Post,* August 24, 1992.

45. Durch, "Introduction to Anarchy: Humanitarian Intervention and 'State-Building' in Somalia," in Durch, ed., *UN Peacekeeping,* 319.

46. See Oberdorfer, "U.S. Took Slow Approach"; "The Path to Intervention," *Washington Post,* December 6, 1992; Powell, *My American Journey,* 550.

47. NSD 74, November 24, 1992, National Security Directives File, Bush Library; also Ordway to Scowcroft, December 3, 1992, Somalia File 3, Ordway Files, NSC Files, ibid.; and "Core Talking Points on Somalia," undated, Box 2, FOIA 98-0101, ibid.

48. Anthony Lewis, "Death at Bush's Door," *New York Times,* October 9, 1992.

49. Bush in *Public Papers, 1992,* 2192; Wright, "World View."

50. The Defense Planning Guidance originated in the office of Undersecretary of Defense for Policy Paul Wolfowitz. Its authors included Zalmay Khalilzad, later U.S. ambassador to Afghanistan and Iraq.

51. Report quoted in "Excerpts from Pentagon's Plan," *New York Times,* March 8, 1992.

52. *National Security Strategy,* 1991, 2; Amy Kaslow, "Bush Points to Trade Successes as He Jumps into the Election Race," *Christian Science Monitor,* August 24, 1992; *Public Papers, 1992,* 18.

53. "Helping the Jobless," *Journal of Commerce,* June 15, 1992; "How the Candidates Stand on Trade Issues," *Seattle Times,* February 24, 1992; Kaslow, "Bush Points to Trade Successes."

54. Baker to Bush, February 28, 1990, Box 1, William Pryce Files, NSC Files, Bush Library; *Public Papers, 1992,* 18.

55. "How the Candidates Stand on Trade Issues," *Seattle Times,* February 24, 1992; Richard Gephardt, "This Trade Pact Is Wrong," *USA Today,* September 16, 1992; H. Erich Heinemann, "Fixing America's Job Machine," *Journal of Commerce,* August 19, 1992; "Excerpts from Third Presidential Debate," *Boston Globe,* October 20, 1992.

56. "The New Pentagon Paper," *Washington Post,* May 27, 1992; Barton Gellman, "Aim of Defense Plan Supported by Bush but President Says He Has Not Read Memo," *Washington Post,* March 12, 1992; "Pentagon's New World View," *Washington Post,* May 24, 1992.

Chapter 4. The Successor to Containment

1. Holbrooke memo to Lake, Berger, Gore, and Clinton, reprinted in Holbrooke, *To End a War,* 42; *Public Papers, 1992,* 1798, 1838.

2. Gwen Ifill, "Clinton Seeking Forceful Image as a Leader in Foreign Affairs," *New York Times,* June 28, 1992.

3. Gwen Ifill, "Baker's Role, Clinton's Vision," *New York Times,* August 14, 1992; Thomas Friedman, "Turning His Sights Overseas, Clinton Sees a Problem at 1600 Pennsylvania Avenue," *New York Times,* April 2, 1992.

4. Samuel Huntington to Will Marshall, June 17, 1992, Box 11, Papers of Anthony Lake, Library of Congress; *Public Papers, 1992,* 1799.

5. Powell, *My American Journey,* 547; Christopher, *Chances of a Lifetime,* 172–73.

6. See Amy Kaslow, "Diverse Group of 'Insiders' Tapped for Cabinet Jobs," *Christian Science Monitor,* December 28, 1992.

7. Senate Foreign Relations Committee, *Nomination of Madeleine K. Albright,* January 21, 1993, 25.

8. Jason Deparle, "The Man inside Clinton's Foreign Policy," *New York Times,* August 20, 1995; "Press Briefing by Anthony Lake and General Wesley Clark," May 5, 1994, White House, Office of the Press Secretary.

9. Lake, "From Containment to Enlargement," 4; Thomas Friedman, "Clinton's Foreign Policy: Top Adviser Speaks Up," *New York Times,* October 31, 1993. A theoretical treatment of the "democratic peace" is Russett's *Grasping the Democratic Peace.*

10. Senate Armed Services Committee, *Nomination of Honorable Les Aspin,* January 7, 1993, 30; Joe Klein, "Hail to the Chiefs," *Newsweek,* February 8, 1993, 31. The "vital interests" quote is from a question asked of Aspin. A senator inquired, "You could use force even when vital interests are not at stake?" to which Aspin responded, "Yes."

11. Morris, *Behind the Oval Office,* 246.

12. Senate Foreign Relations Committee, *Nomination of Warren M. Christopher,* 19–21.

13. Ibid., 21.

14. Friedman, "Clinton's Foreign Policy."

15. Ibid.

16. Talbott, *The Russia Hand,* 133–34.

17. Senate Foreign Relations Committee, *Nomination of Christopher,* 20, 21, 23, 24; Senate Armed Services Committee, *Consideration of Honorable Les Aspin,* 6.

18. Senate Armed Services Committee, *Nomination of Aspin,* 30, 31–32.

19. Senate Foreign Relations Committee, *Nomination of Christopher,* 22.

20. Garten, "Clinton's Emerging Trade Policy," 182–89.

21. Gwen Ifill, "In Depressed Middle West, Clinton Ridicules President on Economy," *New York Times,* October 3, 1992.

22. Ibid.; Williams, *The Tragedy of American Diplomacy;* Kolko, *The Politics of War.*

23. Senate Foreign Relations Committee, *Nomination of Albright,* 10, 12, 13, 32.

24. Reich, *Locked in the Cabinet,* 48–53.

25. *Public Papers, 1993,* 115; Wharton in Senate Foreign Relations Committee, *Foreign Policy Implications of the North American Free Trade Agreement,* October 27, 1993, 6.

26. U.S. Department of State, *Dispatch,* September 13, 1993, 626; *Public Papers, 1993,* 491.

27. Reich, *Locked in the Cabinet,* 56–57, 67.

28. *Congressional Record,* 103rd Cong., 2nd sess., vol. 139, pt. 16:23860.

29. Orme, "Myth versus Facts," 2; Krugman, "Uncomfortable Truth about NAFTA," 14.

30. "Administration Pressed to Win NAFTA Converts," *Congressional Quarterly,* October 2, 1993, 1620; "Clinton Turns up Volume on NAFTA Sales Pitch," *Congressional Quarterly,* October 23, 1993, 2963.

31. "Perot Gores His Own Ox in Debate," *Congressional Quarterly,* November 13, 1993, 3105. Republicans favored the treaty, 132–43; Democrats opposed it, 156–102. One independent voted against NAFTA.

32. See, for instance, "It Won't Be Easy but Clinton Can Parlay NAFTA Success into Approval of GATT," *Washington Post,* August 21, 1994.

33. Michael Kelly, "Surrender and Blame," *New Yorker,* December 19, 1994, 47; Joanna Neuman, "Clinton Stealing Bush's Foreign Policy Thunder," *USA Today,* August 11, 1992.

34. Holbrooke, *To End a War,* 50–52; Gallup poll, January 29, 1993, Gallup Database. Fifty-seven percent favored sending ground troops to create peace; 35 percent opposed the proposal.

35. Powell, *My American Journey,* 547–48, 561; Albright, *Madam Secretary,* 279; Tom Post, Margaret Warner, and Eleanor Clift, "The Road to Indecision," *Newsweek,* May 24, 1993, 20–21.

36. Gallup/EBRI poll, February 1993, USGALLUP.EBRI43.Q14, iPoll Database; "Clinton's Challenge," *New York Times,* January 1, 1993. For general support of a humanitarian policy, see ABC News/*Washington Post* poll, February 28, 1993, USABCWP.93–497.R61B, iPoll Database.

37. *Nightline,* November 4, 1992, ABC News transcript; "Clinton Begins Taking Reins," *Atlanta Journal and Constitution,* May 5, 1992; Blumenthal, *The Clinton Wars,* 60.

38. "Ugly Choices in Bosnia," *Washington Post,* February 2, 1993; Lake notes of meeting, February 2, 1993, Box 43, Lake Papers; Owen, *Balkan Odyssey,* 106–8.

39. U.S. Department of State, *Dispatch,* February 15, 1993, 81, and March 1, 1993, 121.

40. *Public Papers, 1993,* 244, 350–51, 364–65.

41. Clinton, *My Life,* 512; Michael Gordon, "12 in State Dept. Ask Military Move against the Serbs," *New York Times,* April 23, 1993; Powell quoted in John Newhouse, "No Exit, No Entrance," *New Yorker,* June 28, 1993, 49.

42. Anthony Lewis, "No Place to Hide," *New York Times,* April 9, 1993; U.S. Department of State, *Dispatch,* May 10, 1993, 321; Newhouse, "No Exit, No Entrance," 49.

43. *Public Papers, 1993,* 577.

44. U.S. Department of State, *Dispatch,* May 24, 1993, 368; Lake notes of meetings, April 29 and May 8, 1993, Box 43, Lake Papers; Clinton, *My Life,* 513; Post et al., "The Road to Indecision," 21.

45. Clinton to Senate leaders, October 20, 1993, reprinted in Vitas and Williams, eds., *U.S. National Security Policy and Strategy, 1987–1994,* 252–53. For a more complete account of Clinton and Bosnia, see Daalder, *Getting to Dayton.*

46. U.S. Department of State, *Dispatch,* April 19, 1993, 270, and May 3, 1993, 312; Senate Armed Services Committee, *International Peacekeeping and Peace Enforcement,* July 14, 1993, 11–12. See chapter 5, this volume, for an extended discussion of the intervention in Somalia.

47. Barton Gellman, "Wider UN Police Role Supported," *Washington Post,* August 5, 1993. See also Steven Holmes, "Clinton May Let U.S. Troops Serve under UN Chiefs," *New York Times,* August 18, 1993.

48. See, for instance, "New World Army," *New York Times,* March 6, 1992.

49. Ibid.; Powell quoted in Daalder, "Knowing When to Say No," in Durch, ed., *UN Peacekeeping,* 43–44.

50. U.S. Department of State, *Dispatch,* June 28, 1993, 464, and August 9, 1993, 567; *Public Papers, 1993,* 565.

51. "Somalia Goals Lost in Warlord Search, Critics of UN Say," *Miami Herald,* July 15, 1993.

52. *Public Papers, 1993,* 987; Clinton address to the United Nations, September 27, 1993, *Weekly Compilation of Presidential Documents, 1993,* 1908; Lake, "From Containment to Enlargement," 12.

53. Lake, "From Cotainment to Enlargement," 5, 12; U.S. Department of State, *Dispatch,* September 27, 1993, 665–68.

54. Lake, "From Containment to Enlargement," 2, 5, 11–14.

Chapter 5. Unmaking Enlargement

1. *Public Papers, 1993,* 102.

2. "Hope Restored?" *New Yorker,* March 8, 1993, 4–6.

3. *Public Papers, 1993, 565–66.*

4. Notes of meeting with Powell, June 16, 1993, Box 43, Lake Papers.

5. Colman McCarthy, "When Peacemakers Turn Warmakers," *Washington Post,* June 26, 1993; "Drawing the Line in Somalia," *New York Times,* June 20, 1993.

6. *Public Papers, 1993,* 840.

7. Senate Foreign Relations Committee, *U.S. Policy in Somalia,* July 29, 1993, 17.

8. Stephen Rosenfeld, "Who'll Be the Global Cop?" *Washington Post,* September 24, 1993; "Limiting Intervention: The Risks of Going Too Far," *USA Today,* September 28, 1993; "Foreign Policy by the Seat of the Pants," *Washington Times,* September 27, 1993.

9. Lake, "From Containment to Enlargement," 3.

10. Albright, *Madam Secretary,* 222; Senate Armed Services Committee, *U.S. Participation in Somalia Peacekeeping,* October 19–20, 1993; Clinton, *My Life,* 552–53; *Public Papers, 1993,* 867.

11. Gallup poll, October 10, 1993, Gallup Database; *Congressional Record,* 103rd Cong., 2nd sess., vol. 139, 17:H24857; "What Senators Said," *Congressional Quarterly,* October 16, 1993, 2827.

12. *Congressional Record,* 103rd Cong., 2nd sess., vol. 139, 133:H7382; ibid., S13077.

13. U.S. Department of State, *Dispatch,* November 15, 1993, 790.

14. Stephanopoulos, *All Too Human,* 214.

15. *Public Papers, 1993,* 713; "Talking Points for Conversation with Admiral Howe," October 17, 1993, Box 44, Lake Papers.

16. Anthony Lake, "The Limits of Peacekeeping," *New York Times,* February 6, 1994; "The Clinton Administration's Policy on Reforming Multilateral Peace Operations," May 1994, Presidential Security Directives Collection, Part II, NSA; *A National Security Strategy of Engagement and Enlargement,* July 1994, 10.

17. Des Forges, *Leave None to Tell the Story,* 1–20, 31–301; Mamdani, *When Victims Become Killers.*

18. "National Intelligence Daily," April 7, 1994, Humanitarian Intervention Collection, NSA; "Talking Points on Rwanda/Burundi," April 11, 1994, ibid.; Embassy in Kigali to the Department of State, April 8, 1994, ibid.; John Darnton, "Revisiting Rwanda's Horrors with a Former National Security Adviser," *New York Times,* December 14, 2004.

19. PDD 25, "Policy on Reforming Multilateral Peace Operations," May 1994, Presidential Security Directives Collection, NSA.

20. State Department to various embassies, April 8, 1994, Humanitarian Intervention Collection, NSA; Darnton, "Revisiting Rwanda's Horrors."

21. Discussion Paper, May 1, 1994; "Rwanda Interagency Telecon," May 11, 1994; Frank Wisner to Sandy Berger, May 5, 1994, Humanitarian Intervention Collection, NSA; Senate Foreign Relations Committee, *Crisis in Central Africa,* July 26, 1994, 66–68.

22. Gallup poll, December 7, 1994, Gallup Database. For the range of estimates, see des Forges, *Leave None to Tell the Story,* 15–16.

23. *Public Papers, 1994,* 830, 1057.

24. Human Rights Watch, *Silencing a People,* 1–3, 37–46, 53–124; Dupuy, *Haiti in the New World Order,* 139.

25. Clinton quoted in Lake notes of meeting, October 18, 1993, Box 44, Lake Papers; Albright in Hyland, *Clinton's World,* 62.

26. State Department cable quoted in "Mixing the Signals," *Newsweek,* May 16, 1994, 41; U.S. Department of State, *Dispatch,* May 23, 1994, 325; Pezzullo in Senate Foreign Relations Committee, *U.S. Policy toward Haiti,* March 8, 1994, 93; Douglas Jehl, "U.S. Sees New Policy on Haitian Refugees as Buying Time," *New York Times,* May 10, 1994.

27. Senate Foreign Relations Committee, *U.S. Policy toward Haiti,* June 28, 1994, 8, 23.

28. U.S. Department of State, *Dispatch,* August 15, 1994, 555; Elaine Sciolino, "Top U.S. Officials Divided in Debate on Invading Haiti," *New York Times,* August 4, 1994.

29. Ann Devroy and John Goshko, "Clinton May Request Reservists for Haiti," *Washington Post,* September 13, 1994.

30. *Public Papers, 1994,* 1558.

31. Ibid., 1567.

32. See the September 26, 1994, cover of *Time* and table of contents of *Newsweek.*

33. Thomas Friedman, "President Vows Victory on Trade," *New York Times,* September 28, 1994.

34. "Key Panel Moves GATT Pact," *Congressional Quarterly,* August 20, 1994, 2438; *Congressional Record,* 103rd Cong., 2nd sess., vol. 140, pt. 21, 30139.

35. Keith Bradshers, "Panel Clears GATT Accord without Fast-Track

Proviso," *New York Times,* August 3, 1994; Moynihan quoted in Thomas Friedman, "President Mulls Deal on Trade," *New York Times,* September 10, 1994.

36. Springer and Molina, "The Mexican Financial Crisis," 57–81.

37. Christopher in Senate Foreign Relations Committee, *Mexico's Economic Situation,* January 26, 1995, 55; Sanders in House Committee on Banking and Financial Services, *Administration's Response to the Mexican Financial Crisis,* April 6, 1995, 38; Senate Banking Committee, *Mexican Peso Crisis,* January 31–July 14, 1995.

38. Ifill, "Clinton Seeking Image as a Forceful Leader."

39. Quoted in Dan Balz, "Protest Vote Cuts Bush's N.H. Margin," *Washington Post,* February 19, 1992.

40. David Sanger, "Gloom Lifts in U.S. and Falls on Japan," *New York Times,* December 29, 1992.

41. Charles Leadbeater, "Import Fall Lifts Trade Surplus," *Financial Times,* December 15, 1992; Don Oberdorfer and Jim Hoagland, "Japan Envoy Wary of U.S. Sanctions," *Washington Post,* February 14, 1993.

42. U.S. Department of State, *Dispatch,* May 24, 1992, 380.

43. Armacost, *Friends or Rivals,* 176; David Sanger, "Japan's Growing Trade Surplus Is a Minus in U.S. Equation," *New York Times,* February 5, 1993; *Weekly Compilation of Presidential Documents, 1993,* 1289. In some sense, the reliance on numerical indicators gave the lie to Clinton's claim that his program represented "free" trade; "objective criteria" seemed a formula for managed trade.

44. Quoted in David Sanger, "Disputes on U.S. Trade Grow in Japan," *New York Times,* January 18, 1993; William Dawkins, "Plaudits Pile up at Home for Hardline Hosokawa," *Financial Times,* February 14, 1994; Hook, Gibson, Hughes, and Dobson, *Japan's International Relations,* 106–8; Hunsberger, ed., *Japan's Quest.*

45. Thomas Friedman, "Playing Poker: Clinton Says Economy Is All Aces," *New York Times,* July 10, 1994; *Public Papers, 1994,* 230.

46. "Right and Wrong on Trade," *New York Times,* August 4, 1994.

47. Peter Behr, "U.S.-Japan Trade Talks Start Slowly," *Washington Post,* September 8, 1994; Peter Behr, "Proving the Pudding of Freer Trade," *Washington Post,* October 9, 1994, emphasis added; see also Michiyo Nakamoto, Nancy Dunne, and Richard Waters, "Japan and U.S. Reach Partial Agreement on Trade," *Financial Times,* October 3, 1994.

48. Quoted in Hyland, *Clinton's World,* 134.

49. Senate Finance Committee, *Managing Global and Regional Trade Policy,* 7.

50. U.S. Department of State, *Dispatch,* August–September 1997, 5, and March–April 1997, 30.

51. *Public Papers, 1997,* 1149–50.

52. "Freer Trade Gets an Unfriendly Reception," *Business Week,* September 22, 1997, 34; John Maggs, "Before and NAFTA," *New Republic,* September 1, 1997, 11; Tim Sherrock, "Union's Rank and File Put up Steely Opposition to Fast Track," *Journal of Commerce,* October 27, 1997, 1.

53. House Committee on International Relations, *Fast Track,* November 6, 1997, 8; "What's the Big Deal?" *U.S. News and World Report,* November 24, 1997, 32.

54. "What's the Big Deal?"; "Will the World Slump?" *Economist,* November 15, 1997, 15; Gallup poll, February 25, 1996, www.institution.gallup.com.

55. Thomas Friedman, "Roll Over Hawks and Doves," *New York Times,* February 2, 1997.

56. For theoretical overviews, see Peet, *Unholy Trinity,* 155–60; Dicken, "A New Geo-Economy"; Castells, "The Global Economy"; and Brown, "The Idea of World Community," in Held and McGrew, eds., *The Global Transformations Reader,* 251–73, 453–61.

57. U.S. Department of State, *Dispatch,* September 30, 1996, 483, and September 1997, 5–6.

58. Held, *Global Transformations,* 184–87, 210–33; Greider, *One World, Ready or Not,* especially 261–63; Stiglitz, *Globalization and Its Discontents;* Peralta, "The Globalization of Inequality in the Information Age," in de Ruijter, Fortman, and van Seters, eds., *Globalization and Its New Divides,* 50–64; Youngs, "International Relations as We Enter the Twenty-first Century," in Youngs and Kofman, eds., *Globalization,* 5–6.

59. Greider, *One World, Ready or Not,* 11–12, 40. See also Hedley, *Running out of Control,* especially 26–32.

60. Suer, *Global Order and Global Disorder,* 140–45; Peet, *Unholy Trinity,* 90–110; Goff, "It's Got to be Sheep's Milk or Nothing!" in Helleiner and Pickel, *Economic Nationalism in a Globalizing World;* Kim, ed., *East Asia and Globalization,* especially 56–61, 163–64, 210–12; Adhiriki, "The Globalisation Mantra," and Kelegama, "Globalisation: A South Asian Perspective," in Adhiriki, ed., *Globalisation: South Asian Perspectives,* 13–15, 36–39.

61. Thomas Friedman, "Buchanan for President," *New York Times,* December 24, 1995; Rodrik, *Has Globalization Gone Too Far,* 2; Mander, "Facing the Rising Tide," in Mander and Goldsmith, eds., *The Case against the Global Economy,* 3–4.

62. Aaron Zitner, "Increasing Global Trade Raises Insecurity," *Boston Globe,* December 2, 1999; Casey Corr, "A Global Convergence Zone for Anyone with a Gripe," *Seattle Times,* December 1, 1999.

63. Bob Deans, "With Nod to Protests, Clinton Chides WTO," *Atlanta Journal and Constitution,* December 2, 1999; Steven Greenhouse and Joseph Kahn, "U.S. Effort to Add Labor Standards to Agenda Fails," *New*

York Times, December 3, 1999; "U.S. Fails to Reach Many of Its Goals at World Trade Talks," *St. Louis Post-Dispatch,* December 4, 1999; Robert A. Jordan, "Battle in Seattle Sent a Message," *Boston Globe,* December 7, 1999; Martin Wolf, "In Defence of Global Capitalism," *Financial Times,* December 8, 1999; Joseph Kahn and David Sanger, "Impasse on Trade Delivers a Stinging Blow to Clinton," *New York Times,* December 5, 1999.

64. Senate Finance Committee, *Managing Global and Regional Trade Policy,* 8; Gallup poll, April 9, 2000, Gallup Database. Forty-five percent believed that free trade was negative because it cost jobs; 42 percent still saw it as a boon to exports.

65. Rielly, "The Public Mood at Mid-Decade," 82, 86.

Chapter 6. Whither Foreign Policy?

1. Susan Shirk and Richard Bush to Richard Holbrooke, July 26, 1992, Box 11, Lake Papers.

2. Holbrooke, "Japan and the United States: Ending the Unequal Partnership," 41–58.

3. Clinton in *Public Papers, 1993,* 1019–27; U.S. Department of State, *Dispatch,* September 6, 1993, 612, and October 18, 1993, 728.

4. *Public Papers, 1993,* 1053–56; U.S. Department of State, *Dispatch,* August 2, 1993, 549.

5. Edward Walsh, "Clinton Indicts Bush's World Leadership," *Washington Post,* October 2, 1992.

6. U.S. Department of State, *Dispatch,* April 5, 1993, 218; see also Lake notes of meeting with Lord, March 8, 1993, Box 43, Lake Papers.

7. Manning, "The United States in North Korean Foreign Policy," in Kim, ed., *North Korean Foreign Relations,* 142–43.

8. Senate Foreign Relations Committee, *Threat of North Korean Nuclear Proliferation,* February 6, 1992, 100–102.

9. Senate Foreign Relations Committee, *U.S. Policy toward North Korea,* March 3, 1994, 24.

10. Tarnoff and Davis to Christopher, November 6, 1993, North Korea Collection, NSA; Clinton in *Public Papers, 1993,* 2058. The most complete treatment of the North Korean crisis is Wit, Poneman, and Gallucci, *Going Critical.*

11. Jay Peterzell, "A Game of Nuclear Roulette," *Time,* January 10, 1994, 28–29; Senate Armed Services Committee, *Consideration of William J. Perry,* February 2, 1994, 21; Lake, *Confronting Backlash States,* 2.

12. R. Jeffrey Smith, "North Korean Conduct in Inspection Draws Criticism of U.S. Officials," *Washington Post,* March 10, 1994; Kim, "The Making of China's Korea Policy in the Era of Reform," in Lampton, ed., *Making of Chinese Foreign and Security Policy,* 371–407; David Sanger, "U.S. Revising North Korea Strategy," *New York Times,* November 22, 1993.

13. "Senate Leaders Support Action against North Korea," *Washington Post,* May 16, 1994; Clinton in *Public Papers, 1994,* 1039; Michael Gordon, "White House Asks Global Sanctions on North Koreans," *New York Times,* June 3, 1994.

14. Tom Post, "Looking for Leverage," *Newsweek,* June 13, 1994, 23; *Public Papers, 1994,* 1080–81.

15. *Public Papers, 1994,* 1086–88.

16. R. Jeffrey Smith, "White House Disputes Carter on North Korea," *Washington Post,* June 18, 1994. Since the beginning of the second North Korean nuclear crisis in late 2002, the issue of whether North Korea had earlier violated the 1994 agreed framework has been hotly debated. For the most part, Clinton's advisers did not think so, and as late as 2002, the CIA averred that the agreement remained intact. See "Review of United States Policy toward North Korea: Findings and Recommendations," October 12, 1999; testimony by William Perry before the Senate Foreign Relations Committee, October 12, 1999, http://www.state.gov; and untitled CIA report, November 2002, North Korea Collection, NSA.

17. *National Security Strategy,* 1995, 28; John F. Harris and Kevin Sullivan, "U.S., Japan Update Alliance and Upgrade Role for Tokyo," *Washington Post,* April 17, 1994.

18. Rone Tempest, "Perry Visit to China Resumes U.S. Contact," *Chicago-Sun Times,* October 17, 1994; Sheila Tefft, "U.S. Defense Chief Forges Close Ties to China's Veiled Military Leaders," *Christian Science Monitor,* October 19, 1994.

19. For instance, "News Conference with President Bill Clinton and Prime Minister Paul Keating of Australia," Federal News Service transcript, September 14, 1993.

20. State Department Briefing Paper, October 5, 1993, PRC Collection, NSA; Suettinger, *Beyond Tiananmen,* 178.

21. Christopher to Clinton, November 15, 1993, PRC Collection, NSA; Elaine Sciolino, "China Rejects Call from Christopher for Rights Gains," *New York Times,* March 13, 1994.

22. Fewsmith, *China since Tiananmen,* 75–99; Nathan and Ross, *The Great Wall and the Empty Fortress,* 188–90; Sciolino, "China Rejects Call from Christopher."

23. Perry to JCS and others, August 1994; "Most Favored Nation Status of the People's Republic of China," June 17, 1994, PRC Collection, NSA; Lord testimony to the House Foreign Affairs Committee, FDCH congressional testimony transcript, June 15, 1994.

24. Linda Chavez, "Clinton Bungling on China," *USA Today,* August 9, 1995.

25. *Congressional Record,* 104th Cong., 1st sess., vol. 141, 118:H7277, H7289.

26. Christopher, *Chances of a Lifetime,* 243; Swaine, "Chinese Decision-Making Regarding Taiwan," in Lampton, ed., *Making of Chinese Foreign and Security Policy,* 319–21.

27. Michael Dobbs, "Christopher Treads Lightly on China Policy," *Washington Post,* August 1, 1995; Perry speech, February 13, 1996, PRC Collection, NSA; *Public Papers, 1996,* 2137.

28. Beijing to Christopher, March 15 and 16, 1996, PRC Collection, NSA; Perry and Carter, *Preventive Defense,* 92–101; Suettinger, *Beyond Tiananmen,* 253.

29. "Getting It Right on China," *New York Times,* February 28, 1995; Lieberthal, "A New China Strategy," 35–49; Muravchik, "Clintonism Abroad," 36–40.

30. Anthony Lewis, "The End of an Era," *New York Times,* May 24, 1993.

31. McFaul, *Russia's Unfinished Revolution,* 123–203.

32. Christopher in Senate Foreign Relations Committee, *Nomination of Warren Christopher,* 26; Senate Foreign Relations Committee, *U.S. Policy on Ukrainian Security,* June 24, 1993, 4–26.

33. Simes, "Reform Reaffirmed," and Lipton, "Reform Endangered," 38–77; Nixon quoted in Crowley, *Nixon off the Record,* 173, 176.

34. U.S. Department of State, *Dispatch, 1993 Supplement,* 3, 21.

35. Talbott, *The Russia Hand,* 102.

36. Elaine Sciolino, "U.S. to Offer Plan," *New York Times,* October 21, 1993.

37. Asmus and Kugler, "Building a New NATO," 28–40; see also notes of Clinton's meeting with Chancellor Helmut Kohl of Germany, July 11, 1994, Box 48, Lake Papers; "German DM Backs NATO Membership for Ex–Soviet Bloc States," *Agence France Press,* October 8, 1993; "East European States Need Clear Prospect of NATO Membership: Kohl," *Agence France Press,* January 18, 1994; "Germany Is Keen to See NATO Expand to Include Poland, Czech Republic, Slovakia," *Agence France Press,* November 30, 1994; Goldgeier, *Not Whether but When,* 20.

38. Steven Erlanger, "Russia Warns NATO on Expanding East," *New York Times,* November 26, 1993; Roger Cohen, "Yeltsin Opposes Expansion of NATO in Eastern Europe," *New York Times,* October 2, 1993.

39. Michael Gordon, "U.S. Opposes Move to Rapidly Expand NATO Membership, but Officials Are Divided," *New York Times,* January 2, 1994.

40. Senate Armed Services Committee, *Department of Defense Authorization for Appropriations for Fiscal Year 1994,* 80, 97.

41. Roger Cohen, "NATO and Russia Clash on Future Alliances," *New York Times,* December 10, 1993; Christopher, *Chances of a Lifetime,* 276, 280.

42. Zbigniew Brzezynski, "A Bigger—and Safer—Europe," *New York Times,* December 1, 1993; *Public Papers, 1994,* 40.

43. Talbott in House Committee on Foreign Affairs, *U.S. Policy toward the New Independent States,* 19; Slocombe in Senate Armed Services Committee, *Future of NATO,* May 1, 2002, 4.

44. Brown, "The Flawed Logic of NATO Expansion," 41.

45. Daniel Williams, "Yeltsin, Clinton Clash over NATO's Role," *Washington Post,* December 6, 1994; Holbrooke in Senate Armed Services Committee, *Future of NATO,* 27.

46. "What Next in Bosnia?" *Philadelphia Inquirer,* July 18, 1995; William Pfaff, "Who Should Carry the Big Stick in Bosnia?" *Chicago Tribune,* July 18, 1995; *Congressional Record,* 104th Cong., 1st sess., vol. 141, 91: S7743.

47. U.S. Department of State, *The Road to Dayton,* 6–21; Thomas Lippman and Ann Devroy, "Clinton's Policy Evolution," *Washington Post,* October 22, 1995; Steven Engleberg, "How Events Drew U.S. into Balkans," *New York Times,* August 19, 1995; Albright, *Madam Secretary,* 292–95; Holbrooke, *To End a War,* 73–74, 92; Stephanopoulos, *All Too Human,* 383.

48. James Williams, "Serbs Say Hospital Hit by UN Shells," *Washington Post,* September 10, 1995; Christopher in Senate Armed Services Committee, *Situation in Bosnia,* 195. Critics pointed out that the Dayton plan was not entirely dissimilar from Vance-Owen. On the impact of the Croatian offensive on the peace talks, see Burg and Shoup, *The War in Bosnia-Herzegovina,* 326–27, 357.

49. Talbott, *The Russia Hand,* 180.

50. McFaul, *Russia's Unfinished Revolution,* 279–84; Bennett, *The Rise, Fall, and Reprise of Soviet-Russian Military Interventionism,* 328–47, especially 346–47.

51. Jeff Jacoby, "Chechnya: The Fruits of U.S. Silence," *Boston Globe,* January 19, 1995; *Congressional Record,* 141st Cong., 1st sess., vol. 141, 77:S6425, 53:S4327, 76:S6315–16.

52. U.S. Department of State, *Dispatch,* June 17, 1996, 317. Yeltsin also benefited from the fact that several prominent Russian businessmen, convinced that a communist victory would lead to their ruin, cooperated to give him greater access to Russian television. McFaul, *Russia's Unfinished Revolution,* 292–94.

53. McFaul, *Russia's Unfinished Revolution,* 324–26; Kotkin, *Armageddon Averted,* 134–45.

54. House Committee on International Relations, *The Threat from Russian Organized Crime,* April 30, 1996, 5.

55. Kissinger in Senate Armed Services Committee, *U.S. National Secu-*

rity Strategy, February 2, 1995, 6; "Excerpts from Prepared Dole Speech on Foreign Policy," *New York Times,* June 26, 1996; John F. Harris, "Clinton Vows Wider NATO in Three Years," *Washington Post,* October 23, 1996.

56. Stanley Fisher, "1.6 Billion: Just a Start," *New York Times,* April 6, 1993; "The Yeltsin Problem," *New York Times,* January 9, 1995; Kamp, "The Folly of Rapid NATO Expansion," 114–29; "Three Basics on Bosnia," *Christian Science Monitor,* May 13, 1993; "A Turning Point for Europe—and U.S.," *Los Angeles Times,* March 4, 1993; "Clinton Faces Hard Sell on Bosnian Extension," *Chicago Tribune,* December 19, 1997; "How to Get out of Bosnia in Five Years, Not Five Decades," *Los Angeles Times,* December 24, 1997.

57. David Hoffman, "Israel Floats New Option on Mideast," *Washington Post,* August 29, 1993; *Public Papers, 1993,* 1463–66. On Oslo, see Buchanan, *Peace with Justice.*

58. James Collins, "Striking Back," *Time,* July 5, 1993, 20–21; *Public Papers, 1993,* 938–39.

59. U.S. Department of State, *Patterns of Global Terrorism, 1993,* 1; House Committee on International Relations, *U.S. Policy toward Iran,* November 9, 1995, 10; Pollack, *The Persian Puzzle,* 255–61.

60. Indyk, "Back to the Bazaar," 76–77.

61. Lake, *Confronting Backlash States,* 4; see also Pollack, *Persian Puzzle,* 261.

62. Pollack, *The Gathering Storm,* 57, 71.

63. Ann Devroy, "President, Dole Divide over Foreign Policy," *Washington Post,* March 2, 1995; Jim Hoagland, "How CIA's Secret War on Saddam Hussein Collapsed," *Washington Post,* June 26, 1997; Deutch in Senate Select Committee on Intelligence, *Iraq,* September 19, 1996, 6; Pollack, *The Gathering Storm,* 72.

64. Hoagland, "How CIA's Secret War Collapsed." See also Baer, *See No Evil,* 171–213.

65. Pollack, *The Gathering Storm,* 84; Deutch in Senate Select Committee on Intelligence, *Iraq,* 4; Howard Fineman and Tara Sonenshire, "Standing Tall, for Now," *Newsweek,* September 16, 1996, 44; *Congressional Record,* vol. 142, S10016.

66. Martin Indyk, "Dual Containment: U.S. Policy toward Iran and Iraq," Federal News Service transcript, February 24, 1994; Pollack, *The Persian Puzzle,* 263, 273–75.

67. Robert Greenberger, "Clinton Officials to Study Tougher Sanctions on Iran," *Wall Street Journal,* April 3, 1995; Elaine Sciolino, "Christopher Proposes Tighter Curbs on Trade with Iran," *New York Times,* April 1, 1995; Gingrich address to the American Israel Public Affairs Committee, FDCH political transcript, April 9, 1995; Thomas Ricks, "Gingrich Blasts

Clinton's Plans for Pentagon," *Wall Street Journal,* February 9, 1995; David Rogers, "Gingrich Wants Funds Set Aside for Iran Action," *Wall Street Journal,* October 27, 1995; Pollack, *The Persian Puzzle,* 273–75.

68. Tim Weiner, "U.S. Plan to Change Iran Leaders Is an Open Secret before It Begins," *New York Times,* January 26, 1996.

69. Pollack, *The Persian Puzzle,* 282–92; Clarke, *Against All Enemies,* 118, 120. The situation improved somewhat between 1997 and 1999, when the rise of a moderate Iranian government led to a series of conciliatory statements and a brief consideration of U.S.-Iran rapprochement. When Iranian conservatives reined in the moderates beginning in 1999, however, Tehran-Washington relations returned to their usual frostiness.

70. Elaine Sciolino, "Two Neighbors Agree," *New York Times,* July 26, 1994; Ross, *The Missing Peace,* 172–75.

71. Bar-Siman-Tov, "Peace Policy as Domestic and Foreign Policy," in Sofer, ed., *Peacemaking in a Divided Society;* Rubin, *The Transformation of Palestinian Politics,* 162–86.

72. "Asad and Clinton Speak: New Commitment to Peace," *New York Times,* January 17, 1994; Ross, *The Missing Peace,* 153, 219; Christopher, *Chances of a Lifetime,* 221–22; Rabil, *Embattled Neighbors,* 203–10.

73. Ross, *The Missing Peace,* 244, 256.

74. Haass, "The Middle East: No More Treaties," 61–62.

75. Warren Christopher, "Diplomacy that Can't Be Delegated," *New York Times,* December 30, 2004; Ross, *The Missing Peace,* 257.

76. PDD 29, September 16, 1994, Presidential Directives Collection, Series II, NSA.

77. Ibid.

78. Senate Select Committee on Intelligence, *Current and Projected National Security Threats,* February 22, 1996, 5.

79. U.S. Department of State, *Dispatch,* February 1997, 21.

80. Senate Select Committee on Intelligence, *Current and Projected National Security Threats,* February 5, 1997, 29.

81. Deutch in Senate Select Committee on Intelligence, *Current and Projected National Security Threats,* February 22, 1996, 5; U.S. Department of State, *Dispatch,* June 10, 1996, 293–96.

82. Senate Foreign Relations Committee, *Foreign Policy Overview,* August 1, 1996, 10.

83. Blumenthal, *The Clinton Wars,* 154.

84. *Washington Post,* August 30, 1996.

85. Hyland, "A Mediocre Record," 70–75; Commission on America's National Interests, *America's National Interests,* 1. Mandelbaum, "Foreign Policy as Social Work," 16–32, offers another critical view.

86. *New York Times,* August 14, 1995.

Chapter 7. Post–Bumper Sticker Diplomacy

1. In the next chapter, I discuss the political and rhetorical ramifications of Clinton's approach.

2. Morris, *Behind the Oval Office,* 246.

3. Alison Mitchell, "Maine Republican Is Seen as Leader for Defense Post," *New York Times,* November 15, 1996; Alison Mitchell, "Clinton Still Studying Choices for National Security Team," *New York Times,* December 5, 1996.

4. Warren Strobel, "Clinton Taps Chiefs for Pentagon, State," *Washington Post,* December 6, 1996.

5. John Harris, "Little-Known Insiders Gaining Prominence on Clinton Team," *Washington Post,* December 6, 1996; James Bennett, "A Trusted Adviser, and a Friend," *New York Times,* December 6, 1996.

6. Joanna McGeary, "Mix and Match," *Time,* December 16, 1996, 29–30.

7. Senate Select Committee on Intelligence, *Current and Projected National Security Threats,* February 5, 1997, 4, 43.

8. Hughes in ibid., 14, 15, 11; "Confirmation of Former Senator William Cohen to Be Secretary of Defense," Federal News Service transcript, January 22, 1997.

9. Talbott remarks in Washington, D.C., FDCH political transcript, October 20, 1997; Albright in Senate Foreign Relations Committee, *Nomination of Secretary of State,* January 9, 1997, 81.

10. Senate Foreign Relations Committee, *Nomination of Secretary of State,* 37.

11. Ibid., 20–27, 78.

12. See *A National Security Strategy for a New Century,* October 1998, and December 1999, 2, Terrorism Collection, NSA; see also Senate Armed Services Committee, *Worldwide Threats,* February 2, 1999, 15, 28.

13. "Bosnian Serbs Threaten to Attack U.S. Troops," *New York Times,* July 8, 1996; Mike O'Connor, "Bosnian Rulers Are Terrorizing the Opposition," *New York Times,* August 17, 1996; "Remarks by Secretary of Defense William Perry at the Hudson Institute," Federal News Service transcript, December 5, 1996.

14. Senate Armed Services Committee, *Nominations before the Senate Armed Services Committee,* 31, 26; Philip Shenon, "Cohen Says U.S. Troops Will Leave Bosnia in '98," *New York Times,* March 5, 1997.

15. "Croats Fire on Muslims in Bosnia," *New York Times,* February 11, 1997; "Croats Evict 100 Muslims in Bosnia," *New York Times,* February 12, 1997.

16. Holbrooke, *To End a War,* 347; Steven Erlanger, "How Bosnia Policy Set Stage for Albright-Cohen Conflict," *New York Times,* June 12, 1997; *Public Papers, 1997,* 680.

17. John Harris, "Berger Says U.S. Must Stay Involved in Bosnia," *Washington Post,* September 24, 1997; *Public Papers, 1997,* 1795.

18. Jim Hoagland, "NATO Plans Worry Russia's Premier," *Washington Post,* February 4, 1997; *Public Papers, 1997,* 131; Madeleine Albright, "Why Bigger Is Better," *Economist,* February 15, 1997, 21–23; Talbott, *The Russia Hand,* 232.

19. Talbott, *The Russia Hand,* 233.

20. Ibid., 238–41.

21. Andrew Nagorski, "Misplaying a Strong Hand," *Newsweek,* May 12, 1997, 2; Richard Beeston, "Russians Attack Yeltsin over NATO Concessions," *London Times,* March 24, 1997.

22. Steven Erlanger, "U.S. to Back Baltic Membership in NATO, but Not Anytime Soon," *New York Times,* January 12, 1998; Steven Erlanger, "Clinton and 3 Baltic Leaders Sign Charter," *New York Times,* January 17, 1998.

23. Leurdijk and Zandee, *Kosovo from Crisis to Crisis,* 16–24.

24. Eagleburger to Belgrade, December 24, 1992, reprinted in Auerswald and Auerswald, eds., *The Kosovo Conflict,* 65; Gelbard in Senate Foreign Relations Committee, *Crisis in Kosovo,* May 6, 1998, 8.

25. Albright, *Madam Secretary,* 598–99; Primakov, *Russian Crossroads,* 183; Jonathan Landay, "NATO Tries to End a War," *Christian Science Monitor,* June 15, 1998.

26. U.S. Department of State, *Dispatch,* August 1998, 16–17; Steven Lee Myers, "U.S. Urging NATO to Step up Plans to Act against Yugoslavia," *New York Times,* September 24, 1998; Eric Schmitt, "Republicans Criticize Clinton on Kosovo," *New York Times,* October 3, 1998; Talbott, *The Russia Hand,* 300.

27. Senate Armed Services Committee, *U.S. Policy and NATO Military Operations in Kosovo,* February 25 and April 15, 1999, 11; Bruce Nelan, "Troops or Consequences," *Time,* February 8, 1999, 38–39.

28. Daalder and O'Hanlon, *Winning Ugly,* 85; Albright, *Madam Secretary,* 635–36.

29. *Public Papers, 1999,* 451–53; Barton Gellman, "In the End, Allies See No Credible Alternative," *Washington Post,* March 23, 1999.

30. Lambeth, *NATO's Air War for Kosovo,* covers aerial combat in Kosovo.

31. *Public Papers, 1999,* 451–53; David Filipov, "Moscow Escalates the War of Words," *Boston Globe,* April 10, 1999.

32. *Congressional Record,* 106th Cong., 1st sess., vol. 145, 46:S3094; Paris, "Kosovo and the Metaphor War," 423.

33. John Harris, "Clinton Says He Might Send Ground Troops," *Washington Post,* May 19, 1999; Jane Perlez, "Clinton and the Joint Chiefs to Discuss Ground Invasion," *New York Times,* June 2, 1999; Steven Erlanger,

"Allies Were Nearing Kosovo Ground War," *New York Times,* November 7, 1999. Interpretations differ as to whether it was airpower or Clinton's threat of ground troops that convinced Milosevic to quit. Consult Stigler, "A Clear Victory for Air Power," 124–57; Lambeth, *NATO's Air War for Kosovo.*

34. Michael Gordon, "Kremlin versus Its Army," *New York Times,* June 12, 1999; Talbott, *The Russia Hand,* 344–46; Bill Powell, "The Russian Army's Ominous 'Mistake,'" *Newsweek,* June 21, 1999, 42; Katharine Q. Seelye, "U.S. Leaders Are Shocked but Accept Russia Story," *New York Times,* June 12, 1999.

35. Clark, *Waging Modern War,* 394–99; Bradley Graham, "NATO Insubordination in Kosovo Is Recalled," *Washington Post,* September 10, 1999; Talbott, *The Russia Hand,* 347; Michael Dobbs, "NATO Occupies Tense Kosovo Capital," *Washington Post,* June 13, 1999.

36. Talbott, *The Russia Hand,* 347–48; Fareed Zakaria, "Victory, but at a Price," *Newsweek,* June 14, 1999, 29; Ambrosio, *Challenging America's Global Preeminence,* 89–93; Sakwa, "Putin's Foreign Policy," in Gorodetsky, ed., *Russia between East and West,* 183–85. The most significant of these resolutions pertained to Iraq in 1998 and 2003, Kosovo in 1998 and 1999, and China's human rights status. I discuss Iraq and China in the following chapters.

37. Black, *Vladimir Putin and the New World Order,* 303–10; Sakwa, "Putin's Foreign Policy," 183–85; Lee Hockstader, "Russia, China Sign New Friendship Pact," *Washington Post,* April 24, 1997; John Pomfret, "Beijing and Moscow to Sign Pact," *Washington Post,* January 13, 2001; Susan Glasser, "Presidents of Russia, China Sign Pact," *Washington Post,* July 17, 2001.

38. R. W. Apple, "Clinton's Peace Strategy," *New York Times,* December 2, 1995.

39. Peacemaking in this sense (referring to negotiations) should not be confused with the military peacemaking of 1993.

40. Robert Pelletreau, "News Briefing on U.S. Foreign Policy and the Middle East," FDCH political transcript, December 18, 1996; Ross, *The Missing Peace,* 300.

41. "Looking Ahead: Two U.S. Documents," *New York Times,* January 17, 1997, emphasis added; Thomas Lippman, "Accord Assures Continued U.S. Role in Middle East," *Washington Post,* January 16, 1997.

42. Barari, *Israeli Politics and the Middle East Peace Process,* 120–24; Berlin, *The Path to Geneva,* 64–66; Steven Erlanger and Alison Mitchell, "A Meeting that Transformed the U.S. Stance in the Mideast," *New York Times,* August 9, 1997; Ross, *The Missing Peace,* 338–39; U.S. Department of State, *Dispatch,* August–September 1997, 20.

43. Ross, *The Missing Peace,* 435, 487.

44. Barari, *Israeli Politics and the Middle East Peace Process,* 129–30;

Albright, *Madam Secretary,* 744; Ross, *The Missing Peace,* 558–87; Rabil, *Embattled Neighbors,* 217–19.

45. "Interview of President Clinton by Israeli TV," Federal News Service transcript, July 27, 2000; Ross, *The Missing Peace,* 692, 710.

46. Clinton, *My Life,* 929–44; Ross, *The Missing Peace,* 722, 742, 801; Albright, *Madam Secretary,* 751, 775.

47. On Clinton's involvement, see also Quandt, *Peace Process,* 324–25, 374, 378.

48. Campbell statement to the House International Relations Committee," FDCH political transcript, September 24, 1998.

49. William Perry, "Review of United States Policy toward North Korea," October 12, 1999, www.state.gov.

50. Ibid.

51. Remarks of State Department official Wendy Sherman to the Senate Foreign Relations Committee, March 21, 2000, www.state.gov; Department of State Fact Sheet, June 19, 2000, www.state.gov; Albright, *Madam Secretary,* 715–18.

52. Albright, *Madam Secretary,* 726–29; Steven Mufson, "Clinton Stop in North Korea Unlikely, Official Says," *Washington Post,* November 4, 2000. On Kim's economic situation, see Nanto, "North Korea's Economic Crisis," in Kihl and Kim, eds., *North Korea: The Politics of Regime Survival,* 119–21.

53. "Talking Points for Ivanov Telephone Call," October 29, 2000, North Korea Collection, NSA; Albright, *Madam Secretary,* 718–19, 730–31, 733–34.

54. Clinton, *My Life,* 929, 938; Albright, *Madam Secretary,* 734–35.

55. Ross, *The Missing Peace,* 4; Albright, *Madam Secretary,* 734, 751, 794.

56. Blumenthal, *The Clinton Wars,* 487.

57. Indyk, "Back to the Bazaar," 75–88.

58. Albright, *Madam Secretary,* 455; Thomas Lippman, "Albright Pessimistic as Mideast Trip Ends," *Washington Post,* September 16, 1997.

59. Albright, *Madam Secretary,* 792.

60. Eric Schmitt, "Pentagon Offers New Budget Cuts," *New York Times,* February 9, 1993; Peter Grier, "White House and U.S. Military Are Not in Step—So Far," *Christian Science Monitor,* February 17, 1993.

61. Senate Armed Services Committee, *Department of Defense Authorization for Fiscal Year 2000,* 203.

62. Senate Armed Services Committee, *Department of Defense Authorization for Fiscal Year 1996,* 33.

63. Ibid., 34.

64. Perry in ibid., 29, emphasis added; Cohen in Senate Armed Services Committee, *Department of Defense Authorization for 2000,* 207. In 1999,

the defense budget totaled $279 billion, compared with $382 million in 1989. For Cohen's remarks, see address by William Cohen, Federal News Service transcript, May 15, 2000.

65. On this management strategy, see Perry and Carter, *Preventive Defense,* 175–215.

66. Cohen quoted in Bacevich, *American Empire,* 138.

67. For alternative explanations of Clinton's foreign policy, see Bacevich, *American Empire;* Haass, "The Squandered Presidency"; and Goldman and Berman, "Engaging the World."

Chapter 8. The Politics of Foreign Policy

1. U.S. Department of State, *Dispatch,* November 1997, 19.

2. Here, I use the term *pragmatism* only to pose a contrast with the moralistic tone of enlargement. Clinton's critics charged that the president's strategy was less than pragmatic, a debate I discuss later in this chapter.

3. Senate Foreign Relations Committee, *Nomination of Secretary of State,* January 9, 1997, 37.

4. U.S. Department of State, *Dispatch,* February 1997, 27; *Public Papers, 1997,* 1424–29.

5. Albright in Senate Foreign Relations Committee, *Nomination of Secretary of State,* 51, 61; U.S. Department of State, *Dispatch,* March–April 1997, 23.

6. Bruce Auster, "Conservatives Antsy over China," *U.S. News and World Report,* June 30, 1997; Jesse Helms, "Reality and MFNtasy," *Weekly Standard,* February 24, 1997, 15; Gallup poll, October 27, 1997, Gallup Database.

7. U.S. Department of State, *Dispatch,* June 1997, 14.

8. Fewsmith, *China since Tiananmen,* 205–6; Pearson, "The Case of China's Accession to GATT/WTO," and Gill, "Two Steps Forward, One Step Back," in Lampton, ed., *Making of Chinese Foreign and Security Policy in the Era of Reform,* 267, 283–84, 337–64; David Sanger, "White House Pushing Deal with Beijing," *New York Times,* March 26, 1999.

9. Cox Report, February 1999, available at www.house.gov/coxreport/; Elliot Abrams, "Hapless Abroad," *National Review,* April 5, 1999, 22.

10. David Sanger, "How U.S. and China Failed to Close Trade Deal," *New York Times,* April 5, 1999; Suettinger, *Beyond Tiananmen,* 367; Zhu in *Public Papers, 1999,* 520–21.

11. Philip Shendon, "U.S. to Propose New Criticism of Rights in China," *New York Times,* January 12, 2000.

12. Fewsmith, *China since Tiananmen,* 208–9, 217–19; Tai Ming Cheung, "The Influence of the Gun," in Lampton, ed., *Making of Chinese Foreign and Security Policy,* 61–89. In 1999, 51 percent of Americans believed that it was more important for the United States to take a strong stand

on human rights than to maintain good relations with China, with 43 percent believing the opposite. Gallup poll, March 14, 1999, Gallup Database.

13. "After the China Vote," *Washington Post,* September 23, 2000; William Buckley, "Peking Fatigue," *National Review,* June 19, 2000, 63.

14. Deutch in Senate Select Committee on Intelligence, *Iraq,* 6, 12; James Morrison, "Topple Saddam," *Washington Post,* March 25, 1997; Pollack, *The Gathering Storm,* 86; U.S. Department of State, *Dispatch,* March–April 1997, 5–8.

15. Pollack, *The Gathering Storm,* 87; Ambrosio, *Challenging America's Global Preeminence,* 89–93.

16. Craig Turner, "U.S. Seeks Tougher Sanctions against Iraq," *Los Angeles Times,* October 21, 1997; Robert Reid, "Sanctions on Iraq Divide UN Council," *Washington Times,* October 19, 1997; Steven Lee Myers, "U.S. Will Not Ask to Use Saudi Bases for Raid on Iraq," *New York Times,* February 9, 1998; Bradley Graham, "U.S. Digs in for 'Long-Term' Struggle over Iraq Arms," *Washington Post,* November 26, 1997.

17. Michael Hirsh and John Barry, "A Plan for Saddam," *Newsweek,* November 16, 1998, 54; U.S. Department of State, *Dispatch,* April 1998, 14. Another likely reason for Clinton's caution was the fact that this crisis came just as terrorists bombed the U.S. embassies in Kenya and Tanzania and special prosecutor Kenneth Starr released his report on the Clinton-Lewinsky affair (discussed later).

18. Albright, *Madam Secretary,* 446.

19. Primakov, *Russian Crossroads,* 176.

20. Senate Foreign Relations Committee, *Iraq: Can Saddam Be Overthrown?* March 2, 1998, 8, 25.

21. Slocombe in Senate Armed Services Committee, *U.S. Policy on Iraq,* January 28, 1999, 5; Pollack, *The Gathering Storm,* 96; Tim Weiner, "U.S. Long View on Iraq," *New York Times,* January 3, 1999.

22. Pollack, *The Gathering Storm,* 99; Senate Foreign Relations Committee, *U.S. Policy toward Iraq,* March 9, 1999, 4; Barbara Crossette, "France, in Break with U.S., Urges End to Iraq Embargo," *New York Times,* January 14, 1999.

23. PDD 39, June 21, 1995, Presidential Directives, Series II, NSA; Gati in Senate Select Committee on Intelligence, *Current and Projected National Security Threats,* February 5, 1997, 21.

24. Clarke, *Against All Enemies,* 199–200; James Riser, "Militant Leader Was a U.S. Target since the Spring," *New York Times,* September 6, 1998; "Usama Bin Laden: Islamic Extremist Fighter," January 1996, Terrorism Collection, NSA; Commission on Terrorist Attacks upon the United States, *9/11 Commission Report,* 112, 114.

25. Barton Gellman, "U.S. Strikes Terrorist-Linked Sites in Afghanistan, Factory in Sudan," *Washington Post,* August 21, 1998; Tenet quoted in

Clarke, *Against All Enemies,* 184. I discuss the origins and goals of al Qaeda in chapter 9.

26. "'Our Target Was Terror,'" *Newsweek,* August 31, 1998, 24–29; official quoted in Gellman, "U.S. Strikes."

27. Sharon Lafraniere, "Yeltsin 'Outraged' by Attacks," *Washington Post,* August 22, 1998.

28. William Cohen, "About Last Week," *Washington Post,* August 23, 1998; Clinton in *Public Papers, 1998,* 1465, 1461.

29. Clarke, *Against All Enemies,* 142–45; NSC memo, "Political Military Plan DELENDA," September 1998; CIA Email, May 17, 1999; Steinberg notes on NSC memo, April 2000, quoted in *9/11 Commission Report,* 120, 140.

30. See Clinton, *My Life,* 799–805, for the president's concern on these issues.

31. Sassen, "Governance Hotspots," in Hershberg and Moore, *Critical Views of September 11,* especially 108; Suer, *Global Order and Global Disorder,* especially 140–45; Nassar, *Globalization and Terrorism,* especially 33–37, 103–5.

32. Habeck, *Jihadist Ideology and the War on Terror,* 99–100.

33. Barkawi, *Globalization and War,* 136–37; Jacquard, *In the Name of Osama bin Laden,* 132–35.

34. *National Security Strategy,* 1999, 1; *National Security Strategy,* 2000, iii, 22.

35. Talbott, *Engaging India,* 47; Steven Lee Myers, "Raft of Sanctions," *New York Times,* May 13, 1998; Thomas Lippman and John Ward Anderson, "U.S. Laws Curb Offers to Pakistan," *Washington Post,* May 28, 1998.

36. Paul Warnke, "The Unratified Treaty," *New York Times,* May 14, 1998; Lott quoted in Mary McGrory, "Doomsday and Dalliance," *Washington Post,* June 4, 1998.

37. *Public Papers, 1999,* 769; U.S. Department of State, *Focus on the Issues: Building Peace and Security around the World,* 6.

38. Schlesinger in Senate Armed Services Committee, *Comprehensive Test Ban Treaty,* October 6 and 7, 1999, 62; Kissinger to Jesse Helms, printed in *Congressional Record,* 106th Cong., 2nd sess., October 13, 1999, S12509.

39. Senate Foreign Relations Committee, *Final Review of the Comprehensive Nuclear Test Ban Treaty,* October 7, 1999, 15.

40. Frank Gaffney, "Test-Ban Treaty Rejection Shows Way for GOP," *Insight on the News,* November 15, 1999, 44; Charles Krauthammer, "Arms Control: The End of an Illusion," *Weekly Standard,* November 1, 1999, 22–24.

41. Kristol and Kagan, "Toward a Neo-Reaganite Foreign Policy," 18–32.

42. Irving Kristol, "The Emerging American Imperium," *Wall Street Journal,* August 18, 1997; Ferguson, *Colossus,* 4; Thomas Ricks, "Empire or Not? A Quiet Debate over U.S. Role," *Washington Post,* August 21, 2001.

43. Berger quoted in Ricks, "Empire or Not"; Kristol, "The Emerging American Imperium."

44. Helms, "Saving the UN," 2–4.

45. U.S. Department of State, *Dispatch,* August–September 1997, 1; Philip Shenon, "Deal to Pay Back UN Dues Collapses over Abortion," *New York Times,* October 16, 1998; Eric Schmitt, "Senate Acts to Pay UN Dues, but Clinton Veto Is Expected," *New York Times,* April 29, 1998.

46. "Pope Kofi's Unruly Flock," *Economist,* August 8, 1998, 19–21; Kofi Annan, "The Unpaid Bill that's Crippling the UN," *New York Times,* March 9, 1998.

47. Senate Foreign Relations Committee and United Nations Security Council, *The Future of U.S.-UN Relations,* January 20–21, 2000, 3, 11.

48. U.S. Department of State, *Dispatch,* December 1997, 20–22.

49. Bolton, "Courting Danger: What's Wrong with the International Criminal Court," 60–71; Helms in Senate Foreign Relations Committee, *Is a UN International Criminal Court in the U.S. National Interest?* 7.

50. "Nations, though Not All of Them, Set up an International Criminal Court," *Manchester Guardian,* July 25, 1998; "A Challenge to Impunity," *Economist,* July 25, 1998, 21.

51. Jeremy Rabkin, "This Court Would Be Criminal," *Weekly Standard,* June 26, 2000, 20.

52. On this general theme, see Mann, *Rise of the Vulcans,* 198–247.

53. Here I distinguish between the general public and the elites (elected officials, newspaper and magazine commentators, and other pundits) of the foreign policy intelligentsia.

54. Walt, "Two Cheers for Clinton's Foreign Policy," 65; Lindsay, "The New Apathy," 4.

55. The important distinction between TMD and NMD is that the former afforded no protection to the American homeland.

56. Senate Select Committee on Intelligence, *Intelligence Analysis of the Long Range Missile Threat to the United States,* December 4, 1996; Helms in Senate Foreign Relations Committee, *ABM Treaty and U.S. Ballistic Missile Defense,* 3.

57. U.S. Department of State, *Dispatch,* October 1998, 12; Talbott, *The Russia Hand,* 377; National Missile Defense Act of 1997, 1–6.

58. Senate Foreign Relations Committee, *Ballistic Missile Threat to the United States,* October 6, 1998, 4; "Executive Summary of the Report of the Commission to Assess the Ballistic Missile Threat to the United States," Section II, http://www.house.gov/hasc/testimony/105thcongress/BMThreat.htm.

59. Senate Foreign Relations Committee, *Ballistic Missiles: Threat and Response,* April–September 1999, 176.

60. Woolsey in Senate Foreign Relations Committee, *ABM Treaty,* 11; Helms quoted in Matthew Rees, "Going Ballistic," *Weekly Standard,* February 8, 1999, 14; Douglas Feith, "Live Missiles and Dead Letters," *National Review,* August 3, 1998, 36–37.

61. Charles Krauthammer, "A World Imagined," *New Republic,* March 15, 1999, 26.

62. Cohen quoted in Steven Lee Myers, "Rethinking a Treat for a New Kind of Enemy," *New York Times,* January 24, 1998; *Public Papers, 1999,* 95; Dana Prient, "Cohen Says U.S. Will Build Missile Defense," *Washington Post,* January 21, 1999.

63. Talbott, *The Russia Hand,* 375–96; Black, *Vladimir Putin and the New World Order,* 64–66; Clinton, *My Life,* 908.

64. The extent of congressional influence during the 1970s is covered most recently in Johnson, *Congress and the Cold War,* 105–43.

65. Talbott, *The Russia Hand,* 133–34.

Chapter 9. Full Circle

1. Rice, "In Defense of the National Interest," 46–62.

2. Terry Neal, "Bush Falters in Foreign Policy Quiz," *Washington Post,* November 5, 1999.

3. Bush remarks at the Reagan Library, Federal News Service transcript, November 19, 1999.

4. Ibid.

5. Rice, "In Defense of the National Interest," 46–62. On this theme, see also Mann, *Rise of the Vulcans,* 198–247.

6. Transcript of Second Presidential Debate, October 11, 2000, Federal News Service transcript; Roberto Suro, "Gore, Bush Defense Plans Short of Military Demands," *Washington Post,* October 28, 2000.

7. "The Bush Foreign Policy Team," *New York Times,* December 16, 2001.

8. *Public Papers, 2001,* 473.

9. Ibid., 336.

10. Boniface, "The Specter of Unilateralism," 155–62.

11. David Sanger, "Powell Sees No Need for Apology," *New York Times,* April 4, 2001; Gallup polls, April 8 and 22, 2001, Gallup Database; Jane Perlez and David Sanger, "Bush Aids Saying Some Hope Is Seen to End Standoff," *New York Times,* April 6, 2001.

12. Cooley, *Unholy Wars,* 9–105; Gunaratna, *Inside al Qaeda,* 19–22; Chipman, "Osama bin Laden and Guerilla War," 163–70.

13. Gunaratna, *Inside al Qaeda,* 28–29; Habeck, *Jihadist Ideology,* 19, 38, 77; Rubin and Rubin, *Anti-American Terrorism and the Middle East,*

139; Nacos, "The Terror Calculus behind 9–11," 9; Anonymous [Michael Scheuer], *Through Our Enemies' Eyes,* 49–52.

14. Bin Laden quoted in Rubin and Rubin, *Anti-American Terrorism,* 154; Cooley, *Unholy Wars,* 75–105; Habeck, *Jihadist Ideology,* 102–3; Nacos, "The Terror Calculus behind 9–11," 9.

15. Unger, *House of Bush, House of Saud,* 178–80; Gunaratna, *Inside al Qaeda,* 229; bin Laden quoted in Rubin and Rubin, *Anti-American Terrorism,* 138; Habeck, *Jihadist Ideology,* 14; Commission on Terrorist Attacks upon the United States, *9/11 Commission Report,* especially 213–14.

16. Fred Grimm, "A Calamity beyond Measure," *Miami Herald,* September 12, 2001.

17. "Feeling of Invincibility Suddenly Shattered," *Chicago Tribune,* September 12, 2001.

18. Statement by George Tenet to the Senate Select Committee on Intelligence, "World-Wide Threats," FDCH congressional testimony transcript, February 7, 2001; *9/11 Commission Report,* 213–14.

19. Dan Balz and Bob Woodward, "America's Chaotic Road to War," *Washington Post,* January 27, 2002.

20. *9/11 Commission Report,* 326.

21. Ibid., 330; Woodward, *Bush at War,* 58–59.

22. Woodward, *Bush at War,* 43; Steven Mufson and Thomas Ricks, "Call for Broad Action by Some Officials Runs into Concerns about Diplomatic Fallout," *Washington Post,* September 21, 2001; Jane Perlez, David Sanger, and Thom Shanker, "From Many Voices, One Battle Strategy," *New York Times,* September 23, 2001.

23. Dan Balz and Bob Woodward, "'We Will Rally the World,'" *Washington Post,* January 28, 2002; Powell quoted in *9/11 Commission Report,* 335.

24. "Remarks by President George W. Bush and Secretary of State Colin Powell at the Africa Growth and Opportunity Act Forum," Federal News Service transcript, October 29, 2001; James Dao, "Defense Secretary Warns of Unconventional Attacks," *New York Times,* October 1, 2001; Todd Purdum, "Leaders Face Challenges Far Different from Those of Last Conflict," *New York Times,* September 15, 2001; Michael Gordon, "A New War and Its Scale," *New York Times,* September 17, 2001; David Sanger and Don Van Natta Jr., "In Four Days, a National Crisis Changes Bush's Presidency," *New York Times,* September 16, 2001; Dana Milbank, "Crisis Brings Shift in Presidential Style," *Washington Post,* September 14, 2001.

25. Donald Rumsfeld, "A New Kind of War," *New York Times,* September 27, 2001.

26. Steven Ricks and Steve Mulson, "In War on Terrorism, Unseen Fronts May Be Crucial," *Washington Post,* September 23, 2001; Rumsfeld interview, September 30, 2001, http://www.defenselink.mil/transcripts/2001/t09302001_t0930sd.html.

27. Rice, "In Defense of the National Interest," 46.

28. NSPD 9, October 25, 2001, quoted in *9/11 Commission Report,* 334; *Public Papers, 2001,* 1170.

29. Woodward, *Bush at War,* 73; David Sanger and Elizabeth Bumiller, "In One Month, a Presidency Is Transformed," *New York Times,* October 11, 2001; Tenet to various CIA officials, September 16, 2001, Terrorism and U.S. Policy Collection, NSA.

30. *Public Papers, 2001,* 1141–42.

31. Ibid., 1140.

32. Ibid., 1099, 1141. Bush's was a questionable interpretation of al Qaeda's motives. As discussed previously, al Qaeda's goals were much less expansive than Bush suggested, focusing mainly on forcing a U.S. withdrawal from the Middle East and ending U.S. support for certain governments in the region. See Scheuer, *Imperial Hubris.*

33. *Public Papers, 2001,* 1161. For an introduction to the rhetoric of World War II and the Cold War, consult Hinds and Wendt, eds., *The Cold War as Rhetoric,* and Adams, *The Best War Ever,* respectively.

34. *Public Papers, 2001,* 1142.

35. Ibid., 1109.

36. Ibid., 1144.

37. Ibid., 1116. The White House quickly retracted Bush's "crusade" remark.

38. Eighty-seven percent rated Bush's speech as "excellent" (62 percent) or "good" (25 percent). In early October, 87 percent approved of Bush's handling of antiterrorism policy. Gallup polls, September 22 and October 7, 2001, Gallup Database.

39. *Public Papers, 2001,* 1141–42.

40. Ibid., 1142.

41. See Hicker, "Money Lust"; Nacos, "Attack on America," especially 35–37.

42. Miles A. Pomper, "In for the Long Haul," *Congressional Quarterly,* September 15, 2001, 2118–19; Karen Foerstaland and David Natter, "Beneath Capital's Harmony, Debate Simmers Patiently," *Congressional Quarterly,* September 22, 2001, 2188.

43. "Democrats for Missile Defense?" *Washington Times,* September 28, 2001; Miles Pomper, "New Map of Friends and Foes," *Congressional Quarterly,* September 22, 2001, 2191.

44. Peter Feaver, "Cold War II," *Weekly Standard,* October 1, 2001, 18; "In for the Long Haul," *New York Times,* September 16, 2001.

45. Rush Limbaugh, "A Nation Roused," *National Review Online,* September 28, 2001; Rich Lowry, "Magnificent," *National Review Online,* September 21, 2001.

46. David Brooks, "Bush's Patriotic Challenge," *Weekly Standard,* Oc-

tober 8, 2001, 28; Jessica Lee, William Welch, and Scott Hillkirk, "'Call to Action' Receives Praise," *USA Today,* September 21, 2001.

47. Max Boot, "The Case for American Empire," *Weekly Standard,* October 15, 2001, 27–30.

48. Gallup polls, September 21 and November 11, 2001, and February 10, March 24, and July 8, 2002, Gallup Database.

49. *National Security Strategy,* 2002, iv, 1, 7 (hereafter cited as *NSS* 2002, followed by the page number).

50. John Gaddis writes, "Definitions of national interest in international affairs tend toward the bland and unexceptionable: they all seem to boil down, in one form or another, to the need to create an international environment conducive to the survival and prospering of the nation's domestic institutions." Gaddis, *Strategies of Containment* (2005), 26–27.

51. "Condoleezza Rice Delivers Remarks to International Students," FDCH political transcript, April 29, 2002; *NSS* 2002, iv–v.

52. Bush speech, "A Distinctly American Internationalism," FDCH political transcript, November 19, 1999; Rice, "In Defense of the National Interest"; *NSS* 2002, 15; James Dao, "Defense Secretary Warns of Unconventional Attacks," *New York Times,* October 1, 2001.

53. Rice, "In Defense of the National Interest," 61. See also Colin Powell, "Briefing for the Press aboard Aircraft en Route to Brussels," http://www.state.gov/secretary/rm/2001/953.htm.

54. Balz and Woodward, "America's Chaotic Road to War"; Bush address at West Point, FDCH political transcript, June 1, 2002; Donald Rumsfeld, "Beyond This War on Terrorism," *Washington Post,* November 1, 2001; Daalder and Lindsay, *America Unbound.*

55. *NSS* 2002, iv.

56. Ibid., 9–10.

57. Bush address at West Point, June 1, 2002.

58. *NSS* 2002, 26–27. In 2006, Bush sought to remove the nuclear issue as a sticking point in U.S.-Indian relations by concluding an agreement ending U.S. sanctions on the Indian nuclear program.

59. *NSS* 2002, v, 28.

60. Ibid., iv, 5–7; Bush address at West Point, June 1, 2002.

61. *Preemption* as practiced by the Bush administration is actually *prevention* in an international relations theory sense, in that *preemption* refers to forestalling an imminent attack, whereas *prevention* entails attacking so that one's enemy cannot gain the capabilities needed to attack.

62. *NSS* 2002, 15.

63. Ibid., v.

64. Rumsfeld, "A New Kind of War."

65. Elizabeth Bumiller, "Bush Pledges Attack on Afghanistan Unless It Surrenders bin Laden Now," *New York Times,* September 21, 2001.

66. *NSS* 2002, 6; Unger, *House of Bush, House of Saud,* 260–63; *Public Papers, 2001,* 1168; Bremer quoted in Cooper, *New Political Religions,* 24.

67. State Department, "The Global War on Terrorism: The First 100 Days," January 12, 2002, Terrorism and U.S. Policy Collection, NSA. This aspect of U.S. policy would gradually change in the years after 9/11, with the Bush administration placing greater emphasis on democracy building and liberalization in the Middle East, but it was largely absent from early planning in the war on terror. See chapter 10.

68. "Colin L. Powell Delivers Remarks on Foreign Policy and National Security Strategy at George Washington University," FDCH political transcript, September 5, 2003; "Dr. Condoleezza Rice Delivers Remarks at Los Angeles Town Hall Breakfast," FDCH political transcript, July 12, 2003; *NSS* 2002, iv.

69. Transcript of Second Presidential Debate, Federal News Service transcript, October 11, 2000.

70. Bush address at West Point, June 1, 2002; see also Bacevich and Prodromou, "God Is Not Neutral," 43–54; Bacevich, *The New American Militarism,* 12–13, 122, 145; Woodward, *Bush at War,* 73.

71. Leffler's "9/11 and American Foreign Policy," 395–413, offers a succinct treatment of the long-standing continuity in U.S. security policy. On this point, see also Bacevich, *American Empire,* ch. 9.

72. Bob Woodward and Dan Balz, "At Camp David, Advise and Dissent," *Washington Post,* January 31, 2002; Bob Woodward and Dan Balz, "A Pivotal Day of Grief and Anger," *Washington Post,* January 30, 2002; Bob Woodward, "Secret CIA Units Playing a Central Combat Role," *Washington Post,* November 18, 2001; Jespersen, "Analogies at War," 419. On the conduct and military implications of the conflict, see Biddle, "Afghanistan and the Future of Warfare," 31–46.

73. The Soviet example was a major factor in determining the administration's war plan. See remarks by Paul Wolfowitz, June 26, 2002, www.defenselink.mil/speeches/2002/s20020626-depsecdef1.html.

74. Albright, *Madam Secretary,* 586.

75. Rocca in Senate Foreign Relations Committee, *Political Future of Afghanistan,* December 6, 2001, 7; Senate Foreign Relations Committee, *Afghanistan Stabilization and Reconstruction: A Status Report,* January 27, 2004, 2–5; Senate Foreign Relations Committee, *Reconstruction of Afghanistan,* 7.

76. Kux, *The United States and Pakistan,* 352–58; Celia Dugger, "U.S. Presses Pakistan," *New York Times,* September 14, 2001.

77. Islamabad to State Department, September 14, 2001, quoted in *9/11 Commission Report,* 331; Jane Perlez, "U.S. Sanctions on Islamabad Will Be Lifted," *New York Times,* September 22, 2001; Bush in *Public Papers,*

2001, 1381; John Burns, "U.S. Officers Are Meeting in Islamabad on War Plans," *New York Times,* September 25, 2001.

78. State Department Country Reports on Human Rights Practices—Uzbekistan, February 25, 2000, http://www.state.gov/www/global/human_rights/1999_hrp_report/uzbekist.html; Senate Foreign Relations Committee, *Contributions of Central Asian Nations to the Campaign against Terrorism,* December 13, 2001; David Stern, "Historic Pact Signed with U.S.," *Financial Times,* October 13, 2001; Rashid, *Jihad,* 184.

79. Don van Natta, "U.S. Recruits Rough Ally to Be a Jailer," *New York Times,* May 1, 2005; Jones in Senate Foreign Relations Committee, *Contributions of Central Asian Nations,* 5.

80. Alan Sipress and Steve Mufson, "U.S. Explores Recruiting Iran into New Coalition," *Washington Post,* September 25, 2001; Bahgat, "Iran, the United States, and the War on Terrorism," 95.

81. St. John, *Libya and the United States,* 158–93; Gary Hart, "My Secret Talks with Libya, and Why They Went Nowhere," *Washington Post,* January 18, 2004; State Department Office of the Coordinator for Counterterrorism, "Overview of State-Sponsored Terrorism," April 30, 2001, www.state.gov; *Public Papers, 2001,* 421; Alan Sipress and Peter Behr, "Bush Says Iran, Libya Sanctions to Stay," *Washington Post,* April 20, 2001.

82. National Foreign Intelligence Board, "Foreign Missile Developments and the Ballistic Missile Threat through 2015," Terrorism and U.S. Policy Collection, NSA; Robert Greenberger, "U.S. Hawks Eye Libya Warily—Weapons May Replace Lockerbie as Reason for Sanctions," *Wall Street Journal,* April 22, 2002; Daniel Williams, "Possible Opening to West Stirs Hope in Libya," *Washington Post,* December 27, 2003; Patrick Tyler, "In a Changed World, Qaddafi Is Changing, Too," *New York Times,* December 20, 2001.

83. "Senior Administration Officials Hold Background Briefing Following President Bush's Remarks Regarding Libya," FDCH political transcript, December 19, 2003; Alan Sipress and John Mintz, "Libya Accepts Responsibility for Bombing over Lockerbie," *Washington Post,* May 1, 2003; White House Office of the Press Secretary Fact Sheet, "The President's National Security Strategy to Combat WMD: Libya's Announcement," December 19, 2003, www.state.gov; Peter Slevin and Glenn Frankel, "Libya's Gaddafi Promises to Give up Banned Weapons," *Washington Post,* December 21, 2003.

84. Ambrosio, *Challenging America's Global Preeminence,* 1–3, 136–45; Black, *Vladimir Putin and the New World Order,* 143–44.

85. Dana Milbank, "Policy Changes? What Policy Changes?" *Washington Post,* March 26, 2002; Colin Powell, statement to the Senate Foreign Relations Committee, July 9, 2002; Anne Applebaum, "How the World Has

Changed, Part I," *Slate,* September 21, 2001, quoted in Miller, "The End of Unilateralism or Unilateralism Redux?" 23.

86. Elaine Sciolino and Patrick Tyler, "Saudi Charges Bush with Failure to Broker Middle East Peace," *New York Times,* November 9, 2001; Unger, *House of Bush, House of Saud,* 244–45; David Sanger, "Bush, Mirroring Call on Taliban, Demands Arafat Stop Extremists," *New York Times,* December 3, 2001. In late 2001, Bush classified Hamas and other Palestinian groups as terrorist organizations and moved to deny them funding.

87. *NSS* 2002, 1; Robert Zoellick, "Countering Terror with Trade," *Washington Post,* September 20, 2001.

Chapter 10. Waging the War on Terror

1. *Public Papers, 2001,* 620; see also David Sanger, "After the Taliban, Who?" *New York Times,* November 25, 2001.

2. House Committee on International Relations, *U.S.–North Korea Relations,* July 26, 2001, 13.

3. Michael Gordon, "Broadening of 'Doctrine,'" *New York Times,* January 30, 2002; Bush remarks, FDCH political transcript, January 29, 2001.

4. *Public Papers, 2002,* 256, 265; Guy Dinmore and Andrew Ward, "Koizumi Joins Bush Warning to North Korea," *Financial Times,* May 24, 2003; Judy Keen, "Bush Has Little Use for Diplomatic Niceties," *USA Today,* March 18, 2003; Bush remarks, January 29, 2001.

5. Meter Slevin and Karin DeYoung, "Stunned U.S. Ponders Next Steps," *Washington Post,* October 17, 2002; Armitage in Senate Foreign Relations Committee, *WMD Developments on the Korean Peninsula,* February 4, 2003, 5.

6. Michael Dobbs, "For Wary White House, a Conflict, Not a Crisis," *Washington Post,* December 29, 2002; Howard French and Don Kirk, "American Policies and Presence Are under Fire in South Korea, Straining an Alliance," *New York Times,* December 8, 2002.

7. Bush remarks, October 22, 2003, http://www.whitehouse.gov/news/releases/2003/10/20031022–7.html.

8. Steven R. Weisman, "North Korea's Nuclear Plans Called 'Unacceptable,'" *New York Times,* December 14, 2002; Rice confirmation hearing, Federal News Service transcript, January 18, 2005; Bryan Knowlton, "U.S. Denounces North Korea after Reports of Missile Test," *New York Times,* May 2, 2005; Glenn Kessler, "North Korea Nuclear Estimate to Rise," *Washington Post,* April 28, 2004; Jacoby testimony before Senate Armed Services Committee, Federal News Service transcript, April 28, 2005.

9. Anthony Faiola and Sachiko Sakamaki, "North Korea Suggests It Will Hold Atomic Test," *Washington Post,* May 10, 2005; James Brooke, "South Korea Pushes to Engage the North, Rejecting U.S. Notion of a Quarantine," *New York Times,* May 15, 2005.

10. Glenn Kessler and Anthony Faiola, "U.S. Envoy Met with North Korean Officials at UN," *Washington Post,* May 20, 2005; David Sanger and Thom Shanker, "North Korea Is Reported to Hint at Talks," *New York Times,* June 6, 2005; Glenn Kessler, "Both Sides Bend to Restart N. Korea Talks," *Washington Post,* July 14, 2005; Joohee Cho, "N. Korea's Kim Says He'll Talk if U.S. Gives Respect," *Washington Post,* June 18, 2005; Glenn Kessler, "N. Korea Agrees to Rejoin Talks," *Washington Post,* July 10, 2005; Joel Brinkley, "Setting the Table for North Korea's Return," *New York Times,* July 11, 2005.

11. Kim, "Sino–North Korean Relations," in Kihl and Kim, eds., *North Korea: The Politics of Regime Survival,* 189–94; Edward Cody, "New Talks on North Korea Open with Fresh Strategy," *Washington Post,* July 26, 2005; Jim Yardley and David Sanger, "U.S. Tries a New Approach in Talks with North Korea," *New York Times,* July 27, 2005; Glenn Kessler and Edward Cody, "North Korea, U.S. Gave Ground to Make Deal," *Washington Post,* September 20, 2005.

12. Philip Pan, "New Round Opens in North Korea Nuclear Talks," *Washington Post,* November 9, 2005; Joseph Kahn, "North Korea and U.S. Spar, Causing Talks to Stall," *New York Times,* November 12, 2005.

13. For instance, McMahon, *Cold War on the Periphery;* Immerman, *The CIA in Guatemala.*

14. Condoleezza Rice, "War on Terror," remarks to the Chicago Council on Foreign Relations, Federal News Service transcript, October 8, 2003; "Media Availability with President George W. Bush and Pakistani President Pervez Musharraf," Federal News Service transcript, June 24, 2003.

15. David Sanger, "U.S. Widens View of Pakistani Link to Korean Arms," *New York Times,* March 14, 2004; "A Tale of Nuclear Proliferation," *New York Times,* February 12, 2004.

16. Sanger, "U.S. Widens View"; Seymour Hersh, "The Deal," *New Yorker,* March 8, 2004, 32–37; Peter Slevin, John Lancaster, and Kamran Khan, "At Least 7 Nations Tied to Pakistani Nuclear Ring," *Washington Post,* February 8, 2004.

17. Bush remarks, February 11, 2004, http://www.whitehouse.gov/news/releases/2004/02/20040211-4.html; "Ambassador Richard A. Bouche Holds State Department Regular News Briefing," FDCH political transcript, February 5, 2004.

18. David Sanger and William Broad, "Web of Trails Leads to Pakistan," *New York Times,* January 4, 2004; "Colin Powell Holds Media Availability en Route to Kuwait," FDCH political transcript, March 18, 2004.

19. Hersh, "The Deal"; "U.S. Speaks Softly to Pakistan," *Christian Science Monitor,* March 5, 2004; Bryan Bender, "Pakistan Lets U.S. Troops Conduct Raids in Frontier," *Boston Globe,* February 21, 2004.

20. Bush remarks, Federal News Service transcript, December 13, 2001.

21. Statement by Robert Walpole to the Senate Governmental Affairs Committee, Federal News Service transcript, March 11, 2002.

22. National Intelligence Estimate, December 2001, "Foreign Missile Developments and the Ballistic Missile Threat through 2015," Terrorism and U.S. Policy Collection, NSA.

23. Flynn, "America the Vulnerable," 60; Esther D'Amico, "Port Vulnerability under a Sea of Scrutiny," *Chemical Week,* June 5, 2002, 25; Biden in Senate Foreign Relations Committee, "The Terrorist Nuclear Threat," Federal News Service transcript, March 6, 2002.

24. "Missile Defense Deployment Announcement," Federal News Service transcript, December 17, 2002; Eric Schmitt, "Antimissile System, in a Limited Form, Is Ordered by Bush," *New York Times,* December 18, 2002.

25. In 2004, the 9/11 Commission reported that these aspects of homeland security remained vulnerable to catastrophic penetration. See *9/11 Commission Report,* ch. 12.

26. "Remarks by U.S. Secretary of Defense Donald Rumsfeld to the National Defense University," Federal News Service transcript, January 31, 2002; Stephen Hadley (later deputy national security adviser and national security adviser to Bush) in Senate Foreign Relations Committee, *Ballistic Missiles: Threat and Response,* April–September 1999, 176; *National Security Strategy to Combat Weapons of Mass Destruction,* 2003, 1, 3.

27. On this issue, see Joseph Cirincione, "A Much Less Explosive Threat," *Washington Post,* March 10, 2002.

28. Ibid.; Brands, *The Devil We Knew,* 182–87; Steinberg, *Lost in Space;* "Northrop Grumman, EADS Team on Missile Defense," *Aerospace Daily and Defense Report,* July 23, 2004; "Northrop's Heavy Artillery," *Business Week,* March 8, 2004, 52–53.

29. Powell testimony to Senate Budget Committee, Federal News Service transcript, February 12, 2002.

30. Letter from Rumsfeld et al. to Clinton, January 26, 1998, http://www.newamericancentury.org/iraqmiddleeast2000–1997.htm#iraq; John Bolton, "Congress vs. Iraq," *Weekly Standard,* January 19, 1998, 17. On this subject, see Mann, *Rise of the Vulcans,* 79–94, 198–247, 332–58.

31. Wilson, *The Politics of Truth,* 286; Woodward, *Plan of Attack,* 24–27; David Martin, "Notes from an Aide to Defense Secretary Rumsfeld Say Iraq Was Considered an Attack Target as Far Back as 9/11 Despite No Evidence of Involvement," CBS News transcript, September 4, 2002; *9/11 Commission Report,* 335.

32. Andrew Gowers, interview with George W. Bush, *Financial Times,* November 14, 2003; Bob Woodward, "A Struggle for the President's Heart and Mind," *Washington Post,* November 17, 2002; Woodward, *Plan of Attack,* 25–26; Gaddis, *Surprise, Security, and the American Experience,* ch. 4. See also Suskind, *The One Percent Doctrine.*

33. Anderson, "One Vietnam War Should Be Enough," 18–19; LaFeber, "The Bush Doctrine," 543, 549–50; Bush address on Iraq, Federal News Service transcript, October 7, 2002.

34. Woodward, *Plan of Attack,* 162; "President George W. Bush's Remarks at the American Enterprise Institute," Federal News Service transcript, February 26, 2003; Garran, *True Believer,* 119.

35. Jason Vest, "Wrong Target," *American Prospect,* online edition, April 1, 2004; Wolfowitz interview, May 10, 2003, http://www.defenselink.mil/transcripts/2003/tr20030509-depsecdef0223.html.

36. "A Policy of Evasion and Deception," *Washington Post,* February 6, 2003; Bush address, October 7, 2002.

37. Meeting of various British officials, July 23, 2002, http://www.downingstreetmemo.com/memo.html; National Intelligence Estimate, October 2002, www.fas.org.irp/cia/product/iraq-wmd.html; John Cochran, "Reason for War?" *ABCnews.com,* April 25, 2003, quoted in Kaufman, "Threat Inflation and the Failure of the Marketplace of Ideas," 8; Pfiffner, "Did President Bush Mislead the Country," 25–46.

38. Gallup polls, September 18, 2002, and January 31, 2003, Gallup Database; "Irrefutable," *Washington Post,* February 6, 2003.

39. Senate Armed Services Committee, *Department of Defense Authorization for Appropriations for Fiscal Year 2004,* February 25, 2003, 241–42.

40. Patrick Tyler and Elaine Sciolino, "Bush's Advisers Split on Scope of Retaliation," *New York Times,* September 20, 2001; Woodward, "Struggle for the President's Heart and Mind."

41. Woodward, *Plan of Attack,* 251; Keith Richburg, "NATO Blocked on Iraq Decision," *Washington Post,* January 23, 2003; Sharon LaFraniere, "Russia Aims for Role as Broker between U.S., Europe," *Washington Post,* February 12, 2003; James Rubin, "Chirac Should Be Told to Accept a Timetable," *Financial Times,* January 31, 2003; David Sanger, "U.S. Says UN Could Repeat Errors of 90's," *New York Times,* March 11, 2003. There has recently emerged evidence that despite Schroeder's opposition, German intelligence officials likely provided their U.S. counterparts with information on Iraqi defenses. See Richard Bernstein and Michael Gordon, "Berlin File Says Germany's Spies Aided U.S. in Iraq," *New York Times,* March 2, 2006.

42. Senate Armed Services Committee, *U.S. Policy on Iraq,* September 19–25, 2002, 126.

43. "George W. Bush Holds New Conference," FDCH political transcript, March 6, 2003; "Report of the Commission on the Intelligence Capabilities of the United States Regarding Weapons of Mass Destruction," March 31, 2005, http://www.nytimes.com/packages/pdf/politics/ 20050331_wmd _report.pdf.

44. Thom Shanker, "Iraq Role Limits Military Ability, Congress Is Told," *New York Times,* May 3, 2005.

45. Susan Sachs, "Protests Are Peaceful in Mideast," *New York Times,* March 21, 2003; Mort Rosenblum, "Arab Populations Enraged by Invasion," Global News Wire—Europe Intelligence Wire, March 24, 2003; El-Ayouty, "Basic Tenets of the Anti-U.S. Ideology," in El-Ayouty, ed., *Perspectives on 9/11,* 133–39.

46. Gunaratna, *Inside al Qaeda,* 8–9; Douglas Jehl, "Iraq May Be Prime Place for Training of Militants, CIA Report Concludes," *New York Times,* June 22, 2005. The mismanagement of the occupation has been the subject of numerous books. See Gordon and Trainor, *Cobra II;* Woodward, *State of Denial.*

47. Black, *Vladimir Putin and the New World Order,* 164–65; Ambrosio, *Challenging America's Global Preeminence,* 151–55; Nathan and Gilley, *China's New Rulers,* 207; Curtis, "Anti-Americanism in Europe," 367; "France's Chirac Calls for Multilateralism, End of 'Law of the Jungle,'" Global News Wire, July 22, 2003; Wall, "The French-American War over Iraq," 123–39. On U.S.-European relations, see also Kagan, *Of Paradise and Power.*

48. NBC News/*Wall Street Journal* poll, November 7, 2005, USNBCWSJ.05NOV.R30A, iPoll Database; Jespersen, "Analogies at War," 411–12.

49. Robert Clow, "Most Believe U.S. Is in Recession," *Financial Times,* September 14, 2001; Gerard Baker, "Outlook Uncertain, Says Greenspan," *Financial Times,* September 21, 2001.

50. Bush in *Public Papers, 2001,* 1172, 1185; Cheney in Robert Reich, "How Did Spending Become Our Patriotic Duty?" *Washington Post,* September 23, 2001.

51. Greg Ip, "Some Economists Shift Focus to Recovery," *Wall Street Journal,* November 21, 2001; Russell Gold, "Consumers Show More Optimism about Economy," *Wall Street Journal,* December 24, 2001; untitled cartoon, *New Yorker,* November 12, 2001, 98; Reich, "How Did Spending."

52. Jim Tharpe, "Negative Ads Dog Senate Race," *Atlanta Journal-Constitution,* October 26, 2002; Bryan Faler, "Osama, Saddam, and Max?" *Washington Post,* October 14, 2002. Republican candidate Tim Johnson used similar tactics in an unsuccessful bid to unseat a Democratic senator from South Dakota. Bryan Faler, "To Win a Senate Seat, Is All Fair in Ads and War?" *Washington Post,* October 6, 2002.

53. Gallup polls, August 21 and October 22, 2002, Gallup Database; Jacobsen, "Terror, Terrain, and Turnout," 1.

54. "U.S. Senator John Kerry Delivers Remarks at a Campaign Event," Federal News Service transcript, October 22, 2004; Zell Miller speech, Federal News Service transcript, September 1, 2004, www.lexis-nexis.com.

55. Cheney remarks, Federal News Service transcript, September 7, 2004.

56. Gallup polls, October 16 and 24, 2004, Gallup Database.

57. Ashcroft testimony to Senate Judiciary Committee, Federal News Service transcript, December 6, 2001.

58. Kevin Galvan, "Rights and Wrongs," *Seattle Times,* December 6, 2001.

59. Robyn Blumner, "Ashcroft's Power to Detain without Charges Continues without Oversight," *St. Petersburg Times,* May 5, 2002; Ronald Dworkin, "The Real Threat to U.S. Values," *London Guardian,* March 9, 2002; George Lardner and Peter Slevin, "Military May Try Terrorism Cases," *Washington Post,* November 14, 2001.

60. Carol Leonnig, "Panel Ignored Evidence on Detainee," *Washington Post,* March 27, 2005; Senate Judiciary Committee, *The USA PATRIOT Act in Practice,* September 10, 2002, 9; Scott Shane, "At Security Agency, News of Surveillance Program Gives Reassurances a Hollow Ring," *New York Times,* December 22, 2005.

61. American Civil Liberties Union, "Civil Liberties after 9/11," http://www.aclu.org/SafeandFree/SafeandFree.cfm?ID=10898&c=207; Sherly Gay Stolberg and Eric Lichtblau, "Senators Thwart Bush Bid to Renew Law on Terrorism," *New York Times,* December 17, 2005; Sherly Gay Stolberg, "Postponing Debate, Congress Extends Terror Law Five Weeks," *New York Times,* December 23, 2005; ABC News/*Washington Post* poll, June 2–June 5, 2005, USABCWP.060705.R26, iPoll Database.

62. Kerry Remarks at a campaign rally, Federal News Service transcript, September 20, 2004.

63. "George W. Bush Delivers Remarks on the War on Terrorism," Congressional Quarterly transcription, July 11, 2005; "Advance Text of Remarks by National Security Adviser Condoleezza Rice at the McConnell Center for Political Leadership," Federal News Service transcript, March 8, 2004; "Condoleezza Rice Delivers Remarks to U.S. Institute of Peace," Federal News Service transcript, August 19, 2004.

64. "Condoleezza Rice Delivers Remarks to U.S. Institute of Peace," Federal News Service transcript, August 19, 2004; "George W. Bush Delivers Remarks on the War on Terrorism," Congressional Quarterly transcription, July 11, 2005; "George W. Bush Delivers Remarks at the UN Security Council Summit," Congressional Quarterly transcription, September 14, 2005.

65. "Advance Text of Remarks by National Security Adviser Condoleezza Rice at the McConnell Center for Political Leadership," Federal News Service transcript, March 8, 2004; George W. Bush, "Inaugural Address," Federal News Service transcript, January 20, 2005.

66. "Remarks by President George W. Bush at the Woodrow Wilson Center," Federal News Service transcript, December 14, 2005; Eric Schmitt and Thom Shanker, "New Name for 'War on Terror' Reflects Wider U.S.

Campaign," *New York Times,* July 26, 2005; "Remarks of President George W. Bush to the American Legislative Exchange Council," Federal News Service transcript, August 3, 2005.

67. Richard W. Stephenson, "President Makes It Clear: Phrase Is 'War on Terror,'" *New York Times,* August 4, 2005; *National Security Strategy,* 2006, sections I and V. See also U.S. Department of Defense, *Quadrennial Defense Review Report, 2006,* especially 1–17.

68. For instance, "President George W. Bush Delivers Remarks in Birmingham, Alabama," FDCH political transcript, November 3, 2003; "George W. Bush Delivers Remarks at the National Urban League Conference," FDCH political transcript, July 28, 2003; Woodward, *Plan of Attack,* 27; America's Place in the World Survey, October 24, 2005, USPSRA.11705 .R15AF2; CBS News poll, August 31, 2005, USCBS.091005A.R66, iPoll Database.

69. Rice testimony, "Hearing of the National Commission on Terrorist Attacks upon the United States," Federal News Service transcript, April 8, 2004; "Dr. Condoleezza Rice Delivers Remarks at Los Angeles Town Hall Breakfast," FDCH political transcript, July 12, 2003.

70. Charles Krauthammer, "Beyond the Cold War," *New Republic,* December 19, 1988, 18.

Conclusion

1. The Cold War's implications for the current state of international affairs are covered in Westad, *The Global Cold War,* especially 396–407.

2. See, for instance, Steel, *Temptations of a Superpower.* A more radical statement is Kolko and Kolko, *The Limits of Power.*

3. For a trenchant critique, see Hanhimaki, "Global Visions and Parochial Politics," 423–47.

Bibliography

Archival Collections

Cold War International History Project Virtual Archive

End of the Cold War Collection

George Bush Presidential Library

Cabinet Affairs File
Files of Marlin Fitzwater
John Sununu Chief of Staff Files
National Security Council Files
National Security Directive Files
National Security Review Files
Presidential MemCon and TelCon Files
Press Office Files
Processed Freedom of Information Case Files
Speechwriting Office File
White House Staff and Office Files

Hoover Institution on War, Revolution, and Peace

Condoleezza Rice–Philip Zelikow Files

Library of Congress, Manuscript Division

Anthony Lake Papers

Miller Center, University of Virginia

REAGAN ADMINISTRATION ORAL HISTORY INTERVIEWS
Frank Carlucci
George Shultz
William Webster

National Security Archive

The Contras, Cocaine, and Covert Operations Collection
Humanitarian Intervention Collection
Iraqgate Collection
North Korea Collection
Nuclear Weapons Collection
Presidential Security Directives Collection, Part I
Presidential Security Directives Collection, Part II
Solidarity Collection
Soviet Estimate Collection
Terrorism and U.S. Policy Collection
U.S.-China Collection
Vaclev Havel Collection

Official Records and Other Published Documents

Other documents pertaining to State and Defense department policy are located at www.state.gov and www.defenselink.gov. Presidential documents are located at www.whitehouse.gov. CIA documents can be accessed at www.fas.org.irp/cia.

ABC News transcripts. www.lexis-nexis.com.

Auerswald, Philip, and David Auerswald, eds. *The Kosovo Conflict: A Diplomatic History through Documents.* Cambridge: Kluwer Law International, 2000.

Commission on Terrorist Attacks upon the United States. *The 9/11 Commission Report: Final Report of the National Commission on Terrorist Attacks upon the United States.* Washington, D.C.: U.S. Government Printing Office, 2004.

Conaghan, Frank. "Allied Contributions in Support of Operations Desert Shield and Desert Storm," July 31, 1991. Washington, D.C.: General Accounting Office, 1991.

Federal Document Clearing House transcripts, 1990–2005. www.lexis-nexis.com.

Federal News Service transcripts, 1990–2005. www.lexis-nexis.com.

Fischer, Benjamin, ed. *At Cold War's End: U.S. Intelligence on the Soviet Union and Eastern Europe, 1989–1991.* Reston, Va.: Central Intelligence Agency, 1999.

Gallup polls, 1989–2005. Gallup Database, www.institution.gallup.com.

House Committee on Armed Services. *Crisis in the Persian Gulf,* December 4–20, 1990. Washington, D.C.: U.S. Government Printing Office, 1991.

House Committee on Banking and Financial Services. *Administration's Re-*

sponse to the Mexican Financial Crisis, April 6, 1995. Washington, D.C.: U.S. Government Printing Office, 1995.

House Committee on Foreign Affairs. *Developments in Eastern Europe, June 1989,* June 27, 1989. Washington, D.C.: U.S. Government Printing Office, 1989.

———. *Developments in Europe, July 1989,* July 27, 1989. Washington, D.C.: U.S. Government Printing Office, 1989.

———. *The Future of UN Peacekeeping Operations,* March 25, 1992. Washington, D.C.: U.S. Government Printing Office, 1992.

———. *The Future of U.S. Foreign Policy in the Post–Cold War Era,* March 24, 1992. Washington, D.C.: U.S. Government Printing Office, 1992.

———. *Review of the International Aspects of President's 1990 Drug Control Strategy,* February 27, 1990. Washington, D.C.: U.S. Government Printing Office, 1990.

———. *Update on the Situation in Haiti,* October 31, 1991. Washington, D.C.: U.S. Government Printing Office, 1992.

———. *U.S. Policy toward the New Independent States.* Washington, D.C.: U.S. Government Printing Office, 1994.

House Committee on International Relations. *The Clinton Foreign Policy Record: An Evaluation,* May 2, 1996. Washington, D.C.: U.S. Government Printing Office, 1996.

———. *Fast Track: On Course or Derailed? Necessary or Not? Part III,* November 6, 1997. Washington, D.C.: U.S. Government Printing Office, 1998.

———. *The Threat from Russian Organized Crime,* April 30, 1996. Washington, D.C.: U.S. Government Printing Office, 1996.

———. *U.S.–North Korea Relations after the Policy Review,* July 26, 2001. Washington, D.C.: U.S. Government Printing Office, 2001.

———. *U.S. Policy toward Iran,* November 9, 1995. Washington, D.C.: U.S. Government Printing Office, 1996.

iPoll Database. Roper Center, University of Connecticut.

Lake, Anthony. *Confronting Backlash States.* Washington, D.C.: U.S. Government Printing Office, 1994.

———. "From Containment to Enlargement." Remarks at Paul Nitze School of International Affairs at Johns Hopkins University, September 21, 1993. Washington, D.C.: U.S. Government Printing Office, 1993.

National Security Strategy of the United States, 1990–2006. Washington, D.C.: White House, 1991–2006.

Public Papers of the Presidents of the United States, 1989–2001. Washington, D.C.: U.S. Government Printing Office, 1990–2002.

Senate Armed Services Committee. *Comprehensive Test Ban Treaty,* October 6 and 7, 1999. Washington, D.C.: U.S. Government Printing Office, 2000.

———. *Consideration of Honorable Les Aspin to Be Secretary of Defense.* Washington, D.C.: U.S. Government Printing Office, 1993.

———. *Consideration of William J. Perry to Be Secretary of Defense,* February 2, 1994. Washington, D.C.: U.S. Government Printing Office, 1994.

———. *Department of Defense Authorization for Fiscal Years 1992 and 1993.* Washington, D.C.: U.S. Government Printing Office, 1991.

———. *Department of Defense Authorization for Appropriations for Fiscal Year 1994 and the Future Years Defense Program,* part 4. Washington, D.C.: U.S. Government Printing Office, 1994.

———. *Department of Defense Authorization for Appropriations for Fiscal Year 2004,* February 25, 2003. Washington, D.C.: U.S. Government Printing Office, 2004.

———. *Department of Defense Authorization for Fiscal Year 1993 and the Future Years Defense Program.* Washington, D.C.: U.S. Government Printing Office, 1992.

———. *Department of Defense Authorization for Fiscal Year 1996 and the Future Years Defense Program,* February 9, 1995. Washington, D.C.: U.S. Government Printing Office, 1996.

———. *Department of Defense Authorization for Fiscal Year 2000 and the Future Years Defense Program.* Washington, D.C.: U.S. Government Printing Office, 1999.

———. *International Peacekeeping and Peace Enforcement,* July 14, 1993. Washington, D.C.: U.S. Government Printing Office, 1993.

———. *National Security Strategy,* February 2, 1995. Washington, D.C.: U.S. Government Printing Office, 1996.

———. *Nomination of Honorable Les Aspin to Be Secretary of Defense,* January 7, 1993. Washington, D.C.: U.S. Government Printing Office, 1994.

———. *Nominations before the Senate Armed Services Committee, First Session, 105th Congress.* Washington, D.C.: U.S. Government Printing Office, 1998.

———. *Situation in Bosnia.* Washington, D.C.: U.S. Government Printing Office, 1995.

———. *Threat Assessment, Military Strategy, and Defense Planning,* March 20, 1992. Washington, D.C.: U.S. Government Printing Office, 1992.

———. *U.S. Participation in Somalia Peacekeeping,* October 19–20, 1993. Washington, D.C.: U.S. Government Printing Office, 1994.

———. *U.S. Policy and NATO Military Operations in Kosovo,* February 25 and April 15, 1999. Washington, D.C.: U.S. Government Printing Office, 2000.

———. *U.S. Policy on Iraq,* January 28, 1999. Washington, D.C.: U.S. Government Printing Office, 1999.

———. *U.S. Policy on Iraq,* September 19–25, 2002. Washington, D.C.: U.S. Government Printing Office, 2003.

———. *Worldwide Threats,* February 2, 1999. Washington, D.C.: U.S. Government Printing Office, 2000.

Senate Banking Committee. *Mexican Peso Crisis,* January 31–July 14, 1995. Washington, D.C.: U.S. Government Printing Office, 1995.

Senate Finance Committee. *Managing Global and Regional Trade Policy without Fast Track Negotiating Authority,* July 14, 1999. Washington, D.C.: U.S. Government Printing Office, 1999.

Senate Foreign Relations Committee. *ABM Treaty and U.S. Ballistic Missile Defense.* Washington, D.C.: U.S. Government Printing Office, 1997.

———. *Administration's Missile Defense Program and the ABM Treaty,* July 24, 2001. Washington, D.C.: U.S. Government Printing Office, 2001.

———. *Afghanistan Stabilization and Reconstruction: A Status Report,* January 27, 2004. Washington, D.C.: U.S. Government Printing Office, 2004.

———. *Ballistic Missiles: Threat and Response,* April–September 1999. Washington, D.C.: U.S. Government Printing Office, 1998.

———. *Ballistic Missile Threat to the United States,* October 6, 1998. Washington, D.C.: U.S. Government Printing Office, 1998.

———. *Contributions of Central Asian Nations to the Campaign against Terrorism,* December 13, 2001. Washington, D.C.: U.S. Government Printing Office, 2002.

———. *Crisis in Central Africa,* July 26, 1994. Washington, D.C.: U.S. Government Printing Office, 1994.

———. *Crisis in Kosovo,* May 6, 1998. Washington, D.C.: U.S. Government Printing Office, 1998.

———. *Final Review of the Comprehensive Nuclear Test Ban Treaty,* October 7, 1999. Washington, D.C.: U.S. Government Printing Office, 2000.

———. *Foreign Policy Implications of the North American Free Trade Agreement and Legislative Requirements for the Side Agreements,* October 27, 1993. Washington, D.C.: U.S. Government Printing Office, 1994.

———. *Foreign Policy Overview,* February 5, 1992. Washington, D.C.: U.S. Government Printing Office, 1992.

———. *Foreign Policy Overview,* August 1, 1996. Washington, D.C.: U.S. Government Printing Office, 1996.

———. *Future of NATO,* May 1, 2002. Washington, D.C.: U.S. Government Printing Office, 2002.

———. *The Future of U.S.-Soviet Relations, 1989.* Washington, D.C.: U.S. Government Printing Office, 1989.

———. *Iraq,* September 19, 1996. Washington, D.C.: U.S. Government Printing Office, 1996.

———. *Iraq: Can Saddam Be Overthrown?* March 2, 1998. Washington, D.C.: U.S. Government Printing Office, 1998.

———. *Is a UN International Criminal Court in the U.S. National Interest?* July 23, 1998. Washington, D.C.: U.S. Government Printing Office, 1998.

———. *Mexico's Economic Situation and U.S. Efforts to Stabilize the Peso,* January 26, 1995. Washington, D.C.: U.S. Government Printing Office, 1995.

———. *Nomination of Madeleine K. Albright to Be United States Ambassador to the United Nations,* January 21, 1993. Washington, D.C.: U.S. Government Printing Office, 1993.

———. *Nomination of Secretary of State,* January 9, 1997. Washington, D.C.: U.S. Government Printing Office, 1997.

———. *Nomination of Warren M. Christopher to Be Secretary of State,* January 13–14, 1993. Washington, D.C.: U.S. Government Printing Office, 1993.

———. *Political Future of Afghanistan,* December 6, 2001. Washington, D.C.: U.S. Government Printing Office, 2002.

———. *Reconstruction of Afghanistan: An Update,* February 12, 2003. Washington, D.C.: U.S. Government Printing Office, 2003.

———. *Relations in a Multipolar World,* November 13, 1991. Washington, D.C.: U.S. Government Printing Office, 1992.

———. *Threat of North Korean Nuclear Proliferation,* February 6, 1992. Washington, D.C.: U.S. Government Printing Office, 1992.

———. *Treaty on the Final Settlement with Respect of Germany,* September 28, 1990. Washington, D.C.: U.S. Government Printing Office, 1990.

———. *United States Policy toward Iraq: Human Rights, Weapons Proliferation, and International Law,* June 15, 1990. Washington, D.C.: U.S. Government Printing Office, 1990.

———. *U.S. Policy in the Persian Gulf,* September 5, 1990. Washington, D.C.: U.S. Government Printing Office, 1990.

———. *U.S. Policy in Somalia,* July 29, 1993. Washington, D.C.: U.S. Government Printing Office, 1993.

———. *U.S. Policy in the Persian Gulf,* January 8, 1991. Washington, D.C.: U.S. Government Printing Office, 1991.

———. *U.S. Policy on Ukrainian Security,* June 24, 1993. Washington, D.C.: U.S. Government Printing Office, 1993.

———. *U.S. Policy toward Haiti,* March 8, 1994. Washington, D.C.: U.S. Government Printing Office, 1994.

———. *U.S. Policy toward Haiti,* June 28, 1994. Washington: U.S. Government Printing Office, 1994.

———. *U.S. Policy toward Iran and Iraq,* March 2 and August 3, 1995. Washington, D.C.: U.S. Government Printing Office, 1996.

———. *U.S. Policy toward Iraq,* March 9, 1999. Washington, D.C.: U.S. Government Printing Office, 1999.

———. *U.S. Policy toward North Korea,* March 3, 1994. Washington, D.C.: U.S. Government Printing Office, 1994.

———. *WMD Developments on the Korean Peninsula,* February 4, 2003. Washington, D.C.: U.S. Government Printing Office, 2003.

Senate Foreign Relations Committee and United Nations Security Council. *Future of U.S.-UN Relations,* January 20–21, 2000. Washington, D.C.: U.S. Government Printing Office, 2000.

Senate Judiciary Committee. *The USA PATRIOT Act in Practice: Shedding Light on the FISA Practice,* September 10, 2002. Washington, D.C.: U.S. Government Printing Office, 2003.

Senate Select Committee on Intelligence. *Current and Projected National Security Threats to the United States and Its Interests Abroad,* February 22, 1996. Washington, D.C.: U.S. Government Printing Office, 1996.

———. *Current and Projected National Security Threats to the United States,* February 5, 1997. Washington, D.C.: U.S. Government Printing Office, 1997.

———. *Intelligence Analysis of the Long Range Missile Threat to the United States,* December 4, 1996. Washington, D.C.: U.S. Government Printing Office, 1997.

U.S. Congress. *Congressional Record,* vols. 136–49. Washington, D.C.: U.S. Government Printing Office, 1990–2004.

U.S. Department of Defense. *Quadrennial Defense Review Report, 2006.* Washington, D.C.: U.S. Government Printing Office, 2006.

U.S. Department of State. *Dispatch,* 1989–1999. Washington, D.C.: U.S. Government Printing Office, 1989–2000.

———. *Focus on the Issues: Building Peace and Security around the World.* Washington, D.C.: State Department Bureau of Public Affairs, 2000.

———. *Patterns of Global Terrorism, 1993–2002.* Washington, D.C.: Department of State, 1994–2003.

———. *The Road to Dayton: U.S. Diplomacy and the Bosnia Peace Process.* Washington, D.C.: Department of State, 1997.

Vitas, Robert, and John Williams, eds. *U.S. National Security Policy and Strategy, 1987–1994: Documents and Policy Proposals.* London: Greenwood Press, 1996.

Weekly Compilation of Presidential Documents, 1990–2003. Washington, D.C.: U.S. Government Printing Office, 1990–2004.

Memoirs

Albright, Madeleine. *Madam Secretary: A Memoir.* London: MacMillan, 2003.

Bibliography

Armacost, Michael. *Friends or Rivals? The Insider's Account of U.S.-Japan Relations*. New York: Columbia University Press, 1996.

Baer, Robert. *See No Evil: The True Story of a Ground Soldier in the CIA's War on Terrorism*. New York: Crown Publishers, 2002.

Baker, James, and Thomas de Frank. *The Politics of Diplomacy: Revolution, War and Peace, 1989–1992*. New York: G. P. Putnam's Sons, 1995.

Berlin, Yossi. *The Path to Geneva: The Quest for a Permanent Agreement, 1996–2004*. New York: RDV Books, 2004.

Blumenthal, Sidney. *The Clinton Wars*. New York: Farrar, Straus and Giroux, 2003.

Bush, George. *All the Best, George Bush*. New York: Scribner, 1999.

Bush, George, and Brent Scowcroft. *A World Transformed*. New York: Vintage Books, 1998.

Chernyaev, Anatoly. *My Six Years with Gorbachev*. Translated by Robert English and Elizabeth Tucker. University Park: Penn State University Press, 2000.

Christopher, Warren. *Chances of a Lifetime*. New York: Scribner, 2001.

Clark, Wesley. *Waging Modern War*. New York: Perseus, 2001.

Clarke, Richard. *Against All Enemies: Inside America's War on Terror*. New York: Free Press, 2004.

Clinton, Bill. *My Life*. New York: Knopf, 2004.

Dallaire, Romeo. *Shake Hands with the Devil: The Failure of Humanity in Rwanda*. Toronto: Random House Canada, 2003.

Gorbachev, Mikhail. *Memoirs*. New York: Random House, 1995.

Holbrooke, Richard. *To End a War*. New York: Random House, 1998.

Matlock, Jack F. *Autopsy on an Empire: The American Ambassador's Account of the Collapse of the Soviet Union*. New York: Random House, 1995.

Morris, Dick. *Behind the Oval Office: Winning the Presidency in the Nineties*. New York: Random House, 1997.

Owen, David. *Balkan Odyssey*. London: Cassell, 1995.

Perot, Ross. *United We Stand: How We Can Take Back Our Country*. New York: Hyperion Books, 1992.

Perry, William, and Ashton Carter. *Preventive Defense: A New Security Strategy for America*. Washington, D.C.: Brookings Institution, 1999.

Pollack, Kenneth. *The Gathering Storm: The Case for Invading Iraq*. New York: Random House, 2002.

———. *The Persian Puzzle: The Conflict between Iran and America*. New York: Random House, 2004.

Powell, Colin, with Joseph Persico. *My American Journey*. New York: Ballantine, 1996.

Primakov, Yevgeny. *Russian Crossroads: Toward the New Millennium.* New Haven, Conn.: Yale University Press, 2004.

Reich, Robert. *Locked in the Cabinet.* New York: Knopf, 1997.

Rice, Condoleezza, and Philip Zelikow. *Germany Unified and Europe Transformed: A Study in Statecraft.* Cambridge, Mass.: Harvard University Press, 1997.

Ross, Dennis. *The Missing Peace: The Inside Story of the Fight for Middle East Peace.* New York: Farrar, Straus and Giroux, 2004.

Stephanopoulos, George. *All Too Human: A Political Education.* Boston: Little, Brown, 1999.

Suettinger, Robert. *Beyond Tiananmen: The Politics of U.S.-China Relations, 1989–2000.* Washington, D.C.: Brookings Institution, 2003.

Talbott, Strobe. *Engaging India: Diplomacy, Democracy, and the Bomb: A Memoir.* Washington, D.C.: Brookings Institution, 2004.

———. *The Russia Hand: A Memoir of Presidential Diplomacy.* New York: Random House, 2002.

Thatcher, Margaret. *Downing Street Years.* London: HarperCollins, 1993.

Wilson, Joseph. *The Politics of Truth: A Diplomat's Memoir.* New York: Carroll and Graf, 2004.

Wit, Joel, Daniel Poneman, and Robert Gallucci. *Going Critical: The First North Korean Nuclear Crisis.* Washington, D.C.: Brookings Institution, 2004.

Books, Articles, and Other Published Works

Adams, Michael C. C. *The Best War Ever: America and World War II.* Baltimore: Johns Hopkins University Press, 1994.

Adhiriki, Ratnakar, ed. *Globalisation: South Asian Perspectives.* Kathmandu: South Asia Watch on Trade, Economy, and Environment, 2000.

Ambrosio, Thomas. *Challenging America's Global Preeminence: Russia's Quest for Multipolarity.* Burlington, Vt.: Ashgate, 2005.

American Civil Liberties Union. *Civil Liberties after 9/11.* Washington, D.C.: American Civil Liberties Union, 2004.

Anderson, David. "One Vietnam War Should Be Enough and Other Reflections on Diplomatic History and the Making of Foreign Policy." *Diplomatic History* 30, no. 1 (January 2006).

Anonymous [Michael Scheuer]. *Through Our Enemies' Eyes: Osama bin Laden, Radical Islam, and the Future of America.* Washington, D.C.: Brassey's, 2002.

Asmus, Ronald, and Richard Kugler. "Building a New NATO." *Foreign Affairs* 72, no. 4 (September–October 1993).

Bacevich, Andrew. *American Empire: The Realities and Consequences of U.S. Diplomacy.* Cambridge, Mass.: Harvard, 2002.

———. *The New American Militarism: How Americans Are Seduced by War*. New York: Oxford University Press, 2005.

Bacevich, Andrew, and Elizabeth Prodromou. "God Is Not Neutral: Religion and U.S. Foreign Policy after 9/11." *Orbis* 48 (Winter 2004).

Bahgat, Gaudat. "Iran, the United States, and the War on Terrrorism." *Studies in Conflict and Terrorism* 26, no. 2 (March–April 2003).

———. "Nonproliferation Success." *World Affairs* 168, no. 1 (Summer 2005).

Barari, Hassan. *Israeli Politics and the Middle East Peace Process, 1988–2002*. New York: Routledge, 2004.

Barkawi, Tarak. *Globalization and War*. New York: Rowman and Littlefield, 2006.

Bar-Siman-Tov, Yaacov. "Peace Policy as Domestic and Foreign Policy: The Israeli Case." In Sasson Sofer, ed., *Peacemaking in a Divided Society: Israel after Rabin*. London: Frank Cass, 2001.

Baum, Richard. *Burying Mao: Chinese Politics in the Age of Deng Xiaoping*. Princeton, N.J.: Princeton University Press, 1994.

Bennett, Andrew. *The Rise, Fall, and Reprise of Soviet-Russian Military Interventionism, 1973–1996*. Cambridge, Mass.: MIT Press, 1999.

Bennett, Christopher. *Yugoslavia's Bloody Collapse: Causes, Course and Consequences*. London: Hurst, 1995.

Beschloss, Michael, and Strobe Talbott. *At the Highest Levels: The Inside Story of the End of the Cold War*. Boston: Little, Brown, 1993.

Biddle, Stephen. "Afghanistan and the Future of Warfare." *Foreign Affairs* 82, no. 2 (March–April 2003).

Black, J. L. *Vladimir Putin and the New World Order*. New York: Rowman and Littlefield, 2004.

Bolton, John R. "Courting Danger: What's Wrong with the International Criminal Court." *National Interest* (Winter 1998–1999).

Boniface, Pascal. "The Specter of Unilateralism." *Washington Quarterly* (Summer 2001).

Boot, Max. *The Savage Wars of Peace: Small Wars and the Rise of American Power*. New York: Basic Books, 2002.

Bose, Meena. *Shaping and Signaling Presidential Policy*. College Station: Texas A&M Press, 1998.

Bose, Meena, and Rosanna Perotti. *From Cold War to New World Order: The Foreign Policies of George H. W. Bush*. Westport, Conn.: Greenwood, 2002.

Boutros-Ghali, Boutros. *An Agenda for Peace*. New York: United Nations, 1992.

Bowden, Mark. *Black Hawk Down: A Story of Modern War*. New York: Atlantic Monthly Books, 1999.

Bowker, Mike, and Phil Williams. *Superpower Détente: A Reappraisal.* London: Royal Institute of International Affairs, 1988.

Brands, H. W. *The Devil We Knew: Americans and the Cold War.* New York: Oxford University Press, 1993.

———. "George Bush and the Gulf War of 1991." *Presidential Studies Quarterly* 34, no. 1 (March 2004).

———. *Since Vietnam: The United States in World Affairs.* New York: McGraw-Hill, 1995.

———. *What America Owes the World.* New York: Columbia University Press, 1998.

Brown, Michael. "The Flawed Logic of NATO Expansion." *Survival* 37, no. 1 (Spring 1995).

Buchanan, Andrew. *Peace with Justice: A History of the Israeli-Palestinian Declaration of Principles on Interim Self-Government Arrangements.* New York: St. Martin's, 2000.

Buchanan, Patrick. "America First—and Second, and Third." *National Interest* (Spring 1990).

———. *A Republic, Not an Empire: Reclaiming America's National Destiny.* Washington, D.C.: Regnery Books, 1998.

Burg, Steven, and Paul Shoup. *The War in Bosnia-Herzegovina: Ethnic Conflict and International Intervention.* Armonk, N.Y.: M. E. Sharpe, 1999.

Campbell, Colin, and Bert Rockman, eds. *The Clinton Legacy.* New York: Seven Bridges Press, 1999.

Chipman, Don. "Osama bin Laden and Guerilla War." *Studies in Conflict and Terrorism* 26, no. 3 (May–June 2003).

Cole, Wayne. *Roosevelt and the Isolationists, 1932–1945.* Lincoln: University of Nebraska Press, 1983.

Commission on America's National Interests. *America's National Interests.* Cambridge, Mass.: Harvard, 1996.

Conniff, Michael. *Panama and the United States: The Forced Alliance.* Athens: University of Georgia Press, 1992.

Cooley, John K. *Unholy Wars: America, Afghanistan, and International Terrorism.* New York: Pluto Press, 2000.

Cooper, Barry. *New Political Religions, or An Analysis of Modern Terrorism.* London: University of Missouri Press, 2004.

Crowley, Monica. *Nixon off the Record.* New York: Random House, 1996.

Curtis, Michael. "Anti-Americanism in Europe." *American Foreign Policy Interests* 26, no. 5 (October 2004).

Daalder, Ivo. *Getting to Dayton: The Making of America's Bosnia Policy.* Washington, D.C.: Brookings Institution, 2000.

Daalder, Ivo, and James Lindsay. *America Unbound: The Bush Revolution in Foreign Policy*. Washington, D.C.: Brookings Institution, 2003.

Daalder, Ivo, and Michael O'Hanlon. *Winning Ugly: NATO's War to Save Kosovo*. Washington, D.C.: Brookings Institution, 2000.

Dallek, Robert. *Franklin Roosevelt and American Foreign Policy, 1932–1945*. New York: Oxford University Press, 1979.

des Forges, Alison. *Leave None to Tell the Story: Genocide in Rwanda*. New York: Human Rights Watch, 1999.

Donnelly, Thomas, Margaret Roth, and Caleb Baker. *Operation Just Cause: The Storming of Panama*. New York: Lexington, 1991.

Dudziak, Mary. *Cold War Civil Rights: Race and the Image of American Democracy*. Princeton, N.J.: Princeton University Press, 2000.

Dunlop, John. "The August 1991 Coup and Its Impact on Soviet Politics." *Journal of Cold War Studies* 5, no. 1 (Winter 2003).

Dupuy, Alex. *Haiti in the New World Order: The Limits of the Democratic Revolution*. Boulder, Colo.: Westview, 1997.

Durch, William, ed. *UN Peacekeeping, American Politics, and the Uncivil Wars of the 1990s*. New York: St. Martin's, 1996.

Dutt, Gargi, and V. P. Dutt. *China after Mao*. New Delhi: Vikas, 1991.

El-Ayouty, Yassin. "Basic Tenets of the Anti-U.S. Ideology on the Arab and Muslim Street." In Yassin El-Ayouty, ed., *Perspectives on 9/11*. London: Praeger, 2004.

Engel, Jeffrey. "The Face of Evil: Rhetoric and War from Thomas Jefferson to George W. Bush." Paper presented at the 2005 Conference of the Society for Historians of American Foreign Relations.

Esposito, John L. *Unholy War: Terror in the Name of Islam*. New York: Oxford University Press, 2002.

Feaver, Peter, and Christopher Gelpi. *Choosing Your Battles: American Civil-Military Relations and the Use of Force*. Princeton, N.J.: Princeton University Press, 2004.

Ferguson, Niall. *Colossus: The Price of America's Empire*. New York: Penguin, 2004.

Fewsmith, Joseph. *China since Tiananmen: The Politics of Transition*. New York: Cambridge University Press, 2001.

Fischer, Beth. *The Reagan Reversal: Foreign Policy and the End of the Cold War*. Columbia: University of Missouri Press, 1997.

Fitzgerald, Frances. *Way out There in the Blue: Reagan, Star Wars, and the End of the Cold War*. New York: Simon and Schuster, 2000.

Flynn, Steven. "America the Vulnerable." *Foreign Affairs* 81, no. 1 (January–February 2002).

Fousek, John. *To Lead the Free World: American Nationalism and the Cultural Roots of the Cold War*. Chapel Hill: University of North Carolina Press, 2000.

Freedman, Lawrence, and Efraim Karsh. *The Gulf Crisis, 1990–1991: Diplomacy and War in the New World Order.* Princeton, N.J.: Princeton University Press, 1993.

Friedman, Norman. *Desert Victory: The War for Kuwait.* Annapolis, Md.: United States Naval Institute, 1991.

Fukuyama, Francis. "The End of History?" *National Interest* (Summer 1989).

Gaddis, John Lewis. *The Long Peace: Inquiries into the History of the Cold War.* New York: Oxford University Press, 1987.

———. *Strategies of Containment: A Critical Appraisal of American National Security Policy during the Cold War.* New York: Oxford University Press, 2005.

———. *Strategies of Containment: A Critical Appraisal of Postwar American National Security Policy.* New York: Oxford University Press, 1982.

———. *Surprise, Security, and the American Experience.* Cambridge, Mass.: Harvard University Press, 2004.

———. *The United States and the Origins of the Cold War.* New York: Columbia University Press, 1972.

———. *We Now Know: Rethinking Cold War History.* New York: Oxford University Press, 1997.

Garran, Robert. *True Believer: John Howard, George Bush, and the American Alliance.* Sydney: Allen and Unwin, 2004.

Garten, Jeffrey. "Clinton's Emerging Trade Policy." *Foreign Affairs* 72, no. 3 (Summer 1993).

———. *A Cold Peace: America, Japan, Germany, and the Struggle for Supremacy.* New York: Times Books, 1992.

Garthoff, Raymond. *The Great Transition: American-Soviet Relations at the End of the Cold War.* Washington, D.C.: Brookings Institution, 1994.

Garton Ash, Timothy. *The Magic Lantern: The Revolution of '89 Witnessed in Warsaw, Budapest, Berlin, and Prague.* New York: Vintage Books, 1993.

Gnesotto, Nicole, and John Roper, eds. *Western Europe and the Gulf.* Paris: Institute for Security Studies, 1992.

Goff, Patricia M. "It's Got to Be Sheep's Milk or Nothing! Geography, Identity, and Economic Nationalism." In Eric Helleiner and Andreas Pickel, eds., *Economic Nationalism in a Globalizing World.* Ithaca, N.Y.: Cornell University Press, 2005.

Goldgeier, James. *Not Whether but When: The U.S. Decision to Expand NATO.* Washington, D.C.: Brookings Institution, 1999.

Gordon, Michael, and Bernard Trainor. *Cobra II: The Inside Story of the Invasion and Occupation of Iraq.* New York: Pantheon, 2006.

Gordon, Philip H., ed. *NATO's Transformation: The Changing Shape of the Atlantic Alliance*. New York: Rowman and Littlefield, 1997.

Gow, James, ed. *Iraq, the Gulf Conflict, and the World Community*. New York: Brassey's, 1993.

Greider, William. *One World, Ready or Not: The Manic Logic of Global Capitalism*. New York: Simon and Schuster, 1997.

Gunaratna, Rohan. *Inside al Qaeda: Global Network of Terror*. New York: Columbia University Press, 2002.

Gwertzman, Bernard, and Michael Kaufman. *The Collapse of Communism*. New York: Random House, 1990.

Haass, Richard. "The Middle East: No More Treaties." *Foreign Affairs* 75, no. 5 (September–October 1996).

———. *The Opportunity: America's Moment to Alter History's Course*. New York: Public Affairs, 2005.

———. "The Squandered Presidency." *Foreign Affairs* 79, no. 3 (May–June 2000).

Habeck, Mary R. *Jihadist Ideology and the War on Terror*. New Haven, Conn.: Yale University Press, 2006.

Halberstam, David. *War in a Time of Peace: Bush, Clinton, and the Generals*. New York: Scribner, 2001.

Haley, P. Edward. *Strategies of Dominance: The Misdirection of U.S. Foreign Policy*. Baltimore: Johns Hopkins University Press, 2006.

Hanhimaki, Jussi. "Global Visions and Parochial Politics: The Persistent Dilemma of the American Century." *Diplomatic History* 27, no. 4 (September 2003).

Haseeb, Dina, and Malak Rouchdy. "Egypt's Speculation in the Gulf Crisis: The Government's Policies and the Opposition Movements." In Haim Bresheeth and Nira Yuval-Davis, eds., *The Gulf War and the New World Order*. New York: Zed Books, 1991.

Hassan, Hamdi. *The Iraqi Invasion of Kuwait*. London: Pluto Press, 1999.

Hedley, R. Alan. *Running out of Control: Dilemmas of Globalization*. Bloomfield, Conn.: Kumarian, 2002.

Held, David. *Global Transformations, Politics, Economics, and Culture*. Stanford, Calif.: Stanford University Press, 1999.

Held, David, and Anthony McGrew, eds. *The Global Transformations Reader: An Introduction to the Globalization Debate*. Oxford: Blackwell, 2000.

Helms, Jesse. "Saving the UN." *Foreign Affairs* 75, no. 5 (September–October 1996).

Hersh, Seymour. *Chain of Command: The Road from 9/11 to Abu Ghraib*. New York: HarperCollins, 2004.

Hicker, Neil. "Money Lust: How Pressure for Profit Is Perverting Journalism." *Columbia Journalism Review* (July–August 1998).

Hinds, Lynn Boyd, and Theodore Otto Wendt, eds. *The Cold War as Rhetoric: The Beginnings, 1945–1950*. New York: Praeger, 1991.

Holbrooke, Richard. "Japan and the United States: Ending the Unequal Partnership." *Foreign Affairs* 70, no. 5 (Winter 1991–1992).

Hong, Soon-Jick. "North Korean Nuclear Crisis: Prospects and Policy Directions." *East Asian Review* 15, no. 3 (Autumn 2003).

Hook, Glenn D., Julie Gibson, Christopher W. Hughes, and Hugo Dobson. *Japan's International Relations: Politics, Economics, and Security*. New York: Routledge, 2001.

Horner, Charles. "America the Victorious." *Commentary* (May 1990).

Human Rights Watch. *Silencing a People: The Destruction of Civil Society in Haiti*. New York: Human Rights Watch, 1993.

Hunsberger, Warren S., ed. *Japan's Quest: The Search for International Recognition, Status, and Role*. Armonk, N.Y.: M. E. Sharpe, 1997.

Hunt, Michael. *Ideology and U.S. Foreign Policy*. New Haven, Conn.: Yale University Press, 1987.

Hyland, William. *Clinton's World: Remaking Foreign Policy*. New York: Praeger, 1999.

———. "A Mediocre Record." *Foreign Policy* 101 (Winter 1995–1996).

Immerman, Robert. *The CIA in Guatemala: The Foreign Policy of Intervention*. Austin: University of Texas Press, 1982.

Indyk, Martin. "Back to the Bazaar." *Foreign Affairs* 81 (January–February 2002).

Isaacson, Walter, and Evan Thomas. *The Wise Men: Six Friends and the World They Made*. New York: Simon and Schuster, 1986.

Jacobsen, Gary. "Terror, Terrain, and Turnout: Explaining the 2002 Midterm Elections." *Political Science Quarterly* 118, no. 1 (Spring 2003).

Jacquard, Roland. *In the Name of Osama bin Laden: Global Terrorism and the bin Laden Brotherhoood*. Durham, N.C.: Duke University Press, 2002.

Jentleson, Bruce. *With Friends Like These: Reagan, Bush, and Saddam, 1982–1990*. New York: Norton, 1994.

Jespersen, T. Christopher. "Analogies at War: Vietnam, the Bush Administration's War in Iraq, and the Search for a Usable Past." *Pacific Historical Review* 74, no. 3 (August 2005).

Johnson, Chalmers. *Blowback: The Costs and Consequences of American Empire*. Revised and expanded edition. New York: Henry Holt, 2004.

Johnson, Robert David. *Congress and the Cold War*. New York: Cambridge University Press, 2005.

Kagan, Robert. *Of Paradise and Power: America and Europe in the New World Order*. New York: Knopf, 2003.

Kamp, Karl-Heinz. "The Folly of Rapid NATO Expansion." *Foreign Policy* 98 (Spring 1995).

Kaplan, Robert D. *Imperial Grunts: The American Military on the Ground*. New York: Random House, 2005.

Kaufman, Chaim. "Threat Inflation and the Failure of the Marketplace of Ideas: The Selling of the Iraq War." *International Security* 29, no. 1 (Summer 2004).

Kennan, George F. "Obituary for the Cold War." *New Perspectives Quarterly* (Summer 1988).

Kennedy, Paul. *The Rise and Fall of the Great Powers: Economic Change and Military Conflict from 1500 to 2000*. New York: Basic Books, 1987.

Khadduri, Majid, and Edmund Ghareeb. *War in the Gulf, 1990–1991: The Iraq-Kuwait Conflict and Its Implications*. New York: Oxford University Press, 1997.

Kihl, Young Whan, and Hong Nack Kim, eds. *North Korea: The Politics of Regime Survival*. Armonk, N.Y.: M. E. Sharpe, 2006.

Kim Samuel, ed. *East Asia and Globalization*. New York: Rowan and Littlefield, 2000.

Kirkpatrick, Jeanne. "A Normal Country in a Normal Time." *National Interest* (Fall 1990).

———. "The Withering away of the State?" *New Perspectives Quarterly* (Winter 1988–1989).

Kochavi, Noam. "Insights Abandoned, Flexibility Lost: Kissinger, Soviet Jewish Immigration, and the Demise of Détente." *Diplomatic History* 29, no. 3 (June 2005).

Kolko, Gabriel. *The Politics of War: The World and U.S. Foreign Policy, 1943–1945*. New York: Random House, 1968.

Kolko, Gabriel, and Joyce Kolko. *The Limits of Power: The World and United States Foreign Policy, 1945–1954*. New York: Harper and Row, 1972.

Kotkin, Stephen. *Armageddon Averted: The Soviet Collapse, 1970–2000*. New York: Oxford University Press, 2001.

Kramer, Mark. "The Collapse of East European Communism and the Repercussions within the Soviet Union, Part I." *Journal of Cold War Studies* 5, no. 4 (Fall 2003).

———. "The Collapse of East European Communism and the Repercussions within the Soviet Union, Part II." *Journal of Cold War Studies* 6, no. 4 (Fall 2004).

Krauthammer, Charles. "The Unipolar Moment." *Foreign Affairs* 70, no. 1 (Winter 1991).

Kristol, William, and Robert Kagan. "Toward a Neo-Reaganite Foreign Policy." *Foreign Affairs* 75, no. 4 (July–August 1996).

Krugman, Paul. "Uncomfortable Truth about NAFTA." *Foreign Affairs* 73, no. 6 (November–December 1993).

Kux, Dennis. *The United States and Pakistan, 1947–2000: Disenchanted Allies*. Baltimore: Johns Hopkins University Press, 2001.

Kuznick, Peter, and James Gilbert, eds. *Rethinking Cold War Culture.* Washington, D.C.: Smithsonian Institution, 2001.

LaFeber, Walter. "The Bush Doctrine." *Diplomatic History* 26, no. 4 (Fall 2002).

Lambeth, Benjamin. *NATO's Air War for Kosovo: A Strategic and Operational Assessment.* Santa Monica, Calif.: Rand Corporation, 2001.

Lampton, David, ed. *Making of Chinese Foreign and Security Policy in the Era of Reform, 1978–2000.* Stanford, Calif.: Stanford University Press, 2001.

Layne, Christopher. "Kant or Cant: The Myth of the Democratic Peace." *International Security* 19, no. 3 (Fall 1994).

Leffler, Melvyn. "9/11 and American Foreign Policy." *Diplomatic History* 29, no. 3 (June 2005).

Leurdijk, Dick, and Dick Zandee. *Kosovo from Crisis to Crisis.* Burlington, Vt.: Ashgate, 2001.

Levering, Ralph B. "Public Opinion, Foreign Policy, and American Politics since the 1960s." *Diplomatic History* 13, no. 3 (Summer 1989).

Lieberthal, Kenneth. "A New China Strategy." *Foreign Affairs* 74, no. 6 (November–December 1995).

Lindsay, James. "The New Apathy." *Foreign Affairs* 79, no. 5 (September–October 2000).

Lipton, David. "Reform Endangered." *Foreign Policy* 90 (Spring 1993).

Lundestad, Geir. *The American Empire and Other Studies of U.S. Foreign Policy in a Comparative Perspective.* New York: Oxford University Press, 1990.

———. "Empire by Invitation? The United States and Western Europe, 1945–1952." *Journal of Peace Research* 23 (September 1986).

———. *The United States and Western Europe since 1945: From "Empire" by Invitation to Transatlantic Drift.* New York: Oxford University Press, 2003.

Maier, Charles. *Dissolution: The Crisis of Communism and the End of East Germany.* Princeton, N.J.: Princeton University Press, 1997.

Mamdani, Mahmood. *When Victims Become Killers: Colonialism, Nativism, and the Genocide in Rwanda.* Princeton, N.J.: Princeton University Press, 2001.

Mandelbaum, Michael. "Foreign Policy as Social Work." *Foreign Affairs* 75, no. 1 (January–February 1996).

Mander, Jerry, and Edward Goldsmith, eds. *The Case against the Global Economy.* San Francisco: Sierra Club Books, 1996.

Manion, Melanie. "Reluctant Duelists: The Logic of the 1989 Protests and Massacre." In Michael Oksenberg, Lawrence Sullivan, and Marc Lambert, eds., *Beijing Spring, 1989: Confrontation and Conflict.* Armonk, N.Y.: M. E. Sharpe, 1990.

Mann, James. *Rise of the Vulcans: The History of Bush's War Cabinet.* New York: Viking, 2004.

Manning, Robert. "The United States in North Korean Foreign Policy." In Samuel Kim, ed., *North Korean Foreign Relations in the Post–Cold War Era.* New York: Oxford University Press, 1998.

Matarese, Susan. *American Foreign Policy and the Utopian Imagination.* Amherst: University of Massachusetts Press, 2001.

McCrisken, Trevor. *American Exceptionalism and the Legacy of Vietnam: U.S. Foreign Policy since 1974.* New York: Palgrave, 2003.

McFaul, Michael. *Russia's Unfinished Revolution: Political Change from Gorbachev to Putin.* Ithaca, N.Y.: Cornell University Press, 2001.

McMahon, Robert J. *The Cold War on the Periphery: The United States, India, and Pakistan, 1947–1965.* New York: Columbia University Press, 1994.

Mead, Walter Russell. *Power, Terror, Peace, and War: American Grand Strategy in a World at Risk.* New York: Knopf, 2004.

Melanson, Richard. *American Foreign Policy since the Vietnam War: The Search for Consensus from Nixon to Clinton.* Armonk, N.Y.: M. E. Sharpe, 2000.

Miller, Steven E. "The End of Unilateralism or Unilateralism Redux?" *Washington Quarterly* (Winter 2002).

Mitchell, Timothy. "American Power and Anti-Americanism in the Middle East." In Andrew Ross and Kristin Ross, eds., *Anti-Americanism.* New York: New York University Press, 2004.

Mueller, John. "The Banality of Ethnic War." *International Security* 25, no. 1 (June 2000).

Muravchik, Joshua. "Clintonism Abroad." *Commentary* (February 1995).

———. "Losing the Peace." *Commentary* (July 1992).

Musallam, Musallam Alu. *The Iraqi Invasion of Kuwait: Saddam Hussein, His State, and International Power Politics.* London: British Academic Press, 1996.

Nacos, Brigitte. "Attack on America: Terrorism as Breaking News." *Political Science Quarterly* 118, no. 1 (Spring 2003).

———. "The Terror Calculus behind 9-11: A Model for Future Terrorism?" *Studies in Conflict and Terrorism* 26, no. 1 (January–February 2003).

Nassar, Jamal. *Globalization and Terrorism: The Migration of Dreams and Nightmares.* New York: Rowman and Littlefield, 2004.

Nathan, Andrew, and Bruce Gilley. *China's New Rulers: The Secret Files.* New York: New York Review of Books, 2002.

Nathan, Andrew, and Robert S. Ross. *The Great Wall and the Empty Fortress: China's Search for Security.* New York: Norton, 1997.

Newhouse, John. *Imperial America: The Bush Assault on the World Order.* New York: Knopf, 2003.

Odom, William E. *The Collapse of the Soviet Military*. New Haven, Conn.: Yale University Press, 1998.

Office of the Chairman of the Joint Chiefs of Staff. *Operation Just Cause: The Planning and Execution of Joint Operations in Panama*. Washington, D.C.: Office of the Chairman of the Joint Chiefs of Staff, 1995.

Orme, William. "Myth versus Facts." *Foreign Affairs* 73, no. 6 (November–December 1993).

Ouimet, Matthew. *The Rise and Fall of the Brezhnev Doctrine in Soviet Foreign Policy*. Chapel Hill: University of North Carolina Press, 2002.

Paris, Roland. "Kosovo and the Metaphor War." *Political Science Quarterly* 117, no. 3 (Fall 2002).

Pastor, Robert. *Congress and the Politics of U.S. Foreign Economic Policy, 1926–1978*. Berkeley: University of California Press, 1980.

Paterson, Thomas, and Les K. Adler. "The Merger of Nazi Germany and Soviet Russia in the American Image of Totalitarianism, 1930s–1950s." *American Historical Review* 75, no. 4 (April 1970).

Patterson, James. *Grand Expectations: The United States, 1945–1974*. New York: Oxford University Press, 1996.

Peet, Richard. *Unholy Trinity: The IMF, World Bank and WTO*. New York: Zed Books, 2003.

Peralta, Athena. "The Globalization of Inequality in the Information Age." In Arie de Ruijter, Bas de Gaay Fortman, and Paul van Seters, eds., *Globalization and Its New Divides*. Amsterdam: Dutch University Press, 2003.

Pfiffner, James. "Did President Bush Mislead the Country in His Arguments for War with Iraq?" *Presidential Studies Quarterly* 34, no. 1 (March 2004).

Postal, Theodore. "Lessons of the Gulf War Experience with Patriot." *International Security* 16 (Winter 1991–1992).

Powell, Colin. "U.S. Forces: Challenges Ahead." *Foreign Affairs* 71, no. 1 (Winter 1992).

Prados, John. *Hoodwinked: The Documents That Reveal How Bush Sold Us a War*. New York: New Press, 2004.

Pryce-Jones, David. *The War That Never Was: The Fall of the Soviet Union*. London: Weidenfield and Nicolson, 1995.

Puddington, Arch. "The Anti–Cold War Brigade." *Commentary* (August 1990).

Quandt, William B. *Peace Process: American Diplomacy and the Arab-Israeli Conflict since 1967*. Berkeley: University of California Press, 2005.

Rabil, Robert G. *Embattled Neighbors: Syria, Israel, and Lebanon*. Boulder, Colo.: Lynne Rienner, 2003.

Rahman, H. *The Making of the Gulf War: Origins of Kuwait's Long-Standing Territorial Dispute with Iraq*. Berkshire, U.K.: Ithaca Press, 1997.

Rashid, Ahmed. *Jihad: The Rise of Militant Islam in Central Asia*. New Haven, Conn.: Yale University Press, 2002.

Remnick, David. *Lenin's Tomb: The Last Days of the Soviet Empire*. New York: Random House, 1993.

Rice, Condoleezza. "In Defense of the National Interest." *Foreign Affairs* 74, no. 2 (April–May 2000).

Rielly, John E. "The Public Mood at Mid-Decade." *Foreign Policy* 98 (Spring 1995).

Rodrik, Dani. *Has Globalization Gone Too Far?* Washington, D.C.: Institute for International Economics, 1997.

Rogel, Carole. *The Breakup of Yugoslavia and the War in Bosnia*. London: Greenwood, 1998.

Ross, Robert S. *Negotiating Cooperation: The United States and China, 1969–1989*. Stanford, Calif.: Stanford University Press, 1995.

Rubin, Barry. *The Transformation of Palestinian Politics: From Revolution to State-Building*. Cambridge, Mass.: Harvard University Press, 1999.

Rubin, Barry, and Judith Colp Rubin. *Anti-American Terrorism and the Middle East: A Documentary Reader*. New York: Oxford University Press, 2002.

Russett, Bruce. *Grasping the Democratic Peace: Principles for a Post–Cold War World*. Princeton, N.J.: Princeton University Press, 1993.

Russett, Bruce, and James Sutterlin. "The UN in a New World Order." *Foreign Affairs* 70, no. 2 (Spring 1991).

Sacochis, Bob. *The Immaculate Invasion*. New York: Viking, 1999.

Sakwa, Richard. "Putin's Foreign Policy: Transforming the 'East.'" In Gabriel Gorodetsky, ed., *Russia between East and West: Russian Foreign Policy on the Threshold of the Twenty-first Century*. London: Frank Cass, 2003.

Sassen, Saskia. "Governance Hotspots: Challenges We Must Confront in the Post–September 11 World." In Eric Hershberg and Kevin Moore, eds., *Critical Views of September 11: Analyses from Around the World*. New York: Free Press, 2002.

Scheuer, Michael. *Imperial Hubris: Why the West Is Losing the War on Terror*. New York: Brassey's 2004.

Schrecker, Ellen, ed. *Cold War Triumphalism: The Misuse of History after the Fall of Communism*. New York: Norton, 2004.

Scobell, Andrew. "Why the People's Army Fired on the People." In Roger Des Forges, Luo Ning, and Wu Yen-bo, eds., *Chinese Democracy and the Crisis of 1989*. Albany: State University of New York Press, 1993.

Scranton, Margaret E. *The Noriega Years: U.S.-Panamanian Relations, 1981–1990*. Boulder, Colo.: Lynne Rienner, 1991.

Sherry, Michael. *In the Shadow of War: The United States since the 1930s*. New Haven, Conn.: Yale University Press, 1995.

Simes, Dmitri. "Reform Reaffirmed." *Foreign Policy* 90 (Spring 1993).

Smith, Tony. *America's Mission: The United States and the Worldwide Struggle for Democracy in the Twentieth Century.* Princeton, N.J.: Princeton University Press, 1994.

Springer, Gary, and Jorge Molina. "The Mexican Financial Crisis: Genesis, Impact, and Implications." *Journal of Interamerican Studies and World Affairs* 37, no. 3 (Summer 1995).

Steel, Ronald. *Temptations of a Superpower.* Cambridge, Mass.: Harvard, 1995.

Stein, Richard Joseph, ed. *U.S. Foreign Policy since the End of the Cold War.* New York: Wilson, 2001.

Steinberg, Gerald M. *Lost in Space: The Domestic Politics of the Strategic Defense Initiative.* Lexington, Mass.: Lexington Books, 1988.

Stent, Angela. *Russia and Germany Reborn: Unification, the Soviet Collapse, and the New Europe.* Princeton, N.J.: Princeton University Press, 1998.

Stigler, Andrew. "A Clear Victory for Air Power: NATO's Empty Threat to Invade Kosovo." *International Security* 27, no. 3 (Winter 2002–2003).

Stiglitz, Joseph. *Globalization and Its Discontents.* New York: Norton, 2002.

St. John, Ronald Bruce. *Libya and the United States: Two Centuries of Strife.* Philadelphia: University of Pennsylvania Press, 2002.

Stokes, Gale. *The Walls Came Tumbling Down: The Collapse of Communism in Eastern Europe.* New York: Oxford University Press, 1993.

Suer, Keith. *Global Order and Global Disorder: Globalization and the Nation-State.* London: Praeger, 2003.

Suskind, Ron. *The One Percent Doctrine: Deep inside America's Pursuit of Its Enemies since 9/11.* New York: Simon and Schuster, 2006.

Thomas, Raju C. C., ed. *Yugoslavia Unraveled: Sovereignty, Self-Determination, Intervention.* New York: Lexington Books, 2003.

Trachtenberg, Marc. *A Constructed Peace: The Making of the European Settlement, 1945–1963.* Princeton, N.J.: Princeton University Press, 1997.

Tuminez, Astrid S. "Nationalism, Ethnic Pressure, and the Breakup of the Soviet Union." *Journal of Cold War Studies* 5, no. 4 (Fall 2003).

Unger, Craig. *House of Bush, House of Saud: The Secret Relationship between the World's Two Most Powerful Dynasties.* New York: Scribner, 2004.

Urban, George R. *Diplomacy and Disillusion at the Court of Margaret Thatcher: An Insider's View.* London: I. B. Taurus, 1996.

Urry, John. "The Global Complexities of September 11th." *Theory, Culture, and Society* 19, no. 4 (Fall 2002).

U.S. Army Center for Military History. *Operation Just Cause: The Incursion into Panama.* Washington, D.C.: U.S. Army Center for Military History, n.d.

Utgoff, Victor A., ed. *The Coming Crisis: Nuclear Proliferation, U.S. Interests, and World Order.* Cambridge, Mass.: MIT Press, 2000.

von Hippel, Karin. *Democracy by Force: U.S. Intervention in the Post–Cold War World.* New York: Cambridge University Press, 2000.

Wall, Irwin. "The French-American War over Iraq." *Brown Journal of International Affairs* 10, no. 2 (Winter–Spring 2004).

Wallander, Celeste. "Western Policy and the Demise of the Soviet Union." *Journal of Cold War Studies* 5, no. 4 (Fall 2003).

Walt, Stephen. "Two Cheers for Clinton's Foreign Policy." *Foreign Affairs* 79, no. 2 (March–April 2000).

Wang, Jianwei. "China's Perception of the Post–Cold War International Environment." In Xiaobing Li, Xiabo Hu, and Yang Zhong, eds., *Interpreting U.S.-China-Taiwan Relations: China in the Post–Cold War Era.* New York: University Press of America, 1998.

Watson, Bruce, and Peter G. Tsouras. *Operation Just Cause: The U.S. Intervention in Panama.* Boulder, Colo.: Westview, 1991.

Watson, William. *The Collapse of Communism in the Soviet Union.* London: Greenwood, 1998.

Wee, Vivienne. "Globalization after 9/11 and the Iraq War." In Chris Nyland and Gloria Davies, eds., *Globalization in the Asian Region.* Cheltenham, U.K.: Elgar, 2004.

Westad, Odd Arne. *The Global Cold War: Third World Interventions and the Making of Our Times.* New York: Cambridge University Press, 2006.

Williams, William A. *The Tragedy of American Diplomacy.* New York: Delta Books, 1972.

Woodward, Bob. *Bush at War.* New York: Simon and Schuster, 2002.

———. *Plan of Attack.* New York: Simon and Schuster, 2004.

———. *State of Denial: Bush at War, Part III.* New York: Simon and Schuster, 2006.

Woodward, C. Vann. "The Age of Reinterpretation." *American Historical Review* 66 (October 1960).

Youngs, Gillian. "International Relations as We Enter the Twenty-first Century." In Gillian Youngs and Eleonore Kofman, eds., *Globalization: Theory and Practice.* New York: Continuum, 2003.

Zlotnick, Marc. "Yeltsin and Gorbachev: The Politics of Confrontation." *Journal of Cold War Studies* 5, no. 1 (Winter 2003).

Documentary

Smith, Martin, and Chris Durrance. *The House of Saud.* Alexandria, Va.: PBS Films, 2005.

Index